Microsoft® Office
2013 IN PRACTICE
outlook
COMPLETE

Michael-Brian Ogawa
UNIVERSITY OF HAWAII

Randy Nordell
AMERICAN RIVER COLLEGE

Mc
Graw
Hill
Education

Microsoft® Office 2013

2013 IN PRACTICE

outlook

COMPLETE

Ogawa
Nordell

MICROSOFT OFFICE Outlook 2013 Complete: IN PRACTICE
Published by McGraw-Hill/Irwin, a business unit of The McGraw-Hill Companies, Inc., 1221 Avenue of the
Americas, New York, NY, 10020. Copyright © 2014 by The McGraw-Hill Companies, Inc. All rights reserved.
Printed in the United States of America. No part of this publication may be reproduced or distributed in any
form or by any means, or stored in a database or retrieval system, without the prior written consent of The
McGraw-Hill Companies, Inc., including, but not limited to, in any network or other electronic storage or
transmission, or broadcast for distance learning.

Some ancillaries, including electronic and print components, may not be available to customers outside the
United States.

This book is printed on acid-free paper.

1 2 3 4 5 6 7 8 9 0 QVS/QVS 1 0 9 8 7 6 5 4 3

ISBN   978-0-07-782393-1
MHID   0-07-782393-1

Senior Vice President, Products & Markets: *Kurt L. Strand*
Vice President, Content Production & Technology Services: *Kimberly Meriwether David*
Director: *Scott Davidson*
Senior Brand Manager: *Wyatt Morris*
Executive Director of Development: *Ann Torbert*
Development Editor II: *Alan Palmer*
Digital Development Editor II: *Kevin White*
Senior Marketing Manager: *Tiffany Russell*
Lead Project Manager: *Rick Hecker*
Buyer II: *Debra R. Sylvester*
Designer: *Jana Singer*
Interior Designer: *Jesi Lazar*
Cover Image: *Corbis Images*
Content Licensing Specialist: *Joanne Mennemeier*
Manager, Digital Production: *Janean A. Utley*
Media Project Manager: *Cathy L. Tepper*
Typeface: *11/13.2 Adobe Caslon Pro*
Compositor: *Laserwords Private Limited*
Printer: *Quad/Graphics*

Library of Congress Cataloging-in-Publication Data

Ogawa, Michael-Brian, 1981-
    Microsoft Office Outlook 2013 complete: in practice / Michael-Brian Ogawa, University of Hawaii,
Randy Nordell, American River College.
      pages cm
    Includes index.
    ISBN 978-0-07-782393-1 (alk. paper)—ISBN 0-07-782393-1 (alk. paper)
    1. Microsoft Outlook. 2. Time management—Computer programs. 3. Personal information
management—Computer programs. 4. Electronic mail systems—Computer programs. I. Nordell, Randy.
II. Title.
HF5548.4.M5255O325 2015
005.5'7—dc23

2013042077

The Internet addresses listed in the text were accurate at the time of publication. The inclusion of a website
does not indicate an endorsement by the authors or McGraw-Hill, and McGraw-Hill does not guarantee the
accuracy of the information presented at these sites.

www.mhhe.com

dedication

To Nicole. I owe my deepest gratitude to you for encouraging me throughout this endeavor. Your love and support made this project successful, as you were always there to keep me moving forward regardless of what you had on your plate. I can hardly wait to spend more time with you!

—M.B. Ogawa

To Kelly. Thank you for your love, support, and encouragement during the seemingly endless hours of writing and editing throughout this project. Your feedback on the content and proofreading were immensely valuable. I could not have done this without you! I'm looking forward to a summer with you without deadlines.

—Randy Nordell

brief contents

contents

about the authors

MICHAEL-BRIAN OGAWA, Ph.D.

Michael-Brian Ogawa, "M.B.," is a faculty member in the Information and Computer Sciences Department at the University of Hawaii at Manoa. He has been an educator for over a decade and worked with students ranging from elementary school through graduate school. M.B. holds a bachelor's degree in Business Administration, a master's degree in Educational Technology, a master's degree in Library and Information Science, and a doctorate in Education from the University of Hawaii at Manoa. M.B. co-authored *Microsoft Outlook 2007: A Professional Approach*, published articles in Educational Technology and School Librarianship, and speaks at a variety of conferences focusing on education. In his spare time, he enjoys spending time with his family, baseball, running, and reading.

RANDY NORDELL, Ed.D.

Randy Nordell is a Professor of Business Technology at American River College in Sacramento, California. He has been an educator for over 20 years and has taught at the high school, community college, and university levels. He holds a bachelor's degree in Business Administration from California State University, Stanislaus, a single subject teaching credential from Fresno State University, a master's degree in Education from Fresno Pacific University, and a doctorate in Education from Argosy University. Randy is the author of *Microsoft Office 2013: In Practice* and *Microsoft Outlook 2010*, and he speaks regularly at conferences on the integration of technology into the curriculum. When he is not teaching, he enjoys spending time with his family, cycling, skiing, swimming, and enjoying the California weather and terrain.

preface

What We're About

We wrote *Microsoft Office Outlook 2013 Complete: In Practice* to meet the diverse needs of both students and instructors. Our approach focuses on presenting Outlook topics in a logical and structured manner, teaching concepts in a way that reinforces learning with practice projects that are transferrable, relevant, and engaging. Our pedagogy and content are based on the following beliefs.

Students Need to Learn and Practice Transferable Skills

Students must be able to transfer the concepts and skills learned in the text to a variety of projects, not simply follow steps in a textbook. Our material goes beyond the instruction of many texts. In our content, students practice the concepts in a variety of current and relevant projects *and* are able to transfer skills and concepts learned to different projects in the real world.

Your Curriculum Drives the Content

The curriculum in the classroom should drive the content of the text, not the other way around. This book is designed to allow instructors and students to cover all the material they need to in order to meet the curriculum requirements of their courses no matter how the courses are structured. *Microsoft Office Outlook 2013 Complete: In Practice* teaches the marketable skills that are key to student success. McGraw-Hill's Custom Publishing site, **Create**, can further tailor the content material to meet the unique educational needs of any school.

Integrated with Technology

Additional textbook resources found on the text's Online Learning Center (**www.mhhe.com/ office2013inpractice**) integrate with the learning management systems that are widely used in many online and on-site courses.

Reference Text

In addition to providing students with an abundance of real-life examples and practice projects, we designed this text to be used as a Microsoft Office 2013 reference source. The core material, uncluttered with exercises, focuses on real-world use and application. Our text provides clear step-by-step instructions on how readers can apply the various features available in Microsoft Outlook in a variety of contexts. At the same time, users have access to a variety of both online and textbook practice projects to reinforce skills and concepts.

Textbook Learning Approach

Microsoft Office Outlook 2013 Complete: In Practice uses the *T.I.P. approach:*
- **T**opics
- **I**nstruction
- **P**ractice

Topics
- Each Outlook section begins with foundational skills and builds to more complex topics as the text progresses.
- Topics are logically sequenced and grouped by topics.
- Student Learning Outcomes (SLOs) are thoroughly integrated with and mapped to chapter content, projects, end-of-chapter review, and test banks.

Instruction (How To)
- How To guided instructions about chapter topics provide transferable and adaptable instructions.
- Because How To instructions are not locked into single projects, this textbook functions as a reference text, not just a point-and-click textbook.

Practice (Pause & Practice and End-of-Chapter Projects)
- Within each chapter, integrated Pause & Practice projects (three to five per chapter) reinforce learning and provide hands-on guided practice.
- In addition to Pause & Practice projects, each chapter has nine comprehensive and practical practice projects: Guided Projects (three per chapter), Independent Projects (three per chapter), and Challenge Projects (three per chapter).
- Pause & Practice and end-of-chapter projects are complete content-rich projects, not small examples lacking context.

Chapter Features

All chapters follow a consistent theme and instructional methodology. Below is an example of chapter structure.

Main headings are organized according to the *Student Learning Outcomes (SLOs)*.

SLO 1.1

Working with Outlook

When most people think of or hear about Microsoft Outlook, their fir
One of the main features in Outlook is handling email, but Outlook is
personal management software that contains the following features:

- *Email*
- *Calendar*
- *Contacts*
- *Tasks*

remember that Outlook is not email but rather a computer software program that handles email acco
Just as your mail carrier is not the mail itself but rather the person who delivers your mail to your h
mailbox, Outlook delivers email received through your existing email account(s). You must have an e
account to use Outlook to send and receive email.

Outlook allows you to create and send email, reply to received email, forward email to other re
ents, save and manage email, and flag and categorize email. Email is also useful as a method of ser
pictures and other types of computer files to others. Most individuals cannot imagine their daily work
personal business without the use of email.

STUDENT LEARNING OUTCOMES (SLOs)

After completing this chapter, you will be able to:

SLO 1.1 Identify the basic components of Microsoft Outlook 2013 (p. O1-2).

SLO 1.2 Navigate throughout the Outlook environment and identify the different panes in the Outlook window (p. O1-6).

SLO 1.3 Distinguish between Outlook being used as a stand-alone program and in a Microsoft Exchange environment (p. O1-13).

SLO 1.4 Distinguish between the different types of email accounts and set up an email account in Outlook (p. O1-14).

SLO 1.5 Use Outlook to create, send, and receive email (p. O1-17).

SLO 1.6 Use attachments in email (p. O1-28).

SLO 1.7 Differentiate email arrangements and icons (p. O1-32).

SLO 1.8 Explain the importance and process of cleaning up an *Inbox* (p. O1-35).

A list of Student Learning Outcomes begins each chapter. All chapter content, examples, and practice projects are organized according to the chapter SLOs.

CASE STUDY

Central Sierra Insurance (CSI) is a multi-office insurance company that handles all lines of commercial and personal insurance policies. As a thriving and growing insurance agency, Central Sierra is regularly hiring qualified personnel to enhance their sales and support staff. CSI encourages its employees to be active in community organizations and events.

Pause & Practice 1-1: You set up an email account using Microsoft Outlook. You will need an email account that is provided by

your school or a free email service such as Gmail.com or Outlook.com.

Pause & Practice 1-2: You send an email message to your instructor and use the *Cc* function to send a copy to yourself. You also read the message, reply to it, and print it for your records.

Pause & Practice 1-3: You reply to a message with an email attachment. You also forward the message to your instructor as an attachment and delete a message.

SLO 1.1 Working with Outlook

The *Case Study* for each chapter is a scenario that establishes the theme for the entire chapter. Chapter content, examples, figures, Pause & Practice projects, and projects throughout the chapter are closely related to this case study content. The three to five Pause & Practice projects in each chapter build upon each other and address key case study themes.

How To instructions enhance transferability of skills with concise steps and screen shots.

HOW TO: Set Up an Email Account

1. Click the **File** tab. The *Backstage* view opens.
2. Click the **Add Account** button. The *Add Account* dialog box opens (Figure 1-21).

1-21 Add account dialog box

3. Enter the following account settings in the text boxes:
   • *Your Name* (as you want it to appear in email)
   • *E-mail Address*

SLO 1.4 Adding an Email Account in Outlook   O1-15

How To instructions are easy-to-follow concise steps. Screen shots and other figures fully illustrate How To topics.

Central Sierra Insurance (CSI) is a multi-office insurance company that handles all lines of commercial and personal insurance policies. As a thriving and growing insurance agency, Central Sierra is regularly hiring qualified personnel to enhance their sales and support staff. CSI encourages its employees to be active in community organizations and events.

your school or a free email service such as Gmail.com or Outlook.com.

Pause & Practice 1-2: You send an email message to your instructor and use the *Cc* function to send a copy to yourself. You also read the message, reply to it, and print it for your records.

Pause & Practice 1-3: You reply to a me...

Pause & Practice projects, which cover two to three of the Student Learning Outcomes in the chapter, provide students with the opportunity to review and practice skills and concepts. Every chapter contains three to five Pause & Practice projects.

> **MORE INFO**
>
> Chapter 2 goes into more detail and covers the special email features available in Outlook. Chapter 6 discusses the use of rules for handling both incoming and outgoing email, and Chapter 7 provides the reader with information about setting up the different types of email accounts.

More Info provides readers with additional information about chapter content.

> **ANOTHER WAY**
>
> The *Ribbon* can be minimized by pressing **Ctrl+F1** or by clicking on the small up arrow in the upper right corner of the Outlook window. You can restore the *Ribbon* by pressing **Ctrl+F1** or by clicking the small up arrow in the upper right corner of the Outlook window and selecting **Show Tabs and Commands**.

Another Way notations teach alternative methods of accomplishing the same task or feature such as keyboard shortcuts.

Marginal Notations present additional information and alternative methods.

End-of-Chapter Projects

Nine learning projects at the end of each chapter provide additional reinforcement and practice for students.

- *Guided Projects (three per chapter):* Guided Projects provide guided step-by-step instructions to apply Outlook features, skills, and concepts from the chapter. Screen shots guide students through the more challenging tasks. End-of-project screen shots provide a visual of the completed project.
- *Independent Projects (three per chapter):* Independent Projects provide students further opportunities to practice and apply skills, instructing students what to do, but not how to do it. These projects allow students to apply previously learned content in a different context.
- *Challenge Projects (three per chapter):* Challenge Projects encourage creativity and critical thinking by integrating Outlook concepts and features into relevant and engaging projects.

Appendices

- *Setting Up Outlook for an On-Site or Online Classroom Environment:* Appendix A presents tips to help you set up your Outlook course whether it is an online or on-site course.
- *Outlook Shortcuts:* Appendix B presents shortcuts available in Microsoft Outlook. Information is in table format for easy access and reference.
- *Outlook Quick Reference Guide:* Appendix C covers global features available in Microsoft Outlook. Information is organized in table format for easy reference to alternative methods and shortcuts.
- *Exchange Server versus Stand-Alone Usage:* Appendix D explains some of the features available in Outlook when using it in an Exchange environment.
- *Quick Tips:* Appendix E includes many useful tips, such as troubleshooting information and using various features effectively.

Online Learning Center: www.mhhe.com/office2013inpractice

Students and instructors can find the following resources at the Online Learning Center, www.mhhe.com/office2013inpractice

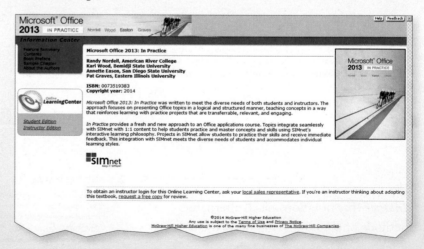

Student Resources

- **_Data Files:_** Files contain start files for all Pause & Practice, Integration, and end-of-chapter projects.
- **_Check for Understanding:_** A combination of multiple choice, matching, and short answer questions are available online to assist students in their review of the skills and concepts covered in the chapter.

Instructor Resources

- **_Instructor's Manual:_** An Instructor's Manual provides teaching tips and lecture notes aligned with the PowerPoint presentations for each chapter.
- **_Test Bank:_** The extensive test bank integrates with learning management systems (LMSs) such as Blackboard, WebCT, Desire2Learn, and Moodle.
- **_PowerPoint Presentations:_** PowerPoint presentations for each chapter can be used in on-site course formats for lectures or can be uploaded to LMSs.
- **_Solution Files:_** Files contain solutions for all Pause & Practice, Integration, Check for Understanding, and end-of-chapter projects.

acknowledgments

REVIEWERS

We would like to thank the following instructors, whose invaluable insights shaped the development of this series.

Frank Abnet
Baker College

Sven Aelterman
Troy University

Nisheeth Agrawal
Calhoun Community College

Jack Alanen
California State University

Doug Albert
Finger Lakes Community College

Lancie Anthony Alfonso
College of Charleston

Farha Ali
Lander University

Beverly Amer
Northern Arizona University

Penny Amici
Harrisburg Area Community College

Leon Amstutz
Taylor University

Chris Anderson
North Central Michigan College

Wilma Andrews
Virginia Commonwealth University

Mazhar Anik
Owens Community College

M. Hashem Anwari
Nova Community College

Ralph Argiento
Guilford Technical Community College

Karen M. Arlien
Bismarck State College

Gary Armstrong
Shippensburg University

Tom Ashby
Oklahoma City Community College

Laura Atkins
James Madison University

William Ayen
University of Colorado

Abida Awan
Savannah State University

Ijaz Awan
Savannah State University

Tahir Aziz
J. Sargeant Reynolds Community College

Mark Bagley
Northwestern Oklahoma State University

Greg Ballinger
Miami Dade College

David Barnes
Penn State Altoona

Emily Battaglia
United Education Institute

Terry Beachy
Garrett College

Michael Beard
Lamar University—Beaumont

Anita Beecroft
Kwantlen Polytechnic University

Julia Bell
Walters State Community College

Paula Bell
Lock Haven University of Pennsylvania

David Benjamin
Pace University

Shantanu Bhagoji
Monroe College

Sai Bhatia
Riverside City College

Cindy Hauki Blair
West Hills College

Scott Blanchard
Rockford Career College

Ann Blackman
Parkland College

Jessica Blackwelder
Wilmington University

James Boardman
Alfred State College

John Bodden
Trident Technical College

Gary Bond
New Mexico State University

Abigail Bornstein
City College of San Francisco

Gina Bowers
Harrisburg Area Community College

Craig Bradley
Shawnee Community College

Gerlinde Brady
Cabrillo College

Gerald Braun
Xavier University

Janet Bringhurst
Utah State University

Brenda Britt
Fayetteville Technical Community College

Annie Brown
Hawaii Community College

Judith Brown
University of Memphis

Menka Brown
Piedmont Technical College

Shawn Brown
Kentucky Community & Technical College

Sylvia Brown
Midland College

Cliff Brozo
Monroe College

Barbara Buckner
Lee University

Sheryl Starkey Bulloch
Columbia Southern University

Rebecca Bullough
College of Sequoias

Kate Burkes
Northwest Arkansas Community College

Sharon Buss
Hawkeye Community College

Angela Butler
Mississippi Gulf Coast Community College

Lynn Byrd
Delta State University

Carolyn Calicutt
Saint Louis Community College

Anthony Cameron
Fayetteville Technical Community College

Eric Cameron
Passaic County Community College

Michael Carrington
Nova Community College

Debby Carter
Los Angeles Pierce College

Cesar Augustus Casas
St. Thomas Aquinas College

Sharon Casseday
Weatherford College

Mary Ann Cassidy
Westchester Community College

Terri Castillo
New Mexico Military Institute

Diane Caudill
Kentucky Community & Technical College

Emre Celebi
Louisiana State University

Jim Chaffee
The University of Iowa Tippie College of Business

Jayalaxmi Chakravarthy
Monroe Community College

Bob Chambers
Endicott College

Debra Chapman
University of South Alabama

Marg Chauvin
Palm Beach Community College

Stephen Cheskiewicz
Keystone College

Mark Choman
Luzerne County Community College

Kungwen Chu
Purdue University

Carin Chuang
Purdue University—North Central

Tina Cipriano
Gateway Technical College

Angela Clark
University of South Alabama

James Clark
University of Tennessee

Steve Clements
Eastern Oregon University

Sandra Cobb
Kaplan University

Paulette Comet
Community College of Baltimore County

Marc Condos
American River College

Ronald Conway
Bowling Green State University

Margaret Cooksey
Tallahassee Community College

Lennie Cooper
Miami Dade College—North

Michael Copper
Palm Beach State College—Lake Worth

Terri Cossey
University of Arkansas

Shannon Cotnam
Pitt Community College

Missie Cotton
North Central Missouri College

Charles Cowell
Tyler Junior College

Elaine Crable
Xavier University

Grace Credico
Lethbridge Community College

Doug Cross
Clackamas Community College

Kelli Cross
Harrisburg Area Community College

Geoffrey Crosslin
Kalamazoo Valley Community College

Christy Culver
Marion Technical College

Urska Cvek
Louisiana State University

Penny Cypert
Tarrant County College

Janet Czarnecki
Brown Mackie College

Don Danner
San Francisco State University

Michael Danos
Central Virginia Community College

Louise Darcy
Texas A&M University

Tamara Dawson
Southern Nazarene University

JD Davis
Southwestern College

Elaine Day
Johnson & Wales University

Jennifer Day
Sinclair Community College

Ralph De Arazoza
Miami Dade College

Lucy Decaro
College of Sequoias

Chuck Decker
College of the Desert

Corey DeLaplain
Keiser University East Campus

Edward Delean
Nova Community College Alexandria

Darren Denenberg
University of Nevada—Las Vegas

Joy DePover
Minneapolis Community & Technical College

Charles DeSassure
Tarrant County Community College

John Detmer
Del Mar College

Michael Discello
Pittsburgh Technical College

Sallie Dodson
Radford University

Veronica Dooly
Asheville-Buncombe Technical Community College

Gretchen Douglas
State University of New York College—Cortland

Debra Duke
Cleveland State University

Michael Dumdei
Texarkana College

Michael Dunklebarger
Alamance Community College

Maureen Dunn
Penn State University

Robert Dusek
Nova Community College

Barbara Edington
St. Francis College

Margaret Edmunds
Mount Allison University

Annette Edwards
Tennessee Technology Center

Sue Ehrfurth
Aims Community College

Donna Ehrhart
Genesee Community College

Roland Eichelberger
Baylor University

Issam El-Achkar
Hudson County Community College

Glenda Elser
New Mexico State University

Emanuel Emanouilidis
Kean University

Bernice Eng
Brookdale Community College

Joanne Eskola
Brookdale Community College

Mohammed Eyadat
California State University—Dominguez Hills

Nancy Jo Evans
Indiana University—Purdue University Indianapolis

Phil Feinberg
Palomar College

Deb Fells
Mesa Community College

Patrick Fenton
West Valley College

Jean Finley
Asheville-Buncombe Technical Community College

George Fiori
Tri-County Technical College Pendleton

Richard Flores
Citrus College

Kent Foster
Winthrop University

Penny Foster
Anne Arundel Community College

Brian Fox
Santa Fe College

Deborah Franklin
Bryant & Stratton College

Judith Fredrickson
Truckee Meadows Community College

Dan Frise
East Los Angeles College

Michael Fujita
Leeward Community College

Susan Fuschetto
Cerritos College

Janos Fustos
Metropolitan State College—Denver

Samuel Gabay
Zarem Golde Ort Technical Institute

Brian Gall
Berks Technical Institute

Lois Galloway
Danville Community College

Saiid Ganjalizadeh
The Catholic University of America

Lynnette Garetz
Heald College Corporate Office

Kurt Garner
Pitt Community College

Randolph Garvin
Tyler Junior College

Deborah Gaspard
Southeast Community College

Marilyn Gastineau
University of Louisiana

Bob Gehling
Auburn University—Montgomery

Amy Giddens
Central Alabama Community College

Tim Gill
Tyler Junior College

Sheila Gionfriddo
Luzerne County Community College

Mostafa Golbaba
Langston University Tulsa

Kemit Grafton
Oklahoma State University—Oklahoma City

Deb Gross
Ohio State University

Judy Grotefendt
Kilgore College

Debra Giblin
Mitchell Technical Institute

Robin Greene
Walla Walla Community College

Nancy Gromen
Eastern Oregon University

Lewis Hall
Riverside City College

Linnea Hall
Northwest Mississippi Community College

Kevin Halvorson
Ridgewater College

Peggy Hammon
Chemeketa Community College

Patti Hammerle
Indiana University—Purdue University Indianapolis

Dr. Bill Hammerschlag
Brookhaven College

Danielle Hammoud
West Coast University Corporate Office

John Haney
Snead State Community College

Ashley Harrier
Hillsborough Community College

Ranida Harris
Indiana University Southeast

Dorothy Harman
Tarrant County College

Marie Hartlein
Montgomery County Community College

Shohreh Hashemi
University of Houston Downtown

Michael Haugrud
Minnesota State University

Rebecca Hayes
American River College

Terri Helfand
Chaffey College

Julie Heithecker
College of Southern Idaho

Gerry Hensel
University of Central Florida—Orlando

Cindy Herbert
Metropolitan Community College

Jenny Herron
Paris Junior College

Marilyn Hibbert
Salt Lake Community College

Will Hilliker
Monroe County Community College

Ray Hinds
Florida College

Rachel Hinton
Broome Community College

Emily Holliday
Campbell University

Mary-Carole Hollingsworth
Georgia Perimeter College

Terri Holly
Indian River State College

Timothy Holston
Mississippi Valley State University

David Hood
East Central College

Kim Hopkins
Weatherford College

Wayne Horn
Pensacola Junior College

Christine Hovey
Lincoln Land Community College

Derrick Huang
Florida Atlantic University

Susan Hudgins
East Central University

Jeff Huff
Missouri State University—West Plains

Debbie Huffman
North Central Texas College

Michelle Hulett
Missouri State University

Laura Hunt
Tulsa Community College

Bobbie Hyndman
Amarillo College

Jennifer Ivey
Central Carolina Community College

Bill Jaber
Lee University

Sherry Jacob
Jefferson Community College

Yelena Jaffe
Suffolk University

Rhoda James
Citrus Community College

Ted Janicki
Mount Olive College

Jon Jasperson
Texas A&M University

Denise Jefferson
Pitt Community College

John Jemison
Dallas Baptist University

Joe Jernigan
Tarrant County College—NE

Mary Johnson
Mt. San Antonio College

Mary Johnson
Lone Star College

Linda Johnsonius
Murray State University

Robert Johnston
Heald College

Irene Joos
La Roche College

Yih-Yaw Jou
University of Houston—Downtown

Jan Kamholtz
Bryant & Stratton College

Valerie Kasay
Georgia Southern University

James Kasum
University of Wisconsin

Nancy Keane
NHTI Concord Community College

Michael Keele
Three Rivers Community College

Debby Keen
University of Kentucky

Judith Keenan
Salve Regina University

Jan Kehm
Spartanburg Community College

Rick Kendrick
Antonelli College

Annette Kerwin
College of DuPage

Manzurul Khan
College of the Mainland

Julia Khan-Nomee
Pace University

Karen Kidder
Tri-State Business Institute

Hak Joon Kim
Southern Connecticut State University

James Kirby
Community College of Rhode Island

Chuck Kise
Brevard Community College

Paul Koester
Tarrant County College

Kurt Kominek
Northeast State Tech Community College

Diane Kosharek
Madison Area Technical College

Carolyn Kuehne
Utah Valley University

Ruth Kurlandsky
Cazenovia College

John Kurnik
Saint Petersburg College

Lana LaBruyere
Mineral Area College

Anita Laird
Schoolcraft College

Charles Lake
Faulkner State Community College

Marjean Lake
LDS Business College

Kin Lam
Medgar Evers College

Jeanette Landin
Empire College

Richard Lanigan
Centura College Online

Nanette Lareau
University of Arkansas Community College Morrilton

David Lee Largent
Ball State University

Linda Lannuzzo
LaGuardia Community College

Robert La Rocca
Keiser University

Dawn D. Laux
Purdue University

Deborah Layton
Eastern Oklahoma State College

Art Lee
Lord Fairfax Community College

Ingyu Lee
Troy University Troy

Kevin Lee
Guilford Technical Community College

Leesa Lee
Western Wyoming College

Thomas Lee
University of Pennsylvania

Jamie Lemley
City College of San Francisco

Linda Lemley
Pensacola State College

Diane Lending
James Madison University

Sherry Lenhart
Terra Community College

Julie Lewis
Baker College—Flint

Sue Lewis
Tarleton State University

Jane Liefert
Middlesex Community College

Renee Lightner
Florida State College

Nancy Lilly
Central Alabama Community College

Mary Locke
Greenville Technical College

Maurie Lockley
University of North Carolina

Haibing Lu
San Diego Mesa College

Frank Lucente
Westmoreland County Community College

Clem Lundie
San Jose City College

Alicia Lundstrom
Drake College of Business

Linda Lynam
Central Missouri State University

Lynne Lyon
Durham Technical Community College

Matthew Macarty
University of New Hampshire

Sherri Mack
Butler County Community College

Heather Madden
Delaware Technical Community College

Susan Mahon
Collin College Plano

Nicki Maines
Mesa Community College

Lynn Mancini
Delaware Technical Community College

Amelia Maretka
Wharton County Junior College

Suzanne Marks
Bellevue Community College

Juan Marquez
Mesa Community College

Carlos Martinez
California State University—Dominguez Hills

Santiago Martinez
Fast Train College

Lindalee Massoud
Mott Community College

Joan Mast
John Wood Community College

Deborah Mathews
J. Sargeant Reynolds Community College

Becky McAfee
Hillsborough Community College

Roberta Mcclure
Lee College

Martha McCreery
Rend Lake College

Sue McCrory
Missouri State University

Brian Mcdaniel
Palo Alto College

Rosie Mcghee
Baton Rouge Community College

Jacob McGinnis
Park University

Mike Mcguire
Triton College

Bruce McLaren
Indiana State University

Bill McMillan
Madonna University

David Mcnair
Mount Wachusett Community College

Gloria Mcteer
Ozarks Technical Community College

Dawn Medlin
Appalachian State University

Peter Meggison
Massasoit Community College

Barbara Meguro
University of Hawaii

Linda Mehlinger
Morgan State University

Gabriele Meiselwitz
Towson University

Joni Meisner
Portland Community College

Dixie Mercer
Kirkwood Community College

Donna Meyer
Antelope Valley College

Mike Michaelson
Palomar College

Michael Mick
Purdue University

Debby Midkiff
Huntington Jr. College of Business

Jenna Miley
Bainbridge College

Dave Miller
Monroe County Community College

Pam Milstead
Bossier Parish Community College

Shayan Mirabi
American Intercontinental University

Johnette Moody
Arkansas Tech University

Christine Moore
College of Charleston

Carmen Morrison
North Central State College

Gary Mosley
Southern Wesleyan University

Tamar Mosley
Meridian Community College

Ed Mulhern
Southwestern College

Carol Mull
Greenville Technical College

Melissa Munoz
Dorsey Business School

Marianne Murphy
North Carolina Central University

Karen Musick
Indiana University—Purdue University Indianapolis

Warner Myntti
Ferris State University

Brent Nabors
Reedley College

Shirley Nagg
Everest Institute

Anozie Nebolisa
Shaw University

Barbara Neequaye
Central Piedmont Community College

Patrick Nedry
Monroe County Community College

Melissa Nemeth
Indiana University—Purdue University Indianapolis

Eloise Newsome
Northern Virginia Community College

Yu-Pa Ng
San Antonio College

Fidelis Ngang
Houston Community College

Doreen Nicholls
Mohawk Valley Community College

Brenda Nickel
Moraine Park Technical College

Brenda Nielsen
Mesa Community College

Phil Nielson
Salt Lake Community College

Suzanne Nordhaus
Lee College

Ronald Norman
Grossmont College

Karen Nunam
Northeast State Technical Community College

Mitchell Ober
Tulsa Community College

Teri Odegard
Edmonds Community College

Michael Brian Ogawa
University of Hawaii

Lois Ann O'Neal
Rogers State University

Stephanie Oprandi
Stark State College of Technology

Marianne Ostrowksky
Luzerne County Community College

Shelley Ota
Leeward Community College

Youcef Oubraham
Hudson County Community College

Paul Overstreet
University of South Alabama

John Panzica
Community College of Rhode Island

Donald Paquet
Community College of Rhode Island

Lucy Parker
California State University—Northridge

Patricia Partyka
Schoolcraft College

James Gordon Patterson
Paradise Valley Community College

Laurie Patterson
University of North Carolina

Joanne Patti
Community College of Philadelphia

Kevin Pauli
University of Nebraska

Kendall Payne
Coffeyville Community College

Deb Peairs
Clark State Community College

Charlene Perez
South Plains College

Lisa Perez
San Joaquin Delta College

Diane Perreault
Tusculum College

Michael Picerno
Baker College

Janet Pickard
Chattanooga State Technical Community College

Walter Pistone
Palomar College

Jeremy Pittman
Coahoma Community College

Morris Pondfield
Towson University

James Powers
University of Southern Indiana

Kathleen Proietti
Northern Essex Community College

Ram Raghuraman
Joliet Jr. College

Patricia Rahmlow
Montgomery County Community College

Robert Renda
Fulton Montgomery Community College
Margaret Reynolds
Mississippi Valley State University
David Richwine
Indian River State College—Central
Terry Rigsby
Hill College
Laura Ringer
Piedmont Technical College
Gwen Rodgers
Southern Nazarene University
Stefan Robila
Montclair State University
Terry Rooker
Germanna Community College
Seyed Roosta
Albany State University
Sandra Roy
Mississippi Gulf Coast Community College—Gautier
Antoon Rufi
Ecpi College of Technology
Wendy Rader
Greenville Technical College
Harold Ramcharan
Shaw University
James Reneau
Shawnee State University
Robert Robertson
Southern Utah University
Cathy Rogers
Laramie County Community College
Harry Reif
James Madison University
Shaunda Roach
Oakwood University
Ruth Robbins
University of Houston—Downtown
Randy Rose
Pensacola State College
Kathy Ruggieri
Lansdale School of Business
Cynthia Rumney
Middle Georgia Technical College
Paige Rutner
Georgia Southern University
Candice Ryder
Colorado State University
Russell Sabadosa
Manchester Community College
Gloria Sabatelli
Butler County Community College
Glenn Sagers
Illinois State University
Phyllis Salsedo
Scottsdale Community College
Dolly Samson
Hawaii Pacific University
Yashu Sanghvi
Cape Fear Community College
Ramona Santamaria
Buffalo State College
Diane Santurri
Johnson & Wales University
Kellie Sartor
Lee College
Allyson Saunders
Weber State University
Theresa Savarese
San Diego City College
Cem Saydam
University of North Carolina
Jill Schaumloeffel
Garrett College
William Schlick
Schoolcraft College
Rory Schlueter
Glendale College

Art Schneider
Portland Community College
Helen Schneider
University of Findlay
Cheryl Schroeder-Thomas
Towson University
Paul Schwager
East Carolina University
Kay Scow
North Hennepin Community College
Karen Sarratt Scott
University of Texas—Arlington
Michael Scroggins
Missouri State University
Janet Sebesy
Cuyahoga Community College Western
Vicky Seehusen
Metropolitan State College Denver
Paul Seibert
North Greenville University
Pat Serrano
Scottsdale Community College
Patricia Sessions
Chemeketa Community College
Judy Settle
Central Georgia Technical College
Vivek Shah
Texas State University
Abul Sheikh
Abraham Baldwin Agricultural College
Lal Shimpi
Saint Augustine's College
Lana Shryock
Monroe County Community College
Joanne Shurbert
NHTI Concord Community College
Sheila Sicilia
Onondaga Community College
Pam Silvers
Asheville-Buncombe Technical Community College
Eithel Simpson
Southwestern Oklahoma State University
Beth Sindt
Hawkeye Community College
Mary Jo Slater
College of Beaver County
Diane Smith
Henry Ford College
Kristi Smith
Allegany College of Maryland
Nadine Smith
Keiser University
Thomas Michael Smith
Austin Community College
Anita Soliz
Palo Alto College
Don Southwell
Delta College
Mimi Spain
Southern Maine Community College
Sri' V. Sridharan
Clemson University
Diane Stark
Phoenix College
Jason Steagall
Bryant & Stratton College
Linda Stoudemayer
Lamar Institute of Technology
Nate Stout
University of Oklahoma
Lynne Stuhr
Trident Technical College
Song Su
East Los Angeles College
Bala Subramanian
Kean University
Liang Sui
Daytona State College

Denise Sullivan
Westchester Community College
Frank Sun
Lamar University
Beverly Swisshelm
Cumberland University
Cheryl Sypniewski
Macomb Community College
Martin Schedlbauer
Suffolk University
Lo-An Tabar-Gaul
Mesa Community College
Kathleen Tamerlano
Cuyahoga Community College
Margaret Taylor
College of Southern Nevada
Sandra Thomas
Troy University
Joyce Thompson
Lehigh Carbon Community College
Jay Tidwell
Blue Ridge Community and Technical College
Astrid Todd
Guilford Technical Community College
Byron Todd
Tallahassee Community College
Kim Tollett
Eastern Oklahoma State College
Joe Torok
Bryant & Stratton College
Tom Trevethan
Ecpi College of Technology
David Trimble
Park University
Charulata Trivedi
Quinsigamond Community College
Alicia Tyson-Sherwood
Post University
Angela Unruh
Central Washington University
Patricia Vacca
El Camino College
Sue van Boven
Paradise Valley Community College
Scott Van Selow
Edison College—Fort Myers
Linda Kavanaugh Varga
Robert Morris University
Kathleen Villarreal
Apollo University of Phoenix
Asteria Villegas
Monroe Community College
Michelle Vlaich-Lee
Greenville Technical College
Carol Walden
Mississippi Delta Community College
Dennis Walpole
University of South Florida
Merrill Warkentin
Mississippi State University
Jerry Waxman
The City University of New York, Queens College
Sharon Wavle
Tompkins Cortland Community College
Rebecca Webb
Northwest Arkansas Community College
Sandy Weber
Gateway Technical College
Robin Weitz
Ocean County College
Karen Welch
Tennessee Technology Center
Marcia Welch
Highline Community College
Lynne Weldon
Aiken Tech College
Jerry Wendling
Iowa Western Community College

Bradley West
Sinclair Community College
Stu Westin
University of Rhode Island
Billie Jo Whary
McCann School of Business & Technology
Charles Whealton
Delaware Technical Community College
Melinda White
Seminole State College
Reginald White
Black Hawk College
Lissa Whyte-Morazan
Brookline College
Sophia Wilberscheid
Indian River State College
Casey Wilhelm
North Idaho College
Amy Williams
Abraham Baldwin Agricultural College
Jackie Williams
University of North Alabama
Melanie Williamson
Bluegrass Community & Technical College
Jan Wilms
Union University
Rhonda Wilson
Connors State College
Diana Wolfe
Oklahoma State University—Oklahoma City
Veryl Wolfe
Clarion University of Pennsylvania
Paula Worthington
Northern Virginia Community College
Dezhi Wu
Southern Utah University
Judy Wynekoop
Florida Gulf Coast University
Kevin Wyzkiewicz
Delta College
Catherine Yager
Pima Community College
Paul Yaroslaski
Dodge City Community College
Annette Yauney
Herkimer County Community College
Yuqiu You
Morehead State University
Bahram Zartoshty
California State University—Northridge
Suzann Zeger
William Rainey Harper College
Steven Zeltmann
University of Central Arkansas
Cherie Zieleniewski
University of Cincinnati—Batavia
Mary Ann Zlotow
College of DuPage
Laurie Zouharis
Suffolk College
Matthew Zullo
Wake Technical Community College

TECHNICAL EDITORS

John Davis
Southern Careers Institute
Deb Giblin
Mitchell Technical Institute
Robert Nichols
College of DuPage
Kathie O'Brien
North Idaho College

Windows 8 and Office 2013 Overview

OFFICE 2013

CHAPTER OVERVIEW

Microsoft Office 2013 and Windows 8 introduce many new features including cloud storage for your files, Office file sharing, and enhanced online content. The integration of Office 2013 and Windows 8 means that files are more portable and accessible than ever when you use *SkyDrive*, Microsoft's free online cloud storage. The new user interface on Office 2013 and Windows 8 allows you to work on tablet computers and smart phones in a working environment that resembles that of your desktop or laptop computer.

STUDENT LEARNING OUTCOMES (SLOs)

After completing this chapter, you will be able to:

SLO 1.1 Use the basic features of Windows 8 and Microsoft Office 2013 products (p. O1-2).

SLO 1.2 Create, save, close, and open Office files (p. O1-12).

SLO 1.3 Print, share, and customize Office files (p. O1-20).

SLO 1.4 Use the *Ribbon*, tabs, groups, dialog boxes, task panes, galleries, and the *Quick Access* toolbar (p. O1-23).

SLO 1.5 Use context menus, mini toolbars, and keyboard shortcuts in Office applications (p. O1-27).

SLO 1.6 Customize the view and display size in Office applications and work with multiple Office files (p. O1-31).

SLO 1.7 Organize and customize Office files and Windows folders (p. O1-34).

CASE STUDY

American River Cycling Club (ARCC) is a community cycling club that promotes fitness. ARCC members include recreational cyclists who enjoy the exercise and camaraderie and competitive cyclists who compete in road, mountain, and cyclocross races throughout the cycling season.

In the Pause & Practice projects, you incorporate many of the topics covered in the chapter to create, save, customize, and share Office 2013 files.

Pause & Practice 1-1: Log into Windows using your Microsoft account, customize the Windows *Start* page, open Office files, create a new file, open and rename an existing file, and share a file.

Pause & Practice 1-2: Modify an existing document, add document properties, customize the *Quick Access* toolbar, export a file as a PDF file, and share a document by sending a link.

Pause & Practice 1-3: Modify the working environment in Office and organize files and folders.

Using Windows 8 and Office 2013

Windows 8 is the *operating system* that makes your computer function and controls the working environment. The Office 2013 software provides you with common application programs such as Word, Excel, Access, and PowerPoint. These applications give you the ability to work with word processing documents, spreadsheets, presentations, and databases in your personal and business projects. Although the Windows 8 operating system and the Office software products work together, they have different functions on your computer.

Windows 8

The operating system on your computer makes all of the other software programs, including Office 2013, function. *Windows 8* has a new user interface—the new *Start page*—where you can select and open a program. Alternatively you can go to the *Windows desktop*, which has the familiar look of previous versions of Windows. You also have the option with Windows 8 to log in to your computer using a Windows account that synchronizes your Windows, Office, and *SkyDrive* cloud storage between computers.

Microsoft Account

In Windows 8 and Office 2013, your files and account settings are portable. In other words, your

Office settings and files can travel with you and be accessed from different computers. You are not restricted to a single computer. When you create a free *Microsoft account* (Live, Hotmail, MSN, Messenger, or other Microsoft service account), you are given a free email account, a *SkyDrive* account, and access to Office Web Apps. If you do not yet have a Microsoft account, you can create one at www.live.com (Figure 1-1).

1-1 Create a Microsoft account

> **MORE INFO**
>
> You will use your Microsoft account for projects in this text.

When you sign in to your computer using Windows 8, you can log in with your Microsoft username and password. Windows uses this information to transfer your Office 2013 settings to the computer you are using and connects you to your *SkyDrive* folder.

Start Page

After logging in to Windows 8 using your Microsoft account (see *Pause & Practice: Office 1-1*, Step 1 on page O1-17), you are taken to the *Start page* (Figure 1-2), which is new to Windows 8. The *Start* page displays different *apps* (applications) as tiles (large and small buttons). Click an app tile to launch a program or task.

Windows 8 uses the term *apps* generically to refer to applications and programs. Apps include the Windows 8 Weather app, Microsoft Excel program, Control Panel, Google Chrome, or File Explorer.

When you start using Windows 8, you can customize your *Start* page. Include the apps you most regularly use, remove the apps you don't want displayed on the *Start* page, and rearrange apps tiles to your preference.

1-2 Windows *Start* page

HOW TO: Customize the Start Page

1. To move an app tile, click and drag the app tile to a new location on the *Start* page. The other app tiles shuffle to accommodate the placement of the app tile.

2. To remove an app tile from the *Start* page, right-click the app tile you want to remove to select it and display your options, and then select **Unpin from Start** (Figure 1-3).

   - When an app tile is selected, a check mark appears in the upper right corner.
   - The app tile is removed from the *Start* page, but the program or task is not removed from your computer.
   - Your options differ depending on the app tile you select.
   - You can right-click multiple app tiles, one after the other, to select and apply an option to all of them.

1-3 App options

3. To add an app tile to the *Start* page, right-click a blank area of the *Start* page and click **All Apps** at the bottom right (Figure 1-4).

4. Right-click the app you want to add to select it and click **Pin to Start** (Figure 1-5).

5. To resize an app tile, right-click the app tile to select it and click **Larger** or **Smaller**.

   - All options do not apply to all apps.

1-4 Display all apps

6. To uninstall an app, right-click the app you want to uninstall to select it and click **Uninstall**.

   - Unlike the unpin option, this option uninstalls the program from your computer, not just your *Start* page.

1-5 Pin selected app to *Start* page

Windows 8 Navigation Options

You can access the Windows 8 options and navigate quickly to other areas from the *Start* page, the Windows desktop, or anywhere on your computer. The **Windows 8 navigation area** and options appear on the right side of your computer monitor when you place your pointer on the small horizontal line at the bottom right corner (Figure 1-6). The following list describes the different options available from the navigation area:

- **Search:** Displays all of the apps available on your computer and opens a search area at the right of your screen.
- **Share:** Displays options for sharing selected apps with other users.
- **Start:** Displays the *Start* page.
- **Devices:** Displays the devices available on your computer.
- **Settings:** Displays options for customizing computer settings; displays power options (Figure 1-7).

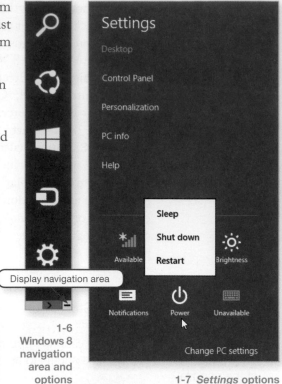

> **ANOTHER WAY**
>
> Click the bottom left corner of your computer screen to toggle between the *Start* page and the desktop.

1-6
Windows 8
navigation
area and
options

1-7 *Settings* options

Desktop and Taskbar

The **Windows desktop** is the working area of Windows and is similar to previous versions of Windows. Click the **Desktop** app tile on the *Start* page to go to the desktop (Figure 1-8). When you install a program on your computer, typically a shortcut to the program is added to the desktop. When you open a program from the *Start* page, such as Microsoft Word, the desktop displays and the program opens.

The *Taskbar* displays at the bottom of the desktop. You can open programs and folders from the *Taskbar* by clicking on an icon on the *Taskbar* (Figure 1-9). You can pin programs and other Windows items, such as the Control Panel or File Explorer, to the *Taskbar*.

1-8 Windows *Desktop* tile on the *Start* page

1-9 *Taskbar* at the bottom of the desktop

HOW TO: Pin a Program to the Taskbar

1. Go to the *Start* page if it is not already displayed.
   - Put your pointer in the bottom right corner of your computer monitor and select **Start** in the navigation area.
   - If you are on the desktop, you can also click the **Start page** icon that appears when you place your pointer in the bottom left corner of your monitor.

2. Right-click a program or Windows item to select it (Figure 1-10).

- A check appears in the upper right of a selected item.
- Options display at the bottom of the *Start* page.

3. Click **Pin to taskbar**.

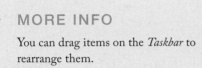

> **MORE INFO**
>
> You can drag items on the *Taskbar* to rearrange them.

1-10 Pin selected item to the *Taskbar*

File Explorer

The **File Explorer** is a window that opens on your desktop where you can browse for files stored on your computer (Figure 1-11). This window displays the libraries and folders on your computer on the left. When you select a library or folder on the left, the contents of the selection are displayed on the right. Double-click a file or folder on the right to open it.

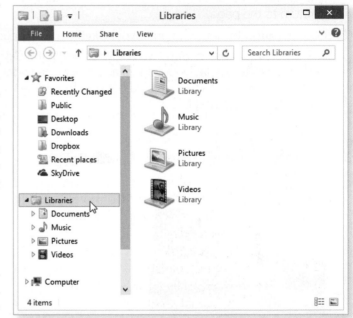

1-11 *File Explorer* window

SkyDrive

SkyDrive is a cloud storage area where you can store files in a private and secure online location that you can access from any computer. With cloud storage you don't have to be tied to one computer, and you don't have to carry your files with you on a portable storage device. When you store your files on *SkyDrive*, the files are actually saved on both your computer and on the cloud. *SkyDrive* synchronizes your files so when you change a file it is automatically updated on the *SkyDrive* cloud.

With Windows 8, the **Sky-Drive folder** is one of your storage location folder options, similar to your *Documents* or *Pictures* folders (Figure 1-12). You can

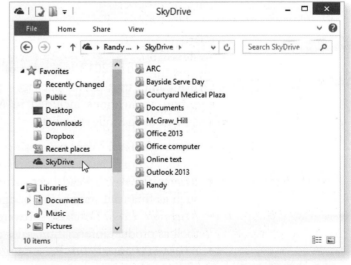

1-12 *SkyDrive* folder

save, open, and edit your *SkyDrive* files from a Windows folder. Your *SkyDrive* folder looks and functions similar to other Windows folders.

In addition to the *SkyDrive* folder on your computer, you can also access your *SkyDrive* files online using an Internet browser such as Internet Explorer, Google Chrome, or Mozilla Firefox. When you access *SkyDrive* online using a web browser, you can upload files, create folders, move and copy files and folders, and create Office files using Office Web Apps (see *Office Web Apps* later in this section).

HOW TO: Use SkyDrive Online

1. Open an Internet browser Window and navigate to the *SkyDrive* website (www.skydrive.com), which takes you to the *SkyDrive* sign in page (Figure 1-13).
   - You can use any Internet browser to access *SkyDrive* (e.g., Internet Explorer, Google Chrome, Mozilla Firefox).
2. Type in your Microsoft account email address and password.
   - If you are on your own computer, check the **Keep me signed in** box to stay signed in to *SkyDrive* when you return to the page.
3. Click the **Sign In** button to go to your *SkyDrive* web page.
   - The different areas of *SkyDrive* are listed under the *SkyDrive* heading on the left (Figure 1-14).
   - Click **Files** to display your folders and files in the folder area.
   - At the top of the page, there are buttons and drop-down menus that list the different actions you can perform on selected files and folders.

1-13 Log in to *SkyDrive* online

1-14 *SkyDrive* online

Office 2013

Microsoft Office 2013 is a suite of personal and business software applications. Microsoft Office comes in different packages and the applications included in each package vary. The common applications included in Microsoft Office and the primary purpose of each are described in the following list:

- *Microsoft Word:* Word processing software used to create, format, and edit documents such as reports, letters, brochures, and resumes.
- *Microsoft Excel:* Spreadsheet software used to perform calculations on numerical data such as financial statements, budgets, and expense reports.
- *Microsoft Access:* Database software used to store, organize, compile, and report information such as product information, sales data, client information, and employee records.
- *Microsoft PowerPoint:* Presentation software used to graphically present information in slides such as a presentation on a new product or sales trends.

- ***Microsoft Outlook:*** Email and personal management software used to create and send email and create and store calendar items, contacts, and tasks.
- ***Microsoft OneNote:*** Note-taking software used to take and organize notes, which can be shared with other Office applications.
- ***Microsoft Publisher:*** Desktop publishing software used to create professional-looking documents containing text, pictures, and graphics such as catalogs, brochures, and flyers.

Office Web Apps

Office Web Apps is free online software from Microsoft that works in conjunction with your online *SkyDrive* account (Figure 1-15). With Office Web Apps, you can work with Office files online, even on computers that do not have Office 2013 installed. This is a useful option when you use a computer at a computer lab or use a friend's computer that does not have Office 2013 installed.

1-15 Office Web Apps

You can access Office Web Apps from your *Sky-Drive* web page and create and edit Word documents, Excel workbooks, PowerPoint presentations, and One-Note notebooks. Office Web Apps is a scaled-down version of Office 2013 and not as robust in terms of features, but you can use it to create, edit, print, share, and insert comments on files. If you need more advanced features, you can open Office Web Apps files in Office 2013.

In *SkyDrive*, you can share files with others. When you share files or folders with others, you establish the access they have to the items you share. You can choose whether other users can only view files or view and edit files. To share a file or folder in your *SkyDrive*, send an email with a link to the shared items or generate a hyperlink that gives access to the shared files to others.

HOW TO: Share an Office Web Apps File

1. Log in to your *SkyDrive* account.
2. Click an Office file to open the file in Office Web Apps.
3. In read-only mode, click the **Share** button above the file. A sharing window opens with different options (Figure 1-16).
   - You can also click the **File** tab and select **Share** on the left.

1-16 Share an Office Web Apps file

4. To send an email, click **Send email**, type the recipient's email address, and type a brief message.
   - Enter a space after typing an email address to add another recipient.
   - Alternatively, you can click **Get a link** to generate a link to send to recipients.
5. Check the **Recipients can edit** box if you want the recipient to be able to edit the file.
   - Deselect this check box if you want recipients to only view the file.
   - You can also require recipients to sign in to *SkyDrive* in order to view or edit the file by checking the **Require everyone who accesses this to sign in** box.
6. Click the **Send** button.
   - Recipients receive an email containing a link to the shared file or folder.
   - A window may open, prompting you to enter a displayed code to prevent unauthorized sharing. Enter the displayed code to return to the sharing window and click **Send**.
7. Click the **X** in the upper right corner or the browser window to exit *SkyDrive*.

Office Web Apps let you synchronously (i.e., at the same time) or asynchronously (i.e., not at the same time) collaborate on an Office file with others who have access to the shared file. If two or more users are working on the same file in Office Web Apps, collaboration information is displayed at the bottom of the Office Web Apps window (Figure 1-17). You are alerted to available updates and told how many people are editing the file.

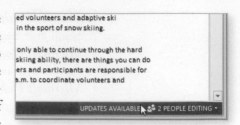

1-17 Collaboration information displayed in the *Status* bar

Click **Updates Available** in the *Status* bar to apply updates to your file. Click **People Editing** to view the names of users who are currently editing the file.

> MORE INFO
>
> The *Status* bar is displayed at the bottom of the application window and is available on all Office applications.

Open an Office Application

When using Windows 8, you click an app tile to open an Office application. If your *Start* page has the Office applications displayed, you can click the **Word 2013**, **Excel 2013**, **Access 2013**, or **PowerPoint 2013** tile to launch the application (Figure 1-18).

If the Office application apps are not on the *Start* page, you can search for the app.

1-18 Launch an Office 2013 application

HOW TO: Search for an App

1. Put your pointer at the bottom right corner of your computer screen to display the Windows 8 navigation options.
2. Click **Search** to display all apps and the *Search* pane on the right (Figure 1-19).
3. Type the name of the application to open (e.g., Access). Windows displays the apps matching the search text.
4. Click the app to launch it.
   - Alternatively, you can click a blank area away from the *Search* pane to close the *Search* pane, scroll through the available apps on your computer, and click an app to launch it.

1-19 Search for an app

> MORE INFO
>
> Add commonly used apps to your Windows *Start* page to save you time.

Office Start Page

In addition to the new *Start* page in Windows 8, most of the Office applications (except Outlook and OneNote) have a new **Start page** that displays when you launch the application (Figure 1-20). From this *Start* page, you can create a new blank file (e.g., a Word document, an Excel workbook, an Access database, or a PowerPoint presentation), create a file from an online template, search for an online template, open a recently used file, or open another file. These options vary depending on the Office application.

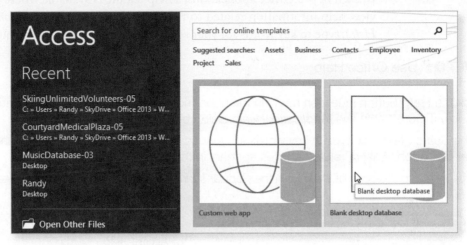

1-20 Access *Start* page

Press the **Esc** key to exit the *Start* page and enter the program. In Access, you have to open an existing database or create a new one to enter the program.

Backstage View

Office 2013 incorporates the **Backstage view** into all Office applications. Click the **File** tab on the *Ribbon* to open the *Backstage* view (Figure 1-21). *Backstage* options vary depending on the Office application. The following list describes some of the common tasks you can perform from the *Backstage* view:

1-21 *Backstage* view in Excel

- **Info:** Displays document properties and other protection, inspection, and version options.
- **New:** Creates a new blank file or a new file from a template or theme.
- **Open:** Opens an existing file from a designated location or a recently opened file.
- **Save:** Saves a file. If the file has not been named, the *Save As* dialog box opens when you select this option.
- **Save As:** Opens the *Save As* dialog box.
- **Print:** Prints a file, displays a preview of the file, or displays print options.
- **Share:** Invites people to share a file or email a file.

- *Export:* Creates a PDF file from a file or saves as a different file type.
- *Close:* Closes an open file.
- *Account:* Displays your Microsoft account information.
- *Options:* Opens the *[Application] Options* dialog box (e.g., Excel Options).

Office 2013 Help

In each of the Office applications, a help feature is available where you can search for a topic and view help information related to that topic. Using the *[Application] Help* dialog box (e.g., *Access Help*), type in key words for your search. Links to online help resources display in the dialog box.

HOW TO: Use Office Help

1. Click the **Help** button (question mark) in the upper right corner of the Office application window (Figure 1-22). The *[Application] Help* dialog box opens (Figure 1-23).

1-22 *Help* button

2. In the *Search* text box, type in key words for your search and press **Enter** or click the **Search** button. A list of related articles appears in the dialog box (Figure 1-24).

   - You can also click one of the links in the *Popular searches* and *Basics and beyond* areas to view related help articles.

1-23 *Access Help* dialog box

1-24 Related articles displayed in the dialog box

3. Click a link to display the article in the dialog box.

   - You can use the *Back*, *Forward*, or *Home* buttons to navigate in the *Help* dialog box.
   - Scroll down to the bottom of the list of articles to use the *Next* and *Previous* buttons to view more articles.

4. Click the **X** in the upper right corner to close the *Help* dialog box.

ANOTHER WAY

F1 opens the *Help* dialog box.

Mouse and Pointers

If you are using Office on a desktop or laptop computer, use your mouse (or touch pad) to navigate around files, click tabs and buttons, select text and objects, move text and objects, and resize objects. The following table lists mouse and pointer terminology used in Office.

Mouse and Pointer Terminology

Term	Description
Pointer	When you move your mouse, the pointer moves on your screen. There are a variety of pointers that are used in different contexts in Office applications. The following pointers are available in most of the Office applications (the appearance of these pointers varies depending on the application and the context used): • *Selection pointer:* Select text or an object. • *Move pointer:* Move text or an object. • *Copy pointer:* Copy text or an object. • *Resize pointer:* Resize objects or table column or row. • *Crosshair:* Draw a shape.
Insertion point	The vertical flashing line where text is inserted in a file or text box. Click the left mouse button to position the insertion point.
Click	Click the left mouse button. Used to select an object or button or to place the insertion point in the selected location.
Double-click	Click the left mouse button twice. Used to select text.
Right-click	Click the right mouse button. Used to display the context menu and the mini toolbar.
Scroll	Use the scroll wheel on the mouse to scroll up and down through your file. You can also use the horizontal or vertical scroll bars at the bottom and right of an Office file window to move around in a file.

Office 2013 on a Tablet

The new user interface in Windows 8 and Office 2013 is designed to facilitate use of Windows and the Office applications on a tablet computer or smart phone. With tablets and smart phones, you use a touch screen rather than using a mouse, so the process of selecting text and objects and navigating around a file is different from when you select and navigate on a desktop or laptop computer. The following table lists some of the gestures used when working on a tablet or smart phone (some of these gestures vary depending on the application used and the context).

Tablet Gestures

Gesture	Used To	How To
Tap	Make a selection or place the insertion point. Double tap to edit text in an object or cell.	
Pinch	Zoom in or resize an object.	
Stretch	Zoom out or resize an object.	
Slide	Move an object or selected text.	
Swipe	Select text or multiple objects.	

Creating, Saving, Closing, and Opening Files

Creating, saving, and opening files is primarily done from the *Start* page or *Backstage* view. These areas provide you with many options and a central location to perform these tasks. You can also use shortcut commands to create, save, and open files.

Create a New File

When you create a new file in an Office application, you can create a new blank file or a new file based on a template (in PowerPoint, you can also create a presentation based on a theme). On the *Start* page, click **Blank [file type]** to create a new blank file in the application you are using (in Word, you begin with a blank document; in Excel, a blank workbook; in Access, a blank desktop database; and in PowerPoint, a blank presentation). From the *Backstage* view, the new file options are available in the *New* area.

HOW TO: Create a New File from the Start Page

1. Open the Office application you want to use. The *Start* page displays when the application opens.
2. From the *Start* page, click **Blank [file type]** or select a template or theme to use for your new blank file. A new file opens in the application you are using.
   - The new file is given a generic file name (e.g., *Document1*, *Book1*, or *Presentation1*). You can name and save this file later.
   - When creating a new Access database, you are prompted to name the new file when you create it.
   - Some templates and themes (in PowerPoint only) are displayed on the *Start* page, but you can search for other online templates and themes using the *Search* text box at the top of the *Start* page.

> **MORE INFO**
>
> **Esc** closes the *Start* page and takes you into the Office application (except in Access).

If you have been using an application already and want to create a new file, you create it from the *Backstage* view.

HOW TO: Create a New File from the Backstage View

1. Click the **File** tab to display the *Backstage* view.
2. Select **New** on the left to display the *New* area (Figure 1-25).
3. Click **Blank [file type]** or select a template or theme to use in your new blank file. A new file opens in the application.
   - The new file is given a generic file name (e.g., *Document1*, *Book1*, or *Presentation1*). You can name and save this file later.
   - When you are creating a new Access database, you are prompted to name the new file when you create it.
   - Some templates and themes (in PowerPoint only) are displayed on the *Start* page, but you can search for other online templates and themes using the *Search* text box at the top of the *Start* page.

1-25 *New* area in Word

Save a File

In Access, you name a file as you create it, but in Word, Excel, and PowerPoint, you name a file after you have created it. When you save a file, you type a name for the file and select the location where the file is saved.

HOW TO: Save a File

1. Click the **File** tab to display the *Backstage* view.
2. Select **Save** or **Save As** on the left to display the *Save As* area (Figure 1-26).
   - If the file has not already been saved, clicking *Save* or *Save As* takes you to the *Save As* area on the *Backstage* view.
3. Select a place to save your file in the *Places* area.
4. On the right, click a folder in the *Recent Folders* area or click the **Browse** button to open the *Save As* dialog box (Figure 1-27).
5. In the *Folder* list on the left, select a location to save the file.
6. In the *File name* area, type a name for the file.
7. In the *Save as type*, select the file type to save.
   - By default, Office selects the file type, but you can change the file type in this area.
8. Click **Save** to close the dialog box and save the file.

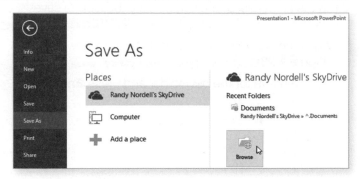

1-26 *Save As* area in PowerPoint

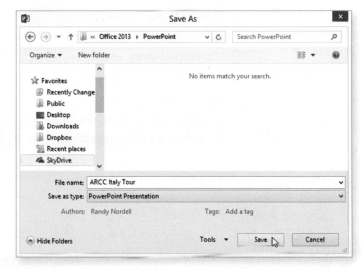

1-27 *Save As* dialog box

Create a Folder

When saving files, it is a good idea to create folders to organize your files. Organizing your files in folders makes it easier to find your files and saves you time when you are searching for a specific file (see *SLO 1.7: Organizing and Customizing Folders and Files* for more information on this topic). When you save an Office file, you can also create a folder in which to store that file.

HOW TO: Create a Folder

1. Click the **File** tab to display the *Backstage* view.
2. Select **Save As** on the left to display the *Save As* area.
3. Select a place to save your file in the *Places* area.
4. On the right, click a folder in the *Recent Folders* area or the **Browse** button to open the *Save As* dialog box.
5. In the *Folder* list at the left, select a location to save the file.
6. Click the **New Folder** button to create a new folder (Figure 1-28).
7. Type a name for the new folder and press **Enter**.

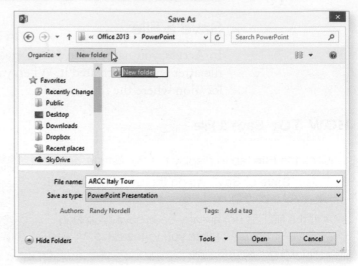

1-28 Create a new folder

> ### ANOTHER WAY
>
> **F12** opens the *Save As* dialog box (except in Access).

Save As a Different File Name

After you have saved a file, you can save it again with a different file name. If you do this, you have preserved the original file and you can continue to revise the second file for a different purpose. For example, you might want to save a different version of a file with a different file name.

HOW TO: Save As a Different File Name

1. Click the **File** tab to display the *Backstage* view.
2. Select **Save As** on the left to display the *Save As* area.
3. Select the location where you want to save your file in the *Places* area.
4. On the right, click a folder in the *Recent Folders* area or the **Browse** button to open the *Save As* dialog box.
5. In the *Folder* list on the left, select a location to save the file.
6. In the *File name* area, type a name for the file.
7. Click **Save** to close the dialog box and save the file.

Office 2013 File Types

When you save an Office file, by default Office saves the file in the most recent file format for that application. You also have the option of saving files in older versions of the Office application you are using. For example, you can save a Word document as an older version to share with or send to someone who uses an older version of Word. Each file has an extension at the end of the file name that determines the file type. The *file name extension* is automatically added to a file when you save it.

The following table lists some of the common file types used in the different Office applications.

Office File Types

File Type	Extension
Word Document	.docx
Word Template	.dotx
Word 97-2003 Document	.doc
Rich Text Format	.rtf
Excel Workbook	.xlsx
Excel Template	.xltx
Excel 97-2003 Workbook	.xls
Comma Separated Values (CSV)	.csv
Access Database	.accdb
Access Template	.accdt
Access Database (2000-2003 format)	.mdb
PowerPoint Presentation	.pptx
PowerPoint Template	.potx
PowerPoint 97-2003 Presentation	.ppt
Portable Document Format (PDF)	.pdf

Close a File

There are a few different methods you can use to close a file.

- Click the **File** tab and select **Close** on the left.
- Press **Ctrl+W**.
- Click the **X** in the upper right corner of the file window. This method closes the file and the program.

When you close a file, you are prompted to save the file if it has not been named or if changes were made after the file was last saved (Figure 1-29). Click **Save** to save and close the file or click **Don't Save** to close the file without saving. Click **Cancel** to return to the file.

1-29 Prompt to save a document before closing

Open an Existing File

You can open an existing file from the *Start* page when you open an Office application or you can open an existing file while you are working on another Office file.

HOW TO: Open a File from the Start Page

1. Open an Office application to display the *Start* page (Figure 1-30).
2. Select a file to open in the *Recent* area on the left.
   - If you select a file in the *Recent* area, the file must be located on the computer or an attached storage device in order to open. If the file has been renamed, moved, or on a storage device not connected to the computer, you received an error message.
3. Alternatively, click the **Open Other [file type]** (e.g., Documents, Workbooks, Files, or Presentations) link to open the *Open* area of the *Backstage* view (Figure 1-31).
4. Select a location in the *Places* area.
5. Select a folder in the *Recent Folders* area or click the **Browse** button to open the *Open* dialog box (Figure 1-32).
6. Select a location from the *Folder* list on the left.
7. Select the file to open and click the **Open** button.

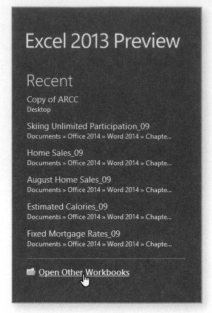

1-30 Open a file from the *Start* page

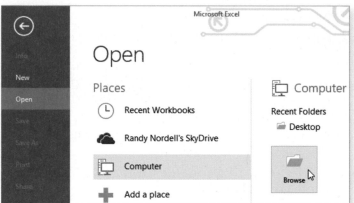

1-31 *Open* area in the *Backstage* view   1-32 *Open* dialog box

To open a file from within an Office application, click the **File** tab to open the *Backstage* view and select **Open** on the left to display the *Open* area. Follow steps 4–7 above to open a file.

You can also open a file from a Windows folder. When you double-click a file in a Windows folder, the file opens in the appropriate Office application. Windows recognizes the file name extension and launches the correct program.

> ### ANOTHER WAY
> **Ctrl+F12** opens the *Open* dialog box when you are in the working area of an Office application (except in Access).

For this project, you log in to Windows using your Microsoft account, customize the Windows *Start* page, create and save a PowerPoint presentation, create a folder, open and rename an Excel workbook, use *Help*, and share a file in *SkyDrive*.

Note to Students and Instructor:
Students: *For this project, you share an Office Web App file with your instructor. You also create a Microsoft account if you don't already have one.*
Instructor: *In order to complete this project, your students need your Microsoft email address. You can create a new Live or Hotmail account for projects in this chapter.*

File Needed: **ARCC2015Budget-01.xlsx**
Completed Project File Names: **[your initials] PP O1-1a.pptx** and **[your initials] PP O1-1b.xlsx**

1. Log in to Windows using your Microsoft account if you are not already logged in.
   a. If you are not logged in to Windows using your Microsoft account, you might need to log out or restart to display the log in page. When Windows opens, type in your Windows account username and password.
   b. If you have not yet created a Microsoft account, open a browser Window and go to www.live.com and click the **Sign up now** link. Enter the required information to create your free Windows account.

2. After logging in to Windows, customize the *Start* page to include Office 2013 apps. If these apps tiles are already on the *Start* page, skip steps 2a–e.
   a. Right-click a blank area of the *Start* page.
   b. Click **All apps** on the bottom right to display the *Apps* area of Windows.
   c. Locate and right-click **Word 2013** to select it (Figure 1-33).
   d. Click **Pin to Start** on the bottom left to add this app to the *Start* page.
   e. Repeat steps 2a–d to pin *Excel 2013*, *Access 2013*, and *PowerPoint 2013* to the *Start* page.

   1-33 Word 2013 selected

3. Return to the *Start* page and arrange apps.
   a. Place your pointer on the bottom right of your screen and select **Start** from the Windows navigation options.

> **ANOTHER WAY**
> Click the bottom left corner of your screen to return to the *Start* page.

   b. Drag the app tiles you added to the *Start* page to your preferred locations.

4. Create a PowerPoint presentation and save in a new folder.
   a. Click the **PowerPoint 2013** app tile on your *Start* page to open the application.
   b. On the PowerPoint *Start* page, click **Blank presentation** to create a new blank presentation (Figure 1-34). A new blank presentation opens.

1-34 Create a new blank PowerPoint presentation

c. Click in the **Click to add title** area and type American River Cycling Club.

d. Click the **File** tab to open the *Backstage* view and click **Save As** on the left to display the *Save As* area.

e. Click *[your name's]* **SkyDrive** in the *Places* area and click **Browse** to open the *Save As* dialog box (Figure 1-35).

f. Click the **New Folder** button to create a new folder in your *SkyDrive* folder.

g. Type American River Cycling Club and press **Enter**.

h. Double-click the folder you created to open it.

i. In the *File name* area, type [your initials] PP O1-1a (Figure 1-36).

j. Click **Save** to close the dialog box and save the presentation.

k. Click the **X** in the upper right corner of the window to close the file and PowerPoint.

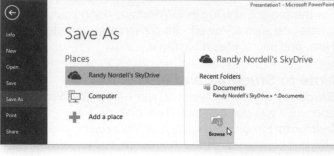

1-35 **Save the file in** *SkyDrive*

1-36 *Save As* **dialog box**

5. Open an Excel file and save as a different file name.

a. Return to the Windows *Start* page.

b. Click the **Excel 2013** app tile to open it.

c. From the Excel *Start* page, click the **Open Other Workbooks** link on the bottom left to display the *Open* area of the *Backstage* view.

d. Click **Computer** in the *Places* area and click **Browse** to open the *Open* dialog box (Figure 1-37).

e. Browse to your student data files and select the **ARCC2015Budget-01** file.

f. Click **Open** to open the workbook.

g. Press **F12** to open the *Save As* dialog box.

h. Click **SkyDrive** in the *Folder* list on the left.

i. Double-click the **American River Cycling Club** folder to open it.

j. In the *File name* area type [your initials] PP O1-1b.

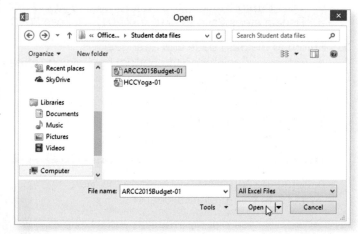

1-37 *Open* **dialog box**

k. Click **Save** to close the dialog box and save the workbook.

6. Use *Excel Help* to find articles about selected topics.

a. Click the **Help** button in the upper right corner of the Excel window. The *Excel Help* dialog box opens.

b. Type pivot table in the *Search* text box and press **Enter**.
c. Click one of the displayed articles and quickly read about pivot tables.
d. Click the **Home** button to return to the home page of Excel help.
e. Type sum function in the *Search* text box and press **Enter**.
f. Click one of the displayed articles and quickly read about sum functions.
g. Click the **X** in the upper right corner to close the *Excel Help* dialog box.
h. Press **Ctrl+W** to close the Excel workbook.
i. Click the **X** in the upper right corner of the Excel window to close Excel.

7. Share an Office Web Apps file on *SkyDrive* with your instructor.
   a. Return to the Windows *Start* page.
   b. Open an Internet browser window and go to the *SkyDrive* (www.skydrive.com) sign-in page (Figure 1-38).
   c. Type in your Microsoft account email address and password and click the **Sign In** button to go to your *SkyDrive* web page.
   d. Click the navigation button on the upper left and select **SkyDrive** (if your *SkyDrive* is not already displayed) (Figure 1-39).
   e. Click the **American River Cycling Club** folder to open it.
   f. Click the **PP O1-1b** Excel workbook to open it in Office Web Apps (Figure 1-40).
   g. Click the **File** tab to open the *Backstage* view.
   h. Click **Share** on the left and select **Share with People**. A sharing window opens with different options (Figure 1-41). Sharing requires the recipient to have a Microsoft account. Also, you might be directed to complete an online form for security purposes the first time you share a file.
   i. Click **Send email**, type your instructor's email address, and type a brief message.
   j. Check the **Recipients can edit** check box.
   k. Click the **Share** button.

8. Select **[your name]** on the upper right of the *SkyDrive* window and select the **Sign out** from the *Account* drop-down list.

1-38 Log in to *SkyDrive* online

1-39 Go to your *SkyDrive*

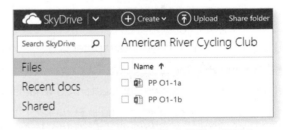

1-40 Open a file in Office Web Apps

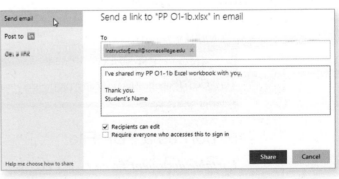

1-41 Share an Office Web App file

Printing, Sharing, and Customizing Files

On the *Backstage* view of any of the Office applications, you can print a file and customize how a file is printed. You can also export an Office file as a PDF file in most of the Office applications. In addition, you can add and customize document properties for an Office file and share a file in a variety of formats.

Print a File

You can print an Office file if you need a paper copy of it. The *Print* area on the *Backstage* view displays a preview of the open file and many print options. For example, you can choose which page or pages to print and change the margins of the file in the *Print* area. Some of the print settings vary depending on the Office application you are using and what you are printing.

HOW TO: Print a File

1. Open the file you want to print from a Windows folder or within an Office program.
2. Click the **File** tab to open the *Backstage* view.
3. Click **Print** on the left to display the *Print* area (Figure 1-42).
   - A preview of the file displays on the right. Click the **Show Margins** button to adjust margins or **Zoom to Page** button to change the view in the *Preview* area. The *Show Margins* button is only available in Word and Excel.
   - On the left a variety of options are listed in the *Settings* area.
   - The *Settings* options vary depending on the Office application you are using and what you are printing.
4. In the *Copies* area, you can change the number of copies to print.
5. The default printer for your computer is displayed in the *Printer* drop-down list.
   - Click the **Printer** drop-down list to select a different printer.
6. In the *Settings* area, you can customize what is printed and how it is printed.
   - In the *Pages* area (*Slides* area in PowerPoint), you can select a page or range of pages (slides) to print.
   - By default all pages (slides) are printed when you print a file.
7. Click the **Print** button to print your file.

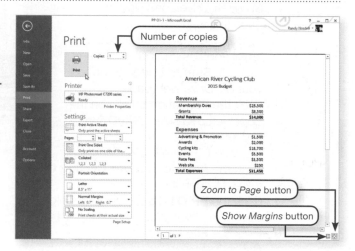

1-42 *Print* area on the *Backstage* view

> **ANOTHER WAY**
>
> **Ctrl+P** opens the *Print* area on the *Backstage* view.

Export as a PDF File

Portable document format, or **PDF**, is a specific file format that is often used to share files that are not to be changed or to post files on a web site. When you create a PDF file from an Office application file, you are actually exporting a static image of the original file, similar to taking a picture of the file.

The advantage of working with a PDF file is that the format of the file is retained no matter who opens the file. PDF files open in Adobe Reader, which is free software that is

O1-20

installed on most computers, or Adobe Acrobat, which is software users have to buy. Because a PDF file is a static image of a file, it is not easy for other people to edit your files. When you want people to be able to view a file but not make changes, PDF files are a good choice.

> **MORE INFO**
> Word 2013 allows you to open PDF files and edit the file as a Word document.

When you export an Office application file as a PDF file, Office creates a static image of your file and prompts you to save the file. The file is saved as a PDF file.

HOW TO: Export a File as a PDF File

1. Open the file you want to export to a PDF file.
2. Click the **File** tab and click **Export** to display the *Export* area on the Backstage view (Figure 1-43).
3. Select **Create PDF/XPS Document** and click the **Create PDF/XPS**. The *Publish as PDF or XPS* dialog box opens.
4. Select a location to save the file.
5. In the *File name* area, type a name for the file.
6. Click **Publish** to close the dialog box and save the PDF file.
   - A PDF version of your file may open. You can view the file and then close it.

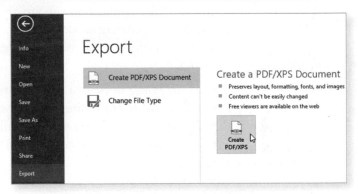

1-43 **Export a file as a PDF file**

Document Properties

Document properties are hidden codes in a file that contain identifying information about that file. Each piece of document property information is called a ***field***. You can view and modify document properties in the *Info* area of the *Backstage* view.

Some document properties fields are automatically generated when you work on a file, such as *Size, Total Editing Time, Created,* and *Last Modified.* But you can modify other document properties fields, such as *Title, Comments, Subject, Company,* and *Author.* You can use document property fields in different ways such as inserting the *Company* field in a document footer.

HOW TO: View and Modify Document Properties

1. Click the **File** tab and click **Info**. The document properties display on the right (Figure 1-44).
2. Click in the text box area of a field that can be edited (e.g., *Add a title* or *Add a tag*) and type your custom document property information.
3. Click the **Show All Properties** link at the bottom to display additional document properties.
   - When all properties are displayed, click **Show Fewer Properties** to display fewer properties.
   - This link toggles between *Show All Properties* and *Show Fewer Properties*.
4. Click the **File** tab to return to the file.

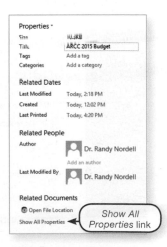

1-44 **Document properties**

Share a File

Windows 8 and Office 2013 have been developed to help you share and collaborate effectively. The *Share* area on the *Backstage* view provides different options for sharing files from within an Office application. When you save a file to your *SkyDrive*, Office gives you a variety of options to share your file (Figure 1-45). Your sharing options vary depending on the Office application you are using. The following list describes some common ways you can share files with others:

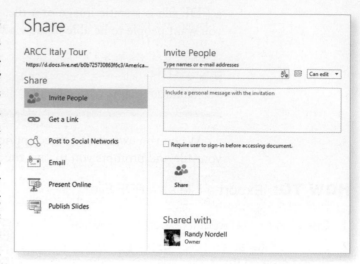

1-45 Share an Office file

- *Invite People* to view or edit your file.
- *Get a Link* to the online file that you can send to others or post online.
- *Post to Social Networks* such as LinkedIn or Facebook.
- *Email* the file as an attachment, link, or PDF file.

> **MORE INFO**
>
> There is not a *Sharing* area on the *Backstage* view in Access.

HOW TO: Share a File

1. Click the **File** tab and select **Share**.
   - If your file is not saved on *SkyDrive*, select **Invite People** and click **Save to Cloud** (Figure 1-46).
   - Save your file to your *SkyDrive* folder.
   - If your file is not saved to *SkyDrive*, you will not have all of the sharing options.
2. Select one of the *Share* options on the left. Additional information is displayed on the right (Figure 1-47).
   - In most of the *Share* options, you can set the permission level to **Can view** or **Can edit**, which controls what others can do with your file.
   - In order to post a file to a social network site, you must connect your social network site to your Microsoft account. Go to the *Account* area of the *Backstage* view to connect to social network sites.

1-46 Save a file to the cloud before sharing

1-47 Share a file on a social network site

Program Options

Using the program options, you can make changes that apply globally to the Office program. For example, you can change the default save location to your *Sky-Drive* folder or you can turn off the *Start* page that opens when you open an Office application.

Click the **File** tab and select **Options** on the left to open the **[Program] Options** dialog box (e.g., Word Options, Excel Options, etc.) (Figure 1-48). Click one of the categories on the left to display the category options on the right. The categories and options vary depending on the Office application you are using.

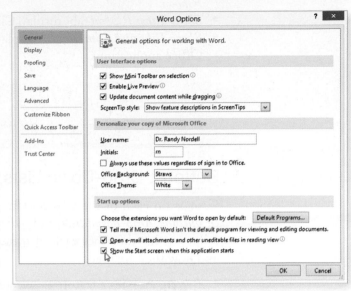

1-48 *Word Options* dialog box

Using the Ribbon, Tabs, and Quick Access Toolbar

You can use the *Ribbon*, tabs, groups, buttons, drop-down lists, dialog boxes, task panes, galleries, and the *Quick Access* toolbar to modify your Office files. This section describes the different tools you can use to customize your files.

The Ribbon, Tabs, and Groups

The *Ribbon*, which appears at the top of an Office file window, displays the many features available to use on your files. The *Ribbon* is a collection of **tabs**. On each tab are *groups* of features. The tabs and groups that are available on each Office application vary. Click a tab to display the groups and features available on that tab.

Some tabs are always displayed on the *Ribbon* (e.g., *File* tab and *Home* tab). Other tabs are *context-sensitive*, which means that they only appear on the *Ribbon* when a specific object is selected in your file. Figure 1-49 displays the context-sensitive *Table Tools Table* tab that displays in Access when you open a table.

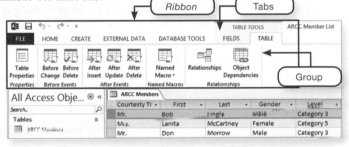

1-49 Context-sensitive *Table Tools Table* tab displayed

Ribbon Display Options

The *Ribbon* is by default displayed when an Office application is open, but you can customize how the *Ribbon* displays. The *Ribbon Display Options* button is in the upper right corner of an Office application window (Figure 1-50). Click the **Ribbon Display Options** button to select one of the three options.

1-50 *Ribbon Display Options*

- ***Auto-Hide Ribbon:*** Hides the *Ribbon*. Click at the top of the application to display the *Ribbon*.
- ***Show Tabs:*** *Ribbon* tabs display. Click a tab to open the *Ribbon* and display the tab.
- ***Show Tabs and Commands:*** Displays the *Ribbon* and tabs, which is the default setting in Office applications.

> **MORE INFO**
>
> **Ctrl+F1** collapses or expands the *Ribbon* to display only tabs.

Buttons, Drop-Down Lists, and Galleries

Groups on each of the tabs contain a variety of ***buttons***, ***drop-down lists***, and ***galleries***. The following list describes each of these features and how they are used:

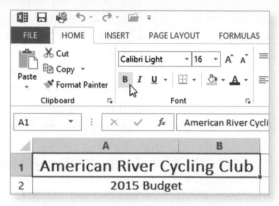

- ***Button:*** Applies a feature to selected text or object. Click a button to apply the feature (Figure 1-51).
- ***Drop-Down List:*** Displays the various options available for a feature. Some buttons are drop-down lists only, which means when you click one of these buttons the drop-down list of options appears (Figure 1-52). Other buttons are ***split***

1-51 *Bold* button in the *Font* group on the *Home* tab

buttons, which have both a button you click to apply a feature and an arrow you click to display a drop-down list of options (Figure 1-53).

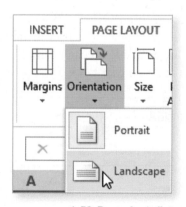

1-52 Drop-down list

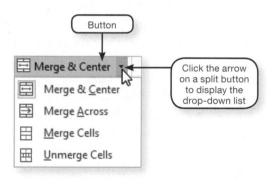

1-53 Split button—button and drop-down list

- ***Gallery:*** Displays a collection of option buttons. Click an option in a gallery to apply the feature. Figure 1-54 is the *Styles* gallery. You can click the **More** button to display the entire gallery of options or click the **Up** or **Down** arrow to display a different row of options.

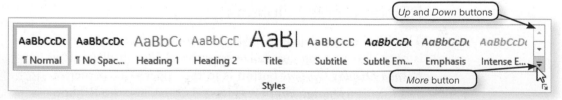

1-54 *Styles* gallery in Word

Dialog Boxes, Task Panes, and Launchers

Not all of the features that are available in an Office application are displayed in the groups on the tabs. Additional options for some groups are displayed in a *dialog box* or *task pane*. A *launcher*, which is a small square in the bottom right of some groups, opens a dialog box or displays a task pane when you click it (see Figure 1-56).

- *Dialog box:* A new window that opens to display additional features. You can move a dialog box by clicking and dragging on the title bar, which is the top of the dialog box where the title is displayed. Figure 1-55 is the *Datasheet Formatting* dialog box that opens when you click the *Text Formatting* launcher in Access.
- *Task pane:* Opens on the left or right of the Office application window. Figure 1-56 is the *Clipboard* pane, which is available in all Office applications. Task panes are named according to their feature (e.g., *Clipboard* pane or *Navigation* pane). You can resize a task pane by clicking and dragging on its left or right border. Click the **X** in the upper right corner to close a task pane.

1-55 *Datasheet Formatting* dialog box

1-56 *Clipboard* pane

ScreenTips

ScreenTips display descriptive information about a button, drop-down list, launcher, or gallery selection in the groups on the *Ribbon.* When you put your pointer on an item on the *Ribbon,* a Screen-Tip displays information about the selection (Figure 1-57). The ScreenTip appears temporarily and displays the command name, keyboard shortcut (if available), and a description of the command.

1-57 ScreenTip

Radio Buttons, Check Boxes, and Text Boxes

Within dialog boxes and task panes there are a variety of features you can apply using radio buttons, check boxes, text boxes, drop-down lists, and other buttons. A *radio button* is a round button that you click to select one option from a list of options. A selected radio button has a solid dot inside the round button. When you see a *check box*, you can use it to select one or more options. A check appears in a check box you have selected. A *text box* is an area where you can type text.

A task pane or dialog box may also include drop-down lists or other buttons that open additional dialog boxes. Figure 1-58 shows the *Page Setup* dialog box in Excel, which includes a variety of radio buttons, check boxes, text boxes, drop-down lists, and other buttons that open additional dialog boxes.

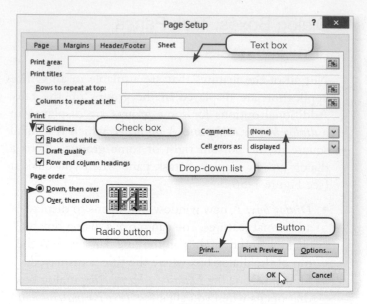

1-58 *Page Setup* dialog box in Excel

Quick Access Toolbar

The ***Quick Access toolbar*** is located above the *Ribbon* on the upper left of each Office application window. It contains buttons you can use to apply commonly used features such as *Save, Undo, Redo,* and *Open* (Figure 1-59). The *Undo* button is a split button. You can click the button to undo the last action performed or you can click the drop-down arrow to display and undo multiple previous actions.

1-59 *Quick Access* toolbar

Customize the Quick Access Toolbar

You can customize the *Quick Access* toolbar to include features you regularly use, such as *Quick Print, New,* and *Spelling & Grammar*. The following steps show how to customize the *Quick Access* toolbar in Word. The customization process is similar for the *Quick Access* toolbar in the other Office applications.

HOW TO: Customize the Quick Access Toolbar

1. Click the **Customize Quick Access Toolbar** drop-down list on the right edge of the *Quick Access* toolbar (Figure 1-60).

2. Select a command to add to the *Quick Access* toolbar. The command appears on the *Quick Access* toolbar.

   - Items on the *Customize Quick Access Toolbar* drop-down list with a check mark are displayed on the *Quick Access* toolbar.
   - Deselect a checked item to remove it from the *Quick Access* toolbar.

3. To add a command that is not listed on the *Customize Quick Access Toolbar,* click the **Customize Quick Access Toolbar** drop-down list and select **More Commands**.

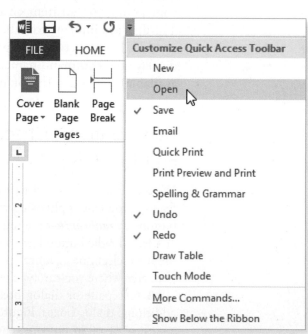

1-60 Customize the *Quick Access* toolbar

The *Word Options* dialog box opens with the *Quick Access Toolbar* area displayed (Figure 1-61).

4. Click the **Customize Quick Access Toolbar** drop-down list on the right and select **For all documents** or the current document.

   • If you select *For all documents*, the change is made to the *Quick Access* toolbar for all documents you open in Word.
   • If you select the current document, the change is made to the *Quick Access* toolbar in that document only.

5. On the left, select the command you want to add.

   • If you can't find the command you're looking for, click the **Choose commands from** drop-down list and select **All Commands**.

6. Click the **Add** button and the command name appears in the list on the right.

7. Add other commands as desired.

8. To rearrange commands on the *Quick Access* toolbar, select the command to move and click the **Move Up** or **Move Down** button.

9. Click **OK** to close the *Word Options* dialog box.

1-61 Customize the *Quick Access* toolbar in the *Word Options* dialog box

---

> **MORE INFO**
>
> To remove an item from the *Quick Access* toolbar, right-click an item and select **Remove from Quick Access Toolbar**.

SLO 1.5

Using a Context Menu, Mini Toolbar, and Keyboard Shortcuts

Most of the formatting and other features you will want to apply to text are available in groups on the different tabs. But many of these features are also available using content menus, mini toolbars, and keyboard shortcuts. You can use these tools to quickly apply formatting or other options to text or objects.

Context Menu

A ***context menu*** is displayed when you right-click text, a cell, or an object such as a picture, drawing object, chart, or *SmartArt* (Figure 1-62). The context menu is a vertical rectangle menu that lists a variety of options. These options are context-sensitive, which means they vary depending on what you right-click.

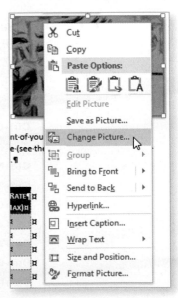

1-62 Context menu

Some options on the context menu are buttons that perform an action (e.g., *Cut* or *Copy*), some are buttons that open a dialog box or task pane (e.g., *Save as Picture* or *Size and Position*), and some are selections that display a drop-down list of selections (e.g., *Bring to Front* or *Wrap Text*).

Mini Toolbar

The ***mini toolbar*** is another context menu that displays when you right-click text, a cell, or an object in your file (Figure 1-63). The mini toolbar is a horizontal rectangle menu that lists a variety of formatting options. These options vary depending on what you right-click. The mini toolbar contains a variety of buttons and drop-down lists. Some mini toolbars automatically display when you select text or an object, such as when you select a row of a table in Word or PowerPoint.

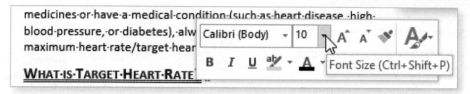

1-63 Mini toolbar

Keyboard Shortcuts

You can also use a ***keyboard shortcut*** to quickly apply formatting or perform actions. A keyboard shortcut is a keyboard key or combination of keyboard keys that you press at the same time. These can include the *Ctrl, Shift, Alt,* letter, number, and function keys (e.g., *F1* or *F7*). The following table lists some common Office keyboard shortcuts.

> **MORE INFO**
>
> See Appendix A for more Office 2013 keyboard shortcuts.

Common Office Keyboard Shortcuts

Keyboard Shortcut	Action or Displays	Keyboard Shortcut	Action or Displays
Ctrl+S	Save	Ctrl+Z	Undo
F12	*Save As* dialog box	Ctrl+Y	Redo or Repeat
Ctrl+O	*Open* area on the *Backstage* view	Ctrl+1	Single space
Shift+F12	*Open* dialog box	Ctrl+2	Double space
Ctrl+N	New blank file	Ctrl+L	Align left
Ctrl+P	*Print* area on the *Backstage* view	Ctrl+E	Align center
Ctrl+C	Copy	Ctrl+R	Align right
Ctrl+X	Cut	F1	*Help* dialog box
Ctrl+V	Paste	F7	*Spelling* pane
Ctrl+B	Bold	Ctrl+A	Select All
Ctrl+I	Italic	Ctrl+Home	Move to the beginning
Ctrl+U	Underline	Ctrl+End	Move to the end

For this project, you work with a document for the American River Cycling Club. You modify the existing document, add document properties, customize the *Quick Access* toolbar, export the document as a PDF file, and share a link to the document.

Note to Instructor:
Students: *For this project, you share an Office Web App file with your instructor.*
Instructor: *In order to complete this project, your students need your Microsoft email address. You can create a new Live or Hotmail account for projects in this chapter.*

File Needed: ***ARCCTraining-01.docx***
Completed Project File Names: ***[your initials] PP O1-2.docx*** and ***[your initials] PP O1-2.pdf***

1. Open Word 2013 and open the ***ARCCTraining-01*** file from your student data files.

2. Save this document as ***[your initials] PP O1-2*** in the *American River Cycling Club* folder in your *SkyDrive* folder.

3. Use a button, drop-down list, and dialog box to modify the document.
   a. Select the first heading, "**What is Maximum Heart Rate?**"
   b. Click the **Bold** button [*Home* tab, *Font* group].
   c. Click the **Underline** drop-down arrow and select **Double underline** (Figure 1-64).
   d. Click the **launcher** in the *Font* group [*Home* tab] to open the *Font* dialog box (Figure 1-65).
   e. In the *Size* area, select **12** from the list or type 12 in the text box.
   f. In the *Effects* area, click the **Small caps** check box to select it.
   g. Click **OK** to close the dialog box and apply the formatting changes.
   h. Select the next heading, "**What is Target Heart Rate?**"
   i. Repeat steps 3b–g to apply formatting to selected text.

4. Add document properties.
   a. Click the **File** tab to display the *Backstage* view.
   b. Select **Info** on the left. The document properties are displayed on the right.
   c. Click in the **Add a title** text box and type ARCC Training.
   d. Click the **Show All Properties** link near the bottom to display more document properties.
   e. Click in the **Specify the subject** text box and type Heart rate training.
   f. Click in the **Specify the company** text box and type American River Cycling Club.
   g. Click the **Show Fewer Properties** link to display fewer document properties.
   h. Click the **Back** arrow on the upper left to close the *Backstage* view and return to the document.

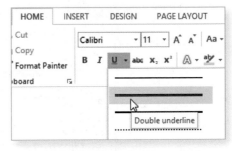

1-64 Apply *Double underline* to selected text

1-65 *Font* dialog box

5. Customize the *Quick Access* toolbar.
   a. Click the **Customize Quick Access Toolbar** drop-down arrow and select **Open** (Figure 1-66).
   b. Click the **Customize Quick Access Toolbar** drop-down arrow again and select **Spelling & Grammar**.
   c. Click the **Customize Quick Access Toolbar** drop-down arrow and select **More Commands**. The *Word Options* dialog box opens (Figure 1-67).
   d. Click the **Customize Quick Access Toolbar** drop-down list on the right and select **For all documents**.

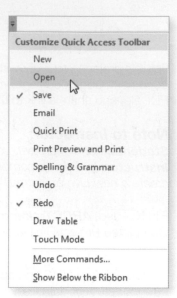

1-66 *Customize Quick Access Toolbar* drop-down list

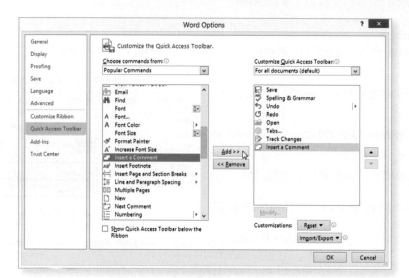

1-67 Customize the *Quick Access* toolbar in the *Word Options* dialog box

   e. In the list of commands at the left, click **Insert a Comment**.
   f. Click the **Add** button to add it to your *Quick Access* toolbar list on the right.
   g. Click **OK** to close the *Word Options* dialog box.
   h. Click the **Save** button on the *Quick Access* toolbar to save the document.

6. Export the file as a PDF file.
   a. Click the **File** tab to go to the *Backstage* view.
   b. Select **Export** on the left.
   c. Select **Create PDF/XPS Document** and click the **Create PDF/XPS** button. The *Publish as PDF or XPS* dialog box opens (Figure 1-68).
   d. Select the **American River Cycling Club** folder in your *SkyDrive* folder as the location to save the file.
   e. In the *File name* area, type [your initials] PP O1-2 if it is not already there.
   f. Deselect the **Open file after publishing** check box if it is checked.

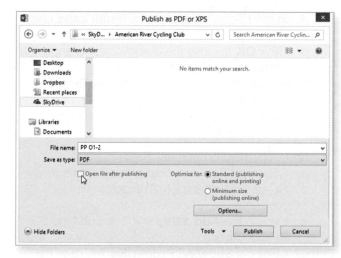

1-68 *Publish as PDF or XPS* dialog box

g. Select the **Standard** (publishing online and printing) radio button.

h. Click **Publish** to close the dialog box and create a PDF version of your file.

7. Get a link to share a document with your instructor.

a. Click the **File** tab to open the *Backstage* view.

b. Select **Share** at the left. Your file is already saved to *SkyDrive* so all of the *Share* options are available.

c. Select **Get a Sharing Link** on the left (Figure 1-69).

d. In the *View Link* area, click the **Create Link** button. A link for the document is created and displayed on the right of the button.

e. Select this link and press **Ctrl+C** to copy the link.

f. Click the **Back** arrow to close the *Backstage* view and return to your document.

8. Save and close the document (Figure 1-70).

9. Email the sharing link to your instructor.

a. Using your email account, create a new email to send to your instructor.

b. Include an appropriate subject line and a brief message in the body.

c. Press **Ctrl+V** to paste the link to your document in the body of the email.

d. Send the email message.

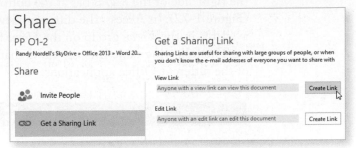

1-69 *Get a Link* to share a file

1-70 PP O1-2 completed

Working with Files

When you work with Office files, there are a variety of views to display your file. You can change how a file is displayed, adjust the display size, work with multiple files, and arrange the windows to view multiple files. Because most people work with multiple files at the same time, Office makes it intuitive to move from one file to another or display multiple document windows at the same time.

File Views

Each of the different Office applications provides you with a variety of ways to view your document. In Word, Excel, and PowerPoint, the different views are available on the *View* tab

(Figure 1-71). You can also change views using the buttons on the right side of the *Status* bar at the bottom of the file window (Figure 1-72). In Access, the different views for each object are available in the *Views* group on the *Home* tab.

The following table lists the views that are available in each of the different Office applications.

1-71 *Workbook Views* group on the *View* tab in Excel

1-72 PowerPoint views on the *Status* bar

File Views

Office Application	Views	Office Application	Views
Word	Read Mode Print Layout Web Layout Outline Draft	**Access** *(Access views vary depending on active object)*	Layout View Design View Datasheet View Form View SQL View Report View Print Preview
Excel	Normal Page Break View Page Layout View Custom Views	**PowerPoint**	Normal Outline View Slide Sorter Notes Page Reading View Presenter View

Change Display Size

You can use the ***Zoom feature*** to increase or decrease the display size of your file. Using *Zoom* to change the display size does not change the actual size of text or objects in your file; it only changes the size of your display. For example, if you change the *Zoom* level to 120%, you increase the display of your file to 120% of its normal size (100%), but changing the display size does not affect the actual size of text and objects in your file. You could also decrease the *Zoom* level to 80% to display more of your file on the screen.

There are a few different ways you can increase or decrease the *Zoom* level on your file. Your *Zoom* options vary depending on the Office application you are using.

- ***Zoom level on the* Status *bar*** (Figure 1-73): Click the + or – buttons to increase or decrease *Zoom* level.

1-73 *Zoom* level area on the *Status* bar in PowerPoint

- ***Zoom group on the View tab*** (Figure 1-74): There are a variety of *Zoom* options in the *Zoom* group. These vary depending on application.

1-74 *Zoom* group in Excel

- *Zoom dialog box* (Figure 1-75): Click the **Zoom** button in the *Zoom* group on *View* tab or click **Zoom level** on the *Status* bar to open the *Zoom* dialog box.

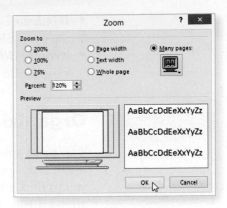

> ### MORE INFO
> The *Zoom* feature is only available in Access in *Print Preview* view when you are working with reports.

1-75 *Zoom* dialog box in Word

Manage Multiple Open Files and Windows

When you are working on multiple files in an Office application, each file is opened in a new window. You can *minimize* an open window to place the file on the Windows *Taskbar* (the bar at the bottom of the Windows desktop), *restore down* an open window so it does not fill the entire computer screen, or *maximize* a window so it fills the entire computer screen. The *Minimize, Restore Down/Maximize,* and *Close* buttons are in the upper right of a file window (Figure 1-76).

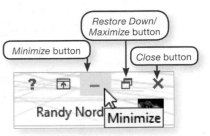

1-76 Window options buttons

> ### MORE INFO
> You can open only one Access file at a time. If you open another Access file, the first one closes.

- *Minimize:* Click the **Minimize** button to hide this window. When a document is minimized, it is not closed. It is collapsed so the window is not displayed on your screen. Click the application icon on the Windows *Taskbar* at the bottom to display thumbnails of open files. You can click an open file thumbnail to display the file (Figure 1-77).
- *Restore Down/Maximize:* Click the **Restore Down/Maximize** button to decrease the size of an open window or maximize the window to fill the entire screen. This button toggles between *Restore Down* and *Maximize.* When

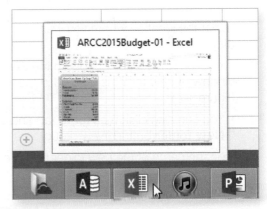

1-77 Display open files on the Windows *Taskbar*

a window is restored down, you can change the size of a window by clicking and dragging on a border of the window. You can also move the window by clicking and dragging on the title bar at the top of the window.
- *Close:* Click the **Close** button to close the window. If there is only one open file, the Office application also closes when you click the *Close* button on the file.

You can switch between open files or arrange the open files to display more than one window at the same time. There are a few ways to do this.

- *Switch Windows button:* Click the **Switch Windows** button [*View* tab, *Window* group] (not available in Access) to display a drop-down list of open files. Click a file from the drop-down list to display the file.

- *Windows Taskbar:* Click an Office application icon on the Windows *Taskbar* to display the open files in that application. Click an open file to display it (see Figure 1-77).
- *Arrange All button:* Click the **Arrange All** button [*View* tab, *Window* group] to display all windows in an application. You can resize or move the open file windows.

Organizing and Customizing Folders and Files

The more you use your computer and create and use files, the more important it is to stay organized. You can do this by using folders to store related files, which makes it easier for you to find, edit, and share your files. For example, you can create a folder for the college you attend. Inside the college folder, you can create a folder for each of your courses. Inside each of the course folders you might create a folder for student data files, solution files, and group projects. Folders can store any type of files, and you are not limited to Office files.

Create a Folder

You can create folders inside of other folders. In *SLO 1.2: Creating, Saving, Closing, and Opening Files,* you learned how to create a new folder when saving an Office file in the *Save As* dialog box. You can also create a folder using a Windows folder.

HOW TO: Create a Windows Folder

1. Open a Windows folder.
   - From the Windows *Start* page, click **File Explorer**, **Computer**, or **Documents** to open a Windows window.
   - Your folders and computer locations are listed on the left.
2. Select the location where you want to create a new folder.
3. Click the **New folder** button on the top left of the window. A new folder is created in the folders area (Figure 1-78).
   - You can also click the **Home** tab and click the **New folder** button [*New* group].
4. Type the name of the new folder and press **Enter**.

1-78 Create a new Windows folder

> **ANOTHER WAY**
> **Ctrl+Shift+N** creates a new folder in a Windows folder.

Move and Copy Files and Folders

You can move or copy files and folders using the *Move to* or *Copy to* buttons on the *Home* tab of a Windows folder. You can also use the move or copy keyboard shortcuts (**Ctrl+X, Ctrl+C, Ctrl+V**) or the drag and drop method. When you move a file or folder, you cut it from one location and paste it in another location. When you copy a file or folder, you create a copy of it and paste it in another location so the file or folder is in two or more locations. If there are files in a folder you move or copy, the files in the folder are moved or copied with the folder.

To move or copy multiple folders or files at the same time, press the **Ctrl** key and select multiple items to move or copy. Use the *Ctrl* key to select or deselect multiple non-adjacent files or folders. You can also use the *Shift* key to select a range of files or folders. Click the first file or folder in a range, press the **Shift** key, and select the last file or folder in the range to select all of the items in the range.

HOW TO: Move or Copy a File or Folder

1. In a Windows folder, select a file or folder to move or copy.
2. Click the **Home** tab to display the tab in the open window.
3. Click the **Move to** or **Copy to** button [*Organize* group] and select the location where you want to move or copy the file or folder (Figure 1-79).

1-79 Move or copy a selected file or folder

   - If the folder you want is not available, select **Choose location** to open the *Move Items* or *Copy Items* dialog box.
   - To use the keyboard shortcuts, press **Ctrl+X** to cut the file or folder or **Ctrl+C** to copy the file or folder from its original location, go to the desired new location, and press **Ctrl+V** to paste it.
   - To use the drag and drop method to move a file or folder, select the file or folder and drag and drop on the new location.
   - To use the drag and drop method to copy a file or folder, press the **Ctrl** key, select the file or folder, and drag and drop on the new location.

> **ANOTHER WAY**
> Right-click a file or folder to display the context menu where you can select **Cut**, **Copy**, or **Paste**.

Rename Files and Folders

When you need to change the name of a file or folder, you can rename these in a Windows folder.

HOW TO: Rename a File or Folder

1. In a Windows folder, select the file or folder you want to rename.
2. Click the **Rename** button [*Home* tab, *Organize* group].
3. Type the new name of the file or folder and press **Enter**.

> **ANOTHER WAY**
> Select a file or folder to rename, press **F2**, type the new name, and press **Enter**. You can also right-click a file or folder and select **Rename** from the context menu.

Delete Files and Folders

You can also easily delete files and folders. When you delete a file or folder, it is moved from its current location to the *Recycle Bin* on your computer, which is the location where deleted items are stored. If a file or folder is in the *Recycle Bin*, you can restore this item to its original location or move it to a different location. You also have the option to permanently delete a file or folder; the item is deleted and not moved to the *Recycle Bin*. If an item is permanently deleted, you do not have the restore option.

There are several ways to delete a file or folder. To ensure that you don't delete anything by mistake, when you delete a file or folder, a confirmation dialog box opens, prompting you to confirm whether or not you want to delete the selected file or folder.

HOW TO: Delete Files and Folders

1. Select the file or folder you want to delete.
   - You can select multiple files and folders to delete at the same time.
2. Click the **Delete** drop-down arrow [*Home* tab, *Organize* group] to display the list of delete options (Figure 1-80).
3. Click **Recycle** or **Permanently delete**. A confirmation dialog box opens.
   - *Recycle* deletes the selected item(s) and moves them to the *Recycle Bin*.
   - *Permanently delete* deletes the item(s) from your computer.
   - The default action when you click the *Delete* button (not the drop-down arrow) is *Recycle*.
4. Click **Yes** to delete.

1-80 Delete selected files and folders

> ## ANOTHER WAY
> Press **Ctrl+D** or the **Delete** key on your keyboard to recycle selected item(s).
> Press **Shift+Delete** to permanently delete selected item(s).

Compressed and Zipped Folders

If you want to share multiple files or a folder of files with classmates, coworkers, friends, or family, you can *zip* the files into a *zipped folder* (also called a *compressed folder*). For example, you can't attach an entire folder to an email message, but you can attach a zipped folder to an email message. Compressing files and folders decreases their size. You can zip a group of selected files, a folder, or a combination of files and folders, and then share the zipped folder with others through email or in a cloud storage location such as *SkyDrive*.

HOW TO: Create a Zipped Folder

1. Select the file(s) and/or folder(s) you want to compress and send.
2. Click the **Zip** button [*Share* tab, *Send* group] (Figure 1-81). A zipped folder is created.
   - The name of the zipped folder is the name of the first item you selected to zip. You can rename this folder.
   - The icon for a zipped folder looks similar to the icon for a folder except it has a vertical zipper down the middle of the folder.

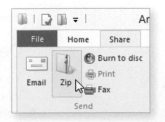

1-81 Create a zipped folder

If you receive a zipped folder from someone via email, save the zipped folder and then you can *extract* its contents. Extracting a zipped folder creates a regular Window folder from the zipped folder.

HOW TO: Extract a Zipped Folder

1. After saving the zipped folder to a location on your computer, select the folder (Figure 1-82).
2. Click the **Extract all** button [*Compress Folder Tools Extract* tab]. The *Extract Compressed (Zipped) Folders* dialog box opens (Figure 1-83).
3. Click **Extract** to extract the folder.
   - Both the extracted folder and the zipped folder display in the folder where they are located.
   - If you check the **Show extracted files when complete** check box, the extracted folder will open after extracting.

1-83 *Extract Compressed (Zipped) Folders* dialog box

1-82 **Extract files from a zipped folder**

For this project, you copy and rename files in your *SkyDrive* folder on your computer, create a folder, move and copy files, create a zipped folder, and rename a zipped folder.

Files Needed: *[your initials] PP O1-1a.pptx*, *[your initials] PP O1-1b.xlsx*, and *[your initials] PP O1-2.docx*
Completed Project File Names: *[your initials] PP O1-3a.pptx*, *[your initials] PP O1-3b.xlsx*, *[your initials] PP O1-3c.docx*, and *ARCC Italy Tour-[current year]* (zipped folder)

1. Open your *SkyDrive* folder.
   a. From the Windows *Start* page, click the **File Explorer** or **Computer** tile to open a Windows folder. If these options are not available on the *Start* page, use *Search* to find and open the *File Explorer* or *Computer* window.

b. Click the **SkyDrive** folder on the left to display the folders in your *SkyDrive* folder.

c. Double click the **American River Cycling Club** folder to open it.

2. Copy and rename files.

a. Select the **[your initials] PP O1-1a** file (this is a PowerPoint file).

b. Click the **Copy to** button [*Home* tab, *Organize* group] and select **Choose Location** to open the *Copy Items* dialog box (Figure 1-84).

c. Select the **American River Cycling Club** folder in your *SkyDrive* folder and click **Copy**.

d. Select the copy of the file (**[your initials] PP O1-1a – Copy**) and click the **Rename** button [*Home* tab, *Organize* group].

e. Type [your initials] PP O1-3a and press **Enter**.

f. Select the **[your initials] PP O1-1b** file (this is an Excel file).

g. Press **Ctrl+C** to copy the file and then press **Ctrl+V** to paste a copy of the file.

h. Rename this file [your initials] PP O1-3b.

i. Right-click the **[your initials] PP O1-2** file (this is a Word file and the third one in the list) and select **Copy** from the context menu.

j. Right-click a blank area of the open window and select **Paste** from the context menu.

k. Rename this file [your initials] PP O1-3c.

1-84 Copy selected file

3. Create a new folder and move files.

a. With the *American River Cycling Club* folder still open, click the **New folder** button on the upper left.

b. Type ARCC Italy Tour and press **Enter**.

c. Select the **[your initials] PP O1-3a** file.

d. Hold down the **Ctrl** key, select the **[your initials] PP O1-3b** and **[your initials] PP O1-3c** files.

e. Click the selected files and drag and drop on the *ARCC Italy Tour* folder (don't hold down the *Ctrl* key while dragging). The files are moved to the *ARCC Italy Tour* folder.

f. Double-click the **ARCC Italy Tour** folder to open it and confirm the files are moved.

g. Click the **Up** or **Back** arrow to return to the *American River Cycling Club* folder.

4. Create a zipped folder.

a. Select the **ARCC Italy Tour** folder.

b. Click the **Zip** button [*Share* tab, *Send* group]. A zipped (compressed) folder is created.

c. Right-click the zipped folder and select **Rename** from the context menu.

d. At the end of the folder name, type - (a hyphen), type the current year, and press **Enter** (Figure 1-85).

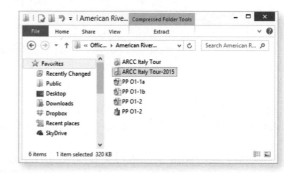

1-85 PP O1-3 completed

5. Email the zipped folder to your instructor.

a. Using your email account, create a new email to send to your instructor.

b. Include an appropriate subject line and a brief message in the body.

c. Attach the **ARCC Italy Tour-[current year]** zipped folder to the email message.

d. Send the email message.

Chapter Summary

1.1 Use the basic features of Windows 8 and Microsoft Office 2013 products (p. O1-2).

- **Windows 8** is the operating system on your computer.
- A **Microsoft account** is a free account you create. When you create a Microsoft account, you are given an email address, a **SkyDrive** account, and access to **Office Web Apps**.
- **SkyDrive** is the **cloud storage** area where you can store files in a private and secure online location.
- In Windows 8, the **SkyDrive folder** is one of your file storage location options.
- The **Start page** in Windows 8 is where you select what you want to do on your computer.
- The **Windows desktop** is the working area of Windows and the **Taskbar** is at the bottom of the desktop. You can pin applications to the Taskbar.
- The **File Explorer** is a window that displays libraries, files, and folders on your computer.
- You can access your *SkyDrive* folders and files using an Internet browser window.
- **Apps** are the applications or programs on your computer. App buttons are arranged in tiles on the Windows 8 *Start* page.
- You can customize the *Start* page to add, remove, or arrange apps.
- **Navigation options** display on the right side of your computer monitor when you put your pointer in the bottom right corner.
- **Office 2013** is application software that contains **Word**, **Excel**, **Access**, **PowerPoint**, **Outlook**, **OneNote**, and **Publisher**.
- **Office Web Apps** is free online software that works in conjunction with your online *SkyDrive* account.
- In *SkyDrive*, you can share Office files with others.
- When you open each of the Office applications, a **Start page** is displayed where you can open an existing file or create a new file.
- In the **Backstage view** in each of the Office applications, you can perform many common tasks such as saving, opening an existing file, creating a new file, printing, and sharing.
- **Office Help** contains searchable articles related to specific topics.

- Use the mouse (or touch pad) on your computer to navigate the pointer on your computer screen. Use the pointer or click buttons to select text or objects.
- When using Office 2013 on a tablet, use the touch screen to perform actions.

1.2 Create, save, close, and open Office files (p. O1-12).

- You can create a new Office file from the *Start* page or *Backstage* view of the Office application you are using.
- When you **save a file** for the first time, you give it a **file name**.
- You can create **folders** to organize saved files, and you can save a file as a different file name.
- A variety of different **file types** are used in each of the Office applications.
- You can close an Office file when you are finished working on it. If the file has not been saved or changes have been made to the file, you are prompted to save the file before closing.
- In each of the Office applications, you can open an existing file from the *Start* page or from the *Backstage* view.

1.3 Print, share, and customize Office files (p. O1-20).

- You can print a file in a variety of formats. The *Print* area on the *Backstage* view lists your print options and displays a preview of your file.
- You can export a file as a **PDF file** and save the PDF file to post to a web site or share with others.
- **Document properties** contain information about a file.
- You can **share** Office files in a variety of ways and allow others to view or edit shared files.
- **Program options** are available on the *Backstage* view. You can use the program options to make global changes to an Office application.

1.4 Use the Ribbon, tabs, groups, dialog boxes, task panes, galleries, and the Quick Access toolbar (p. O1-23).

- The **Ribbon** appears at the top of an Office window. It contains **tabs** and **groups** that allow you to access features you regularly use.

O1-39

- The **Ribbon Display Options** provides different ways the *Ribbon* can be displayed in Office applications.
- Within groups on each tab are a variety of **buttons**, **drop-down lists**, and **galleries**.
- **Dialog boxes** contain additional features not always displayed on the *Ribbon*.
- Click the **launcher** in the bottom right corner of some groups to open a dialog box for that group.
- A **ScreenTip** displays information about commands on the *Ribbon*.
- Dialog boxes contain **radio buttons**, **check boxes**, **drop-down lists**, and **text boxes** you can use to apply features.
- The **Quick Access toolbar**, which contains buttons that allow you to perform commands, is displayed in all Office applications on the upper left.
- You can add or remove commands on the *Quick Access* toolbar.

1.5 Use context menus, mini toolbars, and keyboard shortcuts in Office applications (p. O1-27).

- A **context menu** displays when you right-click text or an object. The context menu contains different features depending on what you right-click.
- The **mini toolbar** is another context menu that displays formatting options.
- You can use **keyboard shortcuts** to apply features or commands.

1.6 Customize the view and display size in Office applications and work with multiple Office files (p. O1-31).

- In each of the Office applications, there are a variety of **views**.
- The **Zoom feature** changes the display size of your file.
- You can work with multiple Office files at the same time and switch between open files.

1.7 Organize and customize Office files and Windows folders (p. O1-34).

- **Folders** store and organize your files.
- You can create, move, or copy files and folders. Files stored in a folder are moved or copied with that folder.
- You can rename a file to change the file name.
- When you delete a file or folder, it is moved to the **Recycle Bin** on your computer by default. Alternatively, you can permanently delete files and folders.
- A **zipped (compressed) folder** makes it easier and faster to email or share multiple files. You can zip files and/or folders into a zipped folder.
- When you receive a zipped folder, you can **extract** the zipped folder to create a regular Windows folder and access its contents.

Check for Understanding

In the **Online Learning Center** for this text (www.mhhe.com/office2013inpractice), there are a variety of resources that can be used to review the concepts covered in this chapter.

The following Online Learning Resources are available in the Online Learning Center:

- Multiple choice questions
- Short answer questions
- Matching exercises

In these projects, you use your *SkyDrive* to store files. If you don't have a Microsoft account, see *SLO 1.1: Using Windows 8 and Office 2013* for information about obtaining a free personal Microsoft account.

Guided Project 1-1

For this project, you organize and edit files for Emma Cavalli at Placer Hills Real Estate. You extract a zipped folder, rename files, manage multiple documents, and apply formatting.
[Student Learning Outcomes 1.1, 1.2, 1.4, 1.5, 1.6, 1.7]

Files Needed: ***CavalliFiles-01*** (zipped folder)
Completed Project File Names: ***[your initials] Office 1-1a.docx***, ***[your initials] Office 1-1b.docx***, ***[your initials] Office 1-1c.xlsx***, and ***[your initials] Office 1-1d.pptx***

Skills Covered in This Project

- Copy and paste a zipped folder.
- Create a new folder in your *SkyDrive* folder.
- Extract a zipped folder.
- Move a file.
- Rename a file.
- Open a Word document.
- Switch between two open Word documents.

- Save a Word document with a different file name.
- Change display size.
- Use a mini toolbar, keyboard shortcut, context menu, and dialog box to apply formatting to selected text.
- Close a Word document.

1. Copy a zipped folder and create a new *SkyDrive* folder.
   a. From the Windows *Start* page, click **File Explorer** or **Computer** to open a Windows folder. If these options are not available on the *Start* page, use *Search* to find and open a Windows folder.
   b. Browse to the location on your computer where you store your student data files.
   c. Select the ***CavalliFiles-01*** zipped folder and press **Ctrl+C** to copy the folder.
   d. Select your **SkyDrive** folder at the left and click the **New folder** button to create a new folder.
   e. Type PHRE and press **Enter**.
   f. Press **Enter** again to open the *PHRE* folder.
   g. Press **Ctrl+V** to paste the copied ***CavalliFiles-01*** zipped folder in the *PHRE* folder.

2. Extract a zipped folder.
   a. Select the ***CavalliFiles-01*** zipped folder.
   b. Click the **Compressed Folder Tools Extract** tab and click the **Extract all** button. The *Extract Compressed (Zipped) Folders* dialog box opens.
   c. Deselect the **Show extracted files when complete** check box.
   d. Click the **Extract** button. The zipped folder is extracted and there are now two *CavalliFiles-01* folders. One folder is zipped and the other is a regular folder.
   e. Select the zipped ***CavalliFiles-01*** folder and press **Delete** to delete the zipped folder.

3. Move and rename files.
   a. With the *PHRE* folder still open, double-click the **CavalliFiles-01** folder to open it.
   b. Click the first file, press and hold the **Shift** key, and click the last file to select all four files.
   c. Press **Ctrl+X** to cut the files from the current location.

d. Click the **Up** button to move up to the *PHRE* folder (Figure 1-86).

e. Press **Ctrl+V** to paste and move the files.

f. Select the ***Cavalli files-01*** folder and press **Delete** to delete the folder.

g. Select the ***CavalliPHRE-01*** file, click the **File** tab, and click the **Rename** button [*Organize* group].

h. Type [your initials] Office 1-1a and press **Enter**.

i. Right-click the ***FixedMortgageRates-01*** file and select the **Rename** from the context menu.

j. Type [your initials] Office 1-1b and press **Enter**.

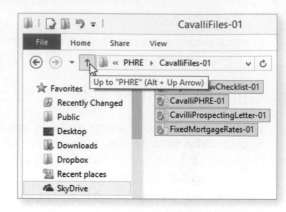

1-86 Go up to the *PHRE* folder

4. Open two Word documents and rename a Word document.

a. Press the **Ctrl** key and click the ***BuyerEscrowChecklist-01*** and ***CavalliProspectingLetter-01*** files to select both files.

b. Press the **Enter** key to open both files in Word.

c. If the *BuyerEscrowChecklist-01* document is not displayed, click the **Switch Documents** button [*View* tab, *Window* group] and select ***BuyerEscrowChecklist-01***. You can also switch documents by selecting the document on the *Taskbar*.

d. Click the **File** tab and select **Save As** at the left.

e. Select **[your name's] SkyDrive** in the *Places* area and select the **PHRE** folder or click **Browse** and select the **PHRE** folder. The *Save As* dialog box opens.

f. Type [your initials] Office 1-1c in the *File name* text box and click **Save**.

g. Press **Ctrl+W** to close the document. The *Cavalli Prospecting Letter_01* remains open.

5. Change display size and edit and rename a Word document.

a. Click the **Zoom In** or **Zoom Out** button at the bottom right of the document window to change the display size to 120% (Figure 1-87). This will vary depending on the current display size.

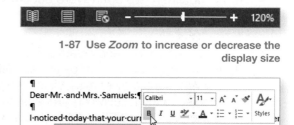

1-87 Use *Zoom* to increase or decrease the display size

b. Select "**Placer Hills Real Estate**" in the first body paragraph of the letter and the mini toolbar is displayed (Figure 1-88).

c. Click the **Bold** button on the mini toolbar to apply bold formatting to the selected text.

1-88 Use the mini toolbar to apply formatting

d. Select the first sentence in the second body paragraph ("**I am also a Whitney Hills** . . . ") and press **Ctrl+I** to apply italic formatting to the selected sentence.

e. Select the text that reads "**Emma Cavalli**," below "Best regards."

f. Right-click the selected text and select **Font** from the context menu to open the *Font* dialog box.

g. Check the **Small Caps** check box in the *Effects* area and click **OK** to close the *Font* dialog box.

h. With "**Emma Cavalli**" still selected, click the **Bold** button [*Home* tab, *Font* group].

i. Press **F12** to open the *Save As* dialog box.

j. Type [your initials] Office 1-1d in the *File name* text box and click **Save**.

k. Click the **X** in the upper right corner of the document window to close the document and close Word.

6. Your *PHRE* folder should contain the files shown in Figure 1-89.

1-89 Office 1-1 completed

Guided Project 1-2

For this project, you modify an Excel file for Hamilton Civic Center. You rename a file, add document properties, use *Help* to search a topic, share the file, and export a file as a PDF file.
[Student Learning Outcomes 1.1, 1.2, 1.3, 1.4]

Note to Students and Instructor:
Students: *For this project, you share an Office file with your instructor.*
Instructor: *In order to complete this project, your students need your Microsoft email address. You can create a new Live or Hotmail account for projects in this chapter.*

File Needed: **HCCYoga-01.xlsx**
Completed Project File Names: **[your initials] Office 1-2.xlsx** and **[your initials] Office 1-2.pdf**

Skills Covered in This Project

- Open Excel and an Excel workbook.
- Create a new *SkyDrive* folder.
- Save an Excel workbook with a different file name.
- Add document properties to a file.

- Use *Microsoft Excel Help* to search for a topic.
- Open a Word document.
- Share a file.
- Export a file as a PDF file.

1. Open Excel 2013 and open an Excel workbook.
   a. From the Windows *Start* page, click **Excel 2013** to open this application. If Excel 2013 is not available on the *Start* page, use *Search* to find and open it.
   b. From the Excel *Start* page, click **Open Other Workbooks** to display the *Open* area of the *Backstage* view.
   c. In the *Places* area, select where your student data files are stored and click the **Browse** button to open the *Open* dialog box.
   d. Browse to the location where your student data files are stored, select the **HCCYoga-01** file, and click **Open** to open the Excel workbook.

2. Save a file as a different file name in your *SkyDrive* folder.
   a. Click the **File** tab to open the *Backstage* view and select **Save As** at the left.
   b. In the *Places* area, select **[your name's] SkyDrive**.
   c. Click the **Browse** button to open the *Save As* dialog box.
   d. Select the **SkyDrive** folder on the left and click the **New folder** button to create a new folder.
   e. Type HCC and press **Enter**.
   f. Double-click the **HCC** folder to open it.
   g. In the *File name* area, type [your initials] Office 1-2 and click **Save** to close the dialog box and save the file.

3. Add document properties to the Excel workbook.
   a. Click the **File** button to open the *Backstage* view and select **Info** on the left. The document properties are displayed on the right.
   b. Put your insertion point in the *Title* text box ("Add a title") and type Yoga Classes.
   c. Click the **Show All Properties** link to display more properties.

O1-43

d. Put your insertion point in the *Company* text box and type Hamilton Civic Center.
e. Click the **back arrow** in the upper left of the *Backstage* window to return to the Excel workbook.

4. Use *Help* to learn about a topic.
   a. Click **Microsoft Excel Help** button (question mark) in the upper right corner of the Excel window or press **F1** to open the *Excel Help* dialog box.
   b. Put your insertion point in the *Search help* text box, type AutoSum, and press **Enter**.
   c. Click the first link and read about *AutoSum*.
   d. Click the **Back** button to return to the search list of articles and click the second link.
   e. Read about *AutoSum* and then click the **X** in the upper right corner to close the *Excel Help* dialog box.

5. Share an Excel workbook with your instructor.
   a. Click the **File** tab and select **Share** at the left.
   b. In the *Share* area, select **Invite People** (Figure 1-90).
   c. Type your instructor's email address in the *Type names or email addresses* area.
   d. In the drop-down list to the right of the email address, select **Can edit**.
   e. In the body, type a brief message.
   f. Click the **Share** button.
   g. Click the **Save** button to save and return to the workbook.

1-90 Invite people to share a file

6. Export the Excel workbook as a PDF file.
   a. Click the **File** button and select **Export** at the left.
   b. In the *Export* area, select **Create PDF/XPS Document** and click the **Create PDF/XPS** button. The *Publish as PDF or XPS* dialog box opens.
   c. Check the **Open file after publishing** check box. The publish location and file name are the same as the Excel file; don't change these.
   d. Click **Publish** to create and open the PDF file (Figure 1-91). The PDF file opens in an Internet browser window in *SkyDrive*.
   e. Close the Internet browser window.

7. Save and close the Excel file.
   a. Click the **Excel** icon on the Windows *Taskbar* to display the Excel file.
   b. Press **Ctrl+S** to save the file.
   c. Click the **X** in the upper right corner of the Excel window to close the file and Excel.

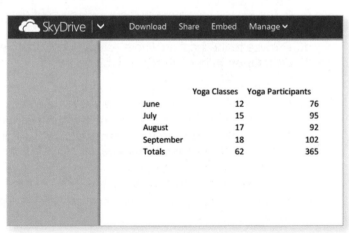

1-91 PDF file displayed in *SkyDrive*

Independent Project 1-3

For this project, you organize and edit files for Courtyard Medical Plaza. You extract a zipped folder, rename files, export a file as a PDF file, and share a file in *SkyDrive*.
[Student Learning Outcomes 1.1, 1.3, 1.6, 1.7]

Note to Students and Instructor:
Students: *For this project, you share an* Office Web App *file with your instructor.*
Instructor: *In order to complete this project, your students need your Microsoft email address. You can create a new Live or Hotmail account for projects in this chapter.*

Files Needed: **CMPFiles-01** (zipped folder)
Completed Project File Names: **[your initials] Office 1-3a.pptx**, **[your initials] Office 1-3a-pdf.pdf**, **[your initials] Office 1-3b.accdb**, **[your initials] Office 1-3c.xlsx**, and **[your initials] Office 1-3d.docx**

Skills Covered in This Project

- Copy and paste a zipped folder.
- Create a new folder in your *SkyDrive* folder.
- Extract a zipped folder.
- Move a file.

- Rename a file.
- Open a PowerPoint presentation.
- Export a file as a PDF file.
- Use *SkyDrive* to share a file.

1. Copy a zipped folder and create a new *SkyDrive* folder.
   a. Using a Windows folder, browse to locate the **CMPFiles-01** zipped folder in your student data files and copy the zipped folder.
   b. Go to your *SkyDrive* folder and create a new folder named Courtyard Medical Plaza within the *SkyDrive* folder.

2. Copy and extract the zipped folder and move files.
   a. Paste the zipped folder in the *Courtyard Medical Plaza* folder.
   b. Extract the zipped folder and then delete the zipped folder.
   c. Open the **CMPFiles-01** folder and move all of the files to the *Courtyard Medical Plaza* folder.
   d. Delete the **CMPFiles-01** folder.

3. Rename files in the *Courtyard Medical Plaza* folder.
   a. Rename the **CMPStayingActive-01** PowerPoint file to [your initials] Office 1-3a.
   b. Rename the **CourtyardMedicalPlaza-01** Access file to [your initials] Office 1-3b.
   c. Rename the **EstimatedCalories-01** Excel file to [your initials] Office 1-3c.
   d. Rename the **StayingActive-01** Word file to [your initials] Office 1-3d.

4. Export a PowerPoint file as a PDF file.
   a. From the *Courtyard Medical Plaza* folder, open the **[your initials] Office 1-3a** file. The file opens in PowerPoint.
   b. Export this file as a PDF file. Don't have the PDF file open after publishing.
   c. Save the file as [your initials] Office 1-3a-pdf and save in the *Courtyard Medical Plaza* folder.
   d. Close the PowerPoint file and exit PowerPoint.

5. Use *SkyDrive* to share a file with your instructor.
   a. Open an Internet browser window and log in to your *SkyDrive* (www. skydrive.com) using your Microsoft account.
   b. Go to your *SkyDrive* files and open the **Courtyard Medical Plaza** folder.
   c. Open the *[your initials] Office 1-3a* file in PowerPoint Web App.
   d. Share this file with your instructor.
   e. Send an email to share the file and include your instructor's email address and a brief message. Allow your instructor to edit the file.
   f. Sign out of *SkyDrive*.

6. Close the Windows folder containing the files for this project (Figure 1-92).

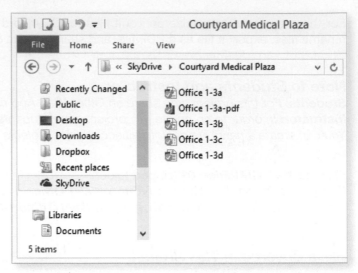

1-92 Office 1-3 completed

Independent Project 1-4

For this project, you modify a Word file for Life's Animal Shelter. You rename the document, add document properties, modify the document, share a link to the document, export a document as a PDF file, and create a zipped folder.
[Student Learning Outcomes 1.1, 1.2, 1.3, 1.4, 1.5, 1.6, 1.7]

Note to Students and Instructor:
Students: *For this project, you share an Office file with your instructor.*
Instructor: *In order to complete this project, your students need your Microsoft email address. You can create a new Live or Hotmail account for projects in this chapter.*

File Needed: *LASSupportLetter-01.docx*
Completed Project File Names: *[your initials] Office 1-4.docx*, *[your initials] Office 1-4.pdf*, and *LAS files* (zipped folder)

Skills Covered in This Project

- Open Excel and an Excel file.
- Create a new *SkyDrive* folder.
- Save a file with a different file name.
- Apply formatting to selected text.
- Add document properties to the file.
- Use *Microsoft Excel Help* to search for a topic.
- Open a Word document.
- Share a file.
- Export a file as a PDF file.

1. Open Word 2013 and open a Word document.
   a. From the Windows *Start* page, open Word 2013.
   b. From the Word *Start* page, open the ***LASSupportLetter-01*** document from your student data files.

2. Create a new folder and save the document with a different file name.
   a. Open the **Save As** dialog box and create a new folder named LAS in your *SkyDrive* folder.
   b. Save this document as [your initials] Office 1-4.

3. Apply formatting changes to the document using a dialog box, keyboard shortcut, and mini toolbar.
   a. Select "**To**" and use the **launcher** to open the *Font* dialog box.
   b. Apply **Bold** and **All caps** to the selected text.
   c. Repeat the formatting on the other three memo guide words: "**From**," "**Date**," and "**Subject**."
   d. Select "**Life's Animal Shelter**" in the first sentence of the first body paragraph and use the keyboard shortcut to apply **bold** formatting.
   e. Select the first sentence in the second body paragraph ("**Would you again consider** . . . ") and use the mini toolbar to apply **italic** formatting.

4. Add the following document properties to the document:
   Title: Support Letter
   Company: Life's Animal Shelter

5. Get a link to share this document with your instructor.
   a. Create and copy an **Edit Link** you can email to your instructor.
   b. Create a new email to send to your professor using the email you use for this course.
   c. Include an appropriate subject line and a brief message in the body.
   d. Paste the link in the body of the email message and send the message.

6. Use the keyboard shortcut to **save** the file before continuing.

7. Export this document as a PDF file.
   a. Save the file in the same location and use the same file name.
   b. Close the PDF file if it opens after publishing.

8. Save and close the Word file and exit Word (Figure 1-93).

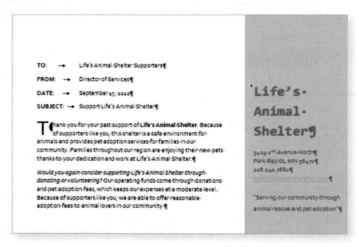

1-93 Office 1-4 completed

9. Create a zipped folder.
   a. Using a Windows folder, open the **LAS** folder in your *SkyDrive* folder.
   b. Select the two files and create a zipped folder.
   c. Rename the zipped folder LAS files (Figure 1-94).

10. Close the open Windows folder.

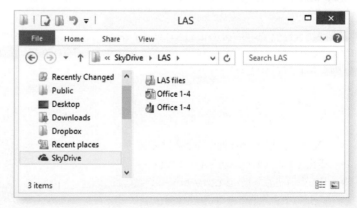

1-94 Office 1-4 completed

Challenge Project 1-5

For this project, you create folders to organize your files for this class and use *SkyDrive* to share a link with your professor.
[Student Learning Outcomes 1.1, 1.7]

Note to Students and Instructor:

Students: *For this project, you share an Office file with your instructor.*
Instructor: *In order to complete this project, your students need your Microsoft email address.*
You can create a new Live or Hotmail account for projects in this chapter.

File Needed: None
Completed Project File Name: Email link to shared folder to your instructor

Using a Windows folder, create *SkyDrive* folders to contain all of the files for this class. Organize your files and folders according to the following guidelines:

- Create a *SkyDrive* folder for this class.
- Create a *Student data files* folder inside the class folder.
- Extract student data files if you have not already done so. Make sure they are in the *Student data files* folder.
- Create a *Solution files* folder inside the class folder.
- Inside the *Solution files* folder, create a folder for each chapter.
- Create a folder to store miscellaneous class files such as the syllabus and other course handouts.

Using an Internet browser, log in to your *SkyDrive* and share your class folder with your instructor.

- In *SkyDrive*, select the check box to the right of your class folder and click the **Share** button.
- Create a link to *View only* the folder.
- Create an email to your professor and include an appropriate subject line and a brief message in the body.
- Paste the link to your *SkyDrive* class folder in the body of the email message and send the email.

Challenge Project 1-6

For this project, you save a file as a different file name, customize the *Quick Access* toolbar, share a file with your professor, and export a file as a PDF file.
[Student Learning Outcomes 1.1, 1.2, 1.3, 1.4]

Note to Students and Instructor:
Students: *For this project, you share an Office file with your instructor.*
Instructor: *In order to complete this project, your students need your Microsoft email address. You can create a new Live or Hotmail account for projects in this chapter.*

File Needed: Use an existing Office file
Completed Project File Name: ***[your initials] Office 1-6***

Open an existing Word, Excel, or PowerPoint file. Save this file in a *SkyDrive* folder and name it ***[your initials] Office 1-6***. If you don't have any of these files, use one from your Pause & Practice projects or select a file from your student data files.

With your file open, perform the following actions:

- Customize the *Quick Access* toolbar to add command buttons. Add commands such as *New*, *Open*, *Quick Print*, and *Spelling* that you use regularly in the Office application.
- Share your file with your instructor. Use *Invite People* and include your instructor's email, an appropriate subject line, and a brief message in the body. Allow your instructor to edit the file.
- Export the document as a PDF file. Use the same file name and save it in the same *SkyDrive* folder as your open file.

Outlook Overview and Email Basics

CHAPTER OVERVIEW

Microsoft Outlook (usually referred to as ***Outlook***) is the most widely used email and personal management software today. It is used in both business and personal environments. Outlook 2013 is part of the Microsoft Office 2013 suite of application software. This book covers the different aspects of Outlook and how this software is used to help manage your electronic communication, schedule your appointments and meetings, organize your personal and business contacts, and arrange your list of to-do items.

This first half of this book (Chapters 1–5) introduces you to all the main features of Outlook; the more advanced and special features of Outlook are presented in the second half of the book (Chapters 6-10). After going through the first half of the book, you will be very proficient in using all the main features in Outlook. The remaining chapters will take you more in depth into each of these areas and introduce you to some of the more advanced aspects of Outlook. After going through this book and practicing what you are learning, you will become the Outlook expert in your workplace, family, and neighborhood. Hopefully, that's a good thing!

Today, most people equate Microsoft Outlook with email, and these two terms have become almost synonymous in their use. Email is an integral part of Outlook, but it is much more than just email, as you will discover as you continue through this text. Most people use email on a daily basis, and Outlook is widely used in both the business and home environment to manage email accounts. It is important to remember that Outlook is not email but rather a computer software program that handles email accounts. Just as your mail carrier is not the mail itself but rather the person who delivers your mail to your home mailbox, Outlook delivers email received through your existing email account(s). You must have an email account to use Outlook to send and receive email.

Outlook allows you to create and send email, reply to received email, forward email to other recipients, save and manage email, and flag and categorize email. Email is also useful as a method of sending pictures and other types of computer files to others. Most individuals cannot imagine their daily work and personal business without the use of email.

STUDENT LEARNING OUTCOMES (SLOs)

After completing this chapter, you will be able to:

SLO 1.1 Identify the basic components of Microsoft Outlook 2013 (p. O1-2).

SLO 1.2 Navigate throughout the Outlook environment and identify the different panes in the Outlook window (p. O1-6).

SLO 1.3 Distinguish between Outlook being used as a stand-alone program and in a Microsoft Exchange environment (p. O1-13).

SLO 1.4 Distinguish between the different types of email accounts and set up an email account in Outlook (p. O1-14).

SLO 1.5 Use Outlook to create, send, and receive email (p. O1-17).

SLO 1.6 Use attachments in email (p. O1-28).

SLO 1.7 Differentiate email arrangements and icons (p. O1-32).

SLO 1.8 Explain the importance and process of cleaning up an *Inbox* (p. O1-35).

CASE STUDY

Central Sierra Insurance (CSI) is a multi-office insurance company that handles all lines of commercial and personal insurance policies. As a thriving and growing insurance agency, Central Sierra is regularly hiring qualified personnel to enhance their sales and support staff. CSI encourages its employees to be active in community organizations and events.

Pause & Practice 1-1: You set up an email account using Microsoft Outlook. You will need an email account that is provided by your school or a free email service such as Gmail.com or Outlook.com.

Pause & Practice 1-2: You send an email message to your instructor and use the *Cc* function to send a copy to yourself. You also read the message, reply to it, and print it for your records.

Pause & Practice 1-3: You reply to a message with an email attachment. You also forward the message to your instructor as an attachment and delete a message.

SLO 1.1

Working with Outlook

When most people think of or hear about Microsoft Outlook, their first thought is email. One of the main features in Outlook is handling email, but Outlook is so much more! It is personal management software that contains the following features:

- *Email*
- *Calendar*
- *Contacts*
- *Tasks*
- *Notes*
- *Journal*

Microsoft Outlook 2013 combines the email, calendar, contacts, tasks, notes, and journal features into one piece of personal management software (Figure 1-1). Each of these different features in Outlook operates as an independent piece of a personal information

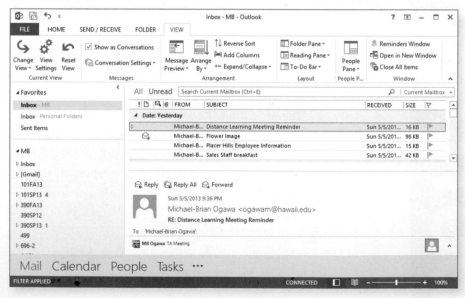

1-1 Outlook interface

management system; yet these different tasks integrate seamlessly together in Outlook. In addition, Outlook can be used in conjunction with Microsoft Word, Excel, Access, and other Microsoft products.

Email

Email is the commonly used term for *electronic mail* (Figure 1-2) Outlook gives users the capability of creating, sending, and receiving email. It can manage a single email account or multiple email accounts. In Outlook, email is activated by clicking on the *Mail* button.

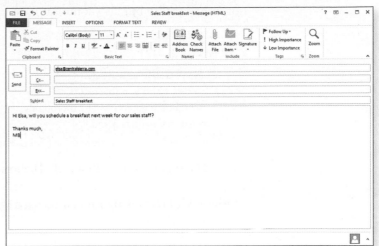

1-2 Email message

> **MORE INFO**
>
> Chapter 2 goes into more detail and covers the special email features available in Outlook. Chapter 6 discusses the use of rules for handling both incoming and outgoing email, and Chapter 7 provides the reader with information about setting up the different types of email accounts.

Calendar

Most individuals organize their daily, weekly, and monthly schedule with some type of calendar. This might be a daily planner you keep with you or a calendar that hangs on your wall at work or at home. *Outlook Calendar* (Figure 1-3) is an electronic calendar that makes it easy to create appointments or events, edit these items, replicate calendar items, set electronic reminders, create meeting requests, and share calendar items with other Outlook users or other devices. Additional information and details can be stored in a calendar item.

1-3 Outlook Calendar

Another advantage of an Outlook calendar is that users can synchronize their work and home calendars. As the popularity of multifunction (smart) cell phones increases, the potential to have your Outlook calendar synchronized between your work, home, and cell phone is not only a reality but also commonplace for working professionals.

> **MORE INFO**
>
> Outlook Calendar will be covered in Chapters 4 and 9 of this text.
>   Outlook Contacts will be thoroughly covered in Chapters 3 and 8.

Contacts

Outlook also provides an area to keep names, email addresses, phone numbers, and other information about business contacts, coworkers, friends, and family. Similar to the way the Outlook calendar replaces the old paper calendar, *Outlook Contacts* (Figure 1-4) allows users to electronically store personal information. It functions as a database, which is a collection of information. One of the many benefits of Outlook Contacts is that it can be used without having any knowledge of the organizational structure or database.

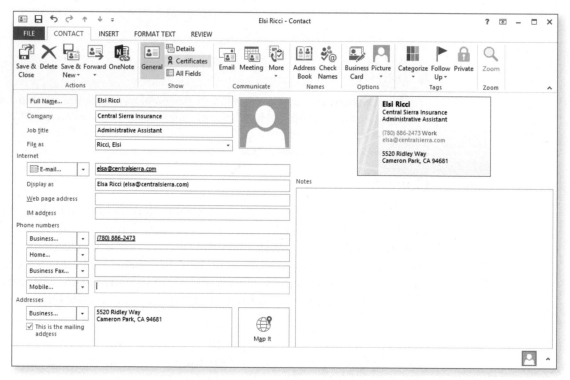

1-4 Outlook contact

Contacts are used to save personal and company information in Outlook and also when populating a recipient list in an email, meeting request, or tasks request.

Tasks

Are you a list person? Do you constantly have a list of things to get done today or this week? Outlook provides a method of keeping track of those things that need to be accomplished with the use of Outlook Tasks. The *Tasks* (Figure 1-5) function is very similar to a notepad that you use to write down your to-do items and then cross them off as they are completed. Tasks are included in the Outlook *To-Do List*, which lists both tasks and emails that have been flagged for some action.

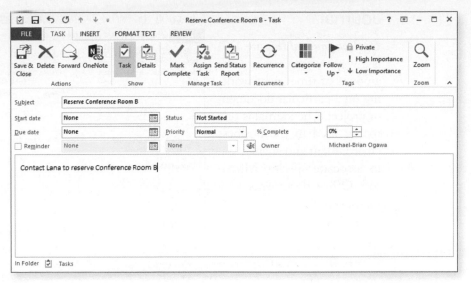

1-5 Outlook task

Some of the advantages of using Outlook Tasks are listed here:

- Tasks are electronic and can be shared between computers and cell phones.
- Many details, which are not typically written down on a piece of paper, can be added to a task.
- Reminders can be set to alert you to an upcoming due date and time for a task.
- A task can be assigned to another Outlook user.

> **MORE INFO**
>
> Outlook tasks and to-do items will be covered in Chapter 5.

Notes

Outlook Notes (Figure 1-6) are used to keep track of information that does not necessarily or neatly fall into the category of a calendar item, contact, or task. Do you ever end the day with a pocket full of scraps of paper with pieces of information written on them? Do you have sticky notes stuck to your computer monitor or refrigerator? Outlook Notes function like electronic sticky notes—actually they look just like them. Notes are an excellent way of storing information such as a user name and password to log into a web site, gift ideas for family and friends, or a list of books you'd like to read.

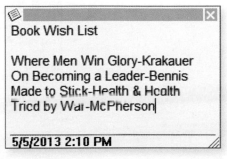

1-6 Outlook note

> **MORE INFO**
>
> Outlook Notes will be covered in Chapter 10.

Journal

Outlook Journal (Figure 1-7) is a way to keep track of the amount of time spent working on a particular document or project. The journal is primarily used in the business environment and enables you to associate specific Microsoft Office documents to a journal entry.

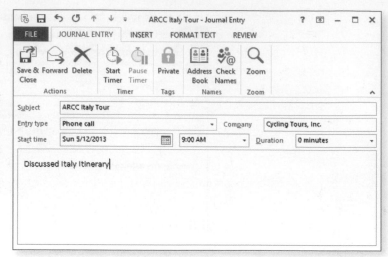

1-7 Outlook journal

> **MORE INFO**
>
> Chapter 10 will teach you how to use the Outlook Journal and provide you with ideas of how this feature might be used in the business setting.

SLO 1.2

Navigating Outlook

The Outlook working environment (Figure 1-8) has a much different look and feel than that of Microsoft Word, Excel, PowerPoint, and Access. The Outlook user interface is divided into multiple sections, called ***panes***. When working with different items in Outlook, you select them by clicking on each item. Selected items are typically highlighted in blue.

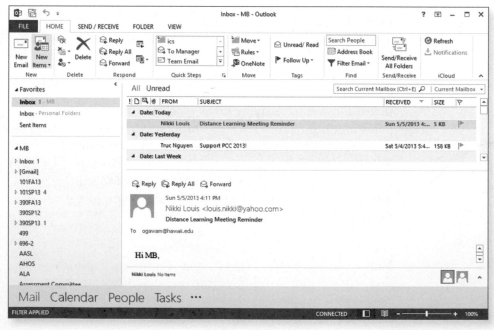

1-8 Outlook environment

As you work through this book and use Outlook, you will become familiar with the Outlook user interface and the different panes available. Outlook has provided much consistency throughout this program to allow you to quickly become comfortable navigating through its working environment.

Outlook Today

Outlook Today (Figure 1-9) is an introductory screen that will provide you with information about your Inbox and other email folders, current calendar items, and upcoming tasks. *Outlook Today* is displayed in the **Folder pane** and is the default view when you open Outlook each time. *Outlook Today* can be customized to meet your personal needs.

1-9 Outlook Today

> **MORE INFO**
>
> Chapter 5 will provide more information about customizing Outlook Today.

Outlook Panes

The Outlook program window is divided into four main panes: *Navigation* pane, *Folder* pane (Figure 1-10), *Reading* pane, and the new *People* pane.

Use the **Navigation pane** to help you navigate through the different features available in Outlook. It is located on the left side of the Outlook window, and the buttons at the bottom of the *Navigation* pane allow you to choose which task you want to work on in Outlook. The main functions in Outlook—**Mail, Calendar, People,** and **Tasks**—are represented by text at the bottom of the *Navigation* pane, while the less commonly used features in Outlook—**Shortcuts, Notes, Folder List,** and **Journal**—are represented by smaller icons which are visible when you click the . . . (more) button.

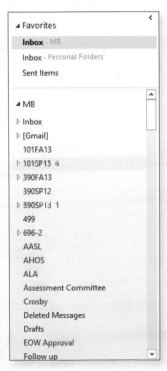

1-10 Navigation pane

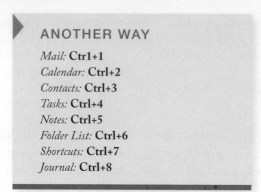
The look of the *Navigation* pane changes depending on the feature chosen, but the large and small navigation buttons at the bottom of the *Navigation* pane remain consistent. The navigation buttons can be customized to better meet your needs. This will be covered in Chapter 5. The width of the *Navigation* pane can be adjusted using the steps outlined in the following *How To* section.

HOW TO: Adjust the Width of the Navigation Pane

1. Click and hold the right border of the *Navigation* pane.
2. Drag the border to the left or right as desired.

The **Folder pane** is the main working area in Outlook and displays the contents of the folder selected in the *Navigation* pane. As a different folder is selected, the contents of the *Folder* pane change. The screenshot in Figure 1-11 is an example of the *Calendar* being selected in the *Navigation* pane, and the selected calendar is displayed in the *Folder* pane.

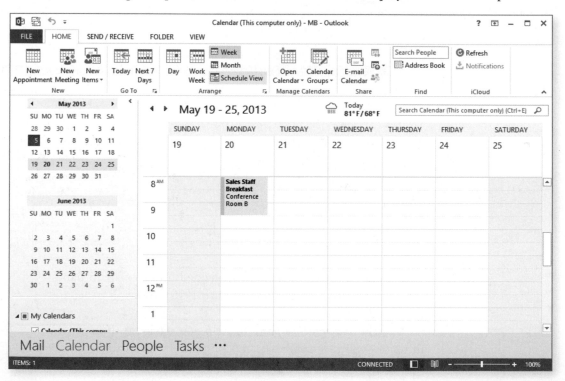

1-11 Calendar displayed in the Folder pane

The **Reading pane** (Figure 1-12) is an optional pane that is available in most of the different main functions in Outlook, although it is primarily used with the *Mail* feature. The *Reading* pane displays the contents of the item selected in the *Folder* pane. The *Reading* pane can be set to appear below or to the right of the *Folder* pane, or it can be turned off. The *Reading* pane will vary depending on the task (e.g., Mail, Calendar, or Contacts) selected in the *Navigation* pane.

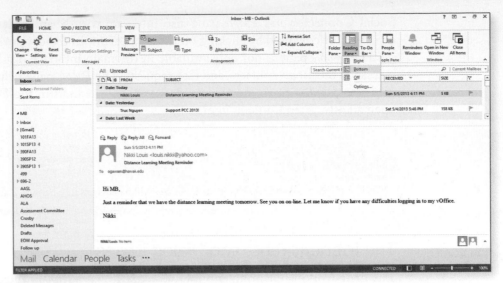

1-12 Reading pane

HOW TO: Change the Location of the Reading Pane

1. Click the **Mail** button in the *Navigation* pane.
2. Click the **View** tab.
3. In the *Layout* group, click the **Reading Pane** button.
4. Choose the desired location: *Right*, *Bottom*, or *Off* (see Figure 1-12).

The *Reading* pane can also be resized in the same manner as the *Navigation* pane. The boundary can be moved to the desired height or width by clicking and holding on the top edge (when the *Reading* pane is displayed at the bottom) or the left edge (when the *Reading* pane is displayed at the right).

The **People pane** (Figure 1-13) is connected with the new **Outlook Social Connector**. The *People* pane provides a collection of information associated with the sender including communication history, meeting requests, attachments, and other social networks. The Outlook

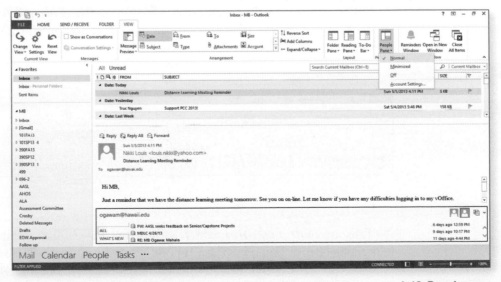

1-13 People pane

Social Connector and *People* pane also integrate with SharePoint. The *People* pane can be expanded or collapsed by clicking on the small arrow in the upper right corner of the pane.

The *People* pane is not only available in the main interface of Outlook but also on email messages, meetings, contacts, and task requests. The *People* pane helps to consolidate all activities associated with an individual into one area. The links in the *People* pane can be used to open an associated Outlook item.

MORE INFO

The *People* pane and *Outlook Social Connector* will be covered in Chapters 2 and 3.

The Ribbon, Tabs, and Dialog Boxes

The main working environment in Outlook 2013 has a **Ribbon** (Figure 1-14), which includes a variety of **tabs**. The *Ribbon* appears at the top of the Outlook window and at the top of any open Outlook item (e.g., email, calendar item, contact, or task). Each tab has a variety of groups, and groups contain a variety of buttons, drop-down lists, and galleries.

1-14 Outlook Ribbon

ANOTHER WAY

The *Ribbon* can be minimized by pressing **Ctrl+F1** or by clicking on the small up arrow in the upper right corner of the Outlook window. You can restore the *Ribbon* by pressing **Ctrl+F1** or by clicking the small up arrow in the upper right corner of the Outlook window and selecting **Show Tabs and Commands**.

When you move your pointer over a button on the *Ribbon*, **ScreenTips** (Figure 1-15) will appear that will tell you what that button represents and provide a shortcut key combination, if available.

1-15 Screen Tip

Tabs are **context sensitive**, which means that the choices of tabs and the content of the tabs change depending on which Outlook item you select. Each tab has different user features available that are divided into **groups**. The size of the buttons in each group will vary depending on the size of the open window.

Some of the groups on each tab have a *launcher* button at the bottom right corner of the group. When the expand button is clicked, the *dialog box* (Figure 1-16) for that particular group opens. The opened dialog box contains additional options for the selected group.

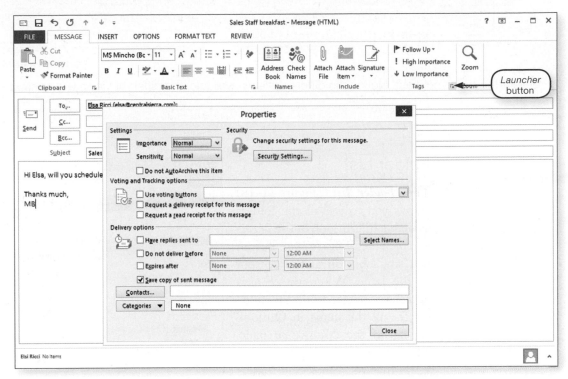

1-16 Dialog box

> **MORE INFO**
>
> The name of the dialog box is not always the same as the name of the group that was expanded. Some dialog boxes contain features that are distributed between a few groups.

> **MORE INFO**
>
> Many of the dialog boxes that you will use in Outlook 2013 are the same as or very similar to the dialog boxes used in previous versions of Outlook.

Views

Each of the different main tasks in Outlook (Mail, Calendar, Contacts, Tasks, Notes, and Journal) has numerous different preset views from which to choose, as well as the option to customize each view or create your own personal view. The selected view will control how the folder selected in the *Navigation* pane will be displayed in the *Folder* pane.

HOW TO: Change to a Different View

1. Click the **View** tab.
2. Click the **Change View** button [*Current View* group] (Figure 1-17).

1-17 Change View button

3. Select the view you want. Notice the different views available; the different views are context sensitive.

Folder List

The *Folder list* (Figure 1-18) allows you to see all the folders available in Outlook in the *Navigation* pane. The *Folders* button is a small button at the bottom of the pane. When the *Folders* button is selected, all the folders for all the items in Outlook appear in the *Navigation* pane. The benefit of viewing the *Folder* list is that you can see all folders available in the folder hierarchy in which they reside, rather than viewing just one set of folders at a time. This view can be used to move folders up or down a level or can be used to drag specific items into a folder.

1-18 Folder list

> **ANOTHER WAY**
>
> **Ctrl+6** displays the *Folder* list in the *Navigation* pane.

> **MORE INFO**
>
> The *Folder* list will be covered more thoroughly in Chapter 6 when we start using multiple folders for email, contacts, and tasks.

Outlook Help

Outlook Help (Figure 1-19) is an online search engine that is available throughout Outlook and will provide you with specific information about topics on which you might have a question or need additional information. The *Microsoft Outlook Help* button is located in the upper right corner of any open Outlook window.

When the *Outlook Help* button is clicked, the *Outlook Help* dialog box opens. You will be given the choice of either typing in keywords related to your search or choosing from a list of common Outlook topics.

1-19 Help function

> ### ANOTHER WAY
>
> The **F1** function key on your computer keyboard opens the *Outlook Help* dialog box.

SLO 1.3

Understanding Outlook Environments

Microsoft Outlook can be used as either a ***stand-alone program*** or in conjunction with a ***Microsoft Exchange Server*** (also referred to as an Exchange server or Exchange). Many individuals use Outlook on their home computer, and this is what is meant by a stand-alone program. Outlook is still part of the Microsoft Office 2013 suite of software and is still capable of performing all the main functions of this personal management software.

Outlook as a Stand-Alone Program

When using Outlook in the home or personal environment, Outlook connects directly with your ***Internet Service Provider*** (***ISP***) and manages your email through the accounts you set up. Outlook can handle a single email account or multiple email accounts. Some of the more advanced and specialty features in Outlook are only available when Outlook is used in conjunction with Exchange.

> ### MORE INFO
>
> Chapter 1 will show you how to set up an email account in Outlook. Managing multiple email accounts will be covered in Chapter 7.

Outlook in an Exchange Environment

In the business environment, Microsoft Outlook is typically connected to a ***Microsoft Exchange Server***. Exchange on a business network handles all the incoming and outgoing mail. Each individual user of Exchange is actually a client of this Exchange network, and the network administrator sets up an account for each individual user. In addition to handling email, Exchange also stores all the data associated with calendars, contacts, tasks, notes, and journals.

Outlook in an Exchange environment has the same user interface as in a stand-alone environment, but Outlook with an Exchange server does allow you more functionality. Some of the enhanced features an Exchange server will enable you to perform include:

- Using voting buttons and tracking responses
- Sending meeting requests and tracking responses
- Recalling messages
- Sharing your calendar, contacts, tasks, and email with others
- Using *MailTips*
- Using a common global contact list

> ### MORE INFO
>
> As you progress through this book, you will be informed when Outlook performs functions differently when using Outlook as a stand-alone program or with Exchange. Also, Appendix D provides a summary of Outlook features unique to an Exchange environment.

SLO 1.4

Adding an Email Account in Outlook

Multiple email accounts can be set up in Outlook. In previous versions of Outlook, only one Exchange account could be connected, but Outlook 2013 gives you the ability to set up multiple Exchange accounts. There are four different types of email accounts that can be set up in Outlook, and Outlook provides you with an *Auto Account Setup Wizard* to walk you through the process of adding an email account to Outlook.

Types of Email Accounts

Microsoft Exchange accounts are used primarily in medium- to large-business settings. These email accounts are set up through the company network or email administrator. An Exchange account has an individual mailbox assigned to each user and resides on an Exchange file server. Outlook connects to the Exchange server to retrieve your email. Exchange accounts use Messaging Application Programming Interface (MAPI) and provide enhanced functionality when used with Outlook. Recalling messages, tracking voting responses, and sharing Outlook with others on your Exchange system are features that are associated with Exchange accounts and Outlook.

POP3 accounts are Internet email accounts that are associated with your Internet service provider (ISP). If you have an ISP such as Comcast or AT&T, you will have an email account (or multiple email accounts) through your provider. This POP3 account can be set up in Outlook to send and receive email. When using Outlook with this type of account, your email messages are downloaded to Outlook.

IMAP accounts are also Internet accounts but are not always associated with an ISP. IMAP accounts create folders on a server to store and organize messages for retrieval by other computers and give you the options to read message headers only and to select which messages to download. These types of accounts are becoming increasingly popular as personal email accounts. Gmail is an example of an IMAP email account.

HTTP accounts use the hypertext transfer protocol used on the web to create, view, send, and receive messages. This type of account is not automatically supported by Outlook but can be configured by installing an add-in. Windows Live Mail is an HTTP account that can be configured to work with Outlook by using the MSN Connector for Outlook.

Add an Email Account

To create, send, and receive email, Outlook must be set up to recognize your email account. In the past, it has been a challenge to get all the specific information needed to set up an email account, but beginning with Outlook 2007, an *Auto Account Setup* (Figure 1-20) feature was added to automatically detect the incoming and outgoing server.

To set up your account, you will need to supply your email address and password to access the account. This will give Outlook the location of your Exchange or Internet mailbox, and your password provides access to the account. An account only needs to be set up once, and it will be stored in Outlook for future use.

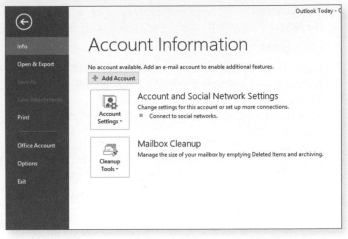

1-20 Account set up

> **MORE INFO**
>
> The first time you open Outlook, you will be prompted to set up an account. The *Add New Account* dialog box automatically opens for you.
>
> Outlook will automatically detect the type of email account being configured.

HOW TO: Set Up an Email Account

1. Click the **File** tab. The *Backstage* view opens.
2. Click the **Add Account** button. The *Add Account* dialog box opens (Figure 1-21).

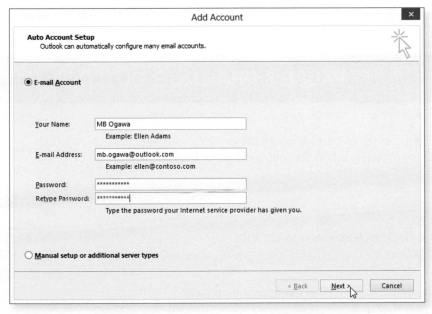

1-21 Add account dialog box

3. Enter the following account settings in the text boxes:
    * *Your Name* (as you want it to appear in email)
    * *E-mail Address*

- *Password*
- *Retype Password*

4. Click **Next**.

5. Outlook will automatically detect your email account and validate it with your password. Three green check marks display when your account has been configured properly (Figure 1-22).

6. Click **Finish** and you're ready to use Outlook.

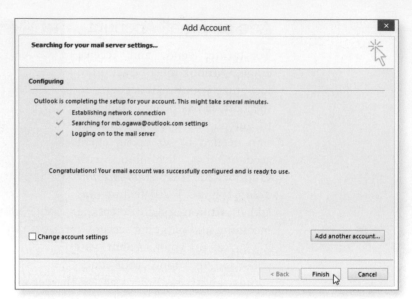

1-22 Successful configuration of an account

> MORE INFO

Chapter 7 will provide additional information on setting up multiple email accounts.

> ANOTHER WAY

An email account can be added to Outlook when Outlook is closed by clicking on **Mail** and then on **Email Accounts** in your computer's *Control Panel*.

PAUSE & PRACTICE: OUTLOOK 1-1

For this Pause and Practice project, you set up an email account using Microsoft Outlook. If you do not have an email account, you can set one up using a free service, such as Outlook (outlook.com) or Gmail (gmail.com).

1. Launch Outlook 2013.

2. Open the *Add Account* dialog box.
   a. Click the **File** tab to open the *Backstage* view and select **Info**.
   b. Click the **Add Account** button.

3. Input your account information.
   a. Type your name, email address, and password in the appropriate fields.
   b. Click **Next**.
   c. If you are using a school email account, you may need to contact your system administrator for the manual setup information.

Creating, Sending, and Receiving Email

Creating and sending an email message is very similar to sending a letter—just much easier and quicker! You select recipients, type the subject of the message, type the message, and send—no stamp or going to the post office.

> **ANOTHER WAY**
>
> **Ctrl+N** opens a new email message when you are in Outlook *Mail*.

Create New Email

To create a new email message, make sure the *Mail* button (Figure 1-23) is selected in the *Navigation* pane and then click the **New Email** button in the *New* group on the *Home* tab. Outlook opens a new email message (Figure 1-24).

> **MORE INFO**
>
> When you click the **New** button or press **Ctrl+N**, Outlook creates a new item of the task selected in Outlook. For example, if you select *Calendar* in the *Navigation* pane and click **New**, you get a new calendar appointment.

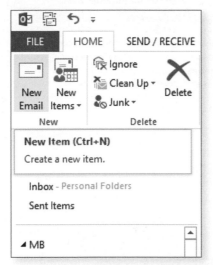

1-23 New mail button

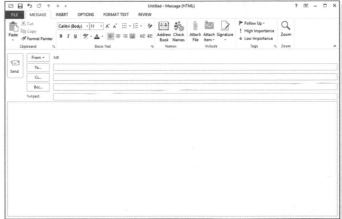

1-24 New email message

Select Recipients

An email message can be sent to one recipient or multiple recipients. You can type the email address into the *To* field or click the **To** button and select from your *Contact* list. If you are typing in the email addresses, separate each email address with a semicolon (;).

When you click the *To* button (Figure 1-25), Outlook opens your *Contacts*. A single recipient can be chosen or multiple recipients can be selected.

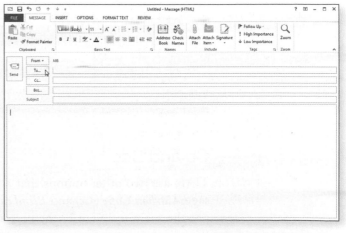

1-25 Select the **To** button

HOW TO: Select Recipients

1. Click the **Mail** button in the *Navigation* pane.
2. Click the **New Email** button to open a new email message.
3. Click the **To** button on the new email message. The *Select Names* dialog box opens.
   - You can also type in an email address in the *To* field.
4. Select recipient(s) (Figure 1-26).

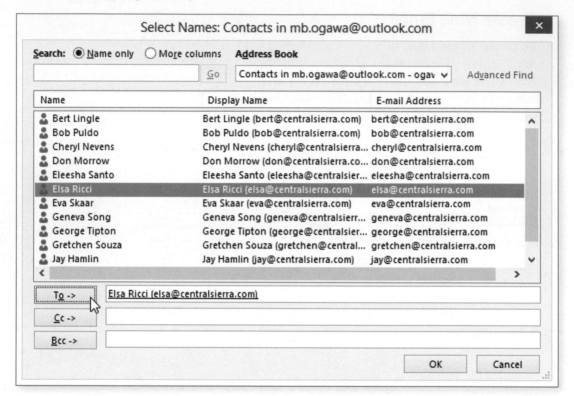

1-26 Select recipients from contacts list

5. Click the **To** button below the names.
6. Click **OK** to close the *Select Names* dialog box.

> **ANOTHER WAY**
>
> When selecting multiple recipients from the contact list, holding down the **Ctrl** key while clicking allows you to select nonadjacent entries. Using the **Shift** key allows you to select a range of recipients. Click the first item in the range, hold down the **Shift** key, and select the last item in the range. These shortcuts are common throughout many of the Microsoft Office applications.

Cc and Bcc

There are two other options that are available when selecting recipients for your email message: ***Carbon Copy*** (*Cc*) and ***Blind carbon copy*** (*Bcc*) (Figure 1-27). *Cc* is used when someone is not the main recipient of the message, but they need to be kept informed of the contents of the message or ongoing email discussion.

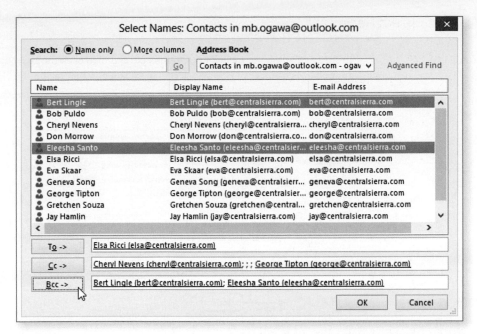

1-27 Select recipients in the Cc and Bcc fields

Bcc is used when you do not want those receiving the email message to see other recipients' email addresses or names (Figure 1-28). When a recipient receives an email, he or she will be able to see other recipients' names and email addresses in both the *To* and *Cc* fields, but the *Bcc* field is hidden.

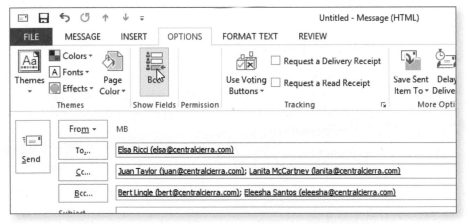

1-28 Select the Bcc option

> ### MORE INFO
>
> Be careful about sharing email addresses with those outside of your organization. *Bcc* is a great feature to provide confidentiality in email by hiding others' email addresses. To send an email, there must be at least one recipient in one of the recipient fields.

The *Cc* button appears on a new message and can be used like the *To* button to select recipients. By default, the *Bcc* button or field is not available when you open a new email message. You can click either the *To* or *Cc* button to open the *Select Names* dialog box. Once this dialog box is open, the *Bcc* field is available.

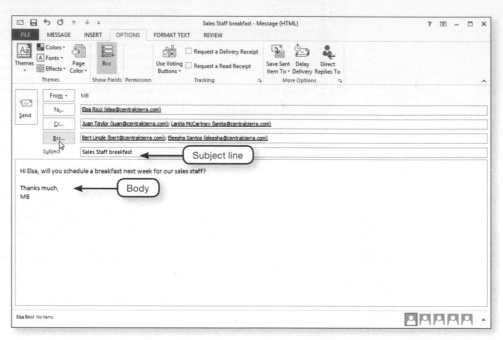

1-29 Select the Bcc button

Subject Line and Body

The **Subject line** alerts recipients to the subject of the email, and the **body** contains the contents of the email (Figure 1-29). When a new email message is created, the email is untitled (top center), but once a subject is typed in, it becomes the message title.

> **MORE INFO**
>
> Use a subject line on every email, and keep it short and descriptive. Your subject line might determine whether or not your message gets read.

Format Text

Outlook provides users with many of the same formatting features that are available in Microsoft Word. These text formatting features can be used in the body of the email message. Many of the commonly used formatting features are available on the *Message* tab in the *Basic Text* group (Figure 1-30). This *Basic Text* group can be expanded (by clicking the small box in the bottom right corner of the group) to open the *Font* dialog box.

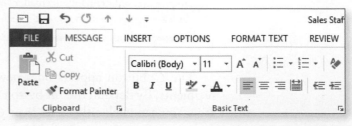

1-30 Formatting options

More formatting options are available by clicking on the *Format Text* tab, which opens this tab for additional formatting features (Figure 1-31).

1-31 Additional formatting options

> **MORE INFO**
>
> Don't overuse text formatting in the body of an email message. Depending on the type of email account the recipient has, some of the text formatting might not be visible to the recipient.

Send an Email

Once you select your recipients and type in the subject and body of the email, you are ready to send the email message. Click the **Send** button to the left of the *To* and *Cc* buttons and your email message will be sent. A copy of it will be automatically saved in the ***Sent Items*** folder in your *Folder* list.

HOW TO: Send an Email Message

1. Click the **New Email** button [*Home* tab, *New* group]. A new email message opens in a new window.
2. Click the **To** button and select the names or email addresses from the *Select Names* dialog box. You can also add recipients to the *Cc* and *Bcc* fields.
3. Click **OK**. The email addresses will appear in the *To, Cc,* and/or *Bcc* fields.
4. Type a brief subject in the *Subject* field.
5. Type a brief message in the body of the message. Remember to always include your name in the body of the email.
6. Click **Send** (Figure 1-32).

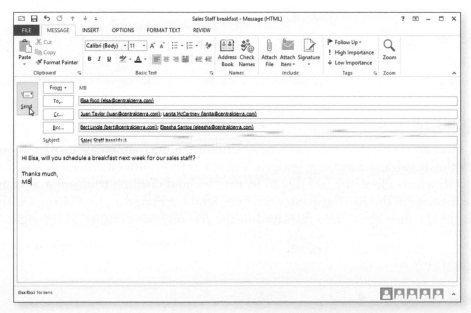

1-32 Sample email message

Save an Email Draft

If you are working on an email and do not have time to finish it or would like to look it over later before sending it, you can save and close the message and it will be available for later use. When you save a message in Outlook, it is kept in the ***Drafts*** folder in the *Folder* list.

To save an unfinished message, click the **Save** button on the ***Quick Access*** toolbar or press **Ctrl+S**. Microsoft Office Outlook automatically saves all unfinished messages for you. By default, unfinished messages are saved to your *Drafts* folder every three minutes (Figure 1-33). You can, however, change this time interval or location.

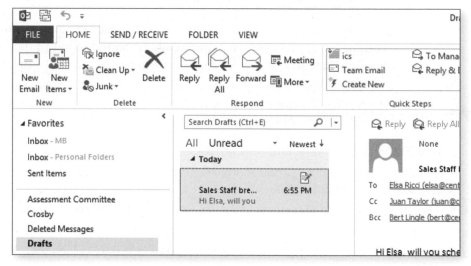

1-33 Saved draft message

Open an Email

When you open an email, it opens into a new window. To open an email in your Inbox, double-click the message; the message opens in a new window. Outlook provides users with a *Reading* pane, which allows the message to be read without opening it in a new window. To view the message in the *Reading* pane, click once on the message in the *Folder* pane and the contents of the message will be displayed in the *Reading* pane (either to the right or at the bottom).

Reply, Reply All, and Forward

When responding to an email, you have three main options: *Reply*, *Reply All*, and *Forward*. **Reply** allows you to send a message to the original sender (Figure 1-34). **Reply All** will let you send a response to the sender and the other email recipients (those in the *To* and *Cc* lines). **Forward** will enable you to forward the email message you received to recipients of your choice.

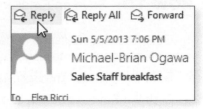

1-34 Reply to a message

Unlike previous versions, Outlook 2013 creates replies and forwarded messages within the Outlook window. If you prefer to write replies in a new window, click the **Pop Out** button in the reply message.

Both *Reply* and *Reply All* will keep the same body and subject line. The body text will be moved down to make room for your message, and the subject will be preceded by "RE:" to indicate this email is a reply. Either the original sender (*Reply*) or the sender and other recipients (*Reply All*) will automatically be in the *To* or *Cc* lines. The difference when using *Forward* is the *To* field will be empty and the subject will include "FW:" in front of the subject (Figure 1-35).

> ☐ Pop Out ☒ Discard
>
> | From ▾ | MB |
> | To... | Elsa Ricci (elsa@centralcierra.com); |
> | Cc... | |
> | Bcc... | |
> | Subject | RE: Sales Staff breakfast |
>
> Thank you for the information!
>
> MB
>
> **From:** Elsa Ricci [mailto:elsa@centralcierra.com]
> **Sent:** Sunday, May 05, 2013 7:06 PM
> **To:** MB Ogawa
> **Subject:** Sales Staff breakfast
>
> The meeting is scheduled.

1-35 Sample reply message

To use any of the response options, open the email and choose either *Reply*, *Reply All*, or *Forward*.

Save an Email in a Windows Folder

When an email message is sent, the original message remains in your Inbox and a copy of the response is automatically saved in the *Sent Items* folder. There might be times when you want to save an important or sensitive email message outside of Outlook. You can save email messages to a different folder on your computer.

HOW TO: Save an Email in a Windows Folder

1. Either click the message to be saved in the *Folder* pane or open the message in a new window.
2. Click the **File** tab. The *Backstage* view opens.
3. Click the **Save As** button to open the *Save As* dialog box (Figure 1-36).
4. Browse to the desired location to save the file.
   - By default, the *File name* will be the subject line of the email. You can change this as desired.
5. Click the **Save** button.

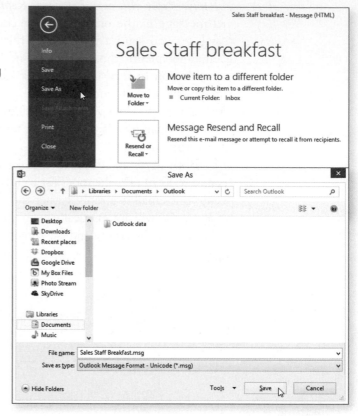

1-36 Save a message

> **ANOTHER WAY**
> **F12** opens the *Save As* dialog box.

Print an Email

If you are on your way to a meeting and need some information from an email in your Inbox, you might want to print the email to take with you. Also, you might want to print the contents of one of your Inbox folders. The *Print* option in Outlook allows you to print either an individual email in ***Memo Style*** or the contents of a folder in ***Table Style***.

HOW TO: Print an Email

1. Select the email or folder to be printed.
2. Click the **File** tab to open the *Backstage* view.

3. Click the **Print** button (Figure 1-37).

4. Select the type of printout you would like in the *Print What* area.

5. Click the **Print** button.

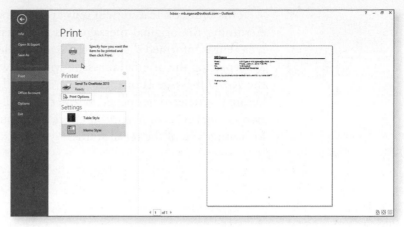

1-37 Print a message

> **ANOTHER WAY**
>
> **Ctrl+P** opens the *Print* area on the *Backstage* view.

Recall an Email Message

Have you ever sent a message and realized, after you pressed the *Send* button, that you omitted information, included incorrect information, or forgot to include an attachment? Outlook provides us imperfect users with a ***Recall*** feature (Figure 1-38) that allows you to recall a message and gives the option of replacing it with a new message.

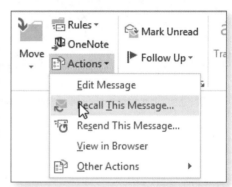

1-38 Recall This Message

HOW TO: Recall an Email Message

1. Locate and open the message to be recalled in your *Sent Items* folder.

2. Click the **Actions** button [*Message* tab, *Move* group].

3. Choose **Recall This Message**. The *Recall This Message* dialog box opens (Figure 1-39).

4. You are given the option to *Delete unread copies of this message* or *Delete unread copies and replace with a new message*. Outlook will also track this action to let you know if the recall was successful.

5. Select one of the options and click **OK**.

   - If you are just deleting unread copies, Outlook performs the recall.
   - If you are replacing the email message with a new one, the original message opens so you can modify it. Press **Send** after editing the message to perform the recall and replace the original message with the new one.

1-39 Recall This Message dialog box

This Outlook feature will only work when used in conjunction with an Exchange server. Assuming the original message has not been read, the original message is deleted and the recipient is informed that you, the sender, deleted the message from his or her mailbox. If you are replacing the original message with a new one, the original message will be deleted when the *Recall* message is opened. The recall will fail if the recipient opens the original message before it is deleted or opened before the recall message. If you have selected the *Tell me if recall succeeds or fails for each recipient* check box, you will receive an email notification in your Inbox informing you of the recall status.

Resend an Email Message

Resending a message is useful if you want to resend a previously sent message. If someone did not receive your original message or if you want to send the same message to new recipients, you can resend a previously sent message rather than creating and sending a new message. The process to resend a message is similar to recalling a message.

HOW TO: Resend an Email Message

1. Locate and open the message to be resent in your *Sent Items* folder.
2. Click the **Actions** button [*Message* tab, *Move* group].
3. Choose **Resend This Message** (Figure 1-40).
4. Select recipients to receive the message.
5. Click **OK**.

1-40 Resend This Message

For this Pause and Practice project, you send an email message to your instructor and use the *Cc* function to send a copy to yourself. You also read the message, reply to it, and print it for your records.

1. Click the **Mail** button in the *Navigation pane*.

2. Create a new email message by clicking the **New Email** button [*Home* tab, *New* group].

3. Enter the following information in the email message fields:

To:	[your instructor's email address]
CC:	[your email address]
Subject:	Central Sierra Information Request
Body:	Hi Don, could you please email me the latest employee information sheet when you have a chance?

   Thank you,

   [your name]

4. Click the **Send** button to send the message.

5. View the message you sent in your Sent Items folder using the *Reading* pane.
   a. Select the message.
   b. Select the *Right* or *Bottom Reading* pane based on your preference [*View* tab, *Layout* group, *Reading Pane* button].

6. Reply to the message.
   a. Click the **Reply** button [*Message* tab, *Respond* group].
   b. Click in the body section of the message and type the following:

      I will look it up and send it to you as soon as I retrieve it.

      [your name]

   c. Click the **Send** button.

7. Print the reply message.
   a. Select the reply message in your Inbox.
   b. Click the **Print** button [*File* tab, *Backstage* view].

8. Print the reply message.
   a. Select the reply message in *Sent Items* folder.
   b. Click the **Print** button [*File* tab, *Backstage* view].

9. Submit the printed copy to your instructor (Figure 1-41).

MB Ogawa

From:	MB Ogawa <mb.ogawa@outlook.com>
Sent:	Monday, May 06, 2013 2:05 AM
To:	mb.ogawa@outlook.com
Subject:	RE: Central Sierra Information Request

I will look it up and send it to you as soon as I retrieve it.

MB

From: MB Ogawa [mailto:mb.ogawa@outlook.com]
Sent: Monday, May 06, 2013 2:03 AM
To: 'Nikki Louis'
Cc: mb.ogawa@outlook.com
Subject: Central Sierra Information Request

Hi Don, could you please e-mail me the latest employee information sheet when you have a chance?

Thank you,
MB

1-41 Completed Pause & Practice 1-2

Handling Attachments

One of the many benefits of email is that a file or multiple files can easily be attached to and sent with an email. Pictures, Word documents, and many other types of files can be attached to an email.

Attach a File

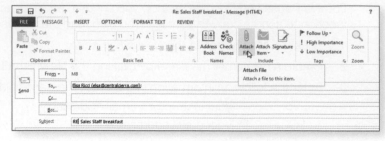

You can attach a file to an email message by clicking on the **Attach File** button (Figure 1-42) on the *Message* tab in the *Include* group.

1-42 Attach File button

There are some types of files and objects that cannot be attached to email. Microsoft Access database files and entire folders cannot be attached to an email message. One way to get around this limitation is to *compress* or *zip* the files or folders and then attach the compressed (zipped) file.

I have sent numerous email messages asking my recipients to refer to an attachment. However, I did not always remember to attach the referenced document to my message. New in 2013, is the **Attachment Reminder** feature. If you forgot to attach a file and reference an attachment in your email message, Outlook will warn you. An *Attachment Reminder* will pop up and allow you to select *Don't Send* or *Send Anyway*. This ensures you attach files to email messages. Selecting *Don't Send* will return you to your message, while selecting *Send Anyway* will send your message as is (Figure 1-43).

1-43 Attachment Reminder

HOW TO: Attach a File

1. When creating, replying to, or forwarding an email, click the **Attach File** button [*Message* tab, *Include* group].
2. Browse through the files on your computer (Figure 1-44).
3. Select the files. The **Ctrl** and **Shift** keys can be used to select multiple files.
4. Click **Insert**. The attached files will appear below the subject line (Figure 1-45).

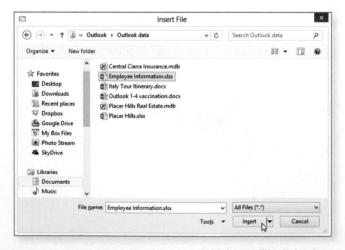

1-44 Insert File dialog box

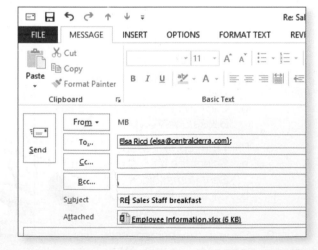

1-45 Attached file

Preview an Attachment

Outlook allows you to preview most types of attachments without opening them. When you click the attachment as shown in Figure 1-45, the attachment will be displayed in the body of the message (Figure 1-46). You can return to the email message by clicking on the **Show Message** button in the *Message* group on the *Attachments* tab.

1-46 Preview an attachment

Open and Save Attachments

Usually when an attachment is received via email, you will want to open and/or save the attachment. It will be located below the subject line in the email.

Outlook 2013 has made attachment handling much easier with the new ***Attachments*** tab. This tab is automatically displayed when the attachment is selected in an email message. Using the *Attachments* tab, you can open, save, print, copy, or remove the attachment.

HOW TO: Open an Attachment

1. With an email message open or in the *Reading* pane, click the attachment to display the *Attachments* tab on the *Ribbon*.
   - When you select the attachment, Outlook usually displays a preview of the attachment in the body of the message.
   - Not all file types will display a preview in the body of the message.
2. Click the **Open** button in the *Actions* group to open the attachment. It opens in a new window (Figure 1-47).

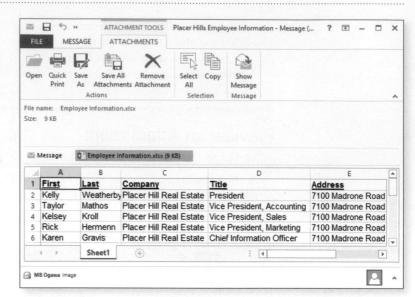

1-47 Opened attachment

> **MORE INFO**
>
> It is important to have virus protection software installed and kept up to date on your computer. Attachments and links in email messages are some of the main ways viruses are spread between computers. Virus protection software could be the best $40–$50 per year you spend.

> **ANOTHER WAY**
>
> An attachment can also be opened by double-clicking on the attachment or by right-clicking the attachment and choosing **Open**.

If an attachment is opened, it can be saved the same way you save any other open document. Typically, you can save an open document by pressing **Ctrl+S** or clicking on the *Save* icon located on the tab or *Quick Access* toolbar. Be sure to specify the location where you want the document saved.

> **ANOTHER WAY**
>
> **Ctrl+S** is the shortcut for save on most software.

An attachment can also be saved without opening it from the email.

HOW TO: Save an Attachment

1. Click the attachment to be saved. The *Attachments* tab opens.
2. Click the **Save As** button in the *Actions* group. The *Save As* dialog box opens.
3. Choose the desired location to save the file and specify a file name.
4. Click **Save**.

Forward an Email as an Attachment

When you forward an email with an attachment, the attachment is automatically included in the email to be forwarded. There might be times where you want to forward an entire email as an attachment rather than forwarding only the contents of the email.

HOW TO: Forward an Email as an Attachment

1. Open the message to be forwarded.
2. On the *Message* tab, click the **More** button in the *Respond* group.
3. Select **Forward as Attachment** (Figure 1-48). A new email opens with the selected email as an attachment. The subject line will be the same as the original message with *FW:* in from indicating that the message is being forwarded (Figure 1-49).

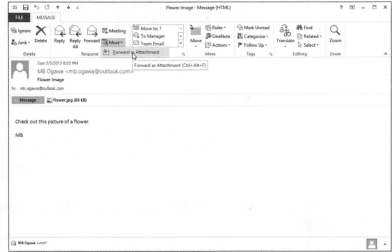

1-49 Forward as Attachment message

1-48 Forward as Attachment button

4. Select recipients and add any necessary information in the body of the message.
5. Press **Send**.

Attach Other Outlook Items

Other Outlook items such as contacts, tasks, calendar items, and Outlook business cards can be attached to an email and sent. These items can be sent either as an attachment or as text in the body of the email.

HOW TO: Attach Other Outlook Items

1. Open a **New** email message.
2. Click the **Insert** tab.

3. Click the *Attach Item* button (Figure 1-50) [*Message* tab, *Include* group] or the *Outlook Item* button [*Insert* tab, *Include* group]. The *Insert Item* dialog box opens.

4. Choose the type of item to be attached (*Business Card*, *Calendar*, or *Outlook Item*).

5. Select the items to be attached. Use the **Ctrl** key to select nonadjacent items or the **Shift** key to select a range of items.

6. Choose whether to insert the items as *Text only* or as an *Attachment* (Figure 1-51).

7. Click **OK**. The Outlook item will be attached to the email message.

1-50 Attach Item button

1-51 Insert an Outlook item as an attachment

> **MORE INFO**
>
> The *Attach Item* button is available in the *Include* group on *Message* tab, and the *Outlook Item* button is available in the *Include* group on the *Insert* tab. Both of these buttons open the *Insert Items* dialog box.

 SLO 1.7

Understanding Arrangement and Icons

As mentioned in *SLO 1.2: Navigating Outlook*, the working environment in Outlook is broken into panes. There are typically four panes open in Outlook: ***Navigation***, ***Folder***, ***Reading***, and ***People***. There is also the ***To-Do bar*** that can be open or collapsed.

In the *Folder* pane, you can arrange emails in numerous different ways to meet your needs and preferences. Outlook also provides users with many ***icons*** to help easily and quickly identify different aspects of an email displayed in the *Folder* pane. The icons on each email in the *Folder* pane can tell you if a message has been read, if it has been replied to or forwarded, if there is an attachment, if it is marked ***important***, if it is ***flagged*** for action, or if it is assigned to a ***category***.

> **MORE INFO**
>
> ***Message options*** will be covered in Chapter 2, which will describe how to use the different features associated with some of the Inbox icons. Chapter 5 will cover how to customize the user interface.

Email Arrangement

Arrangement controls the order in which email messages are displayed in the *Folder* pane. Typically email messages are arranged or sorted with the most recently received email at the top of the list (i.e., arranged by date and time in descending order). The *View* tab provides you with different *View* and *Arrangement* options. Outlook 2013 has upgraded the arrangement options to make it easier to quickly change the arrangement of emails.

Conversation arrangement (Figure 1-52) groups all emails related to a particular email conversation (by subject), which is intended to greatly reduce the number of redundant emails displayed

1-52 Conversation Settings button

in the *Folder* list (Figure 1-53). The *Conversation* arrangement groups these emails together to take up less space in your list of emails and gives you the ability to expand the conversation and see all related messages, including those in the *Sent Items* folder.

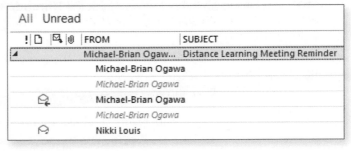

1-53 Conversation arrangement

When there are multiple emails within a conversation, clicking on the small triangle to the left of an email will expand the conversation. The conversation can be collapsed by clicking on the small triangle to the left of the conversation subject in the *Folder* pane.

There are many other preset arrangement options available in Outlook. These can be selected from the *Arrangement* group on the *View* tab.

> **MORE INFO**
>
> When you click the small triangle next to a conversation, the message will be expanded to show the related messages in the current folder. When you click the triangle again, the conversation expands to include related messages in other folders.

Unread/Read Email

When the Inbox (or any other folder) is selected in your *Navigation* pane, the contents of that folder are displayed in the *Folder* pane. The icon to the left of the email shows whether or not the email has been read. When an email has not been read, the email is bold. Once the email has been opened and read, the email will no longer be bold (Figure 1-54).

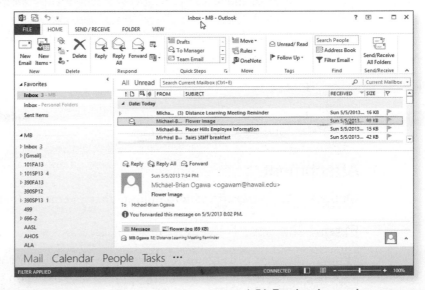

1-54 Read and unread messages

Mark as Unread/Read Email

When an email is opened, Outlook marks it as read. There are times when you might want to mark a message as unread to draw attention to it in the folder or *Folder* pane. Outlook gives you the option of marking an email as **read** or **unread**.

HOW TO: Mark as Unread/Read

1. Select the email in the *Folder* pane to be marked as read or unread.
2. In the *Tags* group on the *Home* tab, click the **Unread/Read** button (Figure 1-55).

1-55 Unread/Read button

> **ANOTHER WAY**
>
> Right-click the email and choose *Mark as Read* or *Mark as Unread*.

> **MORE INFO**
>
> The entire contents of a folder can be marked as read by either right-clicking on the folder and choosing **Mark All as Read** or by clicking on the **Mark All as Read** button in the *Clean Up* group on the *Folder* tab.

Replied to and Forwarded

By scanning your email in the *Folder* pane, you can easily see the response action previously taken on each email. Messages that have been replied to have an envelope icon with an arrow pointing to the left, and those that have been forwarded have an envelope icon with an arrow pointing to the right (Figure 1-56).

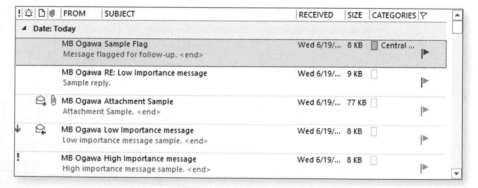

1-56 Sample Inbox

Attachment

Outlook uses a ***paper clip*** icon to indicate that an email has an attachment (Figure 1-56).

Flag

When a message is flagged for follow up or has a flag for recipients, the ***flag*** icon is used. This flag will appear in different shades of red depending on the action of the flag (e.g. *Today*, *Tomorrow*, *This Week*) (Figure 1-56).

Importance

There are three levels of importance that can be set for each email: *high*, *low*, and *normal*. High importance is indicated by a red exclamation point, low importance uses a blue arrow pointed down, and normal importance uses no special icon (Figure 1-56). (Normal importance is the default on all new email messages.)

Category

Categories are used to group Inbox items. Colors are used to distinguish categories, and the category names can be customized to meet your individual needs. Categories are not limited to email messages; they can also be advantageous for grouping contacts, tasks, and calendar items (Figure 1-56).

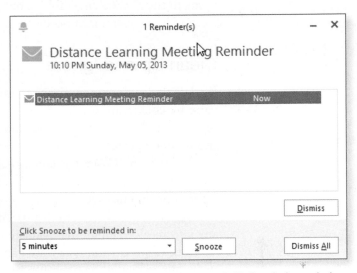

1-57 Reminders window

Reminder

When an email is received that includes a reminder, it is marked with a *small bell* icon. An electronic reminder opens on your computer on the reminder day and time (Figure 1-57). You have the options of opening the email, dismissing the reminder, or snoozing the reminder.

SLO 1.8

Cleaning Up Your Inbox

It is important to manage your Inbox effectively. When you receive mail (postal mail) at home or work, you read it and then determine what action needs to be taken. Bills need to be paid, some information needs to be filed and saved, junk mail is discarded, and other mail is thrown away after you've responded to it. Your email Inbox is very similar. Throughout this text, you will learn about many different tools to help you effectively manage your Inbox. For now, it is important to learn how to delete an email you no longer need.

Delete an Email

Select the emails to be deleted, and then either click the *Delete* button (Figure 1-58) in the *Delete* group on the *Home* tab or press the *Delete* key (not *Backspace*) on your computer keyboard. When an email is deleted, it is not gone forever. It has been moved from your *Inbox* (or the folder it is in) to your *Deleted Items* folder.

1-58 Delete button

> **ANOTHER WAY**
>
> Outlook items can also be deleted by right-clicking on the item and choosing **Delete**, or select an email message in the *Folder* pane and press **Ctrl+D**.

Deleted Items Folder

Deleted Items is a folder (Figure 1-59) in your list of *Mail* folders. Deleted email, contacts, tasks, calendar items, and other Outlook items are stored in this folder when they are deleted from another location. By default, Outlook does not delete the items in the *Deleted Items* folder, but this is not a good location to store items you might need.

Clean Up and Ignore

By default, Outlook now arranges emails displayed in the *Folder* pane by conversation. This helps to both group related items together and reduce the clutter and redundant emails in your Inbox. Two new features added to further manage conversations in Outlook are **Clean Up** and **Ignore**. *Clean Up* will remove redundant messages in an email conversation. *Clean Up* can also be used on an entire folder and subfolders (Figure 1-60). *Ignore* will delete all emails related to a specific conversation and delete any new received email that is related to that conversation.

    Both *Clean Up* and *Ignore* are handy features to help manage the volume of emails you receive. By default when you *Clean Up* or *Ignore* a conversation, the deleted emails are moved to the *Deleted Items* folder.

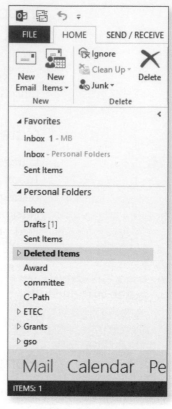

1-59 Deleted Items folder

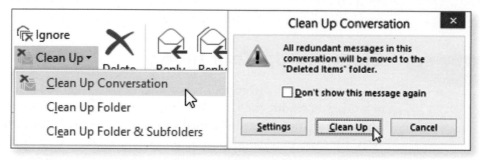

1-60 Clean Up Conversation button and dialog box

Empty Deleted Items

It is a good idea to regularly empty your *Deleted Items* folder. The items in this folder can be manually deleted.

HOW TO: Empty Deleted Items

1. Click the **Deleted Items** folder in the *Navigation* pane.
2. Click the **Folder** tab.
3. Click the **Empty Folder** button (Figure 1-61) in the *Clean Up* group. A dialog box opens confirming that you want to empty the *Deleted Items* folder.
4. Choose **Yes** to delete items in the *Deleted Items* folder.

1-61 Empty Folder button

It is a good idea to have Outlook automatically empty the *Deleted Items* folder each time you exit Outlook. The default settings in Outlook can easily be changed to do this.

HOW TO: Change the Default Setting to Automatically Empty Deleted Items Each Time You Exit Outlook

1. Click the **File** tab to open the *Backstage*.
2. Click the **Options** button on the left. The *Outlook Options* dialog box opens.
3. Click the **Advanced** button on the left.
4. Select the **Empty Deleted Items folder when exiting Outlook** check box (Figure 1-62).
5. Click **OK** to close the *Outlook Options* dialog box.

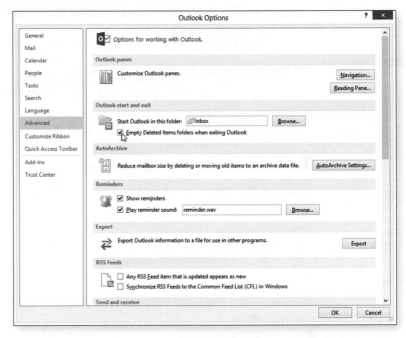

1-62 Empty Deleted Items folder when exiting Outlook option

> **MORE INFO**
>
> The *Outlook Options* dialog box will be referred to throughout this text. This area will allow you to customize the settings in Outlook. *Outlook Options* and other Outlook features are located on the *Backstage* view, which is accessed by clicking on the **File** tab. *Outlook Options* will be covered in Chapter 7.

Even when Outlook items have been deleted and the *Deleted Items* folder has been emptied, Outlook still provides you with the ability to recover deleted items if you are using an Exchange server. The **Recover Deleted Items** button (Figure 1-63) in the *Clean Up* group on the *Folder* tab will allow you to select previously deleted items to recover. These recovered items will be placed in your *Deleted items* folder.

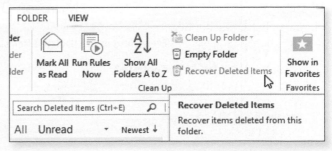

1-63 Recover Deleted Items button

For this Pause and Practice project, you reply to a message with an email attachment. You also forward the message to your instructor as an attachment and delete a message.

File Needed: ***Employee Information.xlsx***
Completed Project File Name: None

---

1. Reply to the message with the subject **Central Sierra Information Request**.
    a. Select the message in your Inbox.
    b. Click the **Reply** button in the message.

2. Add the following text to the body of the message:

    I just found the employee data sheet and attached it to this message.
    [your name]

3. Attach the file ***Employee Information.xlsx*** to the message.

4. Click the **Send** button to send the message.

5. The message will appear in your inbox.

6. Select the message and forward it to your instructor as an attachment.
    a. Click the message to select it.
    b. Click the **Forward as Attachment** option [*Home* tab, *Respond* group, *More* button].
    c. Enter your instructor's email address in the *To* field.
    d. Enter the following text in the body of the message:

    Attached is the requested verification email for the employee data.
    [your name]

    e. Click the **Send** button.

7. Delete the initial reply message that indicated that you would send the message as soon as you retrieved it.
    a. Select the initial reply message in your Inbox.
    b. Click the **Delete** button [*Home* tab, *Delete* group].

8. Empty the *Deleted Items* folder.
    a. Click the **Deleted Items** folder.
    b. Click the **Empty Folder** button [*Folder* tab, *Clean Up* group].
    c. Click **Yes** to confirm the deletion of messages in the *Deleted Items* folder (Figure 1-64).

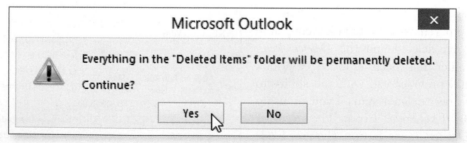

1-64 Confirmation for deleting items

Chapter Summary

1.1 Identify the basic components of Microsoft Outlook 2013 (p. O1-2).

- Outlook includes six major features: *Email, Calendar, Contacts, Tasks, Notes,* and *Journal*.
- *Email:* Gives users the capability of creating, sending, and receiving email. It can manage a single email account or multiple email accounts.
- *Calendar:* An electronic calendar that makes it easy to create appointments or events, edit these items, replicate calendar items, set electronic reminders, create meeting requests, and share calendar items with other Outlook users or other devices.
- *Contacts:* An area to keep names, email, phone numbers, and other information about business contacts, coworkers, friends, and family.
- *Tasks:* An electronic notepad that you use to write down your to-do items and then cross them off as they are completed.
- *Notes:* Electronic sticky notes that are an excellent way of storing information such as a user name and password to log into a web site, gift ideas for family and friends, or a list of books you'd like to read.
- *Journal:* Primarily used in the business environment and enables you to keep track of time spent on a project or document.

1.2 Navigate throughout the Outlook environment and identify the different panes in the Outlook window (p. O1-6).

- *Outlook Today* is the welcome screen for Outlook which provides you with information about your mailbox, calendar items, and task list.
- The *Navigation* pane allows you to quickly switch between different features in Outlook.
- The *Reading* pane allows you to quickly read messages or see details in tasks. This can be shown on the bottom or right of the window.
- The *Ribbon* appears at the top of the Outlook window and includes a variety of *tabs*. Each tab has a variety of *groups;* groups contain buttons, drop-down lists, and galleries.
- You can choose from a variety of preset views to personalize your experience.

- The *Folder list* allows you to see all of the folders in the *Navigation* pane.
- The *Outlook Help* button allows you to quickly search for topics on which you might have a question or need additional information.

1.3 Distinguish between Outlook being used as a stand-alone program and in a Microsoft Exchange environment (p. O1-13).

- Outlook as a standalone program connects directly to your Internet Service Provider and can manage multiple email accounts.
- Outlook is typically connected to an *Exchange Server* in business environments and has the following features:
  - Using voting buttons and tracking responses
  - Sending meeting requests and tracking responses
  - Recalling messages
  - Sharing your calendar, contacts, tasks, and email with others
  - Using MailTips
  - Using a common global contact list

1.4 Distinguish between the different types of email accounts and set up an email account in Outlook (p. O1-14).

- *Microsoft Exchange* accounts are used primarily in medium- to large-business settings. These email accounts are set up through the company network or email administrator. An Exchange account has an individual mailbox assigned to each user and resides on an Exchange file server.
- *POP3* accounts are Internet email accounts that are associated with your Internet service provider (ISP). When using this type of account, Outlook downloads the messages.
- *IMAP* accounts are also Internet accounts but are not always associated with an ISP. IMAP accounts create folders on a server to store and organize messages for retrieval by other computers and give you the option to read message headers only and select which messages to download.
- *HTTP* accounts use the hypertext transfer protocol used on the web to create, view, send, and receive messages. This type of account

is not automatically supported by Outlook but can be configured by installing an add-in.

- You can set up an email account by clicking the **Add Account** button [*File* tab].

1.5 Use Outlook to create, send, and receive email (p. O1-17).

- You select recipients, type the subject of the message, type the message, and send email messages.
- The **To** field indicates who a message is addressed to, while the **Cc** field is used to send a carbon copy of a message to another person. The **Bcc** field is used to send a blind carbon copy of a message to a recipient. *Bcc* is used when you do not want those receiving the email message to see other recipients' email address or names.
- Messages that are sent are automatically copied to the **Sent Items** folder.
- If you are not ready to send an email message, you can save it as a draft to the **Drafts** folder.
- When you read an email message, you can **Reply**, **Reply All**, or **Forward** a message.
- You can save email messages as *.msg* files to a location on your computer.

1.6 Use attachments in email (p. O1-28).

- You can attach files from your computer to email messages.
- You cannot attach a Microsoft Access file or a folder to an email message.
- Most common attachments, such as images, can be previewed by clicking on them within a message.
- Attachments can be saved to your computer.
- Email messages can be forwarded to recipients as attachments.
- You can attach Outlook items, such as business cards, to email messages.

1.7 Differentiate email arrangements and icons (p. O1-32).

- Email messages can be grouped in **Conversations**, which groups all emails related to a particular email conversation. This ensures your email is less cluttered, as only the newest message in a conversation is shown.
- **Unread** messages are bolded, while **read** messages are not. Outlook allows you to mark messages that are read as unread or unread as read. Marking messages as unread ensures they maintain the bold appearance and are easy to pick out.
- A **paper clip** icon is used to indicate that a message has an attachment.
- **Flags** are used to indicate that follow-up on a message is needed.
- You can set the importance of an email messages as high, normal, or low to indicate the priority one should place on the message.
- You can add reminders to email messages that require an action.
- Categories can be used to group emails by similar subjects.

1.8 Explain the importance and process of cleaning up an Inbox (p. O1-35).

- When you delete an email message, it is sent to the **Deleted Items** folder, as opposed to being deleted from your account.
- Emptying your **Deleted Items** folder will delete any messages that were moved to that location.
- **Clean Up** removes redundant messages in an email conversation. *Clean Up* can also be used on an entire folder and subfolders.
- **Ignore** deletes all emails related to a specific conversation and delete any new received email that is related to that conversation.

Check for Understanding

In the **Online Learning Center** for this text (www.mhhe.com/office2013inpractice), there are a variety of resources that can be used to review the concepts covered in this chapter.

The following Online Learning Resources are available in the Online Learning Center:

- Multiple choice questions
- Short answer questions
- Matching exercises

Guided Project 1-1

For this project, you request a meeting with Jay Hamlin of Central Sierra Insurance to discuss ways of attracting new customers. You send an email message to request a meeting and include a *Cc* to yourself so that you can keep this message at the top of your message list.
[Student Learning Outcomes 1.1, 1.2, 1.5, 1.7]

Skills Covered in This Project

- Create a new message.
- Select *To* recipient.
- Select *Cc* recipient.
- Add a subject to a message.

- Add a body to a message.
- Mark a message as low importance.
- Flag a message for follow up.
- Send a message.

---

1. Create a new email message to Jay Hamlin.
   a. Click the **New Email** button [*Home* tab, *New* group].
   b. In the *To* field, type your instructor's email address.
   c. In the *Cc* field, type your email address.
   d. In the *Subject* field, type Attracting New Customers Meeting Request

2. In the body of the message, type the following text:

   Hi Jay, I was wondering if you are available to meet next week to discuss our strategies to attract new customers. I am available on Monday from 2:00 P.M. to 3:00 P.M. or Tuesday from 3:00 P.M. to 4:00 P.M. Please let me know if either of these days work for your schedule. If not, please send me alternative times that you are available.

   Thanks,
   [your name]

3. Mark the message as *Low Importance* and flag the message for follow up.
   a. Click the **Low Importance** button [*Message* tab, *Tags* group].
   b. Click the **Follow Up** [*Message* tab, *Tags* group] and select **Tomorrow**.

4. Click the **Send** button to send the message (Figure 1-65).

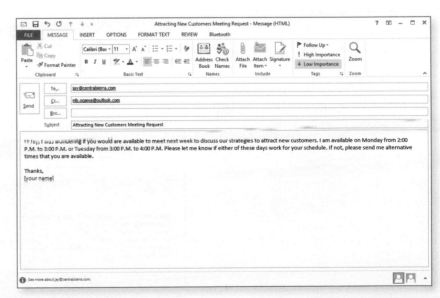

1-65 Completed Guided Project 1-1

Guided Project 1-2

For this project, you follow up with Jay, as he was unable to respond to your first message. You forward your original message to him and ask if he is available to meet.
[Student Learning Outcomes 1.1, 1.2, 1.5, 1.7]

Skills Covered in This Project

- Identify an unread message.
- Open a message.
- Identify a message as low importance.
- Forward a message.
- Select *To* recipient.
- Add a *Bcc* to a message.

- Select *Bcc* recipient.
- Modify the body of a message.
- Remove *Low Importance* tag.
- Mark a message as high importance.
- Send a message.

---

1. Open the message sent in Guided Practice 1-1.
   a. Click the **Mail** button to confirm you are in your Inbox.
   b. Click the message with the subject ***Attracting New Customers Meeting Request***.
   c. The Information bar states, "The message was sent with Low importance."

2. Forward the message to Jay Hamlin and modify the body of the message.
   a. Click the **Forward** button [*Home* tab, *Respond* group].
   b. In the *To* field, type jay@centralsierra.com.
   c. Click the **Bcc** button [*Message* tab, *Show Fields* group] to ensure the *Bcc* field is available.
   d. In the *Bcc* field, type your email address.
   e. In the body of the message, type:

   > Hi Jay, I just wanted to follow up with you regarding our meeting to attract new customers. Are you available next week to meet? Please let me know at your earliest convenience.

   > Thank you,
   > [your name]

   f. Click the **High Importance** button [*Message* tab, *Tags* group].

3. Click the **Send** button to send the message (Figure 1-66).

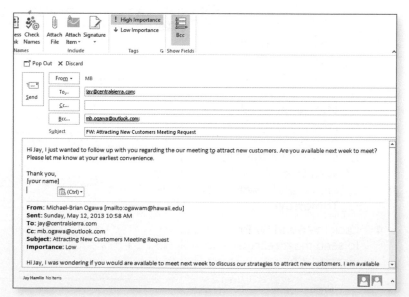

1-66 Completed Guided Project 1-2

Guided Project 1-3

For this project, you reply to the message as Jay Hamlin. You save a draft of your message, save a copy of your message as a *.msg* file, and print a copy of the message.
[Student Learning Outcomes 1.1, 1.2, 1.5, 1.7]

File Needed: None
Completed Project File Name: *[your initials] Outlook 1-3.msg*

Skills Covered in This Project

- Open a message.
- Identify a message as high importance.
- Reply to a message.
- Select a *Cc* recipient.
- Edit the body of a message.

- Save a message as a file .
- Send a message.
- Create a new message.
- Add an attachment to a message.

---

1. Open the message sent in Guided Practice 1-2.
    a. Click the **Mail** button to confirm you are in your Inbox.
    b. Click the message with the subject *FW: Attracting New Customers Meeting Request*.
    c. The Information bar states, "The message was sent with High importance."

2. Forward the message to Jay Hamlin and modify the body of the message.
    a. Click the **Reply** button [*Home* tab, *Respond* group].
    b. Ensure the *To* field has your email address.
    c. In the *Cc* field, type your instructor's email address.
    d. In the body of the message, type:

    Hi [your name], Thanks for checking in with me regarding the meeting about new customers. I accidentally missed your first message. I am available to meet on Tuesday at 2:00 P.M.

    Elsa, could you please schedule the conference room for us next week Tuesday from 2:00 P.M. to 3:00 P.M.

    Jay

3. Save the message to your computer.
    a. Click **Save As** [*File* tab].
    b. Locate the driver and folder where the file is to be stored.
    c. Change the file name to be *[your initials] Outlook 1-3* in the *File Name* area.
    d. Click the **Save** button.

4. Click the **Send** button to send the message.

5. Create a new email message to your instructor.
    a. Click the **New Email** button [*Home* tab, *New* group].
    b. In the *To* field, type your instructor's email address.
    c. In the *Cc* field, type your email address.
    d. In the *Subject* field, type [your initials] Outlook 1-3.

6. In the body of the message, type the following text:

    Hi [instructor's name]. Attached are my three guided practice assignments from Outlook Chapter 1.

    Thanks,
    [your name]

7. Attach the message you saved to your computer to the email message.
    a. Click the **Attach File** button.
    b. Locate the message you saved in step 3.
    c. Select the message and click the **Insert** button (Figure 1-67).

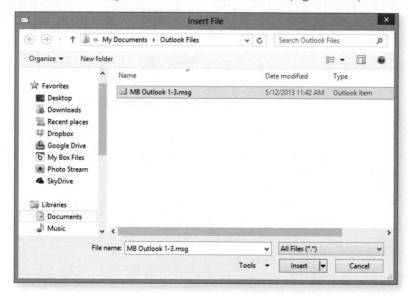

1-67 Attach a saved message

8. Click the **Send** button to send the message (Figure 1-68).

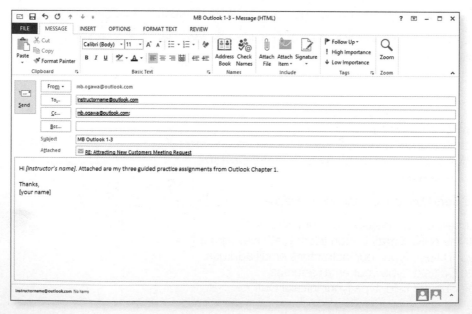

1-68 Completed Guided Project 1-3

Independent Project 1-4

You received a request from Mr. and Mrs. Dodge, over the phone, requesting a vaccination schedule for their newborn child. For this project, you send them an email message with a vaccination schedule. [Student Learning Outcomes 1.1, 1.2, 1.5, 1.6, 1.7]

File Needed: ***Outlook 1-4 vaccination.docx***
Completed Project File Name: None

Skills Covered in This Project

- Create a new message.
- Select a *To* recipient.
- Select a *Cc* recipient.
- Add a subject.
- Add a message.
- Add an attachment to a message.
- Send a message.

1. Create a new email message to the Dodge family using the following information:
   a. In the *To* field, type your partner's email address.
   b. In the *Cc* field, type your email address.

2. In the *Subject* field, type Requested vaccination information for your newborn.

3. Type a short message to the Dodge family indicating that you attached the requested vaccination schedule.

4. Attach the file ***Outlook 1-4 vaccination.docx*** to the message.

5. Send the message (Figure 1-69).

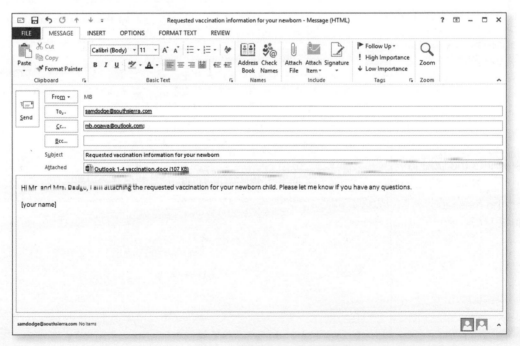

1-69 Completed Independent Project 1-4

Independent Project 1-5

You received a request from Dr. Lee at Courtyard Medical Plaza to verify the message to the Dodge family was sent. For this project, you send him the message that you sent and print a copy for the patient's records.
[Student Learning Outcomes 1.1, 1.2, 1.5, 1.6, 1.7, 1.8]

Skills Covered in This Project

- Open a message.
- Print a message.
- Forward a message as an attachment.
- Select a *To* recipient.

- Select a *Bcc* recipient.
- Add a message.
- Send a message.

---

1. Locate and open the message sent in Independent Project 1-4 with the subject ***Requested vaccination information for your newborn***. The message has a paper clip icon next to it to indicate that it has an attachment.

2. Print the message in a memo format (Figure 1-70).

3. Forward the message as an attachment to the following recipients:
   a. In the *To* field, type your partner's email address.
   b. In the *Cc* field, type your email address.

4. Edit the body of the message to indicate to Dr. Lee that the attached message was sent to the Dodge family.

5. Send the message (Figure 1-71).

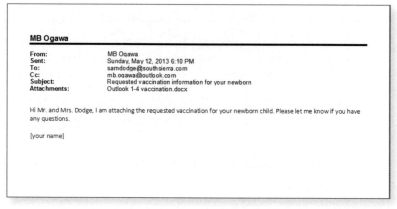

1-70 Printed message in memo format

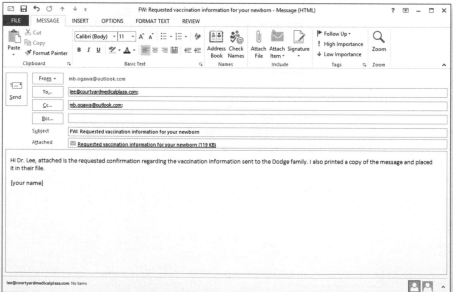

1-71 Completed Independent Project 1-5

Independent Project 1-6

You noticed that your Inbox is becoming cluttered because you included yourself as a *Cc* or *Bcc* on all of your previous messages to the Dodge family and Dr. Lee. For this project, you forward the messages as an attachment to yourself and your instructor to keep it as one message. Next, you clean your Inbox by deleting all previous messages regarding the Dodge family and Dr. Lee.
[Student Learning Outcomes 1.1, 1.2, 1.5, 1.6, 1.7, 1.8]

Skills Covered in This Project

- Open a message.
- Forward a message as an attachment.
- Select a *To* recipient.
- Select a *Cc* recipient.

- Edit the subject.
- Edit the message.
- Send a message.
- Delete messages.

---

1. Locate and open the message sent in Independent Project 1-5 with the subject **FW: Requested vaccination information for your newborn**. The message has a paper clip icon next to it to indicate that it has an attachment.

2. Forward the message as an attachment to the following recipients:
   a. In the *To* field, type your email address.
   b. In the *Bcc* field, type your instructor's email address.

3. Edit the subject of the message to indicate that the message contains all of the Dodge family messages.

4. Edit the body of the message to indicate that the message is a summary of all messages related to the Dodge family.

5. Send the message (Figure 1-72).

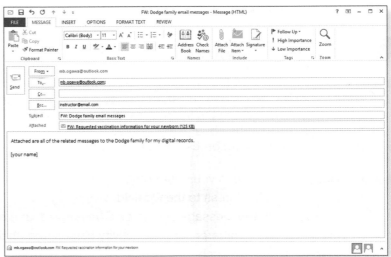

1-72 Message sent for Independent Project 1-6

6. Locate the following messages sent regarding the Dodge family:

   Requested vaccination information for your newborn
   FW: Requested vaccination information for your newborn

7. Delete the two messages listed in step 6 (Figure 1-73).

1-73 Deleting messages for Independent Project 1-6

Challenge Project 1-7

Search for an image online that is representative of you. Compose a message to your instructor with the image as an attachment that explains briefly why and how the image represents you.

Note: Use images that are legal under copyright. You may need to use a search engine, such as http://search.creativecommons.org/ to find licensed content.
[Student Learning Outcomes 1.1, 1.2, 1.5, 1.6, 1.8]

- Send the message to your instructor.
- Add your email address to the *Cc* field.
- The subject of the message should be *Challenge 1-7: Visually Representing [your name]*.
- Include the image as an attachment.
- Explain how the image represents you in three to five sentences.
- Add a citation for the image at the bottom of your message.

Challenge Project 1-8

Compose a message that includes a list of five activities you would like to try in the next five years. For each of the activities you list, compose a short paragraph about that activity and why you find it interesting. Research on the Internet each of the activities you chose. Use your own words when composing the paragraphs about each activity.
[Student Learning Outcomes 1.1, 1.2, 1.5, 1.8]

- Send the message to your instructor.
- Add your email address to the *Cc* field.
- The subject of the message should be *Challenge 1-8: [your name]'s Activities*.
- Use formatting to differentiate the activity names from their description and explanation for wanting to participate in each.

Challenge Project 1-9

Search for a job online that you would like to have. Compose an application letter to the employer highlighting a few reasons why you would be good for the position. The application letter should be short and concise. Attach your resume to the email message.
[Student Learning Outcomes 1.1, 1.2, 1.5, 1.6, 1.8]

- Send the message to your instructor.
- Add your email address to the *Cc* field.
- The subject of the message should be **Challenge 1-9: [your name]'s application for [job name]**.
- Include your resume as an attachment.
- Address the body of the email message to your instructor.
- Include a few reasons why you would be good for the position in the body of the message.

Email Special Features

CHAPTER OVERVIEW

One of the benefits of using Outlook to handle your email accounts is the vast array of features available to customize your messages and the Outlook environment. As your understanding of Outlook increases, you will want to customize your email messages and change some of the default settings in Outlook to more fully meet your needs and preferences.

This chapter will prepare you to customize your email by using some of the different email options available in Outlook. These include marking an email as important, using delivery and read receipts, delaying the delivery of an email, flagging an email for recipients, and many more. You will also learn how to use voting buttons and change the look of your email by using stationery, themes, and signatures. After completing Chapter 1 and this chapter, you will be able to customize Outlook and use email options to meet your personal and professional needs.

STUDENT LEARNING OUTCOMES (SLOs)

After completing this chapter, you will be able to:

SLO 2.1 Differentiate between the types of email formats (p. O2-51).

SLO 2.2 Customize your email using the different types of email options available in Outlook (p. O2-52).

SLO 2.3 Use categories to organize email messages into different groups (p. O2-61).

SLO 2.4 Add *Follow Up* flags to email messages to add reminders to messages (p. O2-64).

SLO 2.5 Use email voting buttons to get responses from recipients and to automatically track responses (p. O2-69).

SLO 2.6 Customize your emails by using signatures, themes, and desktop alerts (p. O2-73).

CASE STUDY

For the Pause & Practice projects, you are working with a partner on a business project. You decided to use email to identify meeting dates and locations. You send and reply to email messages with a partner and use Outlook's email special features to make your tasks easier.

Pause & Practice 2-1: You send a plain text formatted message to a peer to request information about your peer's availability to meet about a business project.

Pause & Practice 2-2: You organize your email messages using categories. You also create a custom follow up flag for your message.

Pause & Practice 2-3: You use voting buttons to determine a good location for your lunch meeting.

Pause & Practice 2-4: You create a signature and insert it in an email message to your partner. You also forward the stream of messages to your instructor.

Understanding Email Format

Not all email accounts operate on the same mail format. Outlook provides flexibility in the type of email messages that are available for different situations. The message format you choose determines the types of formatting features you can use such as fonts, formatted text, colors, styles, bullets, numbering, line spacing, and indents. It is important to note that just because you can and do use some of these advanced formatting features in the body of your email does not mean that the recipient of your email will be able to see them.

There are three different types of mail formats available in Outlook: plain text, Rich Text Format, and Hypertext Markup Language.

Plain Text

All email applications support plain text mail format because it does not include most text formatting features. *Plain text* format does not support bold, italic, or any of the other advanced text formatting features. Pictures cannot be displayed in the body of the message when using plain text format; although, pictures can still be attached to the message and sent.

Hypertext Markup Language

Hypertext Markup Language (HTML) message format is the default format in Outlook. HTML format lets you format the body of your email message similar to a Microsoft Word document. HTML is the most commonly used message format and will allow your recipients to receive a message in the same format as you sent it, unless the recipient's email application supports only plain text formatting.

Outlook Rich Text Format

Rich Text Format (RTF) is unique to Outlook users and is supported in an Exchange environment. This format allows users to use the different formatting features available in Outlook. When using RTF, Outlook automatically converts these messages to Hypertext Markup Language (HTML) by default when you send them to an Internet recipient, so that the message formatting is maintained and attachments are received. It is probably best to use HTML format if you are sending messages outside of an Exchange environment.

Set Default and Change Message Format

As mentioned previously, HTML message format is the default setting in Outlook. The default message format can be changed, and the message format for an individual email can also be changed.

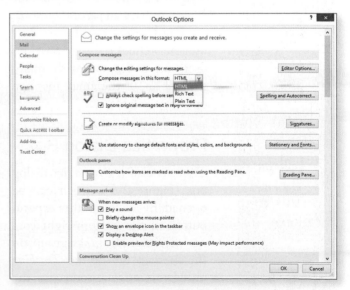

2-1 Outlook Options dialog box

HOW TO: Set Default Message Format

1. Click the **File** tab. The *Backstage* window opens.
2. Click the **Options** button on the left. The *Outlook Options* dialog box opens (Figure 2-1).

3. Click the **Mail** button. The mail options will be displayed.
4. Select the default message desired in the *Compose messages* area.
5. Click **OK** to close the *Outlook Options* dialog box.

If you change the default message setting, then all new emails will have the new default message format.

If you are sending a message to recipients whose email application supports only plain text format, you can change the setting on an individual email rather than changing the default setting.

HOW TO: Change Message Format

1. Open a new email message.
2. Click the **Format Text** tab.
3. In the *Format* group, choose the desired message format (Figure 2-2).

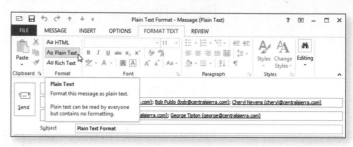

2-2 Select message format

SLO 2.2

Using Message Options

Outlook provides users with a wide variety of message options to enhance an individual email message. The most common message options are available on the *Message* tab. At the bottom right corner of some of the groups is an **expand** button (Figure 2-3). Clicking on the expand button opens a dialog box that includes additional options related to the group. Not all groups have an expand button.

2-3 Expand button

2-4 Options tab

The **Options tab** (Figure 2-4) on a new email message provides users an entire tab with many, but not all, of the email message options available.

Properties Dialog Box

There is also a **Properties** dialog box (Figure 2-5), which can be opened by clicking the **expand** button in the bottom right corner of either the *Tags* group on the *Message* tab or the *Tracking* or *More Options* groups on the *Options* tab.

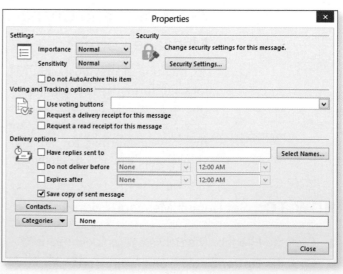

2-5 Properties dialog box

Importance

Outlook offers you the option of marking an email at one of three levels of importance: *normal*, *high*, and *low*. Normal importance is the default setting for all new email messages.

An email message can be marked as **High Importance** to notify your recipients that it is important (Figure 2-6). The **High Importance** button is the red exclamation point in the *Tags* group on the *Message* tab. A message can be marked as **Low Importance** by clicking on the **Low Importance** (blue down arrow) button.

2-6 High Importance tag

When recipients receive an email marked as *High Importance* or *Low Importance*, the email will be marked with the corresponding Inbox icon (Figure 2-7), which alerts them to the importance of the email.

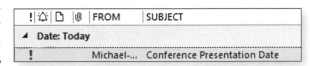

2-7 Message with high importance

Sensitivity

If an email is of a sensitive nature, it can be marked as such to alert recipients. Outlook offers several sensitivity options: *normal* (default setting), *personal*, *private*, and *confidential*. Sensitivity can only be selected from within the *Properties* dialog box; it is not available on any of the new message tabs.

When a recipient receives an email that has been marked as sensitive, there will be a notification in the *InfoBar* (above the *From* line on an open email message). If the message was marked as *Confidential*, the message will read, "Please treat this as Confidential" (Figure 2-8).

2-8 Confidential message

Security

The *security settings* (Figure 2-9) in the *Properties* dialog box provides users with the options of encrypting a message and attachment and including a digital signature. Digital signatures and encryption are available in the *Security Properties* dialog box (Figure 2-10). A *digital signature* is a way of authenticating your email to assure recipients you are who you say you are. The process of *encrypting* a message and attachment scrambles both the message itself and the attached file, which adds a layer of security. The sender uses a *public key* to encrypt a message, and the recipient of an encrypted message must have a *private key* to view the contents of the message and attachment.

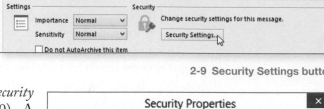

2-9 Security Settings button

2-10 Security Properties dialog box

Delivery and Read Receipts

Have you ever sent out an email and wondered if the recipients had received or read the email? When using Outlook in conjunction with Exchange, *delivery* and *read receipts* can be used to provide you, the sender, with an electronic receipt that an email has been delivered to or opened by its intended recipients. When a delivery or read receipt has been requested (Figure 2-11), the sender will receive an email confirmation that the email has been delivered and/or opened by each recipient.

2-11 Request a Read Receipt

When a recipient receives a message that has a delivery receipt, Outlook automatically generates a receipt that is sent to the sender. If an email has a read receipt request, the recipient receives a notification that a read receipt has been requested (Figure 2-12). The recipient is given the option of sending or declining to send a read receipt.

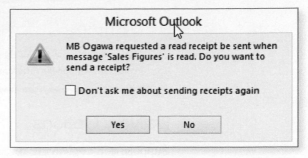

2-12 Read Receipt reply query

Requesting a delivery or read receipt can be done from the *Tracking* group on the *Options* tab or from the *Properties* dialog box (Figure 2-13).

2-13 Request a read receipt for a message in the properties

Outlook uses *tracking* to record this information. Tracking is unique to Exchange and provides the sender with a summary of the receipts received. Once a delivery or read receipt has been received, a *Tracking* button will be available on the original email (usually in the *Sent Items* folder).

HOW TO: View Tracking Results

1. Click the **Sent Items** folder in the *Navigation* pane.
2. Open the sent email that had a delivery or read receipt.
3. Click the **Tracking** button in the *Show* group to view a summary of receipts. The tracking will be displayed in the body of the email (Figure 2-14).
4. Click the **Message** button in the *Show* group to return to the text of the message.

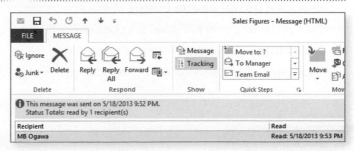

2-14 Tracking a message

Delivery Options

Suppose you are leaving town tomorrow but need to send out an email on Friday, and, since you'll be gone, you want to have replies sent to a coworker in your office. Outlook provides users with customized delivery options. The delivery options include having replies sent to other users, delaying delivery, setting an expiration date and time, and saving the sent email in a different location.

2-15 Save Sent Item To button

Sent email messages are by default saved in the *Sent Items* folder. This location can be changed for an individual email by clicking on the **Save Sent Item To** button in the *More Options* group on the *Options* tab (Figure 2-15). You can choose a folder from the *Folder* list as the location to save this email, use the default folder, or choose to not save the message. This option applies only to the current message.

Delay Delivery (Figure 2-16) is an option that allows you to specify the date and time when an email is to be sent. When this feature is used, an email can be created and sent, and it will stay in your *Outbox* folder until the scheduled delivery date and time. When you click the **Delay Delivery** button, the *Properties* dialog box opens.

2-16 Delay Delivery button

HOW TO: Set the Delay Delivery Option

1. In a new email message, click the **Options** tab.
2. Click the **Delay Delivery** button. The *Properties* dialog box opens (Figure 2-17).

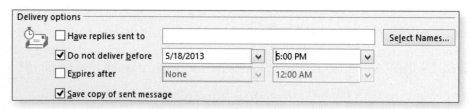

2-17 Delivery options

3. Select the **Do not deliver before** check box.
4. Set the day and time the email is to be delivered.
5. Click **Close** to close the *Properties* dialog box.
6. Click **Send**. The message will be stored in your *Outbox* folder until the specified time to be delivered.

> **MORE INFO**
>
> A rule can also be created to delay the delivery of all emails you send. Rules will be covered in Chapter 6.

There are times when it is beneficial to have other users receive a reply to an email. When the **Direct Replies To** option is selected (Figure 2-18), you can select individuals from your contacts to receive replies from an email you've sent.

2-18 Direct Replies To button

HOW TO: Use the Direct Replies To Feature

1. In a new email message, click the **Options** tab.
2. Click the **Direct Replies To** button. The *Properties* dialog box opens.
3. Click the **Select Names** button (Figure 2-19). The *Have Replies Sent To* dialog box opens.

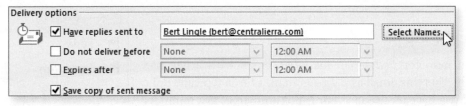

2-19 Direct Replies

4. Select recipients from the contact list and press **OK** to close the *Have Replies Sent To* dialog box.
5. Click **Close** to close the *Properties* dialog box.

> **ANOTHER WAY**
> The *Delay Delivery* and *Direct Replies To* options can be directly accessed from the *Properties* dialog box.

Some emails are time sensitive and are no longer relevant to the recipient after a certain time. The **Expires after** feature lets you set a time for when an email is to expire. When an email has expired, it still remains visible and can be opened from the recipient's Inbox, but it is marked with a strikethrough (Figure 2-20).

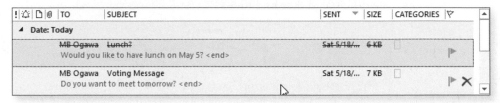

2-20 Expired message

HOW TO: Set an Expiration Day and Time

1. In a new message, click the **expand** button at the bottom right of the *Tags* group on the *Message* tab (Figure 2-21). The *Properties* dialog box opens.

2-21 Expand button

2. Check **Expires after**.

3. Set the date and time the email is to expire (Figure 2-22).

4. Click **Close** to close the *Properties* dialog box.

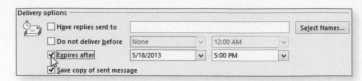

2-22 Set expire date and time

> ▶ **MORE INFO**
>
> When a message has expired, the recipient can still reply to the message.

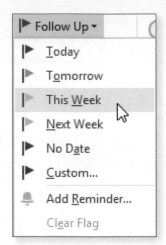

Follow Up Flag

Flagging an item for *Follow Up* marks an email with a flag and automatically lists this email as a *To-Do* item. This is typically done on an email you have received in your Inbox and serves as a reminder that you have to follow up with some action on this email.

An email can be marked for follow up by clicking on the **Follow Up** button in the *Tags* group on the *Message* tab and choosing a flag (Figure 2-23). Email messages marked with a flag will display a flag icon in the *Folder* pane.

2-23 Flag a message
for follow up

Flag for Recipients

A ***Custom flag*** (Figure 2-24) can be used to create a ***Flag for Recipients***. *Flag for Recipients* attaches a flag and message to an email and gives you the option of including a reminder date and time. Outlook provides preset ***Flag to*** messages from which to choose, or you can create your own custom message. If a reminder is set (optional), recipients will receive an Outlook reminder that will open on their computer screen at the designated date and time.

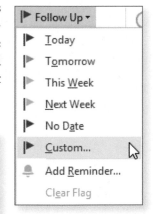

> ▶ **MORE INFO**
>
> The specific follow up options (e.g., *Today*, *This Week*, *Custom*) are only available when using an exchange server. If you are not using an exchange server, you can still add a flag to messages.

2-24 Flag a message for
custom follow up

HOW TO: Flag an Email for the Recipient

1. In a new email, click the **Follow Up** button in the *Tags* group.

2. Select **Custom**. The *Custom* dialog box opens (Figure 2-25).

3. Deselect the **Flag for Me** check box.

4. Select the **Flag for Recipients** check box.

5. Select a **Flag to** message, or type in your own custom message.

6. If you want the recipients to receive a reminder message, select the **Reminder** check box and set a date and time.

7. Click **OK** to close the *Custom* dialog box.

2-25 Custom dialog box

When an email has a *Flag for Recipients*, there will be a notification in the *InfoBar* (above the *From* line on an open email message) visible to both the sender and receiver of the message (Figure 2-26).

2-26 Follow-up message

Permission

The **Permission** option in the *Permission* group on the *Options* tab helps to ensure that sensitive information is not forwarded, printed, or copied. For the permission feature to function properly, your company must enable the **Information Rights Management (IRM)**. If IRM is not enabled for your company, you will not see any options in the *Permission* group.

If the IRM is enabled, the permission can be set to **Do Not Forward** or a custom configuration. When the *Do Not Forward* permission is selected, recipients will receive a notification in the *InfoBar* informing them of the restrictions.

For this Pause and Practice project, you send a plain text formatted message to a peer. The message will request information about your peer's availability to meet about a business project. The message is very important and requires follow up.

1. Create a new email message.
   a. Click the **Mail** button in the *Navigation pane*.
   b. Click the **New Email** button [*Home* tab, *New* group].

2. Click the **Plain Text** button [*Format Text* tab, *Format* group].

3. Enter the following information in the email message fields.
   To: your partner's email address
   Cc: your email address.
   Subject: Business Project Meeting
   Body: Hi [partner name], are you available to meet next week Monday for our business project?

   Thank you,
   [your name]

4. Click the **High Importance** button [*Message* tab, *Tags* group].

5. Click the **Send** button.

6. Open the message your partner sent to you with the subject *Business Project Meeting*.

7. Reply to the email with following message in the body:

   Monday sounds great! Let's meet for lunch.
   [your name]

8. Click the **Request a Read Receipt** option [*Options* tab, *Tracking* group].

9. Click the **Send** button (Figure 2-27).

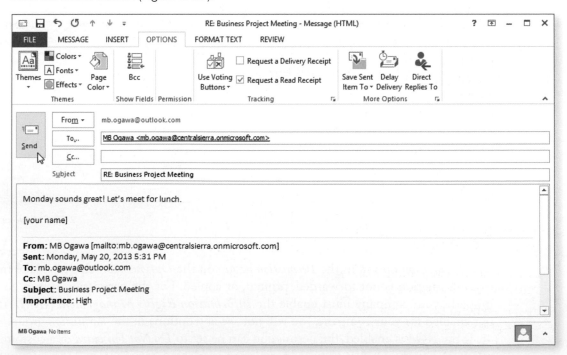

2-27 Completed Pause & Practice 2-1

Using Categories

There might be times when you want to group together related emails, tasks, calendar items, or contacts, but you do not want to create a separate folder in which to store these related items. For example, you might want to group all your cycling buddies' contacts together so they are easy to find or group together tasks and emails related to the upcoming fundraiser at work.

The *Category* feature can be used to mark Outlook items as part of a particular group. One of the useful and unique aspects of categories is that they are global; they can be used throughout Outlook (emails, calendars, contacts, tasks, notes, and journals) to mark different types of Outlook items. Whereas folders are useful for grouping specific items together, they only store one type of Outlook item. Categories are yet another method provided by Outlook to help you organize information. Each of the different areas of Outlook lets you view these Outlook items by category.

> **MORE INFO**
>
> Categories were introduced in Chapter 1.

Customize a Category

Outlook is set up with default categories for your use. These categories are really not all that useful until you customize them to meet your individual needs. Each category has a color, and the default name is the name of the color.

Categories can be used extensively in Outlook both for work and personal use. An instructor can set up categories for each of his or her courses so these categories can be used to mark emails from students, students' contact records, and calendar items and tasks associated with each course. At home, you could have a different category for each member of the family, and one for vacation, church, school, birthdays, anniversaries, and others. When almost all calendar items are marked with a category, it is very easy to visually distinguish by color the category of the event or appointment on the calendar.

The default categories in Outlook are labeled by color. *Customizing* a category is very easy; pick the color of category and rename it. One of the handy features of categories is that you can *rename* or *create* a category anywhere in Outlook and it will be available throughout Outlook. Let's start customizing categories.

2-28 All categories

HOW TO: Customize Categories

1. Click the **Calendar** button in the *Navigation* pane.
2. Click **Month** view.
3. Click any appointment or event on your calendar. The *Appointment* tab will be displayed.
4. Click the **Categorize** button in the *Tags* group and choose **All Categories** (Figure 2-28), or right-click the calendar item and choose **Categorize** and then **All Categories**. The *Color Categories* dialog box opens (Figure 2-29).

5. Click the color of the category to be renamed.

6. Click the **Rename** button.

7. On the left, type the new name of the category and press **Enter** (you can also click another category).

8. Continue to rename categories as desired.

9. Press **OK** when finished. Your categories are now set up and ready to use.

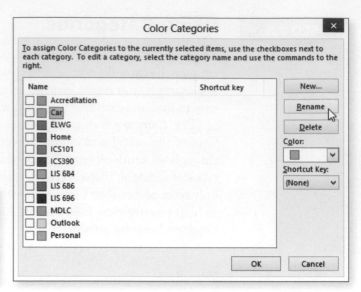

2-29 Rename a category

> **MORE INFO**
>
> The *Color Categories* dialog box can be accessed throughout Outlook. Simply click an email, calendar item, contact, or task and follow the preceding steps.

> **MORE INFO**
>
> When using multiple calendars, you will need to open an appointment to apply a category.

New categories can also be created following a similar process and can be done throughout Outlook. Once your categories are renamed or created, you can assign a category to any Outlook item. You can select or open the item to be categorized. For example, click the **Calendar** button on the *Navigation pane* and select an appointment to be categorized, then click the **Categorize** button in the *Tags* group, and select the category.

HOW TO: Create a New Category

1. Click the **Mail** button in the *Navigation* pane.

2. Select any email in your Inbox.

3. Click the **Categorize** button in the *Tags* group on the *Home* tab and choose **All Categories**, or right-click the mail item and choose **Categorize** and then **All Categories**. The *Color Categories* dialog box opens.

4. Click the **New** button. The *Add New Category* dialog box opens (Figure 2-30).

5. Type the name of the category in the *Name* text box.

6. Click the **Color** drop-down arrow and select a color.

   - You can also add a shortcut key to the category by clicking on the **Shortcut Key** drop-down arrow and selecting an option from the drop-down list.
   - You can apply a category that has a shortcut key assigned by selecting an Outlook item and pressing the shortcut key (e.g., **Ctrl+2**)

7. Click **OK**. The new category is added to your list of categories.

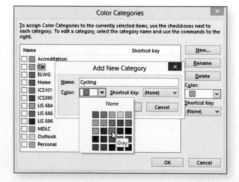 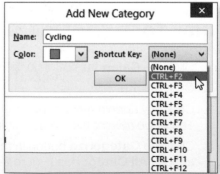

2-30 New category color and shortcut key

Assign a Category

Once your categories are renamed or created, you can assign a category to any Outlook item. You can select or open the item to be categorized, click the **Categorize** button on the tab, and then select the category. You can also right-click the item in the *Folder* pane, choose **Categorize**, and then select the category.

A category can be removed from an Outlook item by following this same process and selecting **Clear All Categories**.

> ### MORE INFO
>
> Outlook items can be assigned to more than one category. When viewing items by category, an item that is assigned to multiple categories will appear in both or multiple category sections; although, it is still only one Outlook item.

View by Categories

When categories have been assigned to Outlook items, you will usually be able to see the color and category when viewing the items in the *Folder* pane (Figure 2-31).

2-31 Outlook calendar folder pane

Within most of the areas in Outlook, you have the option of viewing items by category. This is a filter that can be accessed in the *Advanced View Settings* button in *Current View* group on the *View* tab (Figure 2-32). The *Advanced View Settings: Calendar* dialog box opens. Select the **Filter ...** (more) button to open the *Filter* dialog box and select the *More Choices* tab. Click the **Categories ...** (more) button to select the categories that you would like to be visible (Figure 2-33).

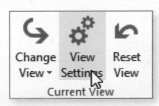

2-32 View Settings button

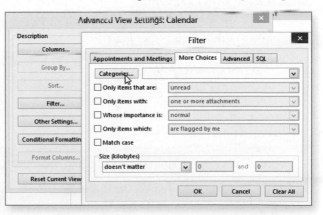

2-33 Categories filter

Set a Quick Click Category

If there is one category you use regularly, this category can be set as the ***Quick Click*** category. By setting a *Quick Click* category, an Outlook item can be quickly added to this category by clicking on the *Categories* field in the *Folder* pane. The *Quick Click* category effectively becomes the default category rather than having to choose a category from the list.

HOW TO: Set a Quick Click Category

1. Click an Outlook item in the *Folder* pane.
2. Click **Categorize** in the *Tags* group and choose **Set Quick Click**. You can also right-click the item in the *Folder* pane, choose **Categorize**, and then **Set Quick Click**. The *Set Quick Click* dialog box opens.
3. Choose the **category** to be used as the *Quick Click* category.
4. Press **OK** (Figure 2-34).

2-34 Set Quick Click dialog box

SLO 2.4

Using Follow Up Flags

Most of you have a stack of to-do items in your office or a pile of papers and bills by your computer at home. At some point you intend to take some kind of action on each of these items. Outlook provides you with *Follow Up* flags (Figure 2-35) to give these items further attention. When an Outlook item is marked with a *Follow Up* flag, it becomes a *To-Do* item.

There are numerous flags available for you to mark items depending on their priority. The types of *Follow Up* flags available in Outlook are:

- *Today*
- *Tomorrow*
- *This Week*
- *Next Week*
- *No Date*
- *Custom*

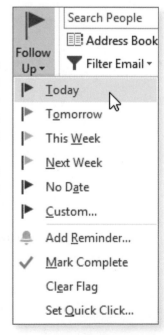

2-35 Follow Up flag

> **MORE INFO**
>
> *Follow Up* flags become a darker shade of red as the marked item approaches its due date. Outlook items marked with a *No Date Follow Up* flag are displayed as dark red, which is the same color as a *Today Follow Up* flag. An Outlook item turns red when it is past its due date.

Apply Follow Up Flag

Follow Up flags can be used on email messages and contacts. Tasks are automatically marked with a *Follow Up* flag based on the due date of the task, but these flags can also be changed.

HOW TO: Apply a Follow Up Flag

1. Open the Outlook item (e.g., email, contact, or task).
2. Click the **Follow Up** button in the *Tags* group (Figure 2-36).

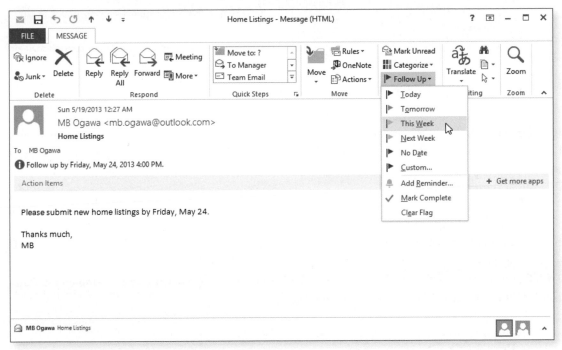

2-36 Apply a This Week Follow Up flag

3. Select the desired **Follow Up flag**. Details of the follow-up status are included in the *InfoBar* of the Outlook item.
4. Close the Outlook item. This marked item is now included in the list of *To-Do* items.

Create a Custom Follow Up Flag

A reminder and/or custom *Follow Up* flag can be added to an Outlook item. If a reminder is set, an electronic reminder will open on your computer screen providing you with details about the marked item.

A custom *Follow Up* flag can be set to give more specific follow-up details on an Outlook item. These include a custom message, start date, due date, and reminder. Outlook provides a few default messages for custom flags, or you can type in your own custom flag message.

HOW TO: Create a Custom Follow Up Flag

1. Open an Outlook item (e.g., email, contact, or task).
2. Click the **Follow Up** button in the *Tags* group.
3. Select *Custom* or *Add Reminder*. The *Custom* dialog box opens (Figure 2-37).
4. Enter the desired details in the *Custom* dialog box.
5. Click **OK** to close the dialog box. Details of the follow-up status are included in the *InfoBar* of the Outlook item.

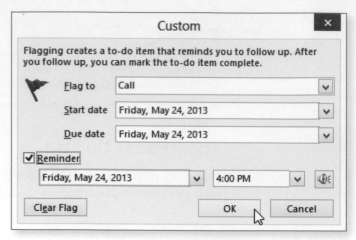

2-37 Custom Follow Up flag

> **MORE INFO**
>
> If you are using a smart phone to synch to Outlook, these reminders will appear on your phone as the item comes due.

Set a Quick Click Follow Up Flag

On the right side of the list of your email messages in the *Folder* pane is a column for *Follow Up* flags. A flag can be added by clicking on this area of the email message without having to select a specific flag.

The ***Quick Click*** flag can be customized to flag the Outlook item with the flag you use most regularly.

HOW TO: Set a Quick Click Follow Up Flag

1. Click the **Follow Up** button in the *Tags* group.
2. Choose **Set Quick Click**. The *Set Quick Click* dialog box opens (Figure 2-38).
3. Choose the desired **Follow Up flag** for *Quick Click* from the list of flag options.
4. Press **OK**.

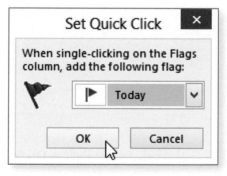

2-38 Quick Click Follow Up flag

To apply the *Quick Click* flag to a selected item, simply click the **Follow Up flag** area of the Outlook item and the *Quick Click* flag will be set on that item.

View To-Do Items

Outlook items marked with a *Follow Up* flag will remain in their location in Outlook (e.g., Inbox, Contacts, or Tasks), but they are also consolidated in the To-Do List (Figure 2-39). As mentioned previously, To-Do items are all Outlook items marked with a *Follow Up* flag and can include email, tasks, and contacts. The To-Do items are also listed in the *To-Do bar*.

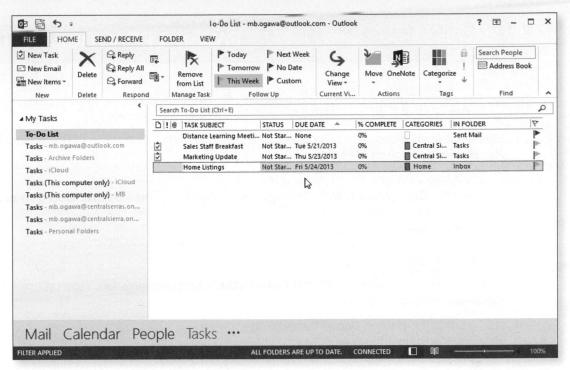

2-39 To-Do List

> MORE INFO

In addition to the To-Do List and the *To-Do bar*, rules and search folders can be used to group items that have been flagged for follow up.

Rules and search folders are covered in chapter 6.

Mark a Flagged Item as Complete

When an Outlook item that has been marked with a *Follow Up* flag has been completed, you can use **Mark Complete** to indicate the item has been completed and the flag will be replaced with a check mark. Or, if the To-Do List is displayed, the item will be crossed out indicating that it has been marked as complete.

The following list explains the numerous ways in Outlook to use *Mark Complete* for an item that has been flagged:

- Click the **flag** icon and the *Mark Complete* check will replace the flag.
- Right-click the item, choose **Follow Up**, and click **Mark Complete**.
- In the To-Do List, click the **Complete** check box to mark an item as completed.
- Open the item, click the **Follow Up** button in the *Tags* group, and choose **Mark Complete**.

> MORE INFO

You can remove a flag (different than marking it as completed) by selecting the Outlook item, opening the **Follow Up** menu, and choosing **Clear Flag**.

For this Pause and Practice project, you organize your email messages using categories. You also create a custom *Follow Up* flag for your message and mark an item as complete.

1. Select the email message you received in *Pause and Practice Outlook 2-1*. The subject is **Re: Business Project Meeting**.

2. Create a new category.
   a. Click the **Categorize** button [*Message* tab, *Tags* group] and select **All Categories . . .**
   b. Click the **New** button.
   c. Type the category name Business Project.
   d. Change the color to red (first row, first column).
   e. Click the **OK** button.

3. With the message selected, click the **Categorize** button [*Message* tab, *Tags* group] and select the **Business Project** category.

4. Add a custom *Follow Up* flag to the message.
   a. Click the **Follow Up** button [*Message* tab, *Tags* group] and select **Custom. . .**
   b. Click the **Start date** drop-down arrow and select **Today**.
   c. Click the **Due date** drop-down arrow and select tomorrow's date.
   d. Click the **Reminder** option.
   e. Click the **OK** button.

5. Click the **Reply** button [*Message* tab, *Respond* group].

6. Reply to the message with following message in the body:

   Sure, are there any foods you like to eat?

   [your name]

7. Click the **Send** button.

8. Open the message your partner sent to you and reply with the following message:

   I like to eat Italian and Japanese cuisine. How about you?

9. Change the subject to My lunch preferences.

10. Click the **Send** button.

11. After receiving the message from your partner, mark the initial reply message as complete.
    a. Locate and click on the first reply from your partner (you categorized it in the beginning of this project).
    b. Click the **Follow Up** button [*Message* tab, *Tags* group] and select **Mark Complete**.

12. If you are not using an exchange server, click the **Tasks** button on the *Navigation pane*.
    a. Click the **To-Do List** under *My Tasks*.
    b. Double-click the email in your *To-Do List*.
    c. Click the **Follow Up** button in the *Tags* group, and choose **Mark Complete**.

13. See Figure 2-40 for the completed Pause & Practice 2-2 project.

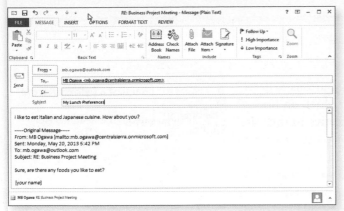
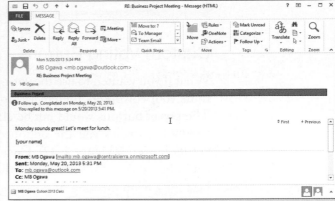

2-40 Completed Pause & Practice 2-2

SLO 2.5

Using Voting Buttons

Voting buttons are a useful way of gathering responses to a question sent via email. The advantage of using voting buttons, rather than having respondents reply to an emailed question, is that you can specify the response choices and Outlook will automatically track and tally the voting responses received. The tracking feature also lets you, the sender of the message, see who has and hasn't voted. You can also export the voting results to Excel.

> **MORE INFO**
> Voting buttons and tracking responses will only work in an Exchange environment.

Preset Voting Buttons

A question can be typed into the body of an email or in the subject line. The *Use Voting Buttons* feature is located on the *Options* tab of a new message. Outlook provides you with preset voting buttons. The preset voting buttons are *Approve;Reject*, *Yes;No*, and *Yes;No;Maybe*.

HOW TO: Use Preset Voting Buttons

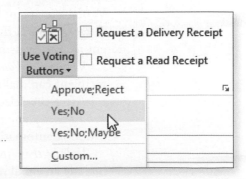

1. In a new email message, click the **Options** tab.
2. Click the **Use Voting Buttons** button.
3. Choose from one of the three preset options (Figure 2-41).
4. Type and send the email.

2-41 Preset voting options

Custom Voting Buttons

What if you wanted to use the voting buttons to determine your coworkers' preferences for lunch on Friday? The preset buttons would not be effective in this case. Outlook provides you the option of creating custom voting buttons (Figure 2-42). Custom voting buttons could be used to find the day of the week that works best for a team meeting or the choice of restaurant for a Friday lunch. As the sender of the message and question, you can create your own custom voting buttons in the *Properties* dialog box by typing each voting option separated by a semicolon.

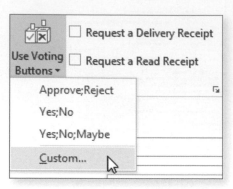

2-42 Custom voting options

HOW TO: Create Custom Voting Buttons

1. In a new email message, click the **Options** tab.
2. Click the **Use Voting Buttons** button.
3. Choose **Custom**. The *Properties* dialog box opens.
4. Select the **Use voting buttons** check box.
5. Select and delete the preset voting buttons (*Accept;Reject*).
6. Type in your voting choices. Separate each choice with a semicolon (Figure 2-43).
7. Click **Close** to close the *Properties* dialog box. The *InfoBar* will inform you that you are using voting buttons on this message.
8. Type and send the email.

2-43 Custom voting buttons

Respond Using Voting Buttons

When a recipient receives an email with voting buttons, there is a *Vote* button to the left of the *Reply* button in the *Respond* group. Also, there is a message in the *InfoBar* alerting the recipient to vote by using the *Vote* button.

When the *Vote* button is clicked, the voting choices appear in a list below the button. The recipient can make his or her selection from the list of choices.

After the selection is made, the recipient can choose one of the following two options: *Send the response now* or *Edit the response before sending*. If *Send the response now* is selected, Outlook automatically replies to the email and includes the recipient's voting selection.

If *Edit the response before sending* is selected, a reply email opens allowing the recipient to include an email response in addition to his or her voting selection. After typing a response in the body, the recipient must send the response.

1. Open the email message that has voting buttons.
2. Click the **Vote** button and make a selection (Figure 2-44).
3. Choose *either Send the response now* or *Edit the response before sending*.

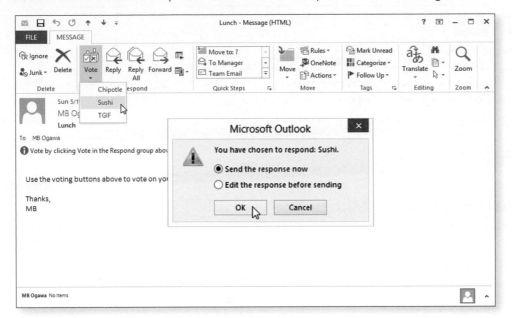

2-44 Voting response

- If you choose *Send the response now*, click **OK** and you are finished and your voting selection has been sent.
- If you chose *Edit the response before sending* and click **OK**, a reply email will automatically open.
- Type any additional information you would like to include in the body of the email.
- Click **Send**.

4. Close the original email.

Track Voting Responses

When recipients respond to an email with voting buttons, the sender of the message will receive the responses. The responses received will include the recipient's voting selection in front of the original subject (Figure 2-45). Also, Outlook uses tracking to record the responses received.

2-45 View voting responses option

HOW TO: Track Voting Responses

1. Open a voting response you received. The voting response is displayed in both the subject line and the *InfoBar*.
2. Click the **InfoBar**, and then click **View voting responses**. The original email message opens. A summary of the voting responses will be displayed in the *InfoBar*, and the individual voting response will be displayed in the body of the message.
3. After you are finished, close both of the open email messages.

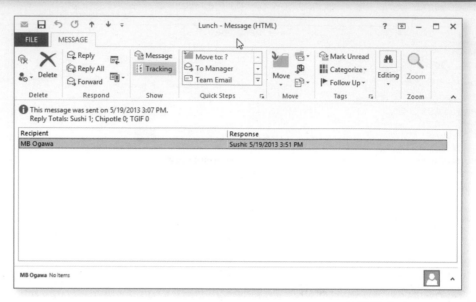

2-46 Voting responses

PAUSE & PRACTICE: OUTLOOK 2-3

For this Pause and Practice project, you use voting buttons to determine a good location for your lunch meeting.

1. Open the message with the subject **My lunch preferences**.

2. Reply to the message using voting options to determine your partner's top choice.
   a. Click the **Reply** button [*Message* tab, *Respond* group].
   b. Click the **Use Voting Buttons** button [*Options* tab, *Tracking* group] and select **Custom**.
   c. Ensure the **Use voting buttons** option is checked. Delete the text in the text field and type French Cuisine; Italian Cuisine; Japanese Cuisine.
   d. Click the **Close** button.
   e. Add the following text to the body of the message:

      Use the voting options above to select your preference. I do not have a preference, so I would like you to choose.

      [your name]

   f. Click the **Send** button.

3. Open your partner's message to you and select *Italian Cuisine*.
   a. Click the **Vote** button [*Message* tab, *Response* group] and select **Italian Cuisine**.
   b. Click the **Send Response Now** radio button and click **OK**.
4. Check your Inbox for the latest message with the voting response (Figure 2-47).

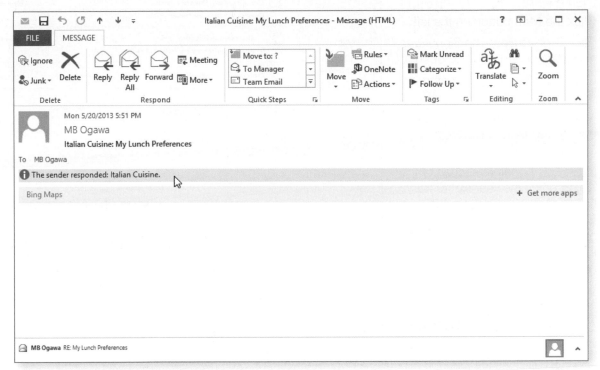

2-47 Completed Pause & Practice 2-3

Customizing Your Email

Have you ever received an email where the body of the message had nice fonts, colors, and background graphics? Most likely, the sender did not spend a huge amount of time customizing the design of the email specifically for you.

As covered in Chapter 1, users have a lot control over how to format the body of an email message. But Outlook also provides users with many features to customize the look of emails by using *signatures*, *stationery*, and *themes*. The default settings can be changed so that each new email created will have a consistent and customized look.

Create a Signature

A *signature* is a saved group of information that can be inserted into the body of an email. Typically, a signature can include the sender's name, title, company, address, and contact information. Signatures can also include logos and graphics. Signatures save time by storing this information so you don't have to type all of it each time you create an email. Signatures can be manually or automatically inserted at the bottom of each new email you create. You can create and save multiple signatures.

HOW TO: Create a Signature

1. Click the **File** tab to open the *Backstage* window.

2. Click **Options** on the left. The *Outlook Options* dialog box opens (Figure 2-48).

3. Click the **Mail** button on the left.

4. Click **Signatures**. The *Signatures and Stationery* dialog box opens.

5. Click **New**. The *New Signature* dialog box opens (Figure 2-49).

6. Type the name for your signature and press **OK** to close the *New Signature* dialog box.

7. In the *Edit signature* section of the dialog box, type your signature information. You can use different fonts, sizes, styles, colors, and alignments to customize your signature.

8. When you are satisfied with your signature, press **Save** (Figure 2-50).

9. Click **OK** to close the *Signatures and Stationery* dialog box.

10. Click **OK** to close the *Outlook Options* dialog box.

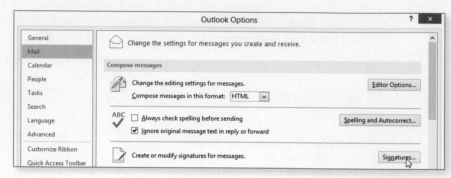

2-48 Outlook Options dialog box

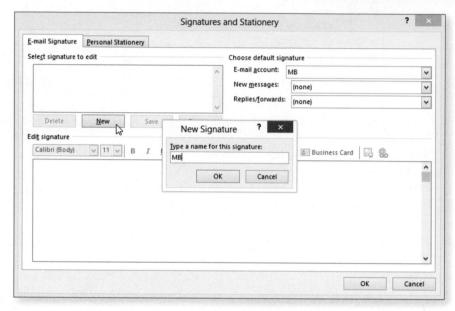

2-49 Signatures and Stationery dialog box

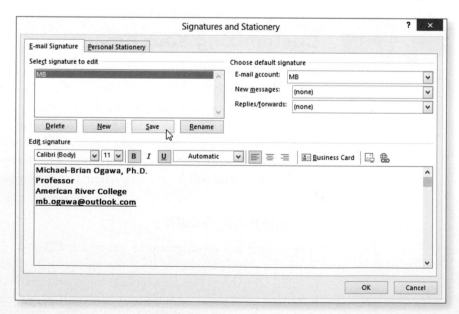

2-50 Sample signature

Set a Default Signature

The default settings on signatures can be changed to automatically insert your signature on all new emails, on all replies and forwards, or on all new emails, replies, and forwards. Or, the default settings can be set to *(none)*.

HOW TO: Set a Default Signature

1. With a new email open, click the **Signatures** button and choose **Signatures**. The *Signatures and Stationery* dialog box opens. (This dialog box can also be opened from the *Backstage* window by choosing **Options**, **Mail**, and then **Signatures**.)

2. In the *Choose default signature* area, set your desired signature defaults (Figure 2-51).

3. Click **OK** to close the *Signatures and Stationery* dialog box.

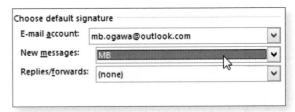

2-51 Default signature

Manually Insert a Signature

Once your signature is saved, it can be inserted into any new message you create, or it can be inserted into any email that you reply to or forward. The *Signature* button will be available in the *Include* group on both the *Message* and *Insert* tabs on any new, replied to, or forwarded email. Be aware that the signature button icon might appear differently depending on the size of the email window.

1. In a new, replied to, or forwarded email, click the **Signature** button in the *Include* group on either the *Message* or *Insert* tab (Figure 2-52).

2. Choose the signature to be inserted into the body of the email.

3. The signature is inserted into the body of the email with a couple of blank lines left above it for the email text.

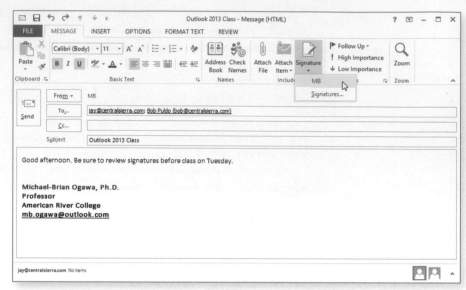

2-52 Signature selection

> **MORE INFO**
>
> Only one signature can be inserted in the body of an email. If you insert a second signature, it will replace the first one.

Themes

Themes are a set of fonts, colors, backgrounds, and fill effects in the body of an email. All emails include a theme. The default setting is the *Office Theme*, which includes a white background with dark and subtle colors. A theme can be selected and customized for each email you create.

The *Themes* group is on the *Options* tab of an email message (Figure 2-53). You can change the theme, color set, font set, effects, and page color to customize the look of your email. *Page color* is the background of the body of an email and is not limited to solid colors; you can change the page color to include a *gradient*, *texture*, *pattern*, or *picture*.

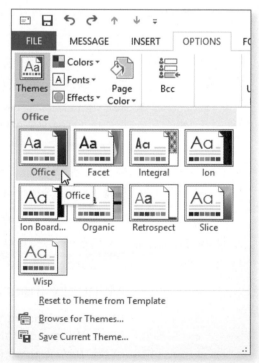

2-53 Themes

> **MORE INFO**
>
> Be careful about making your email message look too fancy and colorful. If you're using email in a business setting, you want your email to look professional. Using a picture as a background will also increase the file size of your email. Sometimes less is more!

Set the Default Theme and Font

To add consistency to your email documents, you might want to change the default settings to control the look of all emails you create. The default settings can be changed to include a theme, consisting of fonts, colors, and background graphics, on all new emails. If you are not using a theme, you can change the default settings on the font, size, style, and color used on all new emails, replies and forwards.

HOW TO: Set the Default Theme and Font

1. Click the **File** tab to open the *Backstage* window.
2. Click the **Options** button on the left. The *Outlook Options* dialog box opens.
3. Click the **Mail** button.
4. Click the **Stationery and Fonts** button. The *Signatures and Stationery* dialog box opens.
5. Click the **Personal Stationery** tab if it is not already displayed (Figure 2-54).

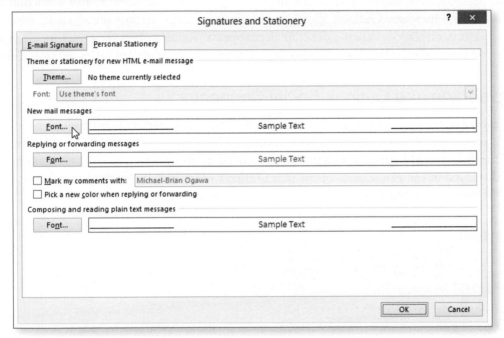

2-54 Personal stationery

6. Set your default preferences for **Theme**, **New mail messages**, and/or **Replying or forwarding messages**.
   - Click the **Font** button under *New mail messages* to modify fonts for new email messages
   - Click the **Font** button under *Replying or forwarding messages* to modify fonts for replies or forwarded messages.
7. Click **OK** to close the *Signatures and Stationery* dialog box.
8. Click **OK** to close the *Outlook Options* dialog box.

> ### MORE INFO
>
> When a default theme is selected, you have the following choices: *Use the theme's font, Use my font when replying and forwarding messages*, or *Always use my fonts*.

Desktop Alerts

A ***desktop alert*** is a notification you receive when a new email arrives in your Inbox (Figure 2-55). The desktop alert appears in a corner of your computer screen and remains there for a few seconds. By default, desktop alerts are turned on. They will also appear when you receive a Meeting Request or Task Request.

2-55 Desktop alert

> **MORE INFO**
>
> Desktop alerts only appear for items received in your Inbox. A rule can be created to have desktop alerts appear when an email is received in other folders. Rules will be covered in Chapter 6.
>   A desktop alert will not appear if you are running a PowerPoint presentation.

The desktop alert notifies you of the name of the sender, the subject, and a portion of the body of the message. Outlook allows you to perform some actions on an email when a desktop alert is displayed. When a desktop alert appears, you can open the email message by clicking on the desktop alert. You can also flag or delete the message from the desktop alert.

People Pane and Outlook Social Connector

The ***People pane*** appears at the bottom of each email message (Figure 2-56) and consolidates other Outlook items associated with an individual. The *People* pane will display email messages, meetings, task requests, attachments, and social network activity as links. Clicking on a link displayed in the *People* pane opens that Outlook item. The *People* pane can also be collapsed or expanded by clicking on the small arrow in the upper right corner of the pane.

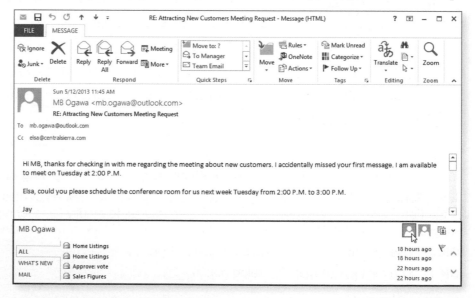

2-56 People pane

If there are multiple recipients of an email, the *People* pane can display items related to each of them. Clicking on one of the picture icons in the top right corner of the *People* pane will allow you to switch between individuals to be displayed in the *People* pane.

The ***Outlook Social Connector (OSC)*** works in conjunction with the *People* pane and can be used to keep track of the social network activity of your personal and business contacts. If your organization is using SharePoint 2013, the OSC can connect with SharePoint to display the activity of your contacts. The OSC can also be used to connect with other social networking sites. To connect to these sites, you will have to download and install an add-in from these sites.

> **MORE INFO**
>
> The *People* pane and Outlook Social Connector will also be discussed in Chapter 3.

PAUSE & PRACTICE: OUTLOOK 2-4

For this Pause and Practice project, you create a signature and insert it in an email message to your peer. You also forward the stream of messages to your instructor.

1. Create a new signature.
   a. Click the **File** tab to open the *Backstage* view and select **Options**. The *Outlook Options* dialog box opens.
   b. Select the **Mail** option.
   c. Click the **Signatures. . .** button. The *Signatures and Stationery* dialog box opens.
   d. Click the **New** button.
   e. Type School Signature and click **OK**.
   f. In the *Edit signature* text area, type:

      [Your Name]
      Student, [Institution Name]
      [your email address]

   g. Select your name and click **Bold** and **Italicize**.
   h. Select the second and third lines of your signature and click **Bold**.
   i. Click the **Save** button.
   j. Click the **OK** button.
   k. Click the **OK** button in the *Outlook Options* dialog box to close it.

2. Select the message from your partner indicating his or her choice, *Italian Cuisine*.

3. Click the **Reply** button to reply to the message including the following information in the email message fields.

   Cc: Your email address
   Body: Thanks, [partner name]. Let's meet at the Italian restaurant on campus for the business project meeting on Monday at noon. See you there!

4. At the end of the body, press the **Enter** key twice.

5. Click the **Signature** button [*Message* tab, *Include* group] and select school signature.

6. Click the **Send** button.

7. Locate and open the message in your Inbox that you sent to your partner and Cc'd to yourself.

8. Click the **Forward** button and enter the following information in the email message fields:
   To: your instructor's email address
   Cc: your email address
   *Subject: **FW: Chapter 2 Pause and Practice***
   Body: Hi [instructor name], this is the Pause and Practice assignments for chapter 2 for class.

9. At the end of the body, press the **Enter** key twice.

10. Click the **Signature** button [*Message* tab, *Include* group] and select school signature.

11. Click the **Send** button (Figure 2-57).

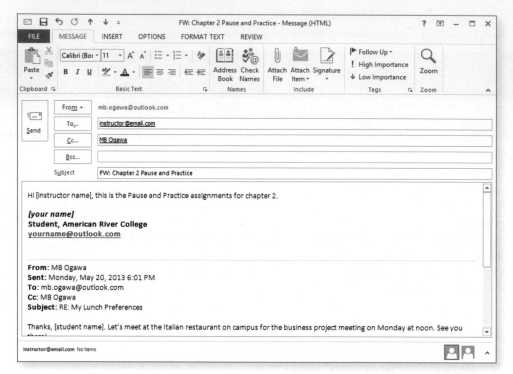

2-57 Completed Pause & Practice 2-4

Chapter Summary

2.1 Differentiate between the types of email formats (p. O2-51).

- There are three types of email formats: Plain text, Hypertext Markup Language, and Rich Text Format.
- **Plain text** format is supported by all email clients. However, it does not support styles such as bold, italic, or underline.
- **Hypertext Markup Language (HTML)** is the default format in Outlook and is most commonly used today. HTML format lets you format the body of your email message similar to a Microsoft Word document.
- **Rich Text Format (RTF)** is unique to Outlook users and is supported in an Exchange environment. This format allows users to use the different formatting features available in Outlook.
- It is probably best to use HTML format if you are sending messages outside of an Exchange environment.

2.2 Customize your email using the different types of email options available in Outlook (p. O2-52).

- There are three levels of importance that can be placed on messages: **high**, **normal**, and **low**. The default level of importance is normal.
- Messages can be marked with different levels of sensitivity. They are **Normal** (default setting), **Personal**, **Private**, and **Confidential**.
- Outlook allows you to apply security settings, such as **digital signatures** and **encryption** on messages.
- You can request **delivery** and and/or **read receipts** when sending messages.
- By using delivery options, you can change where sent items are saved and delay the delivery of messages.
- You can specify who message replies are directed to.
- You can set messages to expire after a specific date.
- Flags for recipients can be used as reminders.
- You can set permissions on messages to prevent others from forwarding messages (requires IRM to be set up by your administrator).

2.3 Use categories to organize email messages into different groups (p. O2-61).

- **Categories** can be used to organize email messages.
- You can create categories based on your needs.
- You can view items within a specific category using the view settings.

2.4 Add *Follow Up* flags to email messages to add reminders to messages (p. O2-64).

- **Follow Up flags** can be used as reminders.
- *Follow Up* flags create To-Do items.

2.5 Use email voting buttons to get responses from recipients and to automatically track responses (p. O2-69).

- **Voting buttons** allow you to quickly gather replies from other users.
- Voting buttons have the following presets: *Approve;Reject*, *Yes;No*, and *Yes;No;Maybe*.
- You can customize the voting buttons to include any choices.
- Voting buttons allow you to automatically track replies, as opposed to manually counting.

2.6 Customize your emails by using signatures, themes, and desktop alerts (p. O2-73).

- **Signatures** allow you to quickly add a group of information to your emails.
- You can create multiple signatures to choose from.
- Signatures can be automatically added to your messages, or you can manually add them.
- **Themes** can be used to quickly improve the aesthetics of your messages.
- **Desktop alerts** appear in the upper right corner of the screen and give you an overview of a message received, meeting request, or task request.
- The **People pane** consolidates multiple Outlook items that are associated with an individual.

Check for Understanding

In the **Online Learning Center** for this text (www.mhhe.com/office2013inpractice), there are a variety of resources that can be used to review the concepts covered in this chapter.

The following Online Learning Resources are available in the Online Learning Center:

- Multiple choice questions
- Short answer questions
- Matching exercises

Guided Project 2-1

For this project, you work as a Real Estate Agent for Placer Hills Real Estate (PHRE). You recently spoke on the phone with a client who is looking to purchase their first home. You follow up with her using email. [Student Learning Outcomes 2.1, 2.2, 2.6]

Skills Covered in This Project

- Select message format.
- Apply a theme.
- Create a signature.
- Add a signature to a message.

---

1. Create a new email message to Katie Binstead.
   a. Click the **New Email** button [*Home* tab, *New* group].
   b. In the *To* field, type your instructor's email address.
   c. In the *Cc* field, type your email address.
   d. In the *Subject* field, type Home of your dreams follow-up.

2. Click the **Rich Text** button [*Format Text* tab, *Format* group].

3. Click the **Themes** button [*Options* tab, *Themes* group] and select **Organic**.

4. Create a new signature.
   a. Click the **File** tab and select **Options**.
   b. Click the **Mail** button on the left.
   c. Click **Signatures**. The *Signatures and Stationery* dialog box opens.
   d. Click **New**. The *New Signature* dialog box opens.
   e. Type [your name] PHRE for your signature and press **OK** to close the *New Signature* dialog box.
   f. Click **OK** to close the *Outlook Options* dialog box.

5. Edit the signature.
   a. Click the **File** tab and select **Options**.
   b. Click the **Mail** button on the left.
   c. Click **Signatures**. The *Signatures and Stationery* dialog box opens.
   d. In the *Edit signature* section of the dialog box, type the following information:

   [your name], Real Estate Agent
   Placer Hills Real Estate

   e. Click the **Save** button.
   f. Click OK to close the Signatures and Stationary dialog box.

6. In the body of the message, type the following text:

   Hi Katie, It was great speaking with you about your ideas for a new home for your family. It is definitely an exciting endeavor. I am looking forward to helping you find the home of your family's dreams.

   Thanks,

7. Press the **Enter** key after the "Thanks" line.

8. Click the **Signature** button [*Message* tab, *Include* group] and select **[your name] PHRE** to insert your signature.

9. Click the **Send** button to send the message (Figure 2-58).

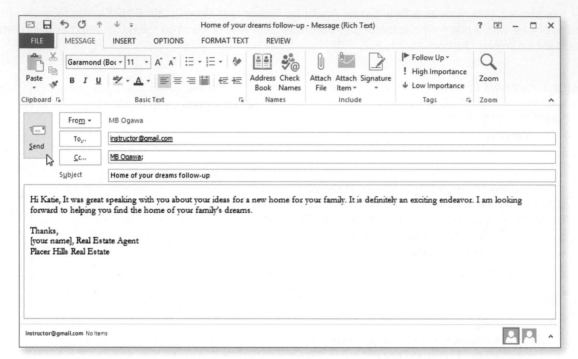

2-58 Completed Guided Project 2-1

Guided Project 2-2

For this project, you follow up with Katie regarding her family's dream home. To help you search for possible options, you ask her to decide on the number of bedrooms her family wants. Since Katie's family is serious about purchasing a home, you create a category for her email messages.
[Student Learning Outcomes 2.1, 2.2, 2.3, 2.5, 2.6]

Skills Covered in This Project

- Create a category.
- Set a Quick Click category.
- Select a message format.
- Apply a theme.
- Add a signature to a message.
- Add custom voting buttons to a message.

1. Open the email message you sent in *Guided Project 2-1*.

2. Create a new category called "Katie" (Figure 2-59).

2-59 Katie category

   a. Click the **Categorize** button [*Message* tab, *Tags* group] and select **All Categories**.
   b. Click the **New** button and type Katie in the *Name* text field.
   c. Click the drop-down arrow next to color and select **yellow**.
   d. Click the **OK** button to close the *Add New Category* dialog box.
   e. Ensure the **Katie** check box is selected and click **OK**.

3. Set the *Katie* category as a *Quick Click*.
   a. Click the **Categorize** button and select **Set Quick Click**.
   b. Click the drop-down arrow and select **Katie**.
   c. Click **OK**.

4. Create a new email message to Katie.
   a. Click the **New Email** button [*Home* tab, *New* group].
   b. In the *To* field, type your instructor's email address.
   c. In the *Cc* field, type your email address.
   d. In the *Subject* field, type Number of bedrooms for property.

5. Click the **Rich Text** button [*Format Text* tab, *Format* group].

6. Click the **Themes** button [*Options* tab, *Themes* group] and select **Organic**.

7. In the body of the message, type the following text:

   Hi Katie, To help me find as many homes as possible for us to check out, could you please use the voting button above to select the number of bedrooms your dream home should have?

   Thanks,

8. Press the **Enter** key after the "Thanks" line.

9. Click the **Signature** button [*Message* tab, *Include* group] and select **[your name] PHRE** to insert your signature.

10. Add voting buttons for two bedrooms, three bedrooms, or four bedrooms to the message.
    a. Click the **Use Voting Buttons** button [*Options* tab, *Tracking* group] and select **Custom**.
    b. Ensure the *Use voting buttons* option is checked and replace the text *Approve;Reject* with 2 bedrooms;3 bedrooms;4 bedrooms.
    c. Click **Close**.

11. Click the **Send** button to send the message (Figure 2-60).

2-60 Completed Guided Project 2-2

Guided Project 2-3

For this project, you send one final message to Katie to confirm a full day of house tours next week on Thursday.
[Student Learning Outcomes 2.1, 2.2, 2.3, 2.4, 2.5, 2.6]

Skills Covered in This Project

- Apply a category to a message.
- Select a message format.
- Apply a theme.

- Add a signature to a message.
- Add preset voting buttons to a message.
- Add a custom Follow Up flag.

1. Open the email message you sent in Guided Project 2-2.
2. Click the **Categorize** button [*Message* tab, *Tags* group] and select **Katie**.
3. Create a new email message to Katie.
   a. Click the **New Email** button [*Home* tab, *New* group].
   b. In the *To* field, type your instructor's email address.
   c. In the *Cc* field, type your email address.
   d. In the *Subject* field, type Property Tour.
4. Click the **Rich Text** button [*Format Text* tab, *Format* group].
5. Click the **Themes** button [*Options* tab, *Themes* group] and select **Organic**.
6. In the body of the message, type the following text:

   > Hi Katie, I would like to confirm that you are available next week Thursday for the property tour? I found 6 homes that could be a good fit for your family. Please use the voting button above to approve or reject this date.
   >
   > Thanks,

7. Press the **Enter** key after the "Thanks" line.
8. Click the **Signature** button [*Message* tab, *Include* group] and select **[your name] PHRE** to insert your signature.
9. Click the **Use Voting Buttons** button [*Options* tab, *Tracking* group] and select **Approve;Reject**.
10. Add a *Follow Up* flag to the message with a reminder to call Katie tomorrow if you do not receive a response.
    a. Click the **Follow Up** button [*Message* tab, *Tags* group] and select **Custom**.
    b. Click the drop-down arrow next to the due date and select tomorrow's date.
    c. Click the **Reminder** check box.
    d. Click the **OK** button.
11. Click the **Send** button to send the message (Figure 2-61).

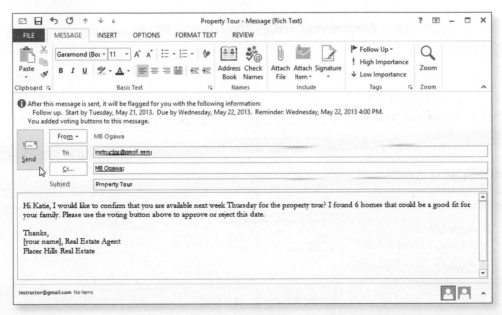

2-61 Completed Guided Project 2-3

Independent Project 2-4

For this project, you are an organizer for the American River Cycling Club (ARCC). You decide to develop a training cycle for the upcoming season. Therefore, you email your members and ask them to vote on a variety of cycling activities to determine priorities for each.
[Student Learning Outcomes 2.1, 2.2, 2.4, 2.5, 2.6]

Skills Covered in This Project

- Select a message format.
- Apply a theme.
- Create a signature.
- Add a signature.
- Add a custom voting button.
- Add a custom voting button.
- Add a *Follow Up* flag

---

1. Create a new message to the ARCC.
   a. In the *To* field, type your instructor's email address.
   b. In the *Cc* field, type your email address.
2. Type ARCC Training Poll in the subject line.
3. Change the message format to **Rich Text Format**.
4. Apply the **Integral** theme to the message.
5. In the body of the message, type the following text:

   > Hi everyone. As we prepare for the upcoming training season, I would like to know which type of training you prefer. If you would like to recommend another type of training, please send me a message containing the type of training. Based on the results of the poll, I will set up a training schedule to accommodate our needs as best as possible.

   > Thanks,

6. Create a signature named **[your name] ARCC**. The signature should have the following format:

   > **[your name]**
   >
   > *Organizer, ARCC*

7. Add the **[your name] ARCC** signature to the message after the "Thanks" line.

8. Add a custom voting button with the following options: **Road;Mountain; Cyclocross**.

9. Add a **Follow Up flag** with a reminder for you in one week.

10. Click the **Send** button to send the message (Figure 2-62).

2-62 Completed Independent Project 2-4

Independent Project 2-5

For this project, you categorize the message sent in Independent Project 2-4. You also share the results of the poll from with the ARCC members.
[Student Learning Outcomes 2.1, 2.2, 2.3, 2.4, 2.6]

Skills Covered in This Project

- Create a category.
- Apply a category to a message.
- Select a message format.
- Apply a theme.
- Add a signature.
- Set the message priority.
- Add a *Follow Up* flag.

---

1. Create a new category called **Cycle Training** using red as the category color and apply it to the message you sent in Independent Project 2-4.

2. Create a new message to the ARCC.
   a. In the To field, type your instructor's email address.
   b. In the Cc field, type your email address.

3. Add the subject Results: ARCC Training Poll.

4. Change the message format to **Rich Text Format**.

5. Apply the **Integral** theme to the message.

6. In the body of the message, type the following text:

   > Hi everyone. Based on the poll, we have the following results.
   > 50% Mountain
   > 25% Road
   > 25% Cyclocross

   > Therefore, we will distribute our training in this manner. A few members also sent me other ideas for training sessions, which I will do my best to incorporate. Please check your email for our schedule.

   > Thanks,

7. Add the **[your name] ARCC** signature to the message after the "Thanks" line.

8. Set the message priority to **low**.

9. Add a **Follow Up flag** with a reminder in three days and a due date in one week.

10. Click the **Send** button to send the message (Figure 2-63).

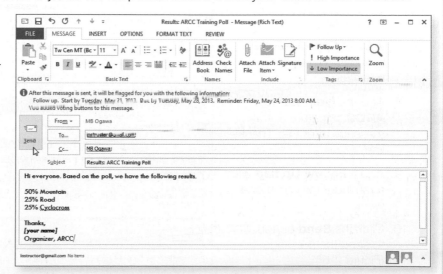

2-63 Completed Independent Project 2-5

Independent Project 2-6

For this project, you familiarize yourself with the basic components of Outlook.
[Student Learning Outcomes 2.1, 2.2, 2.3, 2.4, 2.6]

Skills Covered in This Project

- Apply a category to a message.
- Select a message format.
- Apply a theme.

- Add a preset voting button.
- Add a signature.
- Add a *Follow Up* flag with a reminder.

---

1. Apply the **Cycle Training** category to the message you sent in Independent Project 2-5.

2. Create a new message to the ARCC.
   a. In the *To* field, type your instructor's email address.
   b. In the *Cc* field, type your email address.

3. Add the subject Training Schedule.

4. Change the message format to **Rich Text Format**.

5. Apply the **Integral** theme to the message.

6. In the body of the message, type the following text:

   Hi everyone. Listed below is our training schedule for the upcoming quarter.

   Monday: Mountain
   Tuesday: Road
   Wednesday: Off
   Thursday: Cyclocross
   Friday: Mountain

   Please use the voting button above to approve or reject the schedule. If you reject, please indicate why in the message.

   Thanks,

7. Add an **Approve;Reject** voting button to the message.

8. Add the *[your name] ARCC* signature to the message after the "Thanks" line.

9. Add a **Follow Up flag** with a reminder for you in one week.

10. Click the **Send** button to send the message (Figure 2-64).

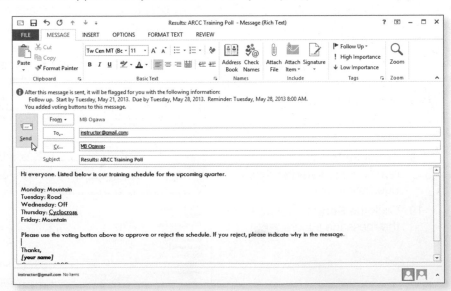

2-64 Completed Independent Project 2-6

Challenge Project 2-7

Compose a message to your instructor to request a meeting regarding your upcoming term paper. This message is of high importance to you. Be sure to use voting options to allow your instructor to quickly select a meeting day.
[Student Learning Outcomes 2.1, 2.2, 2.4, 2.6]

- Send the message to your instructor.
- Add your email address to the *Cc* field.
- The subject of the message should be *Challenge 2-7: Term Paper for ENG 100 Meeting Request*.
- Change the message format to *Rich Text Format*.
- Use voting buttons and the five days of the week to request a day to meet with your instructor.
- Add a *Follow Up* flag to the message and set a reminder for yourself for a week from today.
- Add your signature to the email message.

Challenge Project 2-8

Search for a degree program online that you may be interested in. Develop a set of questions for an academic advisor about the program and how it can suit your educational and lifelong goals. Compose a message to inquire about the program. The application letter should be short and concise.
[Student Learning Outcomes 2.1, 2.2, 2.3, 2.4, 2.6]

- Send the message to your instructor.
- Add your email address to the *Cc* field.
- The subject of the message should be *Challenge 2-8: Potential student inquiry about [educational program]*.
- Change the message format to *HTML Format*.
- Request a delivery receipt.
- Create a category named *School* using a color that you did not assign to a category yet and apply it to the message when you receive it in your Inbox.
- Add a *Follow Up* flag to the message and set a reminder for yourself for a week from today.
- Apply a theme to your email message. The theme should have a professional appearance.
- Print the message and submit it to your instructor.

Challenge Project 2-9

Search online for a job that you would like to have in the future (you may use the position you found in Challenge Project 1-9). Identify a task for your job that requires you to send an email message to coworkers that includes voting options. Compose a message to several coworkers based on the task you identified.

[Student Learning Outcomes 2.1, 2.2, 2.3, 2.4, 2.5, 2.6]

- Send the message to your instructor.
- Add your email address to the *Cc* field.
- The subject of the message should be *Challenge 2-9: Coworkers Inquiry*.
- Change the message format to *Rich Text Format*.
- Add a *Follow Up* flag to the message and set a reminder for yourself for a week from today.
- Categorize your copy of the message using an appropriate category.
- Use voting buttons to automatically track responses based on your inquiry.
- Create and use a signature for your job.
- Apply a theme that is appropriate to the content of the email message.

CHAPTER 3

Contacts

CHAPTER OVERVIEW

Before there were various electronic means to store contact information, a physical paper address book was where we kept information about family, friends, neighbors, and business acquaintances. Typically included were names, addresses, and phone numbers; you might have also included birthdays and anniversaries. Microsoft Outlook provides users with a place to electronically store information for emailing, calling, faxing, or sending letters to individuals.

The Outlook **Contacts** feature gives you the same benefits of a paper address book, but it also has some unique advantages. In addition to standard personal information, contacts can include company information, a picture, and additional notes. Contacts are stored electronically and integrate seamlessly with other Microsoft Office products so you can create envelopes, labels, and letters. Contacts can easily be shared with other Outlook users. Additionally, Outlook Contacts can be synched with cells phones and other electronic devices.

STUDENT LEARNING OUTCOMES (SLOs)

After completing this chapter, you will be able to:

SLO 3.1   Differentiate between the *Contacts* folder and the *Global Address List* (p. O3-94).

SLO 3.2   Create a contact record from different sources (p. O3-95).

SLO 3.3   Enhance contact records by editing contact information and fields (p. O3-102).

SLO 3.4   Use and modify the different contact views (p. O3-107).

SLO 3.5   Create a contact group and produce email from a contact or contact group (p. O3-110).

CASE STUDY

For the Pause & Practice projects, you work with partners in class to create contacts and a contact group to help make communication between you and your classmates more efficient. You also add pictures to contacts to help you match names to faces.

Pause & Practice 3-1: You create a contact with your personal information. You also send it to a partner and create a contact from a business card attached to an email.

Pause & Practice 3-2: You modify your contact to include your picture and a mailing address. You also add a secondary email address.

Pause & Practice 3-3: You create a contact group, update contact information, and send the contact group to your instructor.

SLO 3.1

Understanding Contacts

A *contact* is a set of related information about an individual or organization. This could be as simple as a name and email address with the option of storing additional useful information. Outlook Contacts functions similarly to a database, but you do not need to have a thorough understanding of databases to effectively take advantage of the benefits of Outlook Contacts. Since the *Contacts* folder is similar to a database, it is important to understand some basic database terminology.

Database Lingo

An Outlook contact is commonly referred to as a ***record*** or ***contact record***. A record is a group of related information about an individual or organization. Each individual piece of information in a record is called a ***field***. For example, *Full Name, Company, Job Title,* and *Email address* are all fields in a contact record. A group of related records is called a ***file***. In Outlook, a group of related records can be saved in a *Contact* folder. Folders can be created in Contacts to store a group of related contact records.

Contacts versus Global Address List

If you are using Outlook in a home environment (as a stand-alone program rather than on an Exchange server), your contacts will, by default, be saved in the *Contacts* folder (Figure 3-1). You can choose email recipients from your Contacts (Figure 3-2), and you can also create, edit, and delete records in this list of contacts. When you click the *To* button on a new email, your ***Contacts address book*** opens. This address book lists the names and email addresses of those in your Contacts.

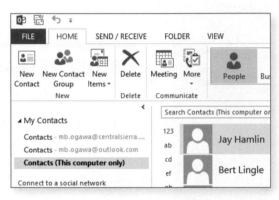

3-1 *Contacts* folder

If you are using Outlook in an Exchange environment, in addition to your Contacts address book, you will also have a ***Global Address List***. This address book contains the contacts for all the individuals in your organization. Your Exchange server administrator will maintain the *Global Address List*. You cannot add contacts to this folder, but you can save contacts from the *Global Address List* to your *Contacts* folder.

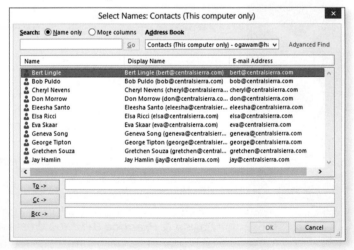

3-2 Choose email recipients from your contacts

> **MORE INFO**
>
> See Chapter 1 for the differences between Outlook as a stand-alone program and Outlook using an Exchange server.

Creating Contacts

As with most Microsoft products, there are numerous methods of accomplishing the same task. Adding contact records to your *Contacts* folder can be accomplished in a number of ways. You can create a new contact from scratch, from the same company as an existing contact, from an email you received, from an electronic business card you received, or from the *Global Address List*.

Create a New Contact

To create a new contact, make sure you have selected the **People** button in the *Navigation* pane. When you click the **New Contact** button on the *Home* tab, a new contact record opens. This new contact will be a blank record, and you will be able to add the contact information desired.

HOW TO: Create a New Contact

1. Click the **People** button in the *Navigation* pane.
2. Click the **New Contact** button on the *Home* tab. A new contact record opens (Figure 3-3).

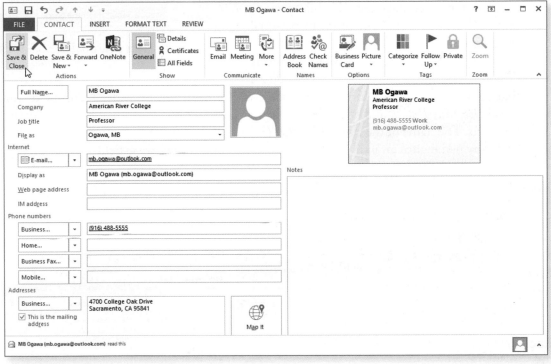

3-3 New Contact dialog box

3. Fill in the desired contact information.
4. Click the **Save & Close** button in the *Actions* group on the *Contact* tab when finished. The contact will be saved in your *Contacts* folder.

> **ANOTHER WAY**
>
> **Ctrl+N** opens a new contact record when you are in Outlook Contacts.
> **Ctrl+Shift+C** opens a new contact record anywhere in Outlook.
> **Ctrl+S** or the *Save* button on the *Quick Access* toolbar saves an open contact.

You can click the **Save & New** button in the *Actions* group on the *Contact* tab (Figure 3-4) to save the current contact in the *Contacts* folder and open a new blank contact.

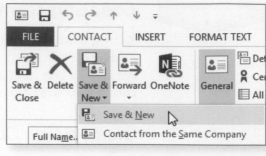

3-4 *Save & New contact option*

Create a New Contact from Same Company

There are times when you are adding contacts from the same company and don't want to have to retype some of the common information such as company name, web page address, and business address. When you are creating a new contact from the same company as an existing contact, you can utilize Outlook's ***Contact from Same Company*** feature (Figure 3-5) which preserves existing company information on a new contact record while providing blank fields for the new contact's personal information.

3-5 *Save & New Contact from the Same Company option*

When the *Contact from Same Company* option is selected, a new contact record opens that contains company information in some of the fields and provides blank fields for *Full Name, Job title, Email,* and other fields that are specific to the individual being added to your Contacts. The name of the contact (in the *Title bar* at the top center of the contact) will be the company name until an individual's name is typed in the *Full Name* field.

HOW TO: Create a New Contact from the Same Company

1. With an existing contact record open, click the drop-down arrow on the **Save & New** button in the *Actions* group on the *Contact* tab.

2. Click the **Contact from the Same Company** button. A new contact record opens with blank fields for the individual's information (Figure 3-6).

3. Fill in the desired information.

4. Click **Save & Close** when done.

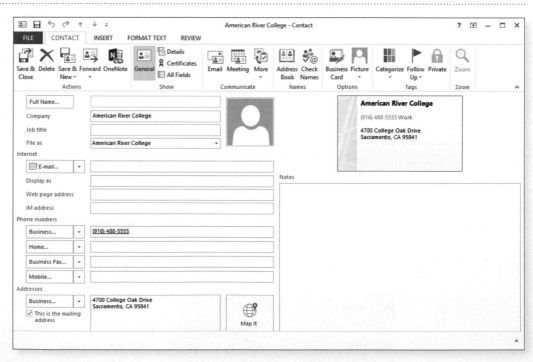

3-6 *New Contact from the Same Company*

Create a Contact from a Received Email

Think of the number of times you have received an email and would have liked to add the sender to your contacts; in Outlook there is a very easy way to do this. The most common and efficient method of adding a contact to your *Contacts* folder is from an email that you receive. When you receive an email from someone that is not currently in your *Contacts* folder, you can easily add this new record without having to manually type in all the information.

HOW TO: Create a Contact from a Received Email

1. Put your pointer over the sender's name in an open email or an email in the *Reading* pane. A communications window will appear.
2. Click the **Open Contact Card** button (Figure 3-7) and then click **Add** (Figure 3-8). A new contact record opens.

3-7 *Open Contact Card*

3-8 Add a contact button

3. The *Full Name, Email,* and *Display as* fields are already filled in with the new contact's information. You can edit existing information or add any additional information (Figure 3-9).
4. Click **Save** when done.

3-9 New contact from email

Create a Contact from an Electronic Business Card

One of the advantages of using Outlook is being able to send and receive contact records between Outlook users. A very effective and easy method of adding contacts to your *Contacts* folder is by having another Outlook user send you a contact as a business card.

HOW TO: Create a Contact from an Electronic Business Card

1. In an open email or an email in the *Reading* pane, click the attached electronic business card (in the attachment area). The *Attachments* tab opens and the attachment will be displayed in the body of the email (Figure 3-10).

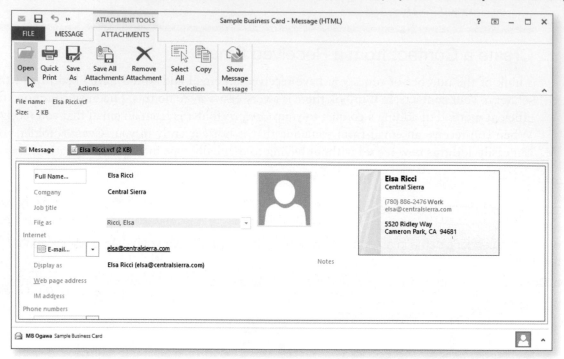

3-10 Business card in the attachments tab

2. Click the **Open** button in the *Actions* group. The contact record opens (Figure 3-11).

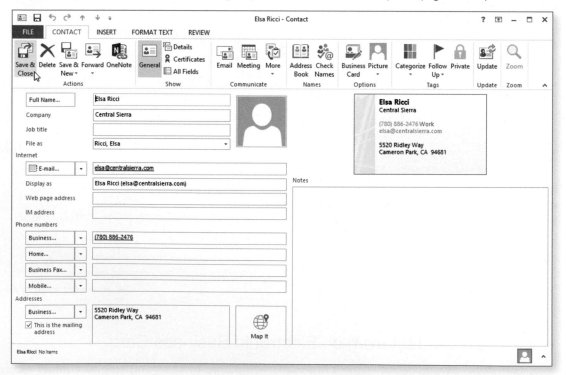

3-11 Business card opened as a contact

3. Make any necessary changes, and then click **Save & Close**.

Add a Contact from the Global Address List

If you are using Outlook in a business environment with an Exchange server, most likely you will have a *Global Address List* populated with contacts from within your organization. This global list is created and maintained by the network administrator who is responsible for maintaining the Exchange server.

The *Global Address List* contains the contact records for all employees in the organization and usually contains **contact groups**. You can add a contact or contact group from the *Global Address List* to your *Contacts* folder.

HOW TO: Add a Contact from the Global Address List

1. In the *Contacts* folder, click the **Address Book** button in the *Find* group on the *Home* tab. The *Address Book* dialog box opens.
2. Click the down arrow on the right side of the *Address Book* drop-down menu (Figure 3-12).
3. Choose **Global Address List**. The list of contacts and contact groups will be displayed.
4. Right-click the contact you want to add to your *Contacts* folder and click **Add to Contacts** (Figure 3-13). The contact record opens in a new window.
5. Click **Save & Close** to save it to your *Contacts* folder.

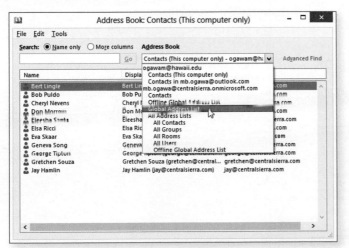

3-12 *Global Address List* option

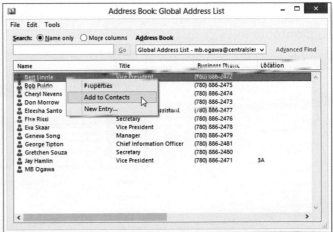

3-13 Add *Global Address* contact to personal contacts

Duplicate Contacts

If you try to add a contact to your *Contacts* folder and it has the same name as an existing contact, Outlook adds a duplicate entry. Outlook allows you to link contacts together into a single entry, which merges the information in each of the records.

HOW TO: Manage Duplicate Contacts

1. Select one of the duplicate contacts and click the **Link Contacts** link (Figure 3-14).
2. Select the contact that you would like to link to and click **OK** (Figure 3-15). You may need to search for the duplicate contact if you do not see it.

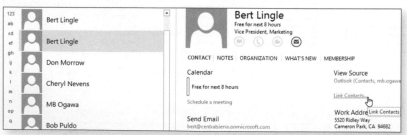

3-14 Link contacts

3-15 Select contacts to link

Linked contacts for Bert Lingle

LINKED CONTACTS

Linking multiple contacts for this person lets you view all their information on one card. You can choose a contact to unlink it.

Bert Lingle
(Address Book)

Bert Lingle
Contacts

LINK ANOTHER CONTACT
Find a contact to link

OK   Cancel

PAUSE & PRACTICE: OUTLOOK 3-1

For this Pause and Practice project, you create a contact with your personal information. You also send it to a partner and create a contact from a business card attached to an email.

1. Click the **People** button in the *Navigation* pane.

2. Create a contact for yourself.
   a. Click the **New Contact** button [*Home* tab, *New* group].
   b. Enter your full name, company (school name), job title (student), and email address in the appropriate fields.
   c. Click the **Save & Close** button [*Contact* tab, *Actions* group].

3. Create a contact for your instructor.
   a. Click the **New Contact** button [*Home* tab, *New* group].
   b. Enter your instructor's full name, company (school name), job title (Professor), and email address in the appropriate fields.
   c. Click the **Save & Close** button [*Contact* tab, *Actions* group].

4. Forward your contact to a partner.
   a. Select your contact.
   b. Click the **As a Business Card** option [*Home* tab, *Share* group, *Forward Contact* button].
   c. Type your partner's email address in the *To* field.
   d. Click the **Send** button.

5. Save your partner's business card to your contacts (Figure 3-16).

3-16 Completed Pause & Practice 3-1

   a. Open the email message that your partner sent with his or her business card.
   b. Double-click the attached business card to open it.
   c. Click the **Save & Close** button [*Contact* tab, *Actions* group].

Editing a Contact Record

Outlook provides you with many fields in a contact record to store information. Not all the information in a contact record has to be completed to save a record. In addition to providing fields to store standard information, Outlook will allow you to change the names of the fields, add multiple email addresses, include a picture, and open a map to the contact's address.

> **MORE INFO**
>
> When creating or editing a contact record, be sure to include the first and last name and begin each name with a capital letter.

Change a Field Name

You can customize many of the fields of a contact record to better meet your needs. Any field with a drop-down menu to the right of the field name is a field name that can be changed. You can select the field name from the choices available. For example, if you would like the mobile (cell) phone number to be listed as the primary phone number, you can change the field from *Mobile* to *Primary*.

HOW TO: Change a Field Name in a Contact Record

1. Change the view to *Business Card* view [*Home* tab, *Current View* group, *Business Card* button].
2. Open the contact record where you want to change a field name.
3. On the field name you would like to change, click the drop-down arrow to the right of the field name (Figure 3-17).
   • A list of available field names opens.
   • Those with a check mark are already being used.
4. Click the desired **field name** to change the field name.

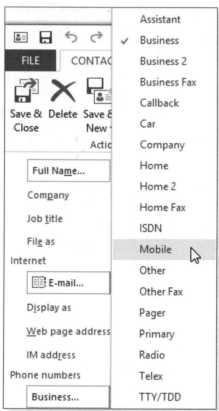

3-17 Change field name

Add an Address

In addition to storing a contact's address, Outlook contact record addresses can be used to generate mailing lists, envelopes, and/or labels. The address field lets you type the address directly into the text box, or an address field dialog box can be opened and the address can be typed into the dialog box. Each contact record can store up to three different addresses. You have the options of business, home, or other addresses.

> **MORE INFO**
>
> If Outlook does not recognize the format in which you type an address, a *Check Address* dialog box opens (Figure 3-18). This will allow you to edit the address.
>
> If you type an email address in a format that Outlook doesn't recognize, a *Check Names* dialog box opens.

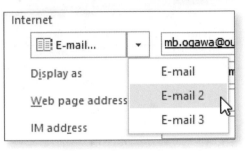

> **ANOTHER WAY**
>
> Any of the field names that are displayed as a button can be clicked on and a dialog box will appear. The information for that field can be typed directly into the dialog box.
>
> Click the **Email** button on a contact record; the *Select Names* dialog box opens and allows you to choose an email address from your *Global Address List*.

3-18 *Check Address* dialog box

Add Multiple Email Addresses

Do you have more than one email account? Outlook will let you store up to three email addresses per contact record. Each email address is added to the Outlook Address Book. The main email address is labeled ***Email***, and the additional email address fields are labeled ***Email 2*** and ***Email 3*** (Figure 3-19).

3-19 Add multiple email addresses

Insert a Picture

To further customize a contact record, you can add a contact's picture. Figure 3-20 is the default image before you customize it. The picture will appear on the contact record when it is open. Also, if you have a picture saved in a contact record and you receive an email from that contact, his or her picture will appear on the email message.

3-20 Default contact picture

HOW TO: Insert a Picture in a Contact Record

1. With a contact record open, click the **picture icon**. The *Add Contact Picture* dialog box opens.

2. Find and select the picture you want on the contact record.

3. Click **OK** to close the dialog box.

4. Click **Save & Close** to close the contact record (Figure 3-21).

3-21 Contact with a picture

If you decide that you do not want the picture on the contact record or that you would like a different picture, you can easily change or delete it.

HOW TO: Change or Remove a Picture

1. Open the contact record.
2. Click the **Picture** button in the *Options* group on the *Contacts* tab.
3. Click either *Change Picture* or *Remove Picture*.
   - If you select *Change Picture,* the *Add Contact Picture* dialog box opens and you can select a new picture.
   - If you select *Remove Picture* (Figure 3-22), the picture will be removed from the contact record. The picture will only be deleted from the contact record, not from your computer.

3-22 *Remove Picture* option

> ### ANOTHER WAY
> You can right-click the picture on the contact record and choose either *Change Picture* or *Remove Picture*.

> ### MORE INFO
> If you use your cell phone to sync with Outlook (not all cell phones will do this), you will have the option to sync your Outlook Contacts. If you receive a phone call from a recipient whose contact record has a picture, the picture will be displayed on the cell phone screen during the incoming call.

Use the Map It Feature

How many times have you used the Internet to get a map or driving directions to a location? You had to go to the web site and type in the address to find the desired information. Microsoft Outlook provides users with a *map* feature (Figure 3-23) that will link an address from a contact record to an interactive Internet map. So, rather than you having to go to a different web site and type in an address, Outlook opens Bing Maps from an address in a contact record with the click of a button (Figure 3-24).

3-23 *Map It* button

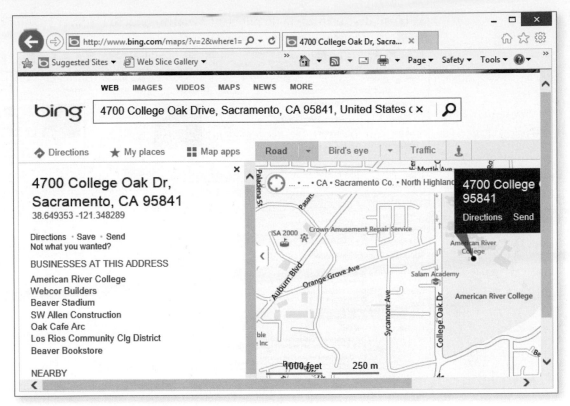

3-24 Bing map

HOW TO: Use the Map It Feature

1. Open an existing contact record that has an address.
2. Click the **Map It** button next to the address in the contact.
3. An Internet window opens with the contact record address mapped.

> **ANOTHER WAY**
> Click the **More** button in the *Communicate* group on the *Contact* tab and choose **Map.**

People Pane

The *People pane*, which is available in the main Outlook interface and on email messages, is also available on contact records (Figure 3-25). This feature provides you with a list of related Outlook activity associated with a contact.

This pane is located at the bottom of the contact record and displays related Outlook items. Clicking on one of the links displayed in the *People pane* opens the selected Outlook item or social networking activity. You can choose how to display or group this information in the *People pane*. Also, the *People pane* can be collapsed or expanded by clicking the small arrow in the upper right corner of the pane.

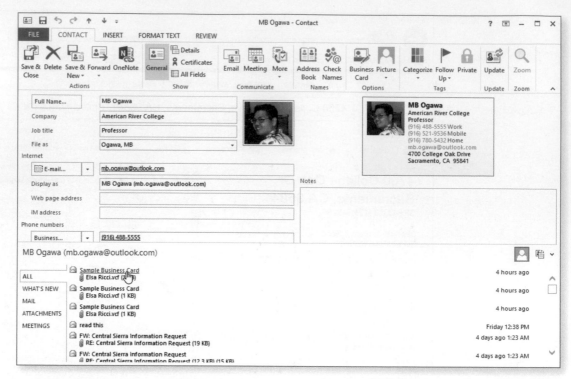

3-25 *People* pane in a contact record

Outlook Social Connector

In addition to consolidating Outlook information related to a contact in the *People* pane, the ***Outlook Social Connector (OSC)*** will also allow you to connect to your social networks such as Facebook, LinkedIn, and MySpace. By using the OSC to connect to your social networks in Outlook, you can view the posts and activity of those in your contacts with whom you are connected on social networks.

By default, Outlook allows you to connect to popular social networks such as Facebook and LinkedIn without a plugin. However, you must install the plugin for other social networking sites, which are available from each provider and provide Outlook with your log in information for the site. This process will vary from site to site.

HOW TO: Connect Outlook to Social Network Accounts

1. Install the plugin from the social networking web site if you are using one other than Facebook, LinkedIn, or a Sharepoint server.

2. Once the plugin is installed, you will be prompted to provide your user name and password.

3. Click the **Connect to social network** link in the *Contacts* folder list (Figure 3-26). The *Social Network Accounts* dialog box opens.

4. Enter your user name and password.

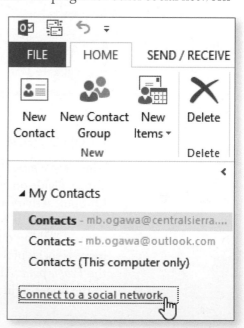

3-26 *Connect to a social network* link

5. Click **Connect** to connect Outlook to your social networking site (Figure 3-27).

6. Click **Finish**.

7. Outlook is now connected to your social networking site, and you will receive a confirmation dialog box. Click **Close** to close this dialog box.

3-27 Enter user name and password for the social network

> **MORE INFO**
>
> This process might be slightly different depending on the social networking site you are setting up in Outlook.

When you open a contact record for a person you are connected with on a social networking site, that contact's activity will be displayed in the *People* pane of the contact record.

Delete a Contact

To delete an existing contact, simply select the contact and press **Delete**. When a contact record is deleted, it is moved to the *Deleted Items* folder where it will stay until it is permanently deleted. If you delete a contact by mistake, you can use the *Undo* button to restore the contact, or you can open the *Deleted Items* folder and drag the contact back to the *Contacts* folder (drag and drop the deleted contact on the *People* button).

> **ANOTHER WAY**
>
> **Ctrl+D** will delete a selected Outlook item.
>
> You can also select the contact and click the **Delete** button on the *Contact* tab or right-click the contact and choose **Delete.**

> **MORE INFO**
>
> You can select a range of contacts by selecting the first contact in a range, holding down the **Shift** key, and selecting the last item in the range. You can also select nonadjacent contact records by holding down the **Ctrl** key and selecting the contacts.

SLO 3.4

Changing and Modifying Views in Contacts

Outlook provides you with preset views in which to display your contacts. These different views display different contact information and varying amounts of information about each contact. The view can be changed by clicking on one of the views in the *Current View* group on the *Home* tab (Figure 3-28).

3-28 Contact views

Contact Views

By default there are five different preset contact views. There are mixed, list, and card views.

- People (*People Card* view)
- Business Card (*Card* view)
- Card (*Card* view)
- Phone (*List* view)
- List (*List* view)

You can change views by selecting a view in the *Current View* group on the *Home* tab. Click the **More** button to display all available views in the *Current View* gallery.

> ### ANOTHER WAY
>
> Click the **View** tab, click **Change View**, and select the view you want.

In the *Arrangement* group on the *View* tab, you are given different options to arrange and sort your contacts. The three preset arrangements are: *Categories, Company,* and *Location.*

Sort Contacts

When viewing contacts in a *List* view, the easiest way to sort or arrange records is to click the column heading. The column by which the records are sorted will be shaded, and the sorting order will be indicated by a small triangle pointing up (ascending order) or down (descending order) (Figure 3-29).

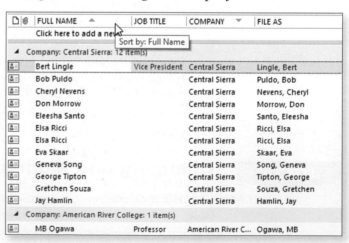

3-29 Sort contacts in a *List* view

Modify a View

As the number of contacts you have stored in Outlook increases, you may want to utilize methods provided by Outlook to help you quickly find a contact. By default, contacts are sorted by last name, but you can group contact records by company or sort them by full name.

In addition, each of the existing contact views can be modified to assist you with finding a contact. You can customize the fields displayed, sort criteria, fonts, font sizes, and styles.

Click the **View Setting** button on the *View* tab to customize the current view.

HOW TO: Modify View Settings

1. Click the **People** button in the *Navigation* pane.
2. Select the desired contacts view in the *Current View* group on the *Contacts* tab.
3. Click the **View** tab.
4. Click the **View Settings** button. The *Advanced View Settings* dialog box for the current view opens (Figure 3-30).
5. Make any desired changes. Each of the buttons on the left opens an additional dialog box.
6. Click **OK** to close the *Advanced View Settings* dialog box.

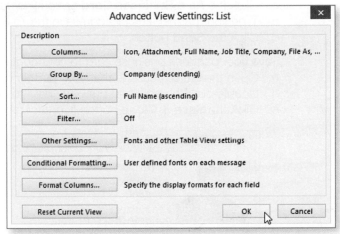

3-30 *Advanced View Settings: List* dialog box

> **MORE INFO**
>
> Feel free to experiment with different views in the *Contacts* folder, because you can easily reset views to their original settings by clicking on the *Reset View* button on the *View* tab or the *Reset Current View* button in the *Advanced View Settings* dialog box.

PAUSE & PRACTICE: OUTLOOK 3-2

For this Pause and Practice project, you modify your contact to include your picture and a mailing address. You also add a secondary email address.

File Needed: A picture of yourself (if you do not have a picture, general picture files are available ***johnsanchez.jpg*** and ***jillricci.jpg***).
Completed Project File Name: None

1. Edit your contact.
   a. Select the **People** button in the *Navigation* pane.
   b. Click **Business Card** view [*Home* tab, *Current View* group].
   c. Double-click your contact.
   d. Select the **Add Picture** option [*Contact* tab, *Options* group, *Picture* button].
   e. Locate your picture and click **OK**. If you do not have a picture, you can use one of the provided images (***johnsanchez.jpg*** or ***jillricci.jpg***) and change it to your image later.
   f. Click the **E-mail** drop-down arrow and select **E-mail 2**.
   g. Type a secondary e-mail address if you have one.
   h. Click the **Business** drop-down arrow under the *Address* section and select **Other**. Click the **This is a mailing address** check box.
   i. Type your school's address.
   j. Click the **Save & Close** button.

2. Forward your updated contact as a business card to a different partner from *Pause & Practice Outlook 3-1*.
   a. Select your contact.
   b. Click the **As a Business Card** option [*Home* tab, *Share* group, *Forward Contact* button].
   c. Type your partner's email address in the *To* field.
   d. Click the **Send** button.

3. Save your partner's business card to your contacts (Figure 3-31).
   a. Open the email message that your partner sent with his or her business card.
   b. Double-click the attached business card to open it.
   c. Click the **Save & Close** button [*Contact* tab, *Actions* group].

3-31 Completed Pause & Practice 3-2

SLO 3.5 # Using Contacts and Contact Groups

One of the most beneficial aspects of the *Contacts* folder is the ability to use this stored information to send emails. An email can be sent to one or more contacts in your *Contacts* folder or the *Global Address List*. You also have the ability to create **contact groups**, which are saved groups of contacts, and send email to the entire contact group.

Send an Email to a Contact

You can send an email to contacts that are stored in your *Contacts* folder in a couple different ways. When you have an email message open, you can click the *To* button and select the contacts from the *Select Names* dialog box. You can also choose contacts from different address books by selecting from the list in the *Address Book* drop-down menu.

HOW TO: Send an Email to a Contact

1. Click the **To** button on an email message (new, reply, or forward). The *Select Names* dialog box opens.

2. Use the *Address Book* drop-down list to select an address book.

3. Select the desired contacts (Figure 3-32).
   - Use **Ctrl** to select non-adjacent contacts.
   - Use **Shift** to select a range of adjacent contacts.

4. Click the **To** button (you can also put contacts in the *Cc* or *Bcc* fields).

5. Click **OK**. Your email recipient list (*To* field) is populated with these contacts.

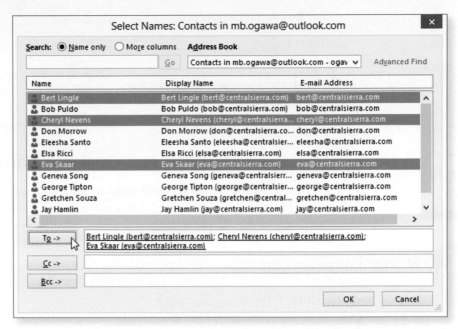

3-32 Select multiple contacts to email

Another way to send a message to a contact is from the contacts in the *Folder* pane. When the *People* button is selected in the *Navigation* pane, your contacts appear in the *Folder* pane. You can create a new email to send to one or more contacts.

HOW TO: Create an Email to a Selected Contact

1. Click the **People** button in the *Navigation* pane.

2. Select the desired contacts.

3. Click the **Email** button in the *Communicate* group on the *Home* tab (Figure 3-33). A new email message opens with the selected contacts in the *To* field.

3-33 Create new email message to selected contacts

3-34 Create new email message to a contact from the *People* view

Forward a Contact as a Business Card

There are times when you will want to send your contact record or another contact record to others via email. You can send this information as an electronic business card attached to an email, and the recipient can easily add the contact record to their *Contacts* folder.

HOW TO: Forward a Contact as a Business Card

1. Click the **People** button in the *Navigation* pane.
2. Select the contacts to be forwarded in the *Folder* pane.
3. Click the **Forward Contact** button in the *Share* group on the *Home* tab.
4. Choose **As a Business Card** (Figure 3-35). A new email opens with the business card attached, and a graphic of the business card will appear in the body of the email (Figure 3-36). This graphic can be deleted.
5. Populate the recipient list and click **Send**.

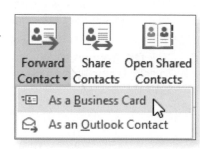

3-35 *Forward Contact As a Business Card*

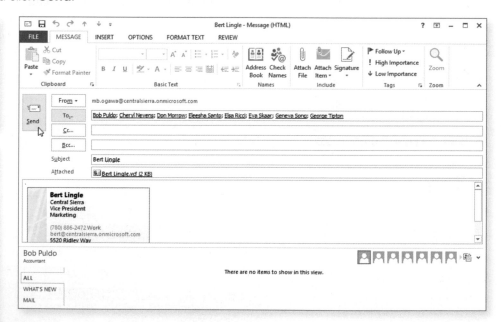

3-36 Attached business card

Create a Contact Group

Contact groups (also known as distribution lists) are commonly used when regularly sending emails to a group of contacts. A contact group is a saved group of contact records. It can include just a few contacts or numerous contacts.

Contact groups are useful to quickly send email to a department, team, or committee. Also, they help to ensure that all members of a group are included in an email and no one is inadvertently left off the recipient list.

Contact groups are named and stored in your *Contacts* folder (or other *Contacts* folder). Most *Global Address Lists* include numerous contact groups that have been created by the Exchange administrator.

HOW TO: Create a Contact Group

1. Click the **People** button in the *Navigation* pane.

2. Click the **New Contact Group** button in the *New* group on the *Home* tab (Figure 3-37). A new *Contact Group* window opens.

3. Type a name for the contact group.

4. Click **Add Members** from the *Member* group and choose **From Outlook Contacts** (Figure 3-38). The *Select Members* dialog box opens.

3-37 *New Contact* Group button

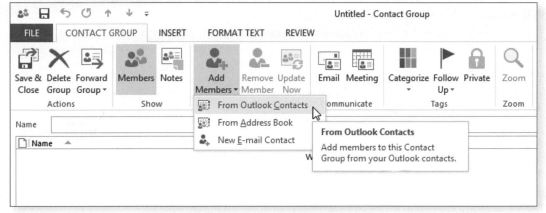

3-38 Select members from *Outlook Contacts* button

5. Select the contacts to be included (Figure 3-39).

6. Click **Members**.

7. Click **OK** to close the *Select Members* dialog box. The contact group is populated with these members.

8. Click **Save & Close** to save the contact group (Figure 3-40).

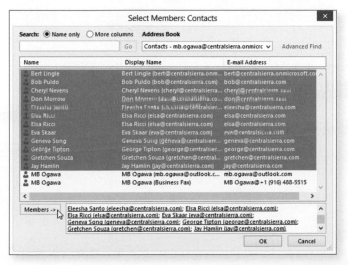

3-39 Select members from Outlook Contacts

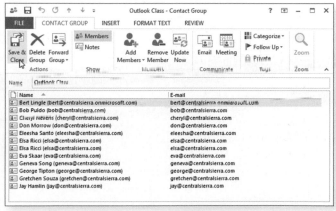

3-40 Contact group members

Send an Email to a Contact Group

A contact group can be used in the same way a contact record is used. On a new email, reply, or forward, you can select a contact group as the recipient by clicking on the *To* button and choosing the contact group from the *Select Names* dialog box. The email message will be sent to all those who are members of the contact group.

You can also create a new message to a contact group directly from your *Contacts* folder.

HOW TO: Send an Email to a Contact Group

1. Click the **People** button in the *Navigation* pane.
2. Select the desired contact group in the *Folder* pane.
3. Click the **Email** button in the *Communicate* group on the *Home* tab (Figure 3-41). A new email opens with the contact group as the recipient.
4. Add a subject and any desired information in the body (Figure 3-42).
5. Click **Send**.

3-41 *Email* button when a contact group is selected

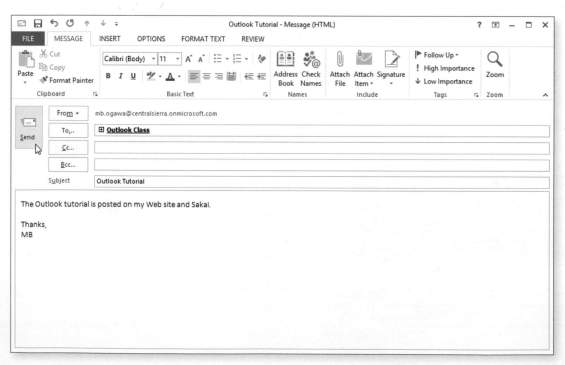

3-42 Email message to a contact group

Modify a Contact Group

You can modify a contact group by opening the contact group and *selecting members*, *removing members*, *adding new members*, or *updating contact information*.

Once a contact group is created, there are times when you might want to either add members or remove members from this list.

HOW TO: Add Members to a Contact Group

1. Click the **People** button in the *Navigation* pane.
2. Open the contact group to be modified.
3. Click the **Add Members** button in the *Members* group and choose **From Outlook Contacts** (Figure 3-43). The *Select Names* dialog box opens.

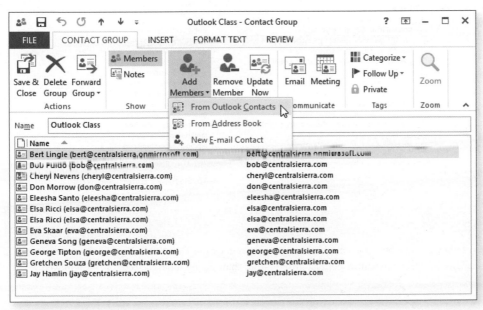

3-43 Add additional members to a contact group

4. Select the contacts to add to your contact group from your *Contacts* folder or the *Global Address List*.

5. Click the **Members** button (Figure 3-44).

6. Click **OK**. The *Select Members* dialog box will close and the new members are now included in your contact group.

7. Click **Save & Close** to save the updated contact group.

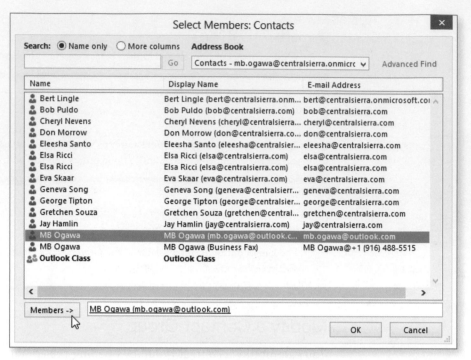

3-44 Select members to add to a contact group

Members can also be easily removed from your contact group.

HOW TO: Remove Members from a Contact Group

1. Click the **People** button in the *Navigation* pane.

2. Open the contact group to be modified.

3. In the body of the contact group, select the members to be removed.

4. Click the **Remove Member** button in the *Members* group (Figure 3-45).

5. Click **Save & Close** to save the updated contact group.

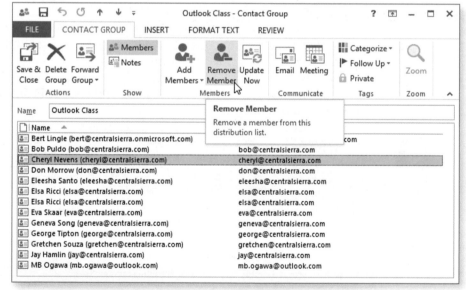

3-45 Remove a member from a contact group

> **MORE INFO**
>
> When removing members from a contact group, *do not* click the *Delete Group* button in the *Actions* group. This will delete the entire contact group rather than the members selected to be removed.

The ***New Email Contact*** option is used to add a member to the contact group who is not currently in your *Contacts* folder.

HOW TO: Add a New Email Contact to a Contact Group

1. Click the **People** button in the *Navigation* pane.

2. Open the contact group to be modified.

3. Click the **Add Members** button in the *Members* group and choose **New Email Contact**. The *Add New Member* dialog box opens.

4. Type in the contact's information. Select the **Add to Contacts** check box, and Outlook will add this contact to your *Contacts* folder.

5. Click **OK** to add the new member to the contact group and to close the *Add New Member* dialog box (Figure 3-46).

6. Click **Save & Close** to save the updated contact group.

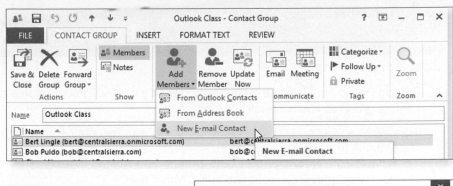

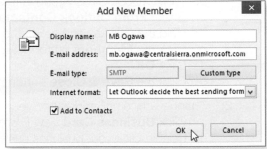

3-46 Add a new contact group member that is not in your contacts list

Update a Contact Group

There will be times when you make changes to a contact in your *Contacts* folder. If this contact is included in a contact group, the changes will not automatically be updated in the contact group. Open the contact group you want to update and click the **Update Now** button in the *Members* group on the *Contact Group* tab to update the members in your contact group to match their contact information in your *Contacts* folder (Figure 3-47).

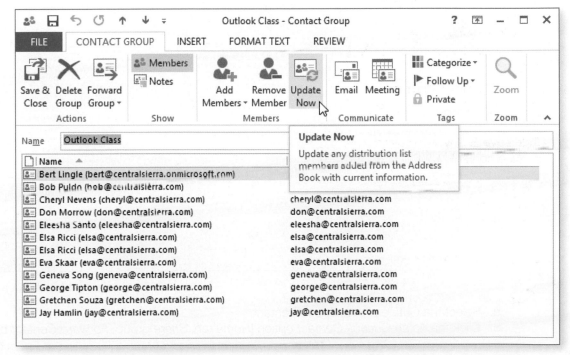

3-47 Update contact group when you modify contact records

For this Pause and Practice project, you create a contact group, update contact information, and send the contact group to your instructor.

1. Create an Outlook contact group including your two partners from *Pause & Practice Outlook 3-1 and 3-2*.
   a. Click the **New Contact Group** button [*Home* tab, *New* group].
   b. Type Outlook Class Group in the *Name* field.
   c. Select **From Outlook Contacts** [*Contact Group* tab, *Members* group, *Add Members* button].
   d. Hold the **Ctrl** key and select the contact information for your two partners and yourself.
   e. Click the **Members** button.
   f. Click **OK**.
   g. Click the **Save & Close** button [*Contact Group* tab, *Actions* group].

2. Change your email address to your personal email address.
   a. Click **Business Card** view [*Home* tab, *Current View* group].
   b. Double-click your business card.
   c. Change your email address to your personal email address.
   d. Click the **Save & Close** button.

3. Update the addresses in the *Outlook Class Group*.
   a. Double-click the business card for *Outlook Class Group*.
   b. Click the **Update Now** button.
   c. Click the **Save & Close** button.

4. Send an email to your instructor with the *Outlook Class Group* contact as an attachment (Figure 3-48).

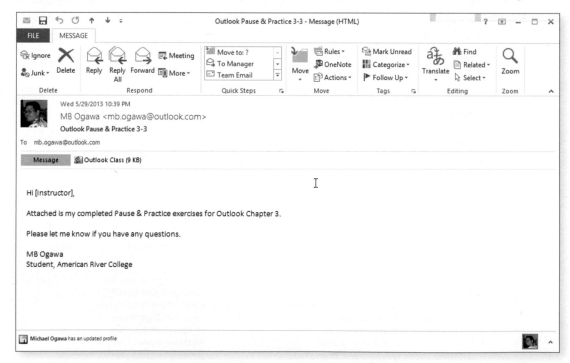

3-48 Completed Pause & Practice 3-3

   a. Select the *Outlook Class Group* contact.
   b. Click the *As an Outlook Contact* option [*Home* tab, *Share* group, *Forward Contact* button].

c. Click the **To** button to open your contacts.
d. Select your instructor and click the **To** button.
e. Click **OK**.
f. Add your email address in the *Cc* field.
g. Change the subject to Outlook Pause & Practice 3-3.
h. Type a short message to your instructor indicating that you attached the completed Pause & Practice exercises.
i. Click the **Send** button.

Chapter Summary

3.1 Differentiate between the *Contacts* folder and the *Global Address List* (p. O3-94).

- An Outlook contact is referred to as a **record** or **contact record**.
- A **record** includes a group of related information about a person such as name, phone number, email address, address, company, and job title.
- Each individual piece of information such as an email address or a phone number is called a **field**.
- Each record is saved to your **Contacts folder**.
- When using Outlook in an Exchange environment, you will have a **Global Address List,** which includes all the members of your organization.

3.2 Create a contact record from different sources (p. O3-95).

- You can create a new contact form using the default template by clicking the *New Contact* button.
- When creating multiple contacts from the same organization, you can use the *Contact from the same Company* option on the *Save & New* button to create a new contact with many of the same fields.
- You can create a contact based on an email you receive.
- A business card can be used to create a contact.
- Contacts in the *Global Address List* (Exchange environments only) can be saved to your personal contacts list.
- You can remove duplicate accounts by linking them.

3.3 Enhance contact records by editing contact information and fields (p. O3-102).

- Field names for specific records can be modified within a record.
- Each record can contain multiple addresses such as business and home.
- Outlook helps you format addresses when it does not recognize the format.
- Each record can contain multiple email addresses.

- You can add pictures to records, which will show up when you receive an email from the contact.
- Outlook can connect to social networks such as LinkedIn and Facebook through the Outlook Social Connector.
- You can receive updates from social networks in the *People* pane.

3.4 Use and modify the different contact views (p. O3-107).

- There are five contact views: *People, Business Card, Card, Phone,* and *List.*
- The **People** view includes all of the contacts' information as **People Cards**. Actions, such as sending an email message, are listed within the People Card.
- The **Business Card** view displays each contact as a business card.
- The **Card** view displays information as cards and is more condensed than the *Business Card* view.
- The **Phone** view displays contacts as a list based on phone number.
- The **List** view displays contacts as a list and includes different company groups.
- You can sort your contacts in list view by clicking the column header (field name).
- The *Advanced View Settings: List* dialog box can be used to customize the sorting of contacts.

3.5 Create a contact group and produce email from a contact or contact group (p. O3-110).

- You can create a contact group, which contains multiple contacts, to send email messages to members.
- When you click the *To* button in a new email message, you can select a contact or contact group instead of manually typing in email addresses.
- When selecting multiple email addresses, you can hold the **Ctrl** key to select non-adjacent contacts and the **Shift** key to select adjacent contacts.
- When selecting a contact or contact group in card or list view, you can click the **Email** button in the *Communicate* group to create new message.

- The *People Card* view includes the email button within the People Card.
- You can forward contacts to others as business cards.
- You can add or remove members from a contact group at any time.

- When you update contact fields, you need to update a contact group to ensure it has the most up-to-date fields.

Check for Understanding

In the **Online Learning Center** for this text (www.mhhe.com/office2013inpractice), there are a variety of resources that can be used to review the concepts covered in this chapter.

The following Online Learning Resources are available in the Online Learning Center:

- Multiple choice questions
- Short answer questions
- Matching exercises

Guided Project 3-1

In this project, you work as an insurance agent for Central Sierra Insurance (CSI). As a new member to the team, you begin setting up your Outlook contacts to make it easy to contact your associates. You will need to work with two partners for this guided project.
[Student Learning Outcomes 3.1, 3.2, 3.5]

Skills Covered in This Project

- Create a new contact.
- Add information in fields.
- Create contacts from the same company.

- Select contacts within the *To* and *Cc* fields of an email.
- Email contacts as a business card.

1. Click the **People** button in the *Navigation* pane.

2. Create a contact for your manager (either one of your partners, but be sure each person creates a unique contact).
   a. Click the **New Contact** button [*Home* tab, *New* group].
   b. Partner with another student and enter his or her full name, company (Central Sierra), job title (Manager), business phone number, and email address in the appropriate fields.
   c. Click the **Contact from the Same Company** option [*Contact* tab, *Actions* group, *Save & New* button].
   d. Create another contact for your other partner. Include his or her full name, company (Central Sierra), job title (Insurance Agent), business phone number, and email address in the appropriate fields.
   e. Click **Save & Close**. Click **Save & Close** for both contacts.

3. Create a new message to your instructor.
   a. Click the **Mail** button in the *Navigation* pane.
   b. Click **New Mail** [*Home* tab, *New* group].
   c. In the *To* field, enter your instructor's email ddress.
   d. In the *Cc* field, enter your email address.
   e. In the *Subject* field, type Outlook Guided Project 3-1
   f. In the message area, type: Dear [instructor name], Attached is my Outlook Guided Project 3-1. Thank you, [your name]

   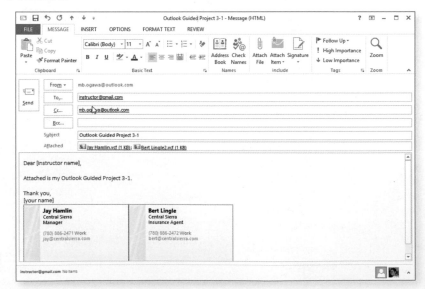

   g. Click the **Business Card** option [*Message* tab, *Include* group, *Attach Item*] and select **Other Business Cards**.
   h. Select the two cards you created and click **OK**.
   i. Your email message should look similar to figure 3-49.
   j. Click the **Send** button.

3-49 Completed Guided Project 3-1

Guided Project 3-2

For this project, you edit your contacts to add additional information. You also add a picture to each of the contacts so that you can easily match your coworkers' faces and names when receiving email. [Student Learning Outcomes 3.1, 3.3, 3.4, 3.5]

Files Needed: **johnsanchez**.jpg and **jillricci**.jpg
Completed Project File Name: None

Skills Covered in This Project

- Edit contacts.
- Include an address in contacts.
- Include a photo in contacts.

- Select contacts within the *To* and *Cc* fields of an email.
- Email contacts as a business card.

1. Edit the two contacts you created in Guided Project 3-1 to include their addresses and pictures.
   a. Click the **Business Card** button [*Home* tab, *Current View* group].
   b. Double-click the first record that you created (your partner that is a manager).
   c. Type the following information in the *Business Address* field:

      5520 Ridley Way
      Cameron Park, CA 94681

   d. Select the **Add Picture** option [*Contact* tab, *Options* group, *Picture* button].
   e. Locate your partner's picture and click **OK**. If you do not have a picture, you can use one of the provided images (**johnsanchez**.jpg or **jillricci**.jpg) and change it to his or her image later.
   f. Click the **Save & Close** button.
   g. Double-click the second record that you created (your partner who is an insurance agent).
   h. Type the following information in the *Business Address* field:

      5520 Ridley Way
      Cameron Park, CA 94681

   i. Select the **Add Picture** option [*Contact* tab, *Options* group, *Picture* button].
   j. Locate your partner's picture and click **OK**. If you do not have a picture, you can use one of the provided images (**johnsanchez.jpg** or **jillricci.jpg**) and change it to his or her image later.
   k. Click the **Save & Close** button.

2. Create a new message to your instructor (Figure 3-50).

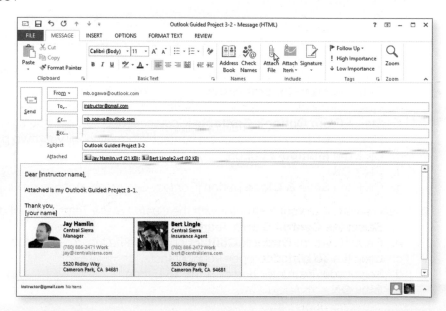

3-50 Completed Guided Project 3-2

    a. Click the **Mail** button in the *Navigation* pane.
    b. Click **New Mail** [*Home* tab, *New* group].
    c. In the *To* field, enter your instructor's email address.
    d. In the *Cc* field, enter your email address.
    e. In the *Subject* field, enter Outlook Guided Project 3-2.
    f. In the message area, type:

       Dear [instructor name],
       Attached is my Outlook Guided Project 3-2.
       Thank you,
       [your name]

    g. Click the **Business Card** option [*Message* tab, *Include* group, *Attach Item*] and select **Other Business Cards**.
    h. Select the two cards you crated and click **OK**.
    i. Click the **Send** button.

Guided Project 3-3

For this project, you create a contact group for your coworker and manager. You also include yourself in the contact group.
[Student Learning Outcomes 3.1, 3.5]

Skills Covered in This Project

- Create a contact group.
- Select contacts within the *To* and *Cc* fields of an email.

- Email a contact group as an Outlook item.

1. Create an Outlook contact group using your two coworkers from Guided Project 3-2.
    a. Click the **New Contact Group** button [*Home* tab, *New* group].
    b. Type Central Sierra Team in the *Name* field.
    c. Select **From Outlook Contacts** [*Contact Group* tab, *Members* group, *Add Members* button].
    d. Hold the **Ctrl** key and select the contact information for your two partners and yourself.
    e. Click the **Members** button.
    f. Click **OK**.
    g. Click the **Save & Close** button [*Contact Group* tab, *Actions* group].

2. Send an email to your instructor with the *Central Sierra Team* contact as an attachment (Figure 3-51).
    a. Select the **Central Sierra Team** contact.
    b. Click the **As an Outlook Contact** option [*Home* tab, *Share* group, *Forward Contact* button].
    c. Click the **To** button to open your contacts.
    d. Select your instructor and click the **To** button.
    e. Click **OK**.

f. Add your email address in the *Cc* field.
g. Change the subject to Outlook Guided Project 3-3.
h. In the message area, type:
    Dear [instructor name],
    Attached is my Outlook Guided Project 3-3.
    Thank you,
    [your name]
i. Click the **Send** button.

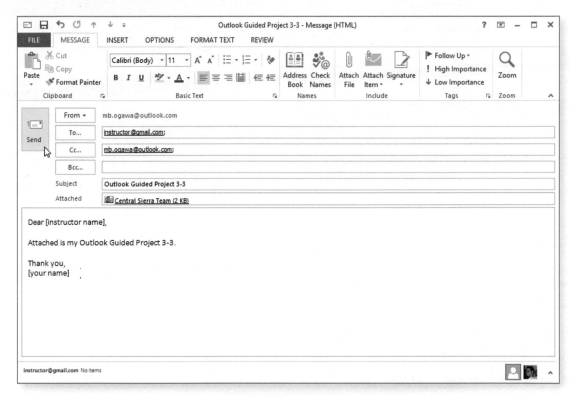

3-51 Completed Guided Project 3-3

Independent Project 3-4

For this project, you work as an academic advisor for Sierra Pacific Community College District (SPCCD), a community college district made up of four individual community colleges. Due to the decentralized nature of the multiple campuses, you realize that it is important that you keep in touch with advisors on the other campuses and you add them to your contacts.
[Student Learning Outcomes 3.1, 3.2, 3.5]

Skills Covered in This Project

- Create contacts.
- Create contacts using the same company.
- Adding information to fields.
- Select contacts within the *To* and *Cc* fields of an email.
- Email contacts as a business card.

1. Create contacts for the following individuals:

Full name	Company	Job title	E-mail	Business Phone
Joy Holland	Sierra Pacific Community College District (North)	Academic Advisor	joy@spccd.edu	209-658-0011
Megan Sharp	Sierra Pacific Community College District (South)	Academic Advisor	megan@spccd.edu	209-658-0891
Jim Hennessey	Sierra Pacific Community College District (East)	Academic Advisor	jim@spccd.edu	209-658-7189
Morgan Santos	Sierra Pacific Community College District (West)	Academic Advisor	morgan@spccd.edu	209-658-5561

2. Send an email to your instructor including the four business cards as attachments.
   a. Include your email address in the *Cc* field.
   b. Type Outlook Independent Project 3-4 in the *Subject* field.
   c. Include a short message indicating that the completed Independent Project is attached to the message (Figure 3-52).

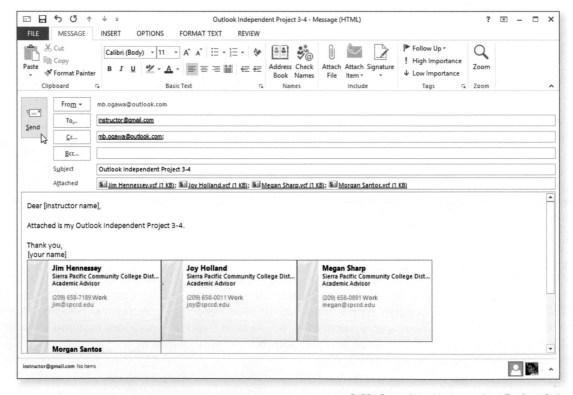

3-52 Completed Independent Project 3-4

Independent Project 3-5

For this project, you familiarize yourself with the basic components of Outlook.
[Student Learning Outcomes 3.1, 3.3, 3.4, 3.5]

Files Needed: **jim.jpg, joy.jpg, megan.jpg,** and **morgan.jpg**
Completed Project File Name: None

Skills Covered in This Project

- Edit contacts.
- Include an address in contacts.
- Include a photo in contacts.
- Add a second email address to contacts.
- Add a mobile phone number to contacts.
- Select contacts within the *To* and *Cc* fields of an email.
- Email contacts as a business card.

1. Edit the four contacts you created in Independent Project 3-4 to include the following:

Full name	Photo	Address	E-mail 2	Mobile Phone
Joy Holland	joy.jpg	7300 College Avenue Student Services, 3F Sacramento, CA 92387	joy@outlook.com	818-298-3987
Megan Sharp	megan.jpg	7300 College Avenue Helmsley Hall, 319 Sacramento, CA 92387	megan@outlook.com	818-459-0091
Jim Hennessey	jim.jpg	7300 College Avenue Hamilton Hall, 210A Sacramento, CA 92387	jim@outlook.com	818-928-9916
Morgan Santos	morgan.jpg	7300 College Avenue POST Bld, 312 Sacramento, CA 92387	morgan@outlook.com	818-298-7620

2. Send an email to your instructor including the four business cards as attachments (Figure 3-53).
   a. Include your email address in the *Cc* field.
   b. Type Outlook Independent Project 3-5 in the *Subject* field.
   c. Include a short message indicating that the completed Independent Project is attached to the message.

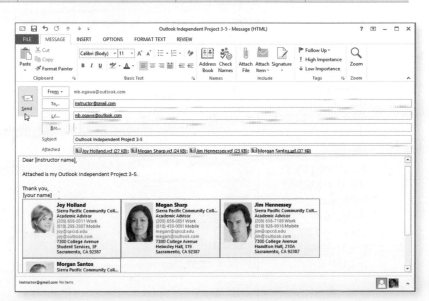

3-53 Completed Independent Project 3-5

Independent Project 3-6

In this project, you continue to familiarize yourself with the basic components of Outlook.
[Student Learning Outcomes 3.1, 3.2, 3.3, 3.4, 3.5]

Skills Covered in This Project

- Create a contact group.
- Add a new contact group member.
- Edit a contact.

- Select contacts within the *To* and *Cc* fields of an email.
- Email a contact group as an Outlook item.

---

1. Create a new contact group with the four advisors called Sierra Pacific Advising Team. Only add their **spccd.edu** email addresses.

2. Add a new member to the contact group with the following information:
    Full Name: John Hays
    E-mail: john@spccd.edu

3. Edit John's contact information to include the following:
    Company: Sierra Pacific Community College District (System)
    Job title: Dean
    E-mail 2: jay@outlook.com
    Business phone: 209-981-2975
    Mobile phone: 818-212-0459
    Photo: **hays.jpg**
    Address:
    7300 College Avenue
    College Hill, 208
    Sacramento, CA 92387

4. Send an email to your instructor including the contact group and Dean Hay's business card as attachments.
    a. Include your email address in the *Cc* field.
    b. Type Outlook Independent Project 3-6 in the *Subject* field.
    c. Include a short message indicating that the completed Independent Project is attached to the message (Figure 3-54).

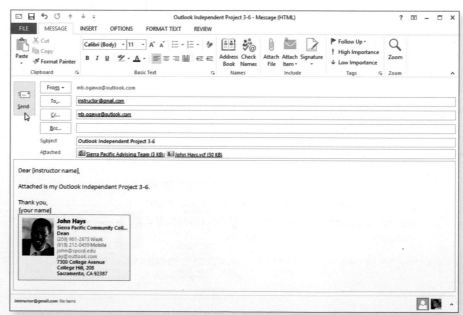

3-54 Completed Independent Project 3-6

Challenge Project 3-7

Develop a contact group for your family and friends to use to send out group updates. Include as much information as possible. If you are concerned about privacy, you can create information for fields that are sensitive.
[Student Learning Outcomes 3.1, 3.2, 3.3, 3.5]

- Create at least five new contacts for friends and family members.
- Use as many fields as possible.
- At minimum, each record should have the full name, email address, phone number, and mailing address completed.
- Include a picture for each contact.
- Create a contact group for the members.
- Use a descriptive name for the group.
- Email the contact group to your instructor as an email attachment.
- Change the subject of your message to **Outlook Challenge Project 3-7**.
- Include a short message indicating why the contact group name is appropriate.

Challenge Project 3-8

Describe an upcoming event in an email message to an organization in which you're a member. Develop contacts and a contact group list for the organization and email it as a file to your instructor.
[Student Learning Outcomes 3.1, 3.2, 3.3, 3.5]

- Create at least five new contacts for your organization.
- Use as many fields as possible. You can create fictitious information for fields that are sensitive.
- At minimum, each record should have the full name and email address of each member.
- Create a contact group for the members.
- Use a descriptive name for the group.
- Write an email message to the organization describing an upcoming event.
- You can use options, such as themes, to improve the aesthetics of the message.
- Save the message as a draft.
- Save the draft as a file.
- Email the contact group to your instructor as an email attachment.
- Include the draft email message as an attachment.
- Change the subject of your message to **Outlook Challenge Project 3-8**.

Challenge Project 3-9

Create a contact group including at least five classmates who are in your study sessions. Incorporate as much information in each record as possible since you may need to get in touch with group members via a variety of means. Write a message to the contact group requesting a study session and use voting buttons to select a specific date.
[Student Learning Outcomes 3.1, 3.2, 3.3, 3.5]

- Create at least five new contacts for your study group.
- Use as many fields as possible.
- At minimum, each record should have a full name, two email addresses, a mobile phone number, and an address.
- Apply a category to each of the contacts and the contact group.
- Create a contact group for the members.
- Use a descriptive name for the group.
- Write an email message to the group requesting a study session on a specific date.
- Use voting buttons to have your group vote on a date.
- Save the message as a draft.
- Save the draft as a file.
- Email the contact group to your instructor as an email attachment.
- Include the draft email message as an attachment.
- Change the subject of your message to **Outlook Challenge Project 3-9**.

Calendar

CHAPTER OVERVIEW

If you use a daily planner or a calendar that hangs on your wall or refrigerator and think you would be lost without it, wait until you start using an Outlook calendar and learn about the many advantages it has over a paper calendar. One of the many advantages to using Microsoft Outlook is that it integrates different Outlook tasks. As personal management software, Outlook not only handles your emails (and multiple email accounts) and contacts but also provides an electronic calendar to be used in conjunction with your email.

In this chapter, you'll learn about many of the features of **Outlook Calendar** and how it integrates with both email and contacts. In future chapters, you will see how calendar items can be used with Tasks, Categories, and the *To-Do bar.* As you progress though this text and continue to utilize Outlook in your daily life for both business and personal use, you will find that Outlook Calendar not only surpasses your expectations but it is an invaluable organizational tool.

STUDENT LEARNING OUTCOMES (SLOs)

After completing this chapter, you will be able to:

SLO 4.1   Identify the different types of calendar items (p. O4-132).

SLO 4.2   Distinguish between different calendar views (p. O4-134).

SLO 4.3   Create and edit calendar items (p. O4-138).

SLO 4.4   Create and use meeting requests (p. O4-144).

CASE STUDY

For the Pause & Practice projects, you begin building your personal calendar by adding a meeting with your instructor and your friend's birthday. You use the features of Outlook to create, modify, and request meetings with others.

Pause & Practice 4-1: For this Pause & Practice project, you create calendar items for an upcoming meeting with your Instructor regarding an assignment. You also create a recurring event for your friend's birthday with a

reminder set a week in advance to ensure you have time to purchase a gift.

Pause & Practice 4-2: You follow up with the two calendar items you created in *Pause & Practice 4-1.* You had an emergency at home, so you decide to send a meeting request to your instructor to Apologize for not being able to make the meeting and reschedule. You also send a meeting request to have lunch with your friend Lynne to give her the gift you purchased.

OUTLOOK

Understanding Calendar Items

Most people who use a calendar to help organize their lives can only imagine having a calendar hanging on their wall or refrigerator instead of keeping all of their appointments on an electronic calendar. But most people who have converted to Outlook Calendar cannot imagine going back to a paper calendar.

An Outlook calendar has many advantages over a paper calendar.

- An Outlook calendar can be viewed in monthly, weekly, daily, or other formats, unlike a paper calendar that has a fixed view.
- Reminders can be set to alert you on your computer or phone about upcoming appointments or events.
- Calendar items can easily be moved, copied, deleted, or set to recur at specific intervals.
- Categories can be used to group calendar items and color them for visual recognition.
- Additional information and details can be included in the body, and items such as contacts and Word documents can be attached to a calendar item.
- Calendar items can be set to recur on a specific interval (daily, weekly, monthly, or yearly).
- Meeting requests can be used to create a meeting on your calendar, invite others to the meeting, and track responses of those attending the meeting.
- Calendars can be synchronized with many cell phones and tablets that have a calendar feature.

There are three main types of calendar items: *appointments*, *events*, and *meeting requests*. Each of these different items has a distinct purpose and use, but all of these items are created in a similar fashion, and you can use the same new calendar item to create each of these different calendar items. For example, an appointment can easily be changed to an event by changing the duration of the calendar item. This consistency makes it easy to learn how to use Outlook Calendar.

Appointments

An *appointment* (Figure 4-1) is a calendar item that has a duration of less than 24 hours, such as a sales meeting, your child's water polo game, or a date with your significant other. This is the most common type of calendar item and can be used for storing all types of appointments or for scheduling blocks of time that are less than a day in length.

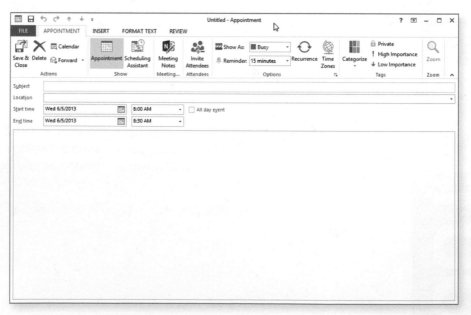

4-1 New appointment

Events

Events (Figure 4-2) are those calendar items that last for 24 hours or more, like vacations, conferences, birthdays, or long holidays.

When a new appointment is open, it can easily be converted to an event by clicking on the **All day event** check box to the right of the *Start time* and *End time*. Conversely, an event can be converted to an appointment by deselecting the **All day event** check box and setting the specific time of the appointment.

4-2 Event

Meeting Requests

A *meeting request* (Figure 4-3) is used to create a calendar item and invite others to this meeting. It looks similar to both an appointment and an event, but the meeting request includes a *To* line used to invite attendees and a *Send* button. A meeting request looks like a combination of a calendar item and a new email and can be either an appointment or event. If you are

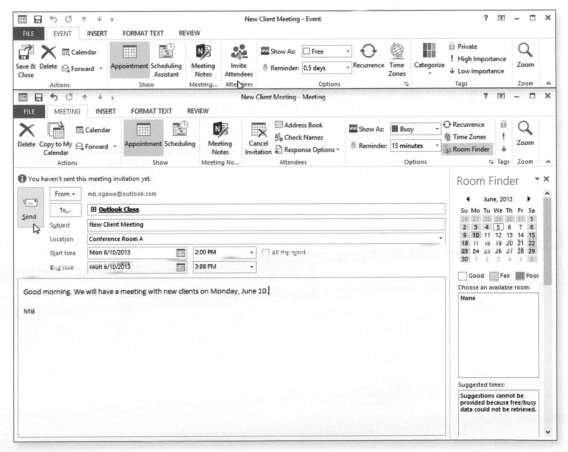

4-3 Meeting request

using an Exchange server, you can select from available rooms if your administrator enabled this feature.

An appointment or event can easily be converted to a meeting request by clicking on the **Invite Attendees** button in the *Attendees* group on the *Appointment* or *Events* tab (the tab name will vary depending on whether the calendar item is an appointment or event).

SLO 4.2

Navigating the Calendar Views

As mentioned previously, one of the advantages of using an Outlook calendar is being able to view the calendar in different formats. There are four main calendar views: *Day*, *Week*, *Month*, and *Schedule*. There are other views available that list calendar items according to specific criteria. You have to experiment with the different views to find the view or views that work best for you. My preference is the *Month* view.

When **Calendar** is selected in the *Navigation* pane, it is displayed in the *Folder* pane. The way the calendar is displayed in the *Folder* pane is dependent upon the calendar view you have selected. The buttons for *Day*, *Week*, *Month*, and *Schedule* view are in the *Arrange* group on the *Home* tab. Also displayed in the *Navigation* pane are the **date navigator** (a thumbnail of a monthly calendar) and the different calendars available (you can have multiple calendars).

> ### MORE INFO
> Tasks and To-Do items will be covered in Chapter 5.

> ### ANOTHER WAY
> **Ctrl+Alt+1** will display the calendar in *Day* view.

Day View

Day view (Figure 4-4) displays the calendar one day at a time with the calendar broken into half-hour segments. Events are displayed at the top of the daily calendar, while appointments appear on the calendar at their scheduled times.

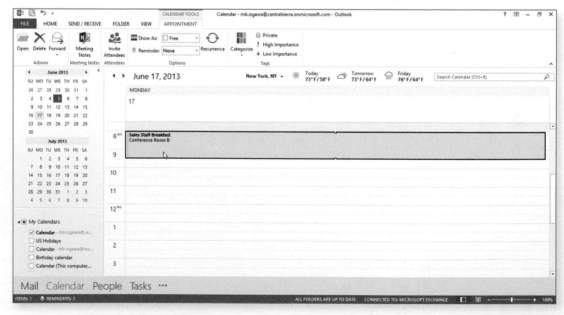

4-4 *Day* view

The date is listed at the top of the calendar, and you can move backward or forward one day at a time on the calendar by clicking on the left or right arrow to the left of the date. You can move to a specific date on the calendar by clicking on the date in the thumbnail calendar provided at the top of the *Navigation* pane.

Week View

Week view (Figure 4-5) has two different display options: **Work Week** or **Week**. *Work Week* view displays a Monday through Friday workweek, while *Week* view displays a Sunday through Saturday week.

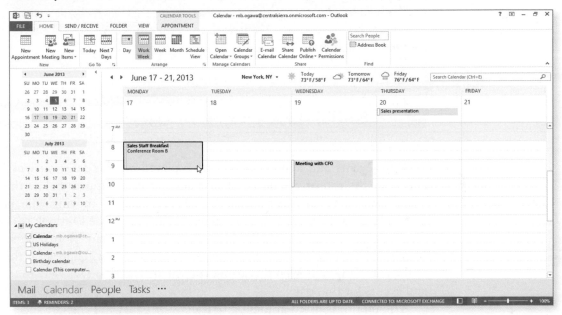

4-5 *Work Week* view

As with *Day* view, *Week* view displays events at the top of the calendar and appointments appear at their set times. The *Daily Task List* is located at the bottom of the *Folder* pane and can either be minimized or turned off.

The date is displayed at the top of the calendar in the *Folder* pane showing the date range for the week. The left and right arrows to the left of the date will move you backward or forward one week at a time.

> ### MORE INFO
>
> Changing work week options, calendar color, and other advanced calendar topics will be covered in Chapter 9.

> ### ANOTHER WAY
>
> **Ctrl+Alt+2** displays the calendar in *Work Week* view.
> **Ctrl+Alt+3** displays the calendar in *Week* view.

Month View

Month view (Figure 4-6) displays an entire month of the calendar. You are given three different options regarding the amount of detail to display on the calendar for each calendar item (*Show Low Detail, Show Medium Detail,* and *Show High Detail*).

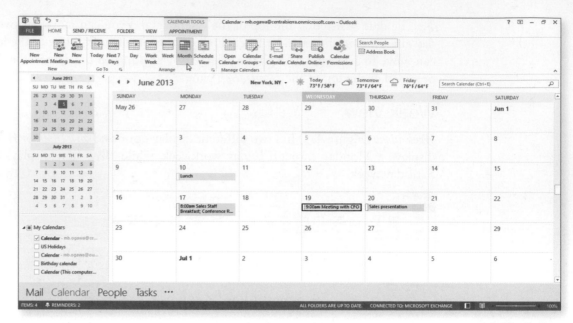

4-6 *Month* view

Both events and appointments are displayed on the dates on which they occur. Events appear at the top of the date cell, and appointments appear below the events. You can see more detail about any of the items on the calendar by moving your pointer over the item. Depending on the size of your computer monitor and the Outlook window, *Month* view will display three or four calendar items on each day. If there are more events or appointments on a certain date than will fit on the calendar, a small arrow will appear at the bottom right corner of the date. If you click on this arrow, you will be taken to *Day* view to see more appointments and events for that day.

The month is listed at the top of the *Folder* pane, and the left and right arrows to the left of the month will move you backward or forward one month at a time.

> **ANOTHER WAY**
>
> **Ctrl+Alt+4** displays the calendar in *Month* view.

> **MORE INFO**
>
> The *Today* button in the *Go To* group on the *Home* tab will always take you to the current day. Also, you can move to a specific day by clicking on the date navigator in the *Navigation* pane.

Schedule View

Schedule view (Figure 4-7) displays your calendar in timeline view in the *Folder* pane. The timeline is displayed horizontally rather than vertically (*Day* and *Week* views). In *Schedule* view you can type a new appointment directly on the calendar, double-click a time slot to open a new appointment, or click the *New Appointment* button on the *Home* tab.

> **ANOTHER WAY**
>
> **Ctrl+Alt+5** displays the calendar in *Schedule* view.

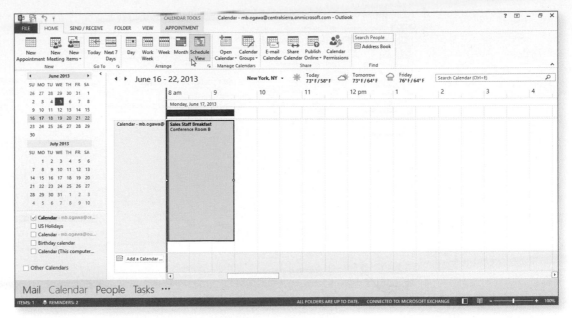

One of the distinct advantages of using the *Schedule* view is the ability to view multiple calendars in the *Folder* pane. When using Outlook in an Exchange environment, it is common to share your calendar with others in your organization. When others have shared their calendars with you, you can select one or more of these shared calendars to be displayed in *Schedule* view, which will help facilitate scheduling meetings, appointments, and events.

> **MORE INFO**
>
> Sharing and opening shared calendars will be covered in Chapter 9.
> Multiple calendars can also be displayed when using *Day, Week, Work Week,* or *Month* views.

Other Views

In addition to the four main calendar views, Outlook also has other preset views available. These different views show calendar items in a list rather than *Day, Week,* or *Month* view. The different preset views are:

- *Calendar* (*Calendar* view)
- *Preview* (*Calendar* view)
- *List* (*List* view)
- *Active* (*List* view)

To access these other views, click **Change View** (Figure 4-8) on the *View* tab and choose the view you want. You can return to *Calendar* view by following the same steps and choosing **Calendar**.

> **MORE INFO**
>
> Any of these views can be customized to better meet your needs. Customizing views will be covered in Chapter 5 and 9.

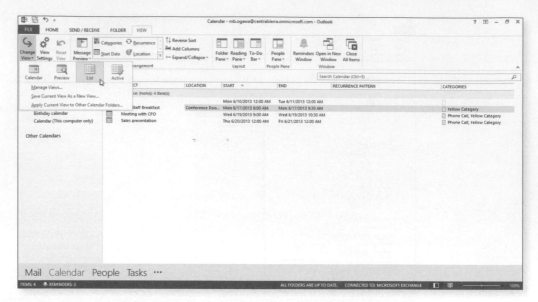

4-8 Additional views

SLO 4.3

Creating and Editing Calendar Items

Creating a calendar item varies depending on the calendar view. In all the calendar views, you can type an appointment directly on the calendar. In *Day* and *Week* views, you can adjust the duration of an appointment by clicking and dragging on the top or bottom edge of the appointment.

Usually the best way to create a calendar item is to open a new calendar item. This will give you more fields to enter detailed information about the appointment or event.

> **ANOTHER WAY**
>
> **Ctrl+N** gives you a new calendar item when you are in your calendar. This shortcut works for all the Outlook tasks. For example, if you're in Contacts and press **Ctrl+N**, you'll get a new contact record. This shortcut works in Mail, Calendar, Contacts, Tasks, Notes, and Journal.

Create an Appointment

When you are in your calendar (it doesn't matter which view), create a new appointment by clicking on the *New Appointment* button on the *Home* tab. The new appointment opens and the date will be the date you were on in the calendar. The date and time can easily be changed.

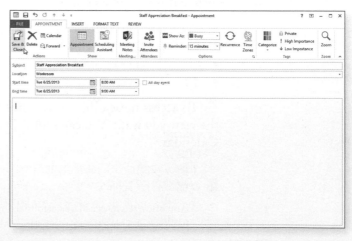

HOW TO: Create an Appointment

1. In your calendar, click the **New Appointment** button on the *Home* tab. A new appointment opens (Figure 4-9).

4-9 New appointment

2. Fill in the *Subject* and *Location* of the appointment. After you enter a subject, the subject appears in the *Title bar* at the top of the open calendar item.

3. Set the *Start time* and *End time* dates and times for this appointment.

4. Enter additional information about this appointment in the body of the new appointment.

5. Click **Save & Close**. The appointment appears on your calendar.

▶ ANOTHER WAY

Ctrl+Shift+A opens a new calendar appointment anywhere in Outlook.

Create an Event

Creating a new event will vary depending on the calendar view. When you are in *Day* or *Week* view, create a new event by double-clicking on the event area at the top of the calendar in the *Folder* pane. In *Month* view, create a new event by double-clicking on the date of the event (or the first day of the event).

An appointment can always be converted to an event by clicking the **All day event** check box to the right of the date and time.

HOW TO: Create an Event

1. Click the **New Appointment** button on the *Home* tab or press **Ctrl+N**. A new appointment opens.

2. Fill in the *Subject* and *Location* of the event.

3. Click the **All day event** check box.
   - The calendar item changes from an appointment to an event (Figure 4-10).
   - In the *Title bar* after the subject, the type of calendar item displays (e.g., *Appointment*, *Event*, or *Meeting*).

4. Set the *Start time* and *End time* dates for this event.

5. Enter additional information about this event in the body of the new appointment.

6. Click **Save & Close**. The event will appear on your calendar.

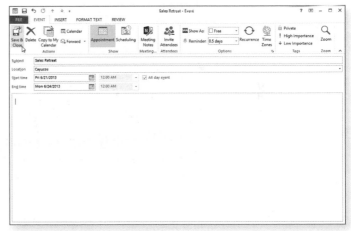

4-10 Event

Reminders

A *reminder* can be set on all calendar items. This reminder opens on your computer screen to remind you of an upcoming appointment, event, or meeting.

The default reminder time for an appointment is 15 minutes before the appointment, and an event is 18 hours before the event. You can easily change the reminder time by clicking on the *Reminder* drop-down menu (Figure 4-11) in the *Options* group on the *Appointment* or *Event* tab. You can also choose to set a specific sound for the reminder. The reminder can also be set to *None*.

When the reminder for an appointment or event comes due, it is displayed on your computer screen (Figure 4-12). The reminder displays the subject of the calendar item, the start date and time, and the location. You are given the options of *Dismiss All, Open Item, Dismiss*, and *Snooze*. If you choose *Snooze*, you can choose to be reminded again in a certain amount of time by clicking on the **Snooze** drop-down menu.

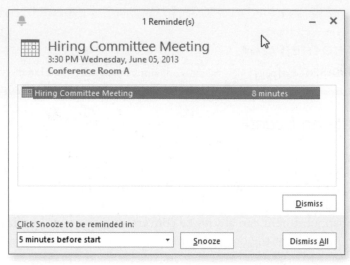

4-12 Reminder window

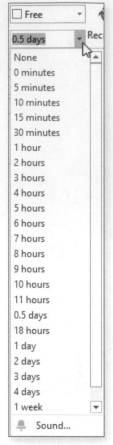

4-11 Reminder drop-down menu

Move and Copy Calendar Items

One of the distinct advantages of using an Outlook calendar is the ability to easily move and replicate calendar items. Many times an appointment is rescheduled, and, when using an Outlook calendar, you can move the item to a new date or time.

To **move** a calendar item, you can open the item from the calendar and change the date and/or time of the item. When you save and close the item, it will be moved to its new date and time on the calendar. If an appointment has been moved to another day and has the same time, you can simply drag and drop the calendar item to the new date on the calendar.

Suppose you have jury duty three days in a row and you don't want to create three separate calendar appointments. To **copy** an existing appointment to another date, you can select the appointment on the calendar, hold down the **Ctrl** key, and drag and drop the appointment on the new date. As you are dragging the calendar item, you will see a small plus sign by the pointer to indicate that you are copying a calendar item rather than moving it (Figure 4-13). The appointment will be copied to the new date.

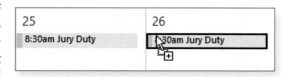

4-13 Copy appointment using **Ctrl** + drag and drop

> ▶ **ANOTHER WAY**
>
> **Ctrl+C** copies a selected calendar item.
> **Ctrl+X** cuts a selected calendar item.
> **Ctrl+V** pastes a copied or cut calendar item to a new location.

Recurring Appointments and Events

When a calendar item has a recurring pattern, it is better to set up the item as a ***recurring appointment*** or ***event*** rather than just copying the item to another location. A recurring appointment or event is typically used for appointments or events that occur on a regular basis such as weekly sales meetings, monthly lunch socials, birthdays, or anniversaries.

A calendar item can be set to recur daily, weekly, monthly, or yearly. The recurring calendar item can be set to end after a certain number of occurrences, end on a certain date, or have no end date.

HOW TO: Create a Recurring Appointment or Event

1. Create a new calendar appointment.

2. Fill in the *Subject, Location, Start time, End time,* and any other needed details in the body.

3. Click the **Recurrence** button in the *Options* group (Figure 4-14). The *Appointment Recurrence* dialog box opens (Figure 4-15).

4. Confirm the correct start and end times in the *Appointment time* section.

5. Set the desired *Recurrence pattern.*

6. Select the *Range of recurrence* for *Start* and *End.*

7. Click **OK** to close the dialog box.

8. Click **Save & Close** to close the recurring appointment.

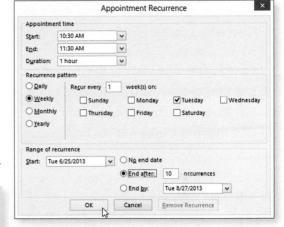

4-14 *Recurrence* button

4-15 *Appointment Recurrence* dialog box

> **ANOTHER WAY**
>
> When a calendar item is open, **Ctrl+G** opens the *Appointment Recurrence* dialog box.

Recurring items can be edited. When you open a recurring item, Outlook will give you two options. ***Open this occurrence*** will allow you to edit that specific calendar item without changing all the recurring items or the recurrence pattern. ***Open the series*** will allow you to edit the entire series of recurring calendar items (Figure 4-16).

4-16 *Open Recurring Item* dialog box

Delete a Calendar Item

You can delete calendar items by selecting the items to be removed from the calendar and either pressing the *Delete* key on your keyboard, clicking on the *Delete* button on the *Appointment* tab, or right-clicking on the calendar item and selecting *Delete.*

When deleting a recurring item, you are given the options to either *Delete Occurrence* or *Delete Series*.

Deleted calendar items are stored in the *Deleted Items* folder and remain there until this folder is permanently emptied. If you delete a calendar item by mistake, you can open the *Deleted Items* folder and drag the calendar item from the *Deleted Items* folder to the *Calendar* button in the *Navigation* pane. The calendar item will be restored to its correct location on the calendar.

> **ANOTHER WAY**
>
> **Ctrl+D** deletes a selected calendar item.

Create a Calendar Item from an Email

There may be times when you receive an email and would like to create a calendar item based on the information in that email. Rather than retyping all the information in the email, you can easily convert it to a calendar item.

HOW TO: Create a Calendar Item from an Email

1. Click the email to be converted to a calendar item (do not open the email).
2. Drag and drop the email on the *Calendar* button in the *Navigation* pane.
3. A new calendar appointment opens. The subject will be the same as the email subject, and the date will be the current date. The body of the new calendar item will contain the information from the body of the email.
4. Edit the calendar item *Start* and *End* dates and times.
5. Edit the body of the calendar item.
6. Click **Save & Close**.

> **ANOTHER WAY**
>
> Select or open an email, click the **Move** button in the *Move* group, and choose **Other Folder.** Select the **Calendar** in the *Move Item to* dialog box and click **OK.** A new calendar appointment opens. When you save and close the appointment, the original email message will be moved to your *Deleted Items* folder.

PAUSE & PRACTICE: OUTLOOK 4-1

In this Pause & Practice project, you create calendar items for an upcoming meeting with your instructor regarding an assignment. You also create a recurring event for your friend's birthday with a reminder set a week in advance to ensure you have time to purchase a gift.

1. Create a new appointment.
   a. Click the **Calendar** button in the *Navigation* pane.
   b. Click the **New Appointment** button [*Home* tab, *New* group].
   c. Enter the following information for the new appointment:
   Subject: Meeting for ENG 100 Paper
   Location: Hamilton Hall 303A
   Start time: Next week Monday's date, 9:00 AM

End time: Next week Monday's day, 10:00 AM
Body: Email copy of paper to the instructor by Friday.

    d. Click the *Reminder* drop-down arrow [*Appointment* tab, *Options* group].

    e. Select **3 days**.

    f. Click the **Save & Close** button.

2. Create a new appointment.

    a. Click the **New Appointment** button [*Home* tab, *New* group].

    b. Enter the following information for the new appointment:

    Subject: Lynne's Birthday

    Location: None

    Start time: July 17 of the current year

    End time: July 17 of the current year

    Click the checkbox for **All day event**.

    Body: Buy Lynne a present. She like sports and tech gadgets.

    c. Click the *Reminder* drop-down arrow [*Appointment* tab, *Options* group].

    d. Select **1 week**.

    e. Click the **Recurrence** button [*Event* tab, *Options* group].

    f. Click the **Yearly** radio button under *Recurrence pattern* and click **OK**.

    g. Click the **Save & Close** button.

      • The two appointments created are displayed in Figure 4-17.

3. Email the two calendar items to your instructor as Outlook items.

    a. Click the **Mail** button in the *Navigation* pane.

    b. Click the **New Email** button [*Home* tab, *New* group].

    c. Enter the following information in your message:

    To: instructor's email address

    Cc: your email address

    Subject: Pause & Practice 4-1

    Body:

    Hi [instructor name],

    Attached are my calendar items for the Pause & Practice 4-1 exercise.

    Sincerely,

    [student name]

    d. Click the **Attach Item** button [*Message* tab, *Include* group] and select **Outlook Item**.

    e. Select the **Calendar** option and locate the two calendar items you created.

    f. Hold the **Ctrl** key and select the two calendar items and click **OK**.

    g. Click **Send**.

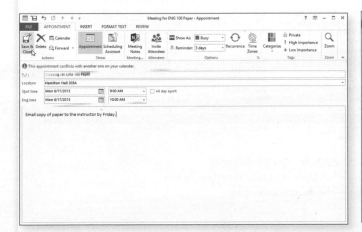 

4-17 Completed Pause & Practice 4-1

Creating and Using Meeting Requests

Suppose you are organizing a meeting within your company and you want to keep track of those who will be attending and those who are not able to make it to the meeting. Outlook provides you with a calendar feature that not only creates a calendar appointment but also sends this appointment to others via email and tracks whether or not they will be attending the meeting.

Meeting requests are used to invite others to a meeting. It can be either an appointment or event. The advantage of using a meeting request over an email to invite attendees to a meeting is that the recipients receive a meeting invitation and are given the options of *Accept, Tentative, Decline,* or *Propose New Time.* When the recipient accepts the meeting request, the meeting is automatically added to the recipient's Outlook calendar and a response is sent to the sender of the meeting request. The meeting request will automatically keep track of attendees' responses.

> ## MORE INFO
>
> Tracking responses for meeting requests only works when used in an Exchange environment.

Create and Send a Meeting Request

Create a meeting request by clicking on the **New Meeting** button on the *Home* tab or by selecting or opening an existing calendar item and clicking on the **Invite Attendees** button in the *Attendees* group (Figure 4-18).

> ## MORE INFO
>
> When sending a meeting request, provide a brief message and your name in the body.

4-18 *Invite Attendees* button

HOW TO: Create and Send a Meeting Request

1. Create a new meeting request by clicking on the **New Meeting** button in the *New* group on the *Home* tab. An existing appointment or event can be converted to a meeting by clicking on the **Invite Attendees** button in the *Attendees* group.

2. Click the **To** button to invite attendees. The *Select Attendees and Resources* dialog box opens (Figure 4-19).

3. Select attendees from your contacts. Attendees can be either *Required* or *Optional* to attend the meeting.

4. Click **OK** to close the dialog box.

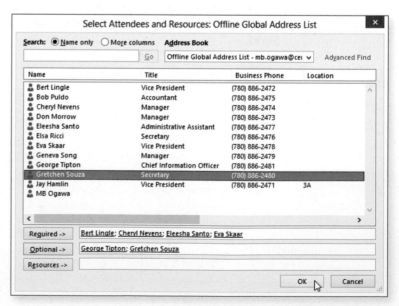

4-19 Select attendees

5. Fill in the *Subject, Location, Start* and *End* times (date and time), and any additional information needed in the body (Figure 4-20).
6. Click **Send** to send the meeting request.

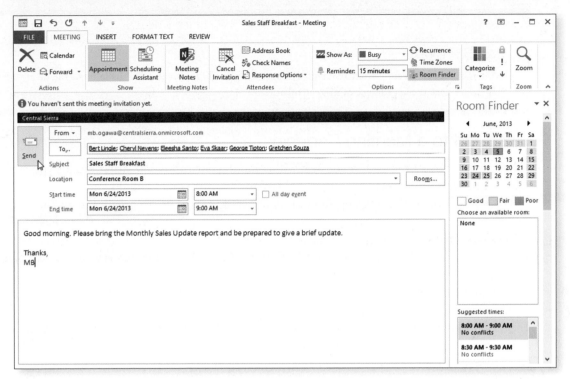

4-20 Filled meeting request

> **MORE INFO**
>
> When you open a new meeting request, it will always be an appointment. The meeting request can be changed to an event by clicking on the **All day event** check box.

> **ANOTHER WAY**
>
> **Ctrl+Shift+Q** opens a new meeting request.

A meeting can also be created directly from a received email. When you receive an email and need to create a meeting based upon the information in that email, you do not have to go to your calendar to create a new meeting. Create a new meeting from this email by clicking the **Reply with Meeting** button

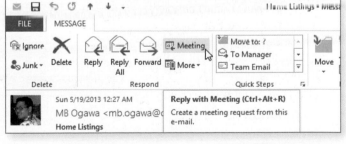

4-21 Create a meeting request from an email message

(**Meeting** button) in the *Respond* group on the *Message* tab (Figure 4-21). The contents of the email message are included in the body of the new meeting. You can add attendees and make any other necessary changes before sending the meeting request.

> ### MORE INFO
>
> When creating a meeting from an email message, it is a good idea to clean up the body of the meeting to enhance the appearance of this calendar item.

Respond to a Meeting Request

When you receive a meeting request, it will come to your Inbox like other emails you receive. The Inbox icon for a meeting request will look different than an email icon.

When you open the meeting request, it will look similar to an email, but in the *Respond* group you are given four additional options: *Accept, Tentative, Decline,* or *Propose New Time.* When one of these responses is selected, a dialog box is opened and you are given the following options: *Edit the Response Before Sending, Send the Response Now,* or *Do Not Send a Response.*

If you choose *Accept, Tentative,* or *Propose New Time,* the meeting request is removed from your Inbox and added to your calendar and a response email is sent to the meeting organizer. If you choose *Decline,* the meeting request is moved from your Inbox to the *Deleted Items* folder and a response is sent to the meeting organizer.

Calendar Preview inserts a snapshot of your calendar in the body of the meeting request so you can view existing calendar items on the day of the new meeting request. Double-clicking on the calendar preview will take you to your calendar.

HOW TO: Respond to a Meeting Request

1. Open the meeting request from your Inbox.

2. Click one of the response buttons in the *Respond* group: *Accept, Decline,* or *Tentative.*

3. Choose *Edit the Response Before Sending* or *Send the Response Now* (Figure 4-22).

   • If you choose *Edit the Response Before Sending,* the email opens and you are able to enter a response in the body of the email before sending.

   • If you choose *Send the Response Now,* the response is automatically sent to the meeting organizer.

4. Click **OK** to close the dialog box.

5. Click **Send** if necessary.

   • If you chose *Accept* or *Tentative,* the response is sent and the meeting request is removed from your Inbox and placed on your calendar.

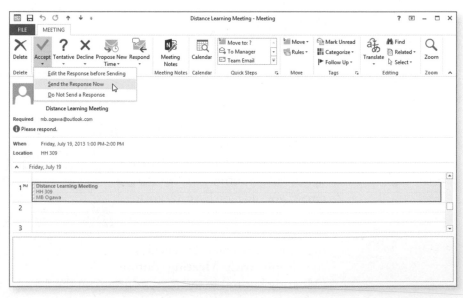

4-22 Respond to a meeting request

Propose a New Time to a Meeting Request

If you can't make a requested meeting at a particular date and time, you have the option of proposing a new time. When you click *Propose New Time* in the *Respond* group, you are given two options: *Tentative and Propose New Time* and *Decline and Propose New Time* (Figure 4-23). The *Propose New Time* dialog box opens. You can propose a new time by either dragging the meeting to a new time slot on the date and time timeline or enter a new date and time in the *Meeting start time* and *Meeting end time* boxes.

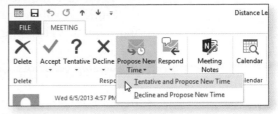

4-23 Propose a new meeting time

HOW TO: Propose a New Time for a Meeting

1. Open the meeting request from your Inbox.
2. Click the **Propose New Time** button and choose either *Tentative and Propose New Time* or *Decline and Propose New Time*. The *Propose New Time* dialog box opens (Figure 4-24).
3. Make changes to the date and/or time.
4. Click **Propose Time**. A *New Time Proposed* meeting request response opens. Notice the proposed changes below the subject line (Figure 4-25).
5. Type a brief message in the body.
6. Click **Send**. The response is sent, and the meeting request is removed from your Inbox and placed on your calendar.

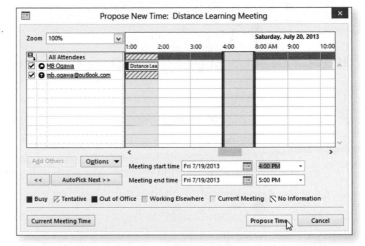

4-24 *Propose New Time* dialog box

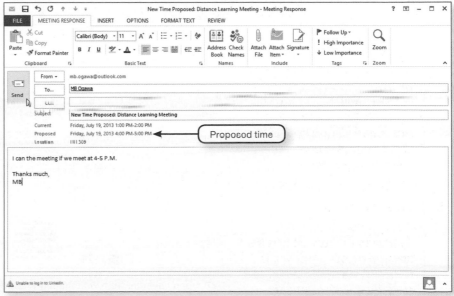

4-25 Proposed meeting time changes

Track Meeting Request Respondents

When you organize a meeting and send out a meeting request, you will receive meeting request responses in your Inbox (Figure 4-26). The responses will tell you the attendance status for each individual.

Outlook will track the responses of those individuals who have responded to your meeting request. When you open, from the calendar, the meeting request you created, Outlook displays a summary of responses in the *Info bar* above the *To* button. Also, you can obtain more detailed tracking information by clicking on the **Tracking** button in the *Show* group on the *Meeting* tab.

4-26 Meeting request acceptance in the Inbox

HOW TO: Track Meeting Request Respondents

1. On your calendar, open the meeting request you created (Figure 4-27).
2. The summary of responses received is displayed in the *Info bar.*
3. Click the **Tracking** button in the *Show* group on the *Meeting* tab. The body of the meeting request displays the names of those invited to the meeting, the attendance status (*Meeting Organizer, Required Attendance,* or *Optional Attendance*), and the response of each individual.
4. Click the **Appointment** button in the *Show* group to close the tracking and return to the meeting request.
5. Click the **X** in the upper right corner to close the meeting request.

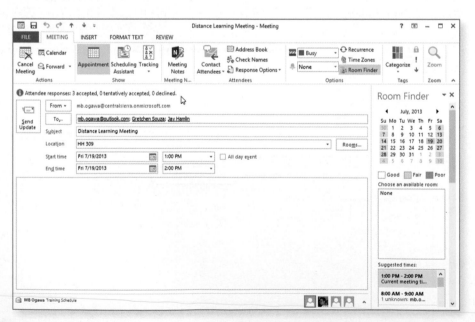

4-27 Open calendar item with meeting responses

4-28 Tracking status

Change and Update a Meeting Request

It is not uncommon for a meeting to have to be rescheduled to a different day, time, or location. Also, you might need to invite additional attendees to a previously scheduled meeting. The meeting organizer can make changes to the meeting and add attendees. When this is done, a ***meeting update*** must be sent to attendees. Attendees will again be given the option of accepting or declining the changes to the meeting.

HOW TO: Change and Update a Meeting Request

1. On your calendar, open the meeting request you created.

2. Make changes to the meeting date and time or location if necessary (Figure 4-29).

3. The **Contact Attendees** button in the *Attendees* group on the *Meeting* tab provides you with the options to add or remove attendees, send a new email message, or send a reply message.

4. After making any necessary changes, click **Send Update**. Changes will be saved to the meeting on your calendar.

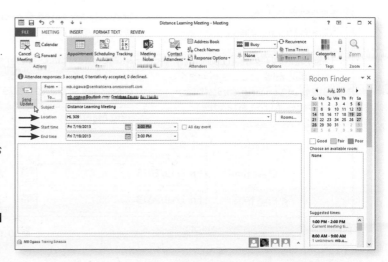

4-29 Updated meeting location and time

Cancel a Scheduled Meeting

Only the meeting organizer can cancel a meeting. When a meeting is canceled, all the attendees will receive a meeting cancellation email. The meeting will be removed from your calendar, and the attendees will have the option of removing the meeting from their calendars.

HOW TO: Cancel a Meeting

1. On your calendar, open the meeting request you created.
2. Click the **Cancel Meeting** button in the *Actions* group (Figure 4-30). The *Send Update* button becomes a *Send Cancellation* button, and there is a message in the *Info bar.*
3. Click the **Send Cancellation** button. The meeting request will be removed from your calendar, and all those invited to the meeting will receive an email notifying them of the meeting cancellation.

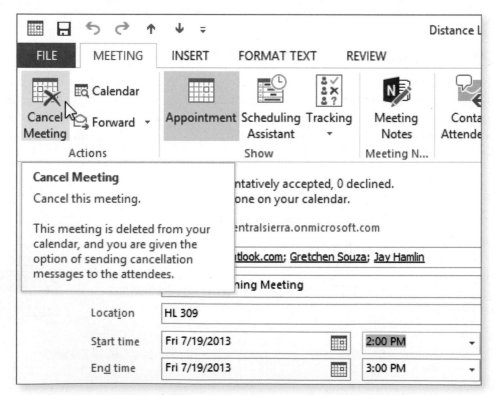

4-30 *Cancel Meeting* button

For this Pause & Practice project, you follow up with the two calendar items you created in *Pause & Practice 4-1.* You had an emergency at home, so you decide to send a meeting request to your instructor to apologize for not being able to make the meeting and to reschedule. You also send a meeting request to have lunch with your friend Lynne to give her the gift you purchased.

1. Click the **Calendar** button in the *Navigation* pane.

2. Create and send a meeting request to your instructor regarding the ENG 100 paper.
   a. Click the **New Meeting** button [*Home* tab, *New* group].
   b. Enter the following information for the new meeting request:
      To: Instructor's email address
      Subject: Reschedule meeting for ENG 100 paper
      Location: Hamilton Hall 303A
      Start time: One day after your initial meeting, 9:00 AM
      End time: One day after your initial meeting, 10:00 AM
      Body:
      Hi [instructor name],
      My apologies; an emergency came up at home and I need to reschedule our meeting. Are you available on Tuesday at the same time? Please use the meeting request response so that it can automatically be added to our calendars.
      Thanks much,
      [your name]
   c. Click the **Send** button.

3. Create and send a meeting request to Lynne regarding her birthday.
   a. Click the **New Meeting** button [*Home* tab, *New* group].
   b. Enter the following information for the new meeting request:
      To: A partner's email address
      Subject: Birthday Lunch
      Location: ARC Student Center Cafe
      Start time: July 17 of the current year at noon
      End time: July 17 of the current year at 1:00 PM
      Body:
      Hi Lynne,
      Are you available for lunch on your birthday? My treat; let's eat at the ARC Student Center Cafe. Use the meeting request response so that it can automatically be added to our calendars.
      [your name]
   c. Click the **Send** button.

4. Open the meeting request to Lynne that you received from your partner.

5. Propose a new meeting time.
   a. Click the **Propose New Time** button [*Meeting* tab, *Respond* group] and select **Tentative and Propose New Time**.
   b. Select **2:00 PM** as the meeting start time and **3:00 PM** as the meeting end time.
   c. Click the **Propose Time** button.
   d. In the body, type:
      Hi [partner name],
      Sorry, I have lunch plans with my mother. How about coffee at the ARC Student Center Café at 2:00 PM?
      Lynne
   e. Click the **Send** button.

6. Locate the message from your partner and open it.

7. Forward the message proposed time message from your partner to your instructor.
   a. Click the **Forward** button [*Meeting Request* tab, *Respond* group].
   b. Enter the following information in the message:
      To: Instructor's email address
      Cc: Your email address
      Subject: Outlook Pause & Practice 4-2
      Body: A short message indicating that you submitted your Pause & Practice project
   c. Click the **Send** button (Figure 4-31).

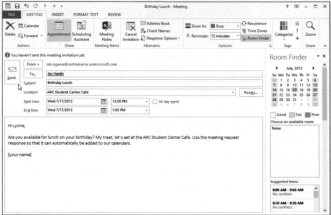

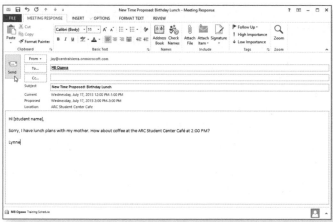

4-31 Completed Pause & Practice 4-2

Chapter Summary

4.1 Identify the different types of calendar items (p. O4-132).

- Unlike paper calendars, an Outlook calendar can be viewed by day, week, month, or other formats.
- You can receive reminders for appointments or events on your computer or mobile device.
- Categories can be used to group certain calendar items together.
- Calendar items can recur at regular intervals.
- Meeting requests can be used to invite others and track their responses.
- Calendars can be synchronized with phones and other mobile devices.
- There are three main types of calendar items: *appointments, events,* and *meeting requests.*
- An *appointment* is a calendar item that has a duration of less than 24 hours.
- *Events* are those calendar items that last for 24 hours or more.
- A *meeting request* is used to create a calendar item and invite others to this meeting.

4.2 Distinguish between different calendar views (p. O4-134).

- Calendars can be displayed in *Day, Week, Month,* or *Schedule* views.
- *Day view* displays the calendar one day at a time with the calendar broken into half-hour segments.
- *Week view* displays the calendar as a *Work Week* or *Week* and breaks the calendar into half-hour segments. The work week is Monday through Friday, while the week is Sunday through Saturday.
- *Month view* displays an entire month of the calendar.
- *Schedule view* displays your calendar horizontally in timeline view in the *Folder* pane.

4.3 Create and edit calendar items (p. O4-138).

- Appointments and events can include a *Subject, Location, Start time, End time,* and additional information in the body.
- Appointments can be converted to events by clicking the **All day event** check box.
- You can add reminders to appointments and events to alert you prior to their start times.
- Calendar items can be moved or copied.
- Recurring appointments or events can be used for items that occur on a regular schedule such as a weekly meeting or a birthday.
- You can drag and drop an email message to the *Calendar* button to create a new calendar item from an email message.

4.4 Create and use meeting requests (p. O4-144).

- *Meeting requests* are used to invite others to a meeting (appointment or event).
- Recipients of meeting requests can respond in the following ways: *Accept, Tentative, Decline,* or *Propose New Time.*
- You can reply to an email message with a meeting request.
- Selecting *Accept, Tentative,* and *Propose New Time* places the meeting time in your calendar.
- Outlook tracks your invitees' responses to your meeting request.
- You can update meeting requests and automatically send an updated message to all recipients.
- Canceling a meeting will delete it from your calendar.
- When you receive a meeting cancellation, the meeting will be marked as canceled in your calendar. You can manually delete the meeting from your calendar since it is not automatically removed with the cancellation.

Check for Understanding

In the **Online Learning Center** for this text (www.mhhe.com/office2013inpractice), there are a variety of resources that can be used to review the concepts covered in this chapter.

The following Online Learning Resources are available in the Online Learning Center:

- Multiple choice questions
- Short answer questions
- Matching exercises

Guided Project 4-1

For this project, you are an administrative assistant at Courtyard Medical Plaza. You manage calendars for several doctors and make appointments on the phone throughout the day. You use Outlook's calendar feature to keep the appointments organized. Today, you received two appointment requests from patients and record them in the calendar.
[Student Learning Outcomes 4.1, 4.2, 4.3]

Skills Covered in This Project

- Create a new appointment.
- Select start and end times.
- Edit the body of an appointment.
- Set a reminder.

---

1. Create a new appointment.
    a. Click the **Calendar** button in the *Navigation* pane.
    b. Select the next day on the calendar.
    c. Click the **New Appointment** button [*Home* tab, *New* group].
    d. Enter the following information for the new appointment:
       Subject: Jim Heely (Dr. Greg Lam)
       Location: Exam Room 1
       Start time: Tomorrow at 8:00 AM
       End time: Tomorrow at 9:00 AM
       Body: Sore throat, cough, fever, nausea
    e. Click the *Reminder* drop-down menu [*Appointment* tab, *Options* group].
    f. Select **5 minutes**.
    g. Click the **Save & Close** button.

2. Create a new appointment.
    a. Click the **New Appointment** button [*Home* tab, *New* group].
    b. Enter the following information for the new appointment:
       Subject: Janice Yoro (Dr. Shirley Louis)
       Location: Exam Room 3
       Start time: Next week Tuesday at 1:00 PM
       End time: Next week Tuesday at 2:00 PM
       Body: Annual check up
    c. Click the *Reminder* drop-down menu [*Appointment* tab, *Options* group].
    d. Select **5 minutes**.
    e. Click the **Save & Close** button.

3. Email the two calendar items to your instructor as Outlook items.
    a. Click the **Mail** button in the *Navigation* pane.
    b. Click the **New Email** button [*Home* tab, *New* group].
    c. Enter the following information in your message:
       To: instructor's email address
       Cc: your email address
       Subject: Outlook Guided Project 4-1

Body:
Hi [instructor name],
Attached are my calendar items for the Guided Project 4-1 exercise.
Sincerely,
[your name]

   d. Click the **Attach Item** button [*Message* tab, *Include* group] and select **Outlook Item**.

   e. Select the **Calendar** option and locate the two calendar items you created.

   f. Hold the **Ctrl** key and select the two calendar items and click **OK**.

   g. Click **Send** (Figure 4-32).

4-32 Completed Guided Project 4-1

Guided Project 4-2

For this project, you send meeting requests to two doctors to ensure they know when they are seeing the patients. Drs. Lam and Louis also indicated that they wanted to set up weekly meetings, so you create a recurring calendar item for the weekly meeting and send the request to both of them.
[Student Learning Outcomes 4.1, 4.2, 4.3, 4.4]

⟿Skills Covered in This Project

- Create a new appointment.
- Select start and end times.
- Edit the body of an appointment.

- Set a reminder.
- Set recurrence.
- Send a meeting request.

---

1. Send a meeting request to Dr. Lam for the upcoming appointment.
   a. Open the appointment with the subject *Jim Heely (Dr. Greg Lam)*.
   b. Click the **Invite Attendees** button [*Appointment* tab, *Attendees* group].
   c. Type a partner's email address in the *To* field.
   d. Click the **Send** button.

2. Send a meeting request to Dr. Louis for the upcoming appointment.
   a. Open the appointment with the subject *Janice Yoro (Dr. Shirley Louis)*.
   b. Click the **Invite Attendees** button [*Appointment* tab, *Attendees* group].
   c. Type a partner's email address in the *To* field.
   d. Click the **Send** button.

3. Create a new appointment.
   a. Click the **Calendar** button in the *Navigation* pane.
   b. Click the **New Appointment** button [*Home* tab, *New* group].
   c. Enter the following information for the new appointment:
      Subject: Weekly Doctors' Meeting
      Location: Conference Room
      Start time: Mondays at 3:00 PM
      End time: Mondays at 4:00 AM
      Body: See agenda sent by administrative assistant.
   d. Click the *Reminder* drop-down menu [*Appointment* tab, *Options* group].
   e. Select **30 minutes**.
   f. Click the **Invite Attendees** button [*Appointment* tab, *Attendees* group].
   g. Type a partner's email address in the *To* field.
   h. Click the **Save & Close** button.
   i. Figure 4-33 includes each of the appointments created.

4. Email the three meeting requests and to your instructor as Outlook items.
   a. Click the **Mail** button in the *Navigation* pane.
   b. Click the **New Email** button [*Home* tab, *New* group].
   c. Enter the following information in your message:
      To: Instructor's email address
      Cc: Your email address
      Subject: Outlook Guided Project 4-2
      Body:
      Hi [instructor name],
      Attached are my meeting requests for the Guided Project 4-2 exercise.
      Sincerely,
      [your name]
   d. Click the **Attach Item** button [*Message* tab, *Include* group] and select **Outlook Item**.
   e. Select the **Sent Items** option and locate the three meeting requests you sent.
   f. Hold the **Ctrl** key and select the three sent mail items and click **OK**.
   g. Click the **Send** button (Figure 4-33).

4-33 Completed Guided Project 4-2

Guided Project 4-3

For this project, you must cancel an appointment for Jim, who stated that he was feeling well enough not to come in. You must also reschedule Janice's annual appointment for the next day, as she just found out that she is in charge of snacks for her son's baseball game.
[Student Learning Outcomes 4.1, 4.2, 4.3, 4.4]

Skills Covered in This Project

- Cancel a meeting request.
- Respond to a meeting request.
- Update a meeting request.

- Accept a meeting request.
- Track meeting request responses.

---

1. Cancel Jim Heely's appointment and send the cancellation to Dr. Lam
   a. Open the appointment with the subject *Jim Heely (Dr. Greg Lam)*.
   b. Click the **Cancel Meeting** button [*Meeting* tab, *Actions* group].
   c. Click the **Send Cancellation** button.

2. Update Janice Yoro's appointment date.
   a. Open the appointment with the subject *Janice Yoro (Dr. Shirley Louis)*.
   b. In the start and end time fields, change the day to Wednesday (keep the same time).
   c. Click the **Send Update** button.

3. Accept the *Weekly Doctors'* meeting request you received.
   a. Open the email with the subject *Weekly Doctors' Meeting*.
   b. Click the **Accept** button [*Meeting* tab, *Respond* group] and select **Send the Response Now**.

4. Click your initial message to ensure you received a response from your partner.

5. Email the three meeting requests to your instructor as Outlook items.
   a. Click the **Mail** button in the *Navigation* pane.
   b. Click the **New Email** button [*Home* tab, *New* group].
   c. Enter the following information in your message:
      To: instructor's email address
      Cc: your email address
      Subject: Outlook Guided Project 4-3
      Body:
      Hi [instructor name],
      Attached are my meeting requests for the Guided Project 4-3 exercise.
      Sincerely,
      [your name]
   d. Click the **Attach Item** button [*Message* tab, *Include* group] and select **Outlook Item**.
   e. Select the **Sent Items** option and locate the meeting cancellation, updated time, and acceptance you sent.
   f. Hold the **Ctrl** key and select the three sent mail items and click **OK**.
   g. Click the **Send** button (Figure 4-34).

4-34 Completed Guided Project 4-3

Independent Project 4-4

For this project, you work as an insurance agent for Central Sierra Insurance (CSI). As an agent, you make and receive many calls to and from clients to set up meetings in person. You also collaborate with a team of insurance agents. You use Outlook's calendar to help you better organize your schedule. [Student Learning Outcomes 4.1, 4.2, 4.3]

Skills Covered in This Project

- Create a new appointment.
- Create a new event.
- Select start and end times.
- Edit the body of an appointment.
- Set a reminder.

1. Create the following appointments:

Subject	Location	Start time	End time	Body	Reminder
Strategic Planning	Conference Room A	Next week Friday, All day event	Next week Friday, All day event	Prepare slides	1 Day

(Continued)

Subject	Location	Start time	End time	Body	Reminder
Dorilyn Sharuma (New Client)	3A	Next week Monday, 9:00 AM	Next week Monday, 11:00 AM	New customer packet.	15 Minutes
Matthew Schmidt (client for 5 years)	3A	Next week Tuesday, 1:00 PM	Next week Tuesday, 1:30 PM	Client just got married. New insurance options.	30 Minutes
Janine Shephard (client for 3 years)	3A	Next week Monday, 2:00 PM	Next week Monday, 3:00 PM	Review current policy to see where she can lower payments.	30 Minute
Clint Howard (Manager)	Mario's Italian Restaurant	Next week Thursday, 12:00 PM	Next week Thursday, 1:30 PM	Lunch meeting about current clients.	2 Hours

2. Email the five calendar items you created to your instructor as email attachments.
   a. Include your email address in the *Cc* field.
   b. Add a short message indicating that the five Outlook calendar items are attached in the message.
   c. Change the subject of your message to **Outlook Independent Project 4-4** (Figure 4-35).

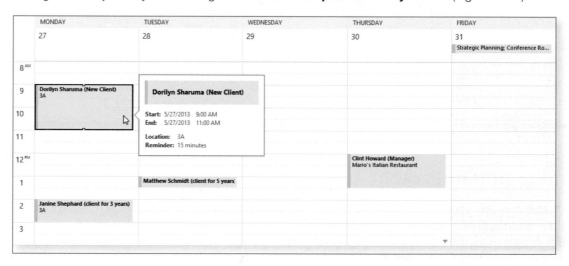

4-35 Completed Independent Project 4-4

Independent Project 4-5

For this project, you categorize all of the calendar items for CSI. You also send out meeting requests to others to ensure everyone is on the same page. You request that your colleague take one of your appointments, as you forgot that you had a doctor's appointment when you decided to meet with Janine because you did not centralize all of your personal and work appointments on one calendar. [Student Learning Outcomes 4.1, 4.2, 4.4]

Skills Covered in This Project

- Create a category.
- Apply categories to calendar items.

- Send meeting requests.
- Modify messages for meeting requests.

---

1. Create a new category called Central Sierra Insurance.

2. Apply the category to the five appointments you created in Independent Project 4-4.

3. Send the strategic planning event to a partner as a meeting request.

4. Send the *Clint Howard (Manager)* appointment as a meeting request to a partner.

5. Send the *Janine Shephard* meeting to a partner and request that he or she take the meeting for you. You forgot that you had a doctor's appointment at that time. Be sure to include a message indicating why you would like your colleague to meet with your client.

6. Email your instructor with your five calendar items and three meeting requests as attachments.
   a. Include your email address in the *Cc* field.
   b. Add a short message indicating that the five Outlook calendar items are attached in the message.
   c. Change the subject of your message to ***Outlook Independent Project 4-5*** (Figure 4-36).

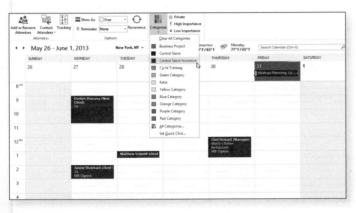

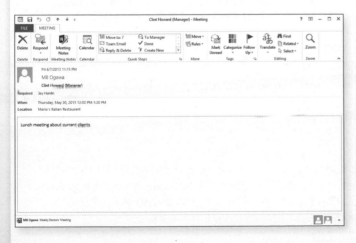

4-36 Completed Independent Project 4-5

Independent Project 4-6

For this project, you add your weekly sales meeting to your calendar. You also respond to the meeting requests you received.
[Student Learning Outcomes 4.1, 4.2, 4.3, 4.4]

Skills Covered in This Project

- Create a new appointment.
- Select start and end times.
- Edit the body of an appointment.
- Set a reminder.
- Set recurrence.

- Apply categories to calendar items.
- Respond to a meeting request.
- Update a meeting request.
- Accept a meeting request.
- Track meeting request responses.

---

1. Create a new appointment with the following information:
   Subject: Weekly Sales Meeting
   Location: Conference Room B
   Start time: Next week Thursday, 4:00 PM
   End time: Next week Thursday, 5:00 PM
   Reminder: 15 minutes
   Recurrence: Weekly with no end date
   Category: Central Sierra Insurance

2. Open the strategic planning event meeting request from your partner and accept it.

3. Open the *Clint Howard* meeting request and tentatively accept and propose a new time 11:30 AM to 1:00 PM. Indicate that you (Clint) have a 1:30 PM appointment.

4. Open the *Janine Shephard* meeting request and decline it. Indicate that you have another meeting at that time and that the sender should check with Chelsea.

5. Email your instructor with the *Weekly Sales Meeting* calendar item and three meeting responses as attachments.
   a. Include your email address in the *Cc* field.
   b. Add a short message indicating that the five Outlook calendar items are attached in the message.
   c. Change the subject of your message to **Outlook Independent Project 4-6** (Figure 4-37).

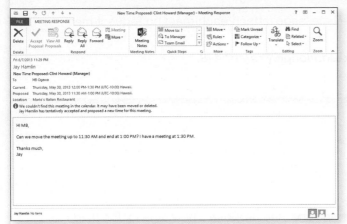
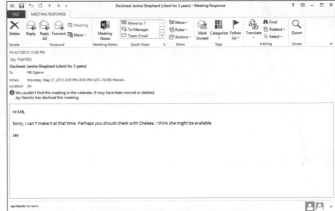

Challenge Project 4-7

Create a calendar for yourself based on your current school, work, and personal schedules for the semester. Be sure to include items such as classes, work, appointments, and events such as birthdays or anniversaries.
[Student Learning Outcomes 4.1, 4.2, 4.3]

- Include your class schedule for the semester.
- Include your work schedule if applicable.
- Include events such as birthdays or anniversaries.
- Use *Recurrence* when applicable.
- Email the calendar to your instructor as an email attachment. Specify the dates to include within the current semester.
- Change the subject of your message to **Outlook Challenge Project 4-7.**

Challenge Project 4-8

Modify the calendar you created in Challenge 4-7 by adding categories and sending out meeting requests. Create at least three categories (school, work, personal). You can add additional categories, such as clubs if it fits your schedule. Send out at least three meeting requests to a partner in class.
[Student Learning Outcomes 4.1, 4.2, 4.3, 4.4]

- Create at least three categories for your calendar and apply them to each item.
- Set up at least three meetings with a partner in class and send the meeting requests.
- Email the calendar to your instructor as an email attachment. Specify the dates to include within the current semester.

- Attach each of the meeting requests to your email message (attach each meeting request message as an Outlook item).
- Change the subject of your message to **Outlook Challenge Project 4-8.**

Challenge Project 4-9

Modify the calendar you created in Challenge Project 4-8 by responding to meeting requests. For the three meeting requests you received, accept one, decline one, and propose a new time for the third one. [Student Learning Outcomes 4.1, 4.2, 4.4]

- Respond to the three meeting requests you received in Challenge Project 4-8.
- Accept one request, decline a request, and propose a new time for the final request.
- Attach each of the meeting request responses to your email message (attach each meeting request message as an Outlook item).
- Change the subject of your message to **Outlook Challenge Project 4-9.**

Tasks, To-Do Items, and User Interface

OUTLOOK

CHAPTER OVERVIEW

So far in this text we have covered the Outlook working environment, and three of the four major components of Outlook: Email, Contacts, and Calendar. The fourth major component of Outlook is **Tasks.**

Many people have a list of tasks to accomplish on any given day or week and enjoy the satisfaction of crossing off tasks that they have completed. Outlook provides a tool that can be used to keep track of your daily tasks. The Tasks feature in Outlook provides you with a place to keep a running list of tasks to be completed. As with calendar items and contacts, Outlook Tasks provides users with many electronic benefits not available on a paper list of tasks, such as electronic reminders, categories, and recurrence. Outlook also allows you to customize the user interface to better meet your needs and preferences.

STUDENT LEARNING OUTCOMES (SLOs)

After completing this chapter, you will be able to:

SLO 5.1 Distinguish between tasks and To-Do items (p. O5-166).

SLO 5.2 Create and use tasks in Outlook (p. O5-167).

SLO 5.3 Understand and customize the *Tasks* views and the *To-Do bar* (p. O5-178).

SLO 5.4 Assign tasks to and accept tasks from other Outlook users (p. O5-180).

SLO 5.5 Customize the user interface in Outlook to better meet your needs (p. O5-187).

CASE STUDY

For the Pause & Practice projects, you are in the early stages of working on a group project for a class you are enrolled in. You take the lead and create tasks for yourself to complete to prepare the group to work together. However, you forgot about a doctor's appointment and need to assign a task to a colleague to help you complete it before its due date.

Pause & Practice 5-1: You create projects based on a class project. You initially set up a handful of tasks to prepare for group work. With a partner, you also email each other and create a task from an email message.

Pause & Practice 5-2: You forgot about a doctor's appointment and assign a task to a group member. You also accept tasks, send updates, and complete a task.

Pause & Practice 5-3: You want to customize Outlook to make it fit your working style. You do this by making Outlook Today your default start screen, add your Inbox to your *Favorites,* and add the *Print* button to the *Quick Access Toolbar.*

O5-165

Understanding Tasks and To-Do Items

Tasks and *To-Do items* are closely related, yet there are some distinct differences. Tasks are those individual items that are kept in the *Tasks* area of Outlook and also appear in the list of To-Do items.

To-Do items are a much broader category of Outlook items. Any email or contact that has a *Flag for Recipient* or includes a *Follow Up* flag will also appear in the **To-Do List** and **To-Do bar.** So, To-Do items are the broader umbrella category under which tasks are included.

Tasks

A task can be created in Outlook to remind you to make a follow-up phone call for an upcoming fundraiser or to order theater tickets for "Wicked", when they go on sale Wednesday. When a task is created, Outlook automatically marks the task with a *Follow Up* flag and the task appears in both the *Task List* (Figure 5-1) and the *To-Do List*.

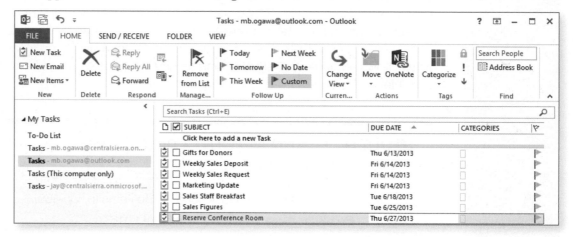

5-1 *Task List*

Task List

The **Task List** is a list of the tasks you have created in Outlook. This list appears in the *Folder* pane when you select *Tasks* in the *My Tasks* area of the *Navigation* pane. The *Task List* includes only tasks and does not include other flagged items in Outlook.

Flagged Items

There might be times when you need to take additional action on an email you received or with a client in your *Contacts*. In addition to a task, which is automatically flagged in Outlook, emails and contacts can also be flagged for follow up. This feature in Outlook provides you with the option of flagging these Outlook items as an additional reminder. When an item is flagged, it will appear as a To-Do item.

To-Do List

As mentioned previously, the **To-Do List** (Figure 5-2) is a broader list of items than the *Task List*. The *To-Do List* includes all Outlook items that have been marked with a flag, which includes tasks, emails, and contacts. The *To-Do List* is available in the *My Tasks* area in the *Navigation* pane of *Tasks*. When the *To-Do List* is selected, the list of To-Do items appears at the right in the *Folder* pane.

5-2 *To-Do List*

> ### MORE INFO
>
> Depending on the types of email accounts you have set up, you might have more than one *Task List* in the *My Tasks* area of the *Navigation* pane. Also, you can create additional task folders.

> ### MORE INFO
>
> The icon for each item in the *To-Do List* shows you what type of Outlook item it is.

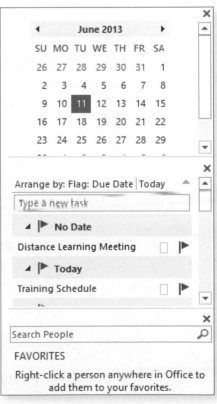

To-Do Bar

The **To-Do bar** (Figure 5-3) is the area of Outlook to the right of the *Folder* pane in Outlook and can be displayed in all the Outlook windows (e.g., *Mail, Calendar, Contacts, Tasks, Notes,* and *Journal*). The *To-Do bar* provides you with a date navigator (calendar thumbnail), upcoming calendar items, and To-Do items. The *To-Do bar* can be customized to show different amounts of information and can be minimized on the right or turned off (*View* tab, *Layout* group, *To-Do Bar* button).

Creating Tasks

Creating a task is similar to creating a new email or calendar item and can be accomplished in a couple of different ways. Some of the benefits of Outlook tasks, compared to a paper list of tasks, are the ability to include additional details with the task, start and due dates, reminders, and recurrence.

5-3 *To-Do bar*

Tasks can also be created from existing information in Outlook. If you receive an email about an upcoming fundraiser for which you are involved, you can create a task from the information included in the email. This can also be done from a calendar item.

Create a New Task

The quickest way to create a new task is to simply type the subject of the task in the *Click here to add a new Task* area above the list of tasks in the *Folder* pane.

HOW TO: Create a New Task in the Folder Pane

1. Click the **Tasks** button in the *Navigation* pane.
2. Click the **Tasks** folder in the *My Tasks* area of the *Navigation* pane.
3. Click the **Click here to add a new Task** area above the *Task List* in the *Folder* pane (Figure 5-4).

5-4 Create a new task in the *Folder* pane

4. Type the subject of the task.
5. Press **Tab** to move to the next field.
   - **Shift+Tab** will move you back one field at a time.
   - Not all task fields are available for editing in the *Task List*.
6. Press **Enter** to complete creating the new task. The task will be listed in the *Task List* in the *Folder* pane.

Another way to create a new task is by clicking on the *New Task* button on the *Home* tab, which opens a new task in a new window. When the new task opens, you can type in a subject and any additional information you desire.

HOW TO: Create a New Task

1. Click the **Tasks** button in the *Navigation* pane.
2. Click the **Tasks** folder in the *My Tasks* area of the *Navigation* pane.
3. Click the **New Task** button in the *New* group on the *Home* tab.
4. Type the subject of the task.
5. Press **Tab** to move to the next field to add the *Start* and *Due* dates and additional information as desired.
   - Press **Save & Close** on the *Task* tab to complete creating the new task (Figure 5-5). The task will be listed in the *Task List* in the *Folder* pane.

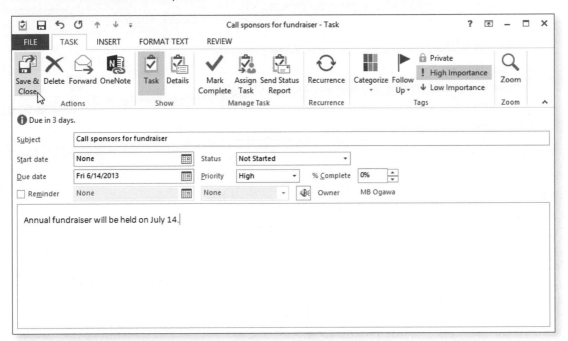

5-5 New *Task* window

> **ANOTHER WAY**
>
> Press **Ctrl+N** to create a new task while in the *Tasks* area. A new task can also be created anywhere in Outlook by pressing **Ctrl+Shift+K.**

> **ANOTHER WAY**
>
> A new task can also be created in the *To-Do bar* by clicking in the **Type a new task** area.

Edit a Task

A task can be edited to include additional information while creating a new task, or an existing task can be opened (by double-clicking on a task in the *Task List* in the *Folder* pane) to add additional information or edit existing information.

A task can include a start date and due date. These dates can be typed in or you can click the drop-down arrow (Figure 5-6) to the right of *Start date* or *Due date* and select from the calendar thumbnail.

The **Status** of the task can be set to *Not Started, In Progress, Completed, Waiting on someone else,* or *Deferred* (Figure 5-7). By default a new task status is set at *Not Started*.

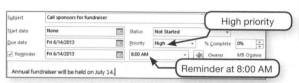

5-7 Task *Status*

The **Priority** of a task can be set to *High, Normal,* or *Low* (Figure 5-8). The priority setting in a task is similar to the **Importance** settings in an email or a calendar item. The default priority setting on a new task is *Normal*.

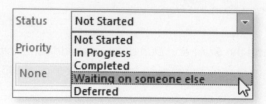

5-6 Task *Start date*

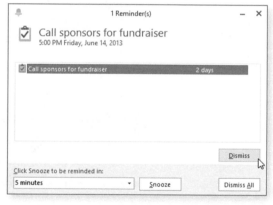

5-8 Reminder and high priority set for task

An electronic **Reminder** (Figure 5-8) can be set to automatically remind you when a task is coming due by clicking the **Reminder** checkbox. The reminder date can be either typed in or selected from the thumbnail calendar when you click the drop-down arrow to the right of the date field. A specific time can also be set.

This reminder opens a reminder window (Figure 5-9) on your computer screen on the date and time you set. You are given the options of *Dismiss All, Open Item, Dismiss,* or *Snooze*. The *Dismiss* button can be used to dismiss the reminder, or the *Dismiss All* button can be used to dismiss the reminder for all items if there is more than one reminder in the reminder list. The task can be opened to view the task specifics, or you can snooze the task for a certain amount of time, after which, the reminder will pop up again on your computer screen.

5-9 Reminder window

> **MORE INFO**
>
> It is not necessary to include a reminder on all items. Include reminders on only those for which you feel a reminder is really important. Reminders can become annoying if they are constantly popping up on your computer screen.

Also, within a task there are other task options available in the *Tags* group on the *Task* tab.

By default, a **Follow Up flag** is set for each new task created based upon the due date of the task. This flag can be changed and a different flag selected from the preset flags, or a custom flag can be created and set for a task (Figure 5-10). These custom flags are similar to those used for emails.

![Call sponsors for fundraiser - Task window showing the Task ribbon with Follow Up flag dropdown open]

5-10 *Follow Up* flag option

    Categories can be used to group tasks (or other Outlook items) by a common category. If you have a list of tasks to be completed for an upcoming fundraiser, a "Fundraiser" category can be created and all tasks pertaining to this fundraiser can be assigned to this category. Tasks can then be viewed by category to show all the tasks grouped and listed by their category.

    A task can also be marked as ***Private.*** This marking does not change any aspect of this task for you, the owner of the task, but rather this feature is important when using Delegates in Outlook. ***Delegates*** are those individuals with whom you share or give permission to some of the areas of your Outlook, such as Calendar or Tasks.

> **MORE INFO**
>
> Categories were briefly introduced in Chapter 2 and will be covered more thoroughly in chapters 8, 9, and 10.
>
> Delegates will be covered in Chapter 9.

Attach a File or an Outlook Item

Another distinct advantage of Outlook Tasks as compared to a paper list of tasks is the ability to attach or include additional resources with a task. If you were creating a task for an upcoming fundraising event, you might want to attach a contact record, an Excel spreadsheet, or an email as a reference and additional information for this task that is to be completed.

    In addition to being able to type additional information in the body of the task, you can also use ***Attach File,*** which could include attachments, such as Word or Excel documents, pictures, or most any other type of attachments you could include in an email. You can also attach an ***Outlook Item*** (Figure 5-11) or a ***Business Card,*** which could include other Outlook items such as a contact record, an email, or a calendar item.

5-11 Attach *Outlook Item* button

HOW TO: Attach a File or an Outlook Item to a Task

1. Open an existing task.
2. Click the **Insert** tab.
3. In the *Include* group, click either *Attach File, Outlook Item,* or *Business Card.* The *Insert* dialog box opens.
4. Browse to the file or Outlook item to be attached or included in the task.
5. Select the files or Outlook items (Figure 5-12).
6. Click *OK* (for *Outlook Item* or *Business Card*) or *Insert* (for *Attach File*). The files or items will be attached to the task.
7. Click **Save & Close** to save and close the task.

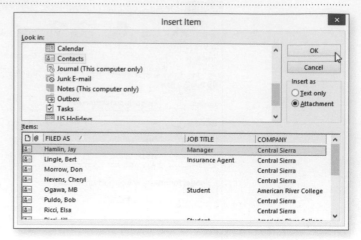

5-12 Select an Outlook item

> **MORE INFO**
>
> A signature can also be included in the body of a task, which might be useful when assigning a task to another Outlook user. Assigning tasks will be covered later in this chapter.

Mark a Task as Complete

Outlook gives you the satisfaction of being able to cross off items on your *Task List* when they are marked as complete. When a task is marked as complete, it remains in your *Task List*, but a line is drawn through it and it is grayed out.

An item can be marked as complete in a number of different ways. When a task is open, it can be marked as completed in the following ways:

- Click the **Mark Complete** button (Figure 5-13) in the *Manage Task* group on the *Task* tab. The task will automatically close, and it will be marked as complete in the *Task List*.

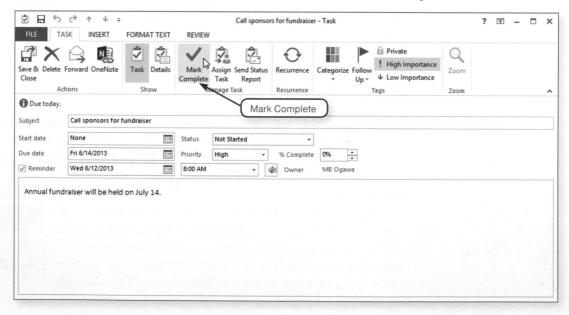

5-13 Mark a task as complete

- Click **Completed** in the *Status* drop-down menu, and then click **Save & Close**.
- In the *% Complete* box, type 100 and click **Save & Close**.

From the *Task List* in the *Folder* pane, a task can be marked as complete in the following ways:

- In the *Task List*, click the **Completed** check box to the left of the task subject (Figure 5-14).
- Right-click the task in the *Task List* and choose **Mark Complete**.
- Select the task in the *Task List* in the *Folder* pane, and click the **Mark Complete** button in the *Current View* group on the *Home* tab.

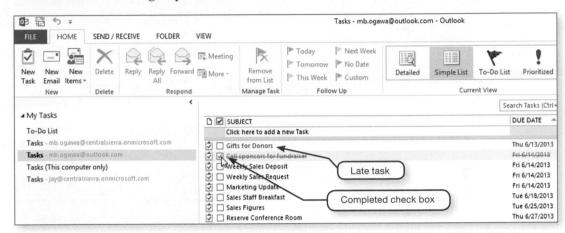

5-14 Completed and late tasks

> **ANOTHER WAY**
>
> In the *To-Do bar*, click on the flag of a task or a To-Do item to mark it as complete.

> **MORE INFO**
>
> An overdue task (see Figure 5-14) will by default appear in red in the *Task List, To-Do List, and To-Do bar*.

Recurring Task

There are times when you have a task that needs to be completed on a regular basis. It could be taking out the trash every Monday night or making a weekly sales deposit at the bank. Rather than having to create a new task each time, Outlook provides a way for you to do this by creating a recurring task.

Recurring tasks are similar to recurring calendar items in that you can specify the recurrence interval (daily, weekly, monthly, or yearly) for the task. The unique aspect of a recurring task is that the task will regenerate itself (i.e., create a new recurring task) once the task is marked as complete. On a recurring calendar item, the recurring item will show up on the calendar every time it recurs, while a recurring task item will only show the current task. The task icon for a recurring task is different than for a regular task.

HOW TO: Create a Recurring Task

1. Create a new task or open an existing task.
2. Click the **Recurrence** button in the *Recurrence* group on the *Task* tab (Figure 5-15). The *Task Recurrence* dialog box opens (Figure 5-16).
3. Set the **Recurrence pattern.**
4. Set the **Range of recurrence.**
5. Click **OK.**

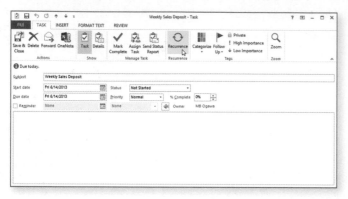

5-15 *Recurrence* button

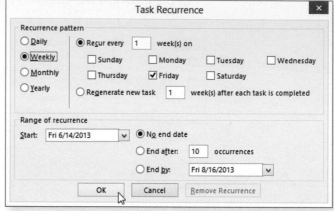

5-16 *Task Recurrence* dialog box

> ### ANOTHER WAY
>
> When a task is open, **Ctrl+G** opens the *Task Recurrence* dialog box.

To regenerate a recurring task, mark the existing recurring task as complete and the recurring task will automatically regenerate itself.

HOW TO: Mark a Recurring Task as Complete

1. Open the recurring task.
2. Click the **Mark Complete** button in the *Manage Task* group on the *Task* tab. The open task will automatically close and regenerate itself in the *Task List* in the *Folder* pane (Figure 5-17).

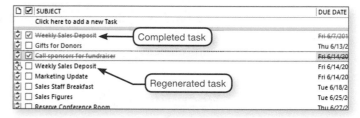

5-17 Completed recurring tasks

> ### ANOTHER WAY
>
> A task can be marked as complete by either clicking on the **Completed** check box for the task in the *Folder* pane or by opening the task and choosing **Completed** in the *Status* drop-down menu.

Create a Task from an Email

There may be times when you receive an email that has some information upon which you must take some action. An email can easily be converted to a task by dragging the email from the list of emails in the *Folder* pane to the *Tasks* button in the *Navigation* pane. The original email will remain in your Inbox.

When this is done, a new task is opened. The subject of the task is the same as the subject of the email, and the body of the email is included in the body of the task. The body of the task also includes the header information (*From, Sent, To,* etc.) at the top of the body of the new task.

The body of the email can be edited to include only the pertinent information, and you can also edit the task to include any additional options such as *Start date, Due date,* or *Reminder.*

HOW TO: Create a Task from an Email

1. Click the **Mail** button in the *Navigation* pane.

2. In the list of emails in the *Folder* pane, click the email to be converted to a task.

3. Drag it to the *Tasks* button in the *Navigation* pane (a small box will appear below the pointer when dragging the email to the *Tasks* button) and release the pointer (Figure 5-18). A new task opens (Figure 5-19).

4. Make any necessary editing changes to the new task.

5. Click **Save & Close.**

5-18 Drag an email to the *Tasks* button to create a new task

> ### ANOTHER WAY
>
> You can also select an email, click the **Move** button in the *Move* group, and choose **Tasks.** When you do this, a new task opens and the entire email message will be an attachment to the task.
>
> Remember when using this method that the email message will no longer be in your list of email messages but will be moved to your *Deleted Items* folder.

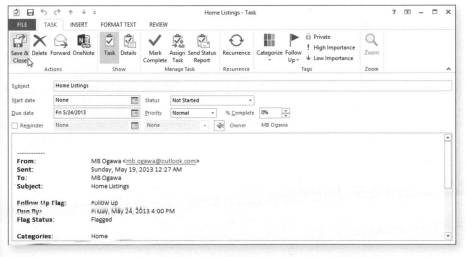

5-19 New task from email

Create a Task from a Calendar Item

There are times when you may need to complete a task prior to an upcoming appointment or event on your calendar. A task can be created from an existing calendar item in a similar fashion as creating a task from an email.

Similar to when an email is converted to a task, the subject of the calendra item will be the subject of the new task. The date of the calendar item will be the due date of the task, and the body of the task will include information from the calendar item (Figure 5-20).

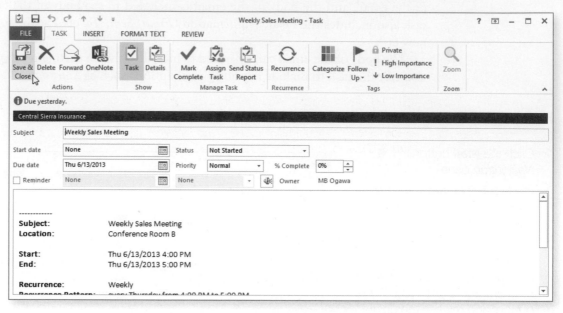

5-20 New task from calendar item

PAUSE & PRACTICE: OUTLOOK 5-1

In this Pause & Practice project, you create projects based on a class project. You initially set up a handful of tasks to prepare for group work. With a partner, you email each other and create a task from an email message.

1. Create a new task.
    a. Click the **Tasks** button in the *Navigation* pane.
    b. Click the **Tasks** folder in the *My Tasks* area of the *Navigation* pane.
    c. Click the **New Task** button in the *New* group on the *Home* tab.
    d. Enter the following information for the new task:
        Subject: Create email list for BUS project
        Start date: Today's date
        Due date: Tomorrow's date
        Reminder: Tomorrow's date at 9:30 AM
        Priority: High
        Message: Collect group email addresses
    e. Click the **Save & Close** button.

2. Email a partner in class to request his or her phone number.

3. Create a new task based on the email message you received regarding the phone number request.
    a. Select the email message your partner sent you regarding the phone number request.
    b. Click and drag the message to the *Tasks* button on the *Navigation* pane.
    c. In the new task window, edit the task in the following way:

Subject: Do not change
Start date: Today's date
Due date: Two days from today
Reminder: Two days from today's date at 9:00 A.M
Priority: High
Message: Edit contacts to include phone numbers

   d. Click the **Save & Close** button.

4. Edit the task with the subject *Create email list for BUS project* to be 50 percent complete.
   a. Double-click the task to open it.
   b. Type 50% in the *% Complete* text box.
   c. Click the **Save & Close** button.

5. Create a new task to email a meeting agenda the day before each meeting.
   a. Click the **New Task** button in the *New* group on the *Home* tab.
   b. Enter the following information for the new task:
     Subject: Create and email meeting agenda
     Start date: None
     Due date: The upcoming Tuesday
     Message: Develop agenda based on previous meeting
   c. Click the **Recurrence** button [*Task* tab, *Recurrence* group].
   d. Set the recurrence to be every Tuesday with no end date.
   e. Click the **OK** button.
   f. Click the **Save & Close** button.

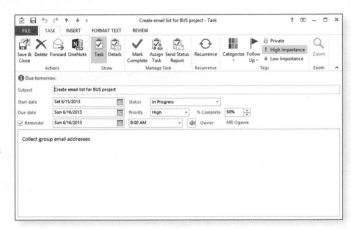

6. Email the three tasks to your instructor as Outlook items.
   a. Click the **Mail** button in the *Navigation* pane.
   b. Click the **New Email** button [*Home* tab, *New* group].
   c. Enter the following information in your message:
     To: Instructor's email address
     Cc: Your email address
     Subject: Outlook Pause & Practice 5-1
     Body: Hi [instructor name],
     Attached are my Outlook items for the Pause & Practice 5-1 exercise.
     Sincerely,
     [your name]
   d. Click the **Attach Item** button [*Message* tab, *Include* group] and select **Outlook Item.**
   e. Select the **Tasks** option and locate the three tasks you created.
   f. Hold the **Ctrl** key and select the three tasks and click **OK.**
   g. Click **Send** (Figure 5-21).

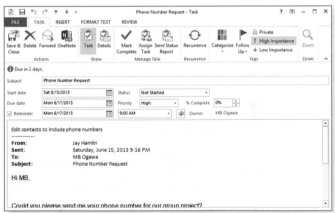

5-21 Completed Pause & Practice 5-1

Viewing Tasks and To-Do Items

Another advantage to using Outlook Tasks as opposed to using a paper list of to-do items is that tasks can be grouped and viewed in a variety of ways. Outlook provides you with many different preset views for grouping and viewing tasks in the *Folder* pane.

Task Views

The different task views are available on both the *Home* and *View* tabs, and you can easily change from one view to another by selecting the drop-down arrow in the *Current View* group on the *Home* tab (Figure 5-22) or by clicking the *Change View* button in the *Current View* group on the *View* tab.

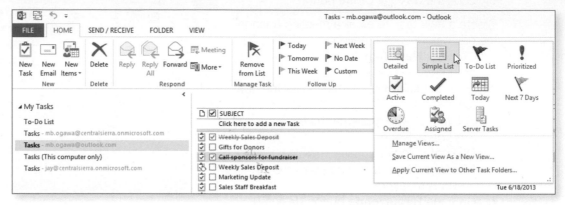

5-22 Change how you view tasks

The preset Task views include:

- *Detailed*
- *Simple List*
- *To-Do List*
- *Prioritized*
- *Active*
- *Completed*
- *Today*
- *Next 7 Days*
- *Overdue*
- *Assigned*
- *Server Tasks*

> **MORE INFO**
>
> Preset views throughout Outlook can be customized, and new views can be created. This topic will be covered in Chapters 8, 9, and 10.

Reading Pane

Just as for email, Outlook provides a *Reading* pane for tasks, which displays the contents of the selected task. The *Reading* pane can be displayed to the right or at the bottom of the *Folder* pane, or it can be turned off (Figure 5-23).

The size of the *Reading* pane can be adjusted by clicking and dragging on the right or left edge of the pane when it is displayed on the right. When the *Reading* pane is displayed at the bottom, the size can be adjusted by dragging the top edge up or down.

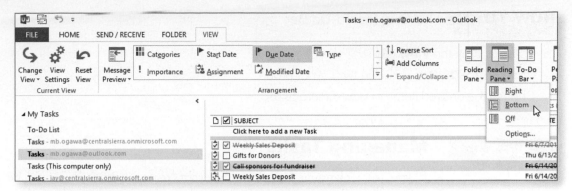

5-23 *Reading* pane options

Tasks in Calendar Views

One of the many advantages of using Outlook is the interconnectedness of the different Outlook components. An example of this is how tasks are connected to the calendar. When you are using your calendar in Outlook, the current tasks are displayed at the bottom of the *Day* and *Week* views in the **Daily Task List** (Figure 5-24), but not in *Month* view. You can turn this feature on or off by selecting an option from the **Daily Task List** button [*View* tab, *Layout* group].

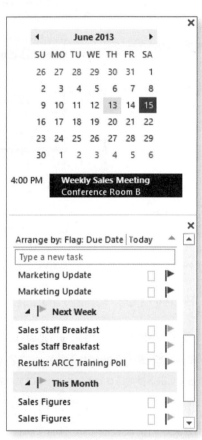

5-24 *Daily Task List*

5-25 *To-Do bar*

Customize the To-Do Bar

The *To-Do bar* (Figure 5-25) provides you with a summary of both your calendar and flagged items in Outlook. It is displayed to the right of the Outlook working environment. The *To-Do bar* has four components: **Date Navigator, Appointments, Task List,** and **People.** The *Task List* includes tasks and flagged items but does not include completed items.

In the *Layout* group on the *View* tab, you are given options for the items to be displayed in the *To-Do bar: Calendar, People, Tasks,* and *Off.* Drag the left edge of the *To-Do bar* to the right or left to adjust its width. You can customize the *To-Do bar* by removing any of the existing components or adjusting the amount of content to be shown.

HOW TO: View Items in the To-Do Bar

1. In *Tasks,* click the **View** tab.
2. Click the **To-Do Bar** button in the *Layout* group.
3. Choose the desired items to view (Figure 5-26).

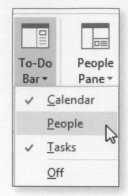

5-26 *To-Do Bar* options

 SLO 5.4 ## Managing Tasks

If you were planning an upcoming event, most likely there would be many tasks to be accomplished prior to the event to ensure success. Each of these jobs could be set up as individual tasks. Others would often be responsible for completing some of the various tasks. Another advantage of Outlook Tasks is its ability to assign tasks to others and track the progress and completion of these tasks.

> **MORE INFO**
>
> Assigning and tracking tasks is available only when using Outlook in an Exchange environment.

Assign a Task

When a task is assigned to another Outlook user, the task request becomes similar to an email. In addition to the other task fields, *To* and *Send* buttons appear on the task request. The *To* button is used to add an Outlook recipient, and the *Send* button is used to send the task request as an email.

HOW TO: Assign a Task

1. Create a new task or open an existing task.
2. Click the **Assign Task** button (Figure 5-27) in the *Manage Task* group on the *Task* tab. A task request email opens.
3. Click the **To** button and choose a recipient.
4. Include a brief message in the body of the task request.
5. Click **Send** (Figure 5-28).

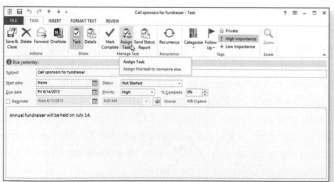

5-27 *Assign Task* button

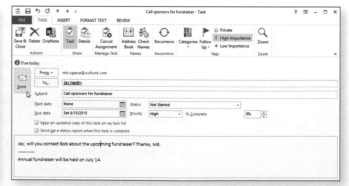

5-28 Assign task to a recipient

> **ANOTHER WAY**
>
> A new task request can be opened anywhere in Outlook by pressing **Ctrl+Shift+U.**

> **MORE INFO**
>
> Assign a task request to only one recipient to ensure responsibility that a task is completed. If multiple individuals are to be assigned a task, think about how you can break the task into smaller parts to assign individually. Also, always include a brief message in the body of the task request.

Accept a Task Request

When a task is assigned to another Outlook user, it is received in the user's Inbox and looks similar to an email. When the recipient opens the task request, he or she has the option to either accept or decline the task request.

When the task request is either accepted or declined, the recipient again has two options: *Edit the response before sending* or *Send the response now*. If *Edit the response before sending* is chosen, the task request recipient will be able to type a message to the task originator before sending the response. If *Send the response now* is chosen, the response to the task request is automatically sent.

When the task request has been accepted and the response has been sent, the task request is removed from the recipient's Inbox and placed in his or her *Task List*. The person accepting the task request is now the owner of this task.

HOW TO: Accept a Task Request

1. Click the **Mail** button in the *Navigation* pane.
2. In your Inbox, open the task request message.
3. Choose **Accept** (Figure 5-29). An *Accepting Task* dialog box opens.
4. Select **Edit the response before sending** (Figure 5-30).

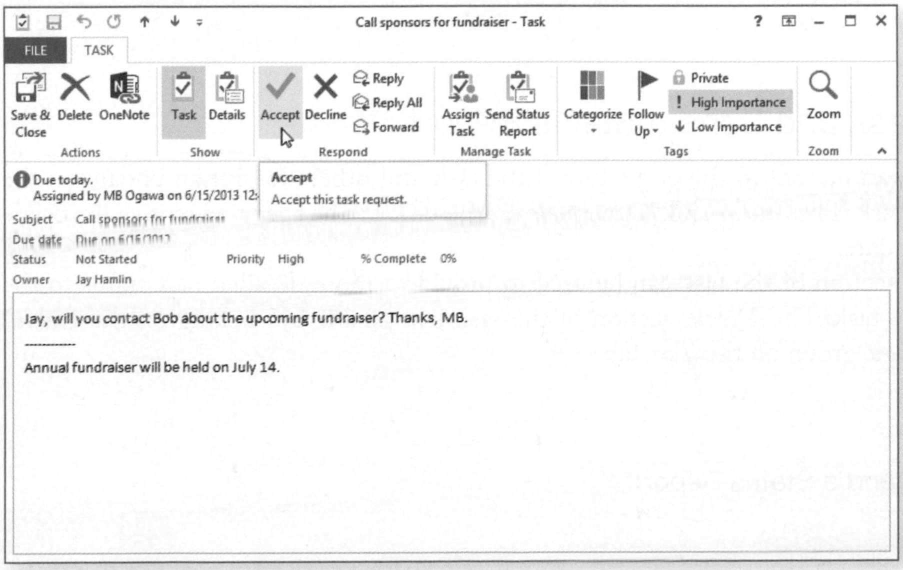

5-29 ***Accept* task button**

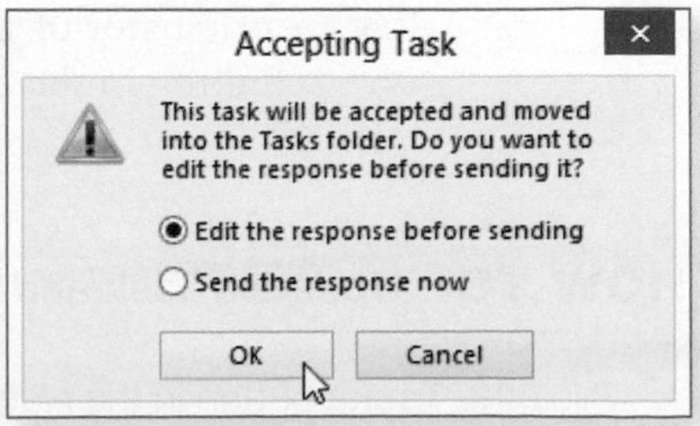

5-30 ***Accepting Task* dialog box**

5. Press **OK** to close the dialog box. The task request response opens, and you can type a response in the body.

6. Press **Send** (Figure 5-31). The task request is removed from your Inbox and moved to your *Task List*. The originator of the task will receive a *Task Accepted* message from you.

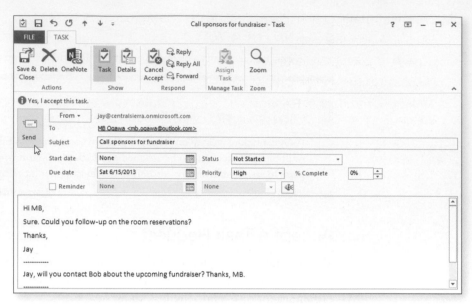

5-31 Completed task response

Task Icons

Different icons are used to help you distinguish between tasks requested, tasks accepted, and tasks declined. These icons will be displayed on your task request emails in your Inbox.

Task Icons

Icon	Icon Name and Description
	Task Request. The task request will be in the recipient's Inbox, and it will have the task icon with a hand at the bottom, indicating that the task is being handed off or assigned, and an envelope icon at the top.
	Task Accepted. When a task recipient accepts a task from you, you receive a *Task Accepted* message in your Inbox. The icon has the task pad with a hand at the bottom and a check at the top.
	Task Declined. When a task recipient declines a task from you, you receive a *Task Declined* message in your Inbox. The icon has the task pad with a hand at the bottom and a red X at the top.

Update a Task and Send a Status Report

A status report can be sent to the originator of the task and others to give an update on the progress of this task. The **Status** and **% Complete** on the task can be specified to give the originator a status update.

The **Details** section of the task can be used to provide a more detailed task status to the originator of the task. The *Details* section of the task is available by clicking on the *Details* button in the *Show* group on the *Task* tab.

HOW TO: Update a Task and Send a Status Report

1. Click the **Tasks** button in the *Navigation* pane.
2. Open the accepted task in your *Task List*.

3. Click the **Details** button (Figure 5-32) in the *Show* group on the *Task* tab.

4. Fill in details for this task.

5. Click the **Task** button in the *Show* group.

6. Fill in the **Status** and **% Complete.**

7. Click the **Send Status Report** button (Figure 5-33) in the *Manage Task* group on the *Task* tab. A *Task Status Report* email is opened. This message contains detailed status report information for the recipients.

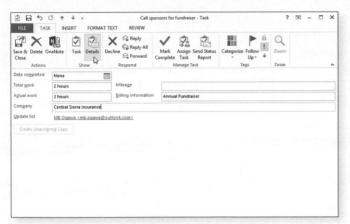

5-32 Task details

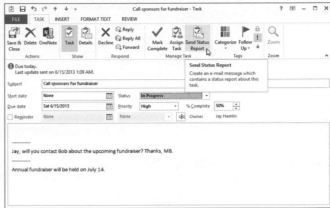

5-33 *Send Status Report* button

8. Include a brief message in the body (Figure 5-34).

9. Select other recipients if necessary. The originator of the task will automatically be a recipient.

10. Click **Send.** The recipients will receive a *Task Status Report* email in their Inboxes.

Complete a Task

As mentioned previously in this chapter, there are many ways to mark a task as completed. When a task is marked as completed, the originator of the task will automatically receive an email informing him or her that the task is complete. In the *Task List* of both the originator and owner of the task, the task will have a line through it to indicate it is a completed task.

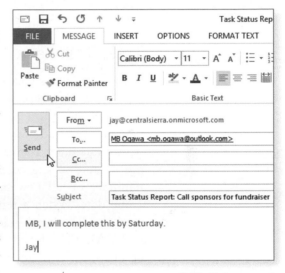

5-34 Status report

> ### ANOTHER WAY
>
> A task can also be marked as complete by selecting the task in the *Folder* pane, clicking on the check box on the task, and then clicking on the **Mark Complete** button (Figure 5-35) in the *Manage Task* group or by right-clicking on the task and choosing **Mark Complete.**

> ### MORE INFO
>
> When you accept a task, make sure you follow through on completing the task. Periodically send a status report to the originator so he or she knows you are working on this task. Be sure to mark the task as complete when finished.

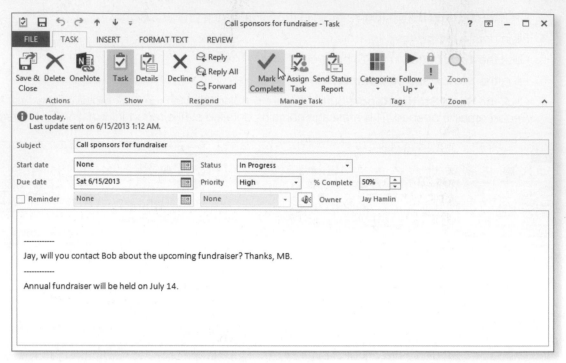

5-35 Mark a task as complete

Task Options

Outlook provides you with the flexibility of customizing some of the default settings for all task items. ***Task options*** are available in the *Outlook Options* dialog box.

By default Outlook does not include a reminder on a new task with a due date. You can change the default setting to include a reminder on all new tasks with a due date. When a reminder is used, the default reminder setting is 8 AM. This default time can be changed to better meet your needs.

The two boxes that are checked in Figure 5-36 pertain to assigning tasks. The first default setting is to keep a copy of an assigned task in your *Task List*. It is a good idea to keep this selected so you have a copy of the task that was assigned to

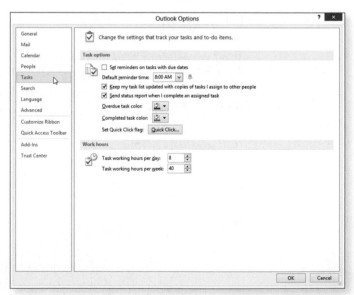

5-36 Outlook task options

someone else. By default Outlook will send a status report to the creator of the task when an assigned task is marked as complete. If you have created a task and assigned it to someone else, it is usually important to get acknowledgment when the task is completed.

The color of overdue and completed tasks can be changed. The default setting is red for overdue tasks and gray for completed tasks. You can set a ***Quick Click*** *Follow Up* flag that will mark a task with the specified flag when it is clicked.

HOW TO: Modify Task Options

1. Click the **File** tab. The *Backstage* window is displayed.
2. Choose **Options** on the left. The *Outlook Options* dialog box opens.
3. Click **Tasks** to change task default settings. The *Task Options* window box opens.
4. Make the desired task option changes.
5. Click **OK** to close the *Task Options* dialog box.
6. Click **OK** to close the *Outlook Options* dialog box.

PAUSE & PRACTICE: OUTLOOK 5-2

For this Pause & Practice project, you assign a task to a group member because you forgot about a doctor's appointment. You also accept tasks, send updates, and complete a task.

1. Assign the task with the subject *Create and email meeting agenda* to your partner.
   a. Click the **Tasks** button in the *Navigation* pane.
   b. Open the task with the subject *Create and email meeting agenda.*
   c. Click the **Assign Task** button [*Task* tab, *Manage Task* group].
   d. In the *To* text area, type your partner's email address (or select it if it is in your contacts).
   e. In the message area, type:
   Hi [partner's name], I have a doctor's appointment this week and will be unable to type up the meeting agenda. Could you please type it up and send it out to the group?
   Thanks,
   [your name]
   f. Click the **Send** button.

2. Accept the task request from your partner.
   a. Click the **Mail** button in the *Navigation* pane.
   b. Open the email message from your partner.
   c. Click the **Accept** button [*Task* tab, *Respond* group].
   d. Select the **Edit the response before sending** radio button and click **OK.**
   e. In the message, type:
   Hi [partner's name], Sure! I will type and send the agenda to the group. I hope all is well with you.
   [your name]
   f. Click the **Send** button.

3. Send an update that the task is 25 percent complete.
   a. Click the **Tasks** button in the *Navigation* pane.
   b. Open the task that you accepted.
   c. Change the *% Complete* to **25%.**
   d. Click the **Send Status Report** button [*Task* tab, *Manage Task* group].
   e. In the email status report, add the following text to the message:
   Hi [partner's name], Just wanted to let you know that I started the agenda and am about 25% through it. Should be finished by the end of the day.
   [your name]
   f. Click the **Send** button.
   g. Click the **Save & Close** button.

4. Complete the task.
   a. Open the task from step 3.
   b. Click the **Mark Complete** button [*Task* tab, *Manage Task* group].

5. Email the task request email, task accepted email, task status report email, and the completed task to your instructor as Outlook items.
   a. Click the **Mail** button in the *Navigation* pane.
   b. Click the **New Email** button [*Home* tab, *New* group].
   c. Enter the following information in your message:
      To: Instructor's email address
      Cc: Your email address
      Subject: Outlook Pause & Practice 5-2
      Body:
      Hi [instructor name],
      Attached are my Outlook items for the Pause & Practice 5-2 exercise.

      Sincerely,
      [your name]
   d. Click the **Attach Item** button [*Message* tab, *Include* group] and select **Outlook Item.**
   e. Select the **Tasks** option and locate the three tasks you created.
   f. Hold the **Ctrl** key and select the three tasks and click **OK.**
   g. Click **Send** (Figure 5-37).

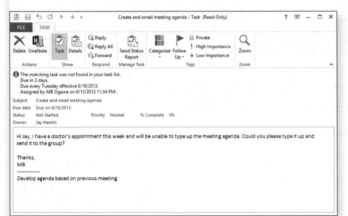

5-37 Completed Pause & Practice 5-2

Customizing Outlook to Fit Your Needs

Now that you are an advanced Outlook user and regularly use the different tasks and special features offered by Outlook, you might want to customize the user interface. You can customize the look and contents of **Outlook Today,** the **Navigation** pane, **Favorites,** and the **Quick Access** toolbar. You can also customized how information is displayed in the *Folder* pane by selecting how fields are displayed.

Outlook Today

Outlook Today is the opening window that is displayed in the *Folder* pane when Outlook is started. It gives you a snapshot of your upcoming calendar, task, and message items. By clicking on an item displayed in *Outlook Today,* you will be taken directly to that item in Outlook.

> **MORE INFO**
>
> You can access *Outlook Today* by clicking on your **Mailbox** folder in the *Navigation* pane.

Outlook Today can be customized to include different amounts of calendar and task items. You can select different mail folders to be displayed, and you can change the overall look and layout of *Outlook Today.*

HOW TO: Customize Outlook Today

1. Click the **Customize Outlook Today** button in the *Folder* pane. The *Customize Outlook Today* screen will be displayed in the *Folder* pane (Figure 5-38).
2. Click the **Startup** check box to have *Outlook Today* automatically displayed each time you open Outlook.
3. In the *Messages* area, you can choose the folders to be displayed in *Outlook Today.*
4. In the *Calendar* area, you can select the number of days to display in *Outlook Today.*
5. In the *Tasks* area, you can customize the tasks to be displayed.
6. In the *Styles* area, you can choose the style of *Outlook Today.*
7. Click **Save Changes.**

5-38 Customize *Outlook Today*

Navigation Pane Options

In the *Navigation* pane, you can choose which buttons are displayed, the order of buttons displayed, and whether a button is large or small. Click the **. . .** (more) button at the bottom of the *Navigation* pane and select **Navigation Options . . .** to open the *Navigation Options* dialog box (Figure 5-39), which provides the following options: *Maximum number of visible items, Compact Navigation,* and reorder each feature.

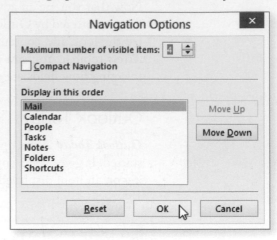

The *Maximum number of visible items* refers to the number of buttons available in the navigation pane without clicking the . . . (more) button to reveal more options. *Compact Navigation* uses icons instead of words for each of the *Navigation Pane* items. This is similar to previous versions of Outlook. You can also change the order of the buttons displayed in the *Navigation* pane by selecting an item and clicking on the *Move Up* or *Move Down* button. The *Reset* button will reset your *Navigation* pane to the original Outlook default settings.

5-39 *Navigation Options* dialog box

Favorites Folders

At the top of the *Navigation* pane above your mail folders is an area called **Favorites** (Figure 5-40). Folders that you regularly use can be added to this area for easy access to the folders. When a folder is placed in the *Favorites* area, the folder is not actually moved to a different location, but rather a link to the folder is created in the *Favorites* area.

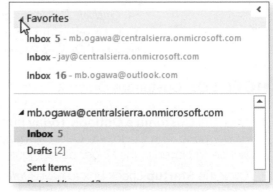

Mail, Search, and *RSS Feeds* folders can be added to the *Favorites* area. Clicking on a folder in the *Favorites* area will display the contents of that folder in the *Folder* pane.

5-40 *Favorites*

HOW TO: Add a Folder to Favorites

1. Click the folder to be added to *Favorites*.
2. Click the **Folder** tab and then click the **Show in Favorites** button in the *Favorites* group.

Folders can be removed from the *Favorites* area by selecting the folder to be removed and clicking the **Show in Favorites** button (Figure 5-41).

5-41 *Show in Favorites* button

> ▶ **ANOTHER WAY**
>
> A folder can also be added to *Favorites* by right-clicking on the folder and choosing **Show in Favorites**. A *Favorites* folder can also be removed this way.

MORE INFO

Customizing the *Quick Access* toolbar can be done in any of the Microsoft Office applications.

Customize the Quick Access Toolbar

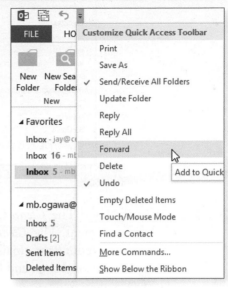

The *Quick Access* toolbar is a set of buttons that quickly access commands in Outlook. For example, the *Save As, Undo,* and *Forward* actions can be performed by clicking on one of these buttons on the *Quick Access* toolbar. This toolbar appears at the top of each open Outlook window just above the *File* tab.

Different commands can be added to this toolbar by clicking the **Customize Quick Access Toolbar** button to the right of the toolbar and selecting the command to be added to the toolbar. More command options are available by clicking **More Commands** in the drop-down menu (Figure 5-42). Commands can be removed from this toolbar by deselecting the item in the *Customize Quick Access Toolbar* list.

5-42 Add *Forward* to the *Quick Access* toolbar

Sort and Arrange Items

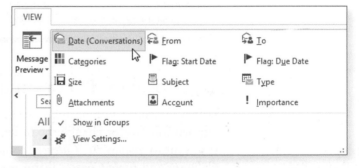

When mail items are displayed in your *Folder* pane, they are typically sorted by date; the most recent item is listed first, and older items are listed below it sequentially. You can change how items are sorted by clicking on one of the arrangement options in the *Arrangement* group on the *View* tab (Figure 5-43).

5-43 Sort email by date

When an arrangement is selected, the items displayed in the *Folder* pane are sorted by that field. For example, if the *Date* arrangement is selected, items will be sorted by the date field. By clicking the **Reverse Sort** button in the *Arrangement* group, items can be sorted in ascending or descending order. The field by which the items are sorted is shaded and a small arrow to the right of the field name in the *Folder* pane indicates whether the sort is ascending or descending.

ANOTHER WAY

Items displayed in the *Folder* pane can also be sorted or arranged by clicking on a column heading in the *Folder* pane.

This ***Conversation arrangement*** (Figure 5-44) groups together related emails (same subject line). When *Conversation* arrangement is used, the related items are grouped together and collapsed so you don't see all the email. When you click the email icon in the *Folder* pane, the conversation group is expanded so you can view all the related emails in that conversation. The intent of this arrangement is to reduce the number of displayed emails in your Inbox.

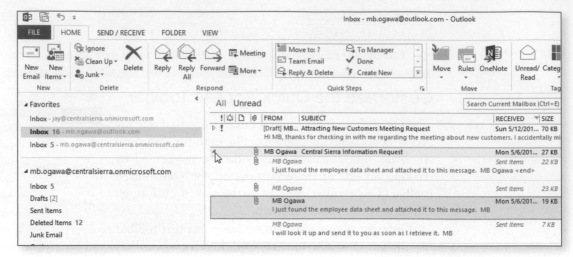

5-44 Email arranged as conversations

The **Clean Up** and **Ignore** features work in conjunction with the *Conversation* arrangement. The *Clean Up Conversation* button in the *Delete* group on the *Home* tab will delete redundant emails from your Inbox, and the *Ignore* button will delete the selected emails in your Inbox and future emails related to the selected conversation.

> **MORE INFO**
>
> Sorting and arranging is not limited to just mail items. You can also sort or use arrangements for any contact, calendar, task, journal, or note views that display items in a list.

Add Columns and Use the Field Chooser

When viewing Outlook items in a list view (e.g., *Phone* view in *Contacts*), you can add or remove columns or change the order of columns to be displayed in the *Folder* pane. Suppose you want to display the *Category* column when viewing your contacts in *Phone* view. The **Add Columns** and **Field Chooser** features allow you to add fields to any list view in Outlook.

HOW TO: Add Columns to a View

1. Click **People** in the *Navigation* pane. *Phone* view displays.

2. Click the **View** tab and then the **Add Columns** button in the *Arrangement* group. The *Show Columns* dialog box opens (Figure 5-45).

3. In the *Available* columns area, select the column to be added and click the **Add** button. Columns can also be removed in this dialog box.

4. You can arrange the display order of columns by clicking on the column on the right and using the *Move Up* or *Move Down* button.

5. Click **OK** to close the *Show Columns* dialog box.

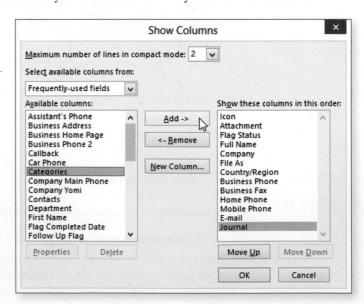

5-45 *Show Columns* dialog box

To display the *Field Chooser* dialog box, right-click any one of the column headings and choose **Field Chooser.** Drag the selected field from the *Field Chooser* dialog box to the desired location in the *Folder* pane (Figure 5-46). When adding fields to the *Folder* pane, a red arrow will appear in the location where the field will be placed.

5-46 *Field Chooser*

You can easily move a field by dragging and dropping the field's column heading to a different location among the column headings. You can also remove a field by dragging and dropping the field below the column headings area in the *Folder* pane.

> **MORE INFO**
>
> In both the *Show Columns* and *Field Chooser* dialog boxes, there are different categories of fields from which to choose.

Show in Groups

When items are shown in a list in the *Folder* pane, Outlook can group the items by the field by which the items are sorted. For example, when items are sorted by date, Outlook will group them by *Today, Yesterday, Last Week, Two Weeks Ago, Three Weeks Ago, Last Month,* and *Older.*

> **ANOTHER WAY**
>
> You can also remove a field from the *Folder* pane by right-clicking on the column heading and choosing **Remove This Column.**

You can change the grouping by selecting a different field (column heading) by which to group the items. Click a column heading to toggle it back and forth between ascending and descending sort order. Clicking on the small triangle to the left of the group name will expand or collapse the group. You can turn off grouping by deselecting **Show in Groups.**

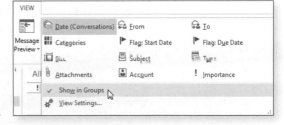

5-47 *Show in Groups* option

HOW TO: Show in Groups

1. Click the **Mail** button in the *Navigation* pane.
2. Click the **View** tab.
3. In the *Arrangements* group, click the **More** button to expand the arrangements (or choose **Arrange By**).
4. Click **Show in Groups** (Figure 5-47). The items displayed in the *Folder* pane are displayed in groups (Figure 5-48).

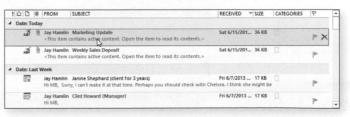

5-48 *Email items grouped by dates*

You can also expand or collapse groups by clicking on the **View** tab and selecting **Expand/Collapse.** You will have the options *of Collapse This Group, Expand This Group, Collapse All Groups,* and *Expand All Groups* (Figure 5-49).

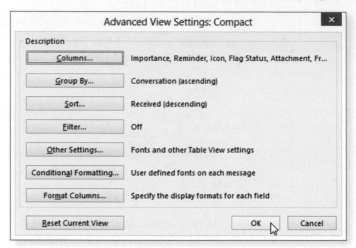

5-49 *Collapse All Groups* option

Customize Views

Outlook also provides you with an **Advanced View Settings** dialog box (Figure 5-50) to further customize how your items are displayed in the *Folder* pane. The *Advanced View Settings* dialog box will allow you to customize the view by which you are currently displaying items in the *Folder* pane. Click the **View Settings** button in the *Current View* group on the *View* tab for the following view options:

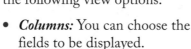

5-50 *Advanced View Settings* dialog box

- **Columns:** You can choose the fields to be displayed.
- **Group By:** You can group and sort by multiple fields.
- **Sort:** You can specify the fields and type of sort to be applied.
- **Filter:** You can create a filter so only certain items are displayed.
- **Other Settings:** You can customize font, size, gridlines, *AutoPreview,* and *Reading* pane options.
- **Conditional Formatting:** You can customize how specific items are displayed in the *Folder* pane. The options in this area will vary depending on the type of Outlook items being displayed in the *Folder* pane.
- **Format Columns:** You can customize the format, width, and alignment of the fields displayed.
- **Reset Current View:** You can reset the view to its original default settings.

> ### ANOTHER WAY
>
> The *Reset View* button in the *Current View* group on the *View* tab will reset the selected view to its original settings.

> ### MORE INFO
>
> When you customize a view, the changes made will be saved and displayed whenever this view is used.

Create a Custom View

For each area of Outlook, you are provided with many different preset views. As discussed, you can modify any of these views to meet your individual needs. The *Manage All Views* dialog box will allow you to customize preset views or create a new custom view for that area of Outlook. Custom views can be saved and used on different folders in Outlook.

HOW TO: Create a Custom View

1. In any area of Outlook, click the **View** tab, choose **Change View,** and then click **Manage Views** (Figure 5-51). The *Manage All Views* dialog box opens (Figure 5-52).

2. Click the **New** button. The *Create a New View* dialog box opens (Figure 5-53).

3. In the *Name of new view* area, type a name for the view.

5-51 *Manage Views* option

5-52 *Manage All Views* dialog box

4. In the *Type of view* area, select **Table.** This selection varies depending on the type of view to be created and the area of Outlook for which you are creating this view.

5. In the *Can be used on* area, click **All Mail and Post folders.** This enables this view to be used on all *Mail and Post* folders.

6. Click **OK.** The *Advanced View Settings* dialog box opens.

7. Click each of the following buttons to customize: **Columns, Group By, Sort, Filter, Other Settings, Conditional Formatting,** and **Format Columns.**

8. When all changes have been made, click **OK** to close the *Advanced View Settings* dialog box (Figure 5-54).

9. Click **Apply View** to apply the new view on the current folder.

10. Click **OK** to close the *Manage All Views* dialog box.

5-53 *Create a New View* dialog box

5-54 Advanced view settings for new view

This new view will now be available for use on all your contact folders (and any other folders you created to use in the new view). You can copy, modify, rename, or delete views from the *Manage All Views* dialog box.

PAUSE & PRACTICE: OUTLOOK 5-3

For this Pause & Practice project, you customize Outlook to make it fit your working style. You make *Outlook Today* your default start screen, add your Inbox to your *Favorites,* and add the print button to the *Quick Access* toolbar. If you prefer not to have these options, feel free to change them back to the default, since there are no submission items. This project should be used to help you customize the Outlook interface to meet your working style.

1. Customize *Outlook Today* and set it to start up when you open Outlook.
   a. Click the **Customize Outlook Today** button in the *Folder* pane. The *Customize Outlook Today* screen will be displayed in the *Folder* pane.
   b. Click the **When starting, go directly to Outlook today** check box.
   c. In the *Messages* area, choose the folders to be displayed in *Outlook Today*.
   d. In the *Calendar* area, select the number of days to display in *Outlook Today*.
   e. In the *Tasks* area, customize the tasks to be displayed.
   f. In the *Styles* area, choose the style of *Outlook Today*.
   g. Click **Save Changes.**

2. Add your Inbox to your *Favorites.*
   a. Right-click on your Inbox.
   b. Select **Show in Favorites.**

3. Add the **Print** button to your *Quick Access* toolbar.
   a. Click the **Customize Quick Access Toolbar** button to the right of the toolbar.
   b. Select the **Print** option (Figure 5-55).

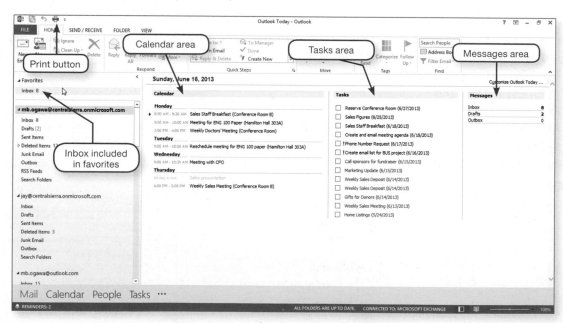

5-55 Completed Pause & Practice 5-3

Chapter Summary

5.1 Distinguish between tasks and To-Do items (p. O5-166).

- **Tasks** are individual items that are kept in the *Tasks* area and also appear in the list of To-Do items.
- **To-Do** items include tasks, flagged email messages, and flagged contacts.
- Tasks can be used to remind you about things that you need to accomplish.
- The **Task List** includes all of the tasks you created.
- **Flagged** items typically indicate that you need to follow up on a particular item. When you flag an item, it appears in the **To-Do List.**
- The *To-Do List* includes both task items and flagged items.
- The *To-Do bar* is located on the right side of the window and includes a date navigator, upcoming calendar items, and To-Do items.

5.2 Create and use tasks in Outlook (p. O5-167).

- You can create a new task from the tasks folder or *New Task* button.
- Tasks include a subject, start date, due date, reminder, status, priority, percent complete, and a message.
- Tasks can include tags such as categories, follow-up flags, and importance.
- You can attach Outlook items and files to tasks.
- Tasks can be marked as completed, which crosses it out in your *Task List.*
- Tasks can be set to recur on a regular basis.
- You can drag and drop email messages and calendar items to the *Tasks* button on the *Navigation* pane to create tasks from different Outlook items.

5.3 Understand and customize the *Tasks* views and the *To-Do bar* (p. O5-178).

- Tasks and To-Do items can be viewed as *Detailed, Simple List, To-Do List, Prioritized, Active, Completed, Today, Next 7 Days, Overdue, Assigned,* or *Server Tasks.*
- Similar to email, you can include the *Reading* pane for tasks.

- You can view tasks in the calendar view if you are viewing the calendar in *Day* or *Week* view.
- The *To-Do bar* can be customized to include the *Calendar, People,* and *Tasks.*

5.4 Assign tasks to and accept tasks from other Outlook users (p. O5-180).

- Tasks can be assigned to others.
- When you receive a **task request,** you have the option to **Accept** or **Decline** the task.
- When accepting a task request, you have two options: *Edit the response before sending* or *Send the response now.*
- While working on a task request, you can send the original task requestor an update of the progress on the task. This can include the **Status***,* **% Complete,** and a **message.**
- Using the details of a task, you can include the amount of hours worked on the task.
- When you mark an accepted task request as **Complete,** it automatically crosses the task off your *Task List* and the task requestor's list
- Outlook allows you to modify the default *Task Options* to meet your particular work style.

5.5 Customize the user interface in Outlook to better meet your needs (p. O5-187).

- **Outlook Today** can be customized to include information that you want available as soon as you launch Outlook.
- The *Navigation* pane can be modified to include more visible items and a *Compact Navigation,* and you can reorder the *Navigation* pane buttons.
- You can include folders that you use often in the **Favorites.**
- The **Quick Access toolbar** can be customized to include buttons you use most often.
- Outlook allows you to sort email and tasks by using a variety of criteria including date received, amongst other criteria.
- You can add additional fields to your tasks, which allow greater sort options.
- Email can be sorted to be viewed in groups, which include weeks and days.
- The **Advanced View Settings** allows for deep customization of views based on many criteria.

Check for Understanding

In the **Online Learning Center** for this text
(www.mhhe.com/office2013inpractice), there are a
variety of resources that can be used to review the
concepts covered in this chapter.

The following Online Learning Resources are available
in the Online Learning Center:

- Multiple choice questions
- Short answer questions
- Matching exercises

Guided Project 5-1

For this project, you coordinate the Cycling Evolution Event for the American River Cycling Club (ARCC). You create tasks that need to be completed in order to prepare for the event.
[Student Learning Outcomes 5.1, 5.2, 5.3]

Skills Covered in This Project

- Create a new task.
- Modify the task subject, start date, due date, reminder, priority, and message.
- Create a task from a calendar appointment.
- Create a recurring task.
- Email task items as attachments.

---

1. Create a new task.
   a. Click the **Tasks** button in the *Navigation* pane.
   b. Click the **Tasks** folder in the *My Tasks* area of the *Navigation* pane.
   c. Click the **New Task** button in the *New* group on the *Home* tab.
   d. Enter the following information for the new task:
      Subject: Call city and county
      Start date: Today's date
      Due date: One week from today
      Reminder: Two days from today at 9:00 AM
      Priority: Normal
      Message: Make arrangements for road path
   e. Click the **Save & Close** button.

2. Create a new calendar appointment.
   a. Click the **Calendar** button in the *Navigation* pane.
   b. Click the **New Appointment** button [*Home* tab, *New* group].
   c. Enter the following information for the new appointment:
      Subject: Cycling Evolution Event
      Location: River City
      Start time: One month from today at 9:00 AM
      End time: One month from today at 12:00 PM
      Body: ARCC half day event
   d. Click the **Save & Close** button.

3. Create a new task based on the appointment you created.
   a. Select the calendar item you created.
   b. Click and drag the calendar item to the *Tasks* button on the *Navigation* pane.
   c. In the new task window, edit the task in the following way:
      Subject: Cycling Evolution Event: Final check
      Start date: None
      Due date: Two days before the event
      Reminder: Three days before the event at 10:00 AM
      Priority: High
      Message: Call city and county to double-check, set up road signs
   d. Click the **Save & Close** button.

4. Create a new task to email the membership each week to give additional details about the event.
    a. Click the **New Task** button in the *New* group on the *Home* tab.
    b. Enter the following information for the new task:
    Subject: Email membership CEE details as they arise
    Start date: None
    Due date: The upcoming Thursday
    Message: Include details such as course, maps, check-in areas, and registration
    c. Click the **Recurrence** button [*Task* tab, *Recurrence* group].
    d. Set the recurrence to be every Thursday at with an end date of the Thursday before the event.
    e. Click the **OK** button.
    f. Click the **Save & Close** button.

5. Email the three tasks to your instructor as Outlook items.
    a. Click the **Mail** button in the *Navigation* pane.
    b. Click the **New Email** button [*Home* tab, *New* group].
    c. Enter the following information in your message:
    To: Instructor's email address
    Cc: Your email address
    Subject: Outlook Guided Project 5-1
    Body:
    Hi [instructor name],
    Attached are my Outlook items
    for the Guided Project 5-1 exercise.
    Sincerely,
    [your name]
    d. Click the **Attach Item** button [*Message* tab, *Include* group] and select **Outlook Item.**
    e. Select the **Tasks** option and locate the three tasks you created.
    f. Hold the **Ctrl** key and select the three tasks and click **OK.**
    g. Click **Send** (Figure 5-56).

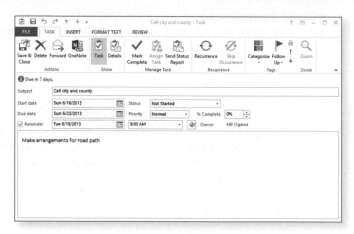

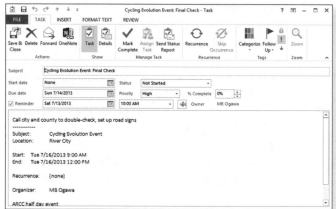

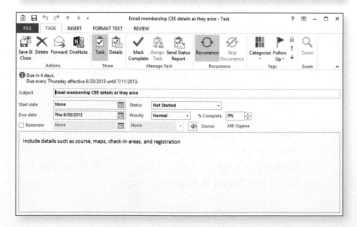

5-56 Completed Guided Project 5-1

Guided Project 5-2

For this project, you enlist the help of others by assigning tasks to them, because you find that the tasks to prepare for the ARCC Cycling Evolution Event are becoming overwhelming.
[Student Learning Outcomes 5.1, 5.3, 5.4]

Skills Covered in This Project

- Edit an existing task.
- Assign a task.
- Edit an assigned task message.
- Mark a task as complete.
- Email task items as attachments.

---

1. Assign the task with the subject *Email membership CEE details as they arise* to your partner.
    a. Click the **Tasks** button in the *Navigation* pane.
    b. Open the task with the subject *Email membership CEE details as they arise.*
    c. Click the **Assign Task** button [*Task* tab, *Manage Task* group].
    d. In the *To* area, type your partner's email address (or select it if it is in your contacts).
    e. In the message area, type:
    Hi [partner's name], I am a bit busy for the next few weeks. Would you be willing to write and send the CEE details to membership as they come up each week?

    Thanks,
    [your name]
    f. Click the **Send** button.

2. Assign the task with the subject *Cycling Evolution Event: Final check* to your partner.
    a. Open the task with the subject *Cycling Evolution Event: Final check.*
    b. Click the **Assign Task** button [*Task* tab, *Manage Task* group].
    c. In the *To* area, type your partner's email address (or select it if it is in your contacts).
    d. In the message area, type:
    "Hi [partner's name], Are you available to perform the final check? My schedule is a bit tight, but can do it if you are not available.

    Thanks,
    [your name]
    e. Click the **Send** button.

3. Complete the task.
    a. Open the task with the subject *Call city and county.*
    b. Click the **Mark Complete** button [*Task* tab, *Manage Task* group].

4. Email the two task request email messages and the completed task to your instructor as Outlook items.
    a. Click the **Mail** button in the *Navigation* pane.
    b. Click the **New Email** button [*Home* tab, *New* group].
    c. Enter the following information in your message:
    To: Instructor's email address
    Cc: Your email address
    Subject: Outlook Guided Project 5-2

Body:

Hi [instructor name],

Attached are my Outlook items for the Guided Project 5-2 exercise.

Sincerely,

[your name]

d. Click the **Attach Item** button [*Message* tab, *Include* group] and select **Outlook Item.**

e. Select the **Tasks** option and locate the three tasks you worked with.

f. Hold the **Ctrl** key and select the two tasks and email message and click **OK.**

g. Click **Send** (Figure 5-57).

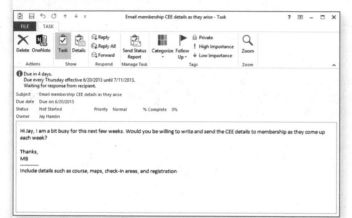

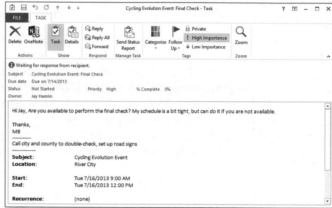

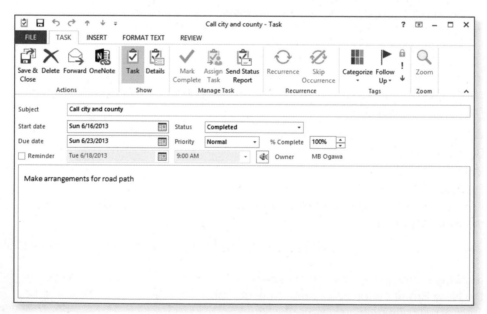

5-57 Completed Guided Project 5-2

Guided Project 5-3

For this project, you respond to task requests you received. Based on your schedule, you are able to accept one, accept one with a minor exception, and decline one.
[Student Learning Outcomes 5.1, 5.3, 5.4]

Skills Covered in This Project

- Accept a task request.
- Modify a reply to a task request.
- Decline a task request.
- Send a status update to a task request.

---

1. Accept the task request with the subject *Email membership CEE details as they arise.*
   a. Click the **Mail** button in the *Navigation* pane.
   b. Open the email message from your partner.
   c. Click the **Accept** button [*Task* tab, *Respond* group].
   d. Select the **Edit the response before sending** radio button and click **OK.**
   e. In the message, type:
      Hi [partner's name], OK. Will be sure to work on this every Thursday till the race!
      [your name]
   f. Click the **Send** button.

2. Send an update that the task is 10 percent complete.
   a. Click the **Tasks** button in the *Navigation* pane.
   b. Open the task that you accepted.
   c. Change the *% Complete* to **10%.**
   d. Click the **Send Status Report** button [*Task* tab, *Manage Task* group].
   e. In the email status report, add the following text to the message:
      Hi [partner's name], Just wanted to let you know that I wrote the draft of the email for this coming Thursday's update.
      [your name]
   f. Click the **Send** button.
   g. Click the **Save & Close** button.

3. Decline the task request with the subject *Cycling Evolution Event: Final Check.*
   a. Click the **Mail** button in the *Navigation* pane.
   b. Open the email message from your partner.
   c. Click the **Decline** button [*Task* tab, *Respond* group].
   d. Select the **Edit the response before sending** radio button and click **OK.**
   e. In the message, type:
      Hi [partner's name], Sorry, I have to drop my daughter off at her softball practice before going to the Cycling Evolution Event. Please take care of the final checks.
      [your name]
   f. Click the **Send** button.

4. Email the task request acceptance message, task decline message, and status update message to your instructor as Outlook items.
   a. Click the **Mail** button in the *Navigation* pane.
   b. Click the **New Email** button [*Home* tab, *New* group].
   c. Enter the following information in your message:
      To: Instructor's email address

Cc: Your email address
Subject: Outlook Guided Project 5-3
Body:
Hi [instructor name],

Attached are my Outlook items for the Guided Project 5-3 exercise.

Sincerely,
[your name]

d. Click the **Attach Item** button [*Message* tab, *Include* group] and select **Outlook Item.**
e. Select the **Messages** option and locate the three tasks you created.
f. Hold the **Ctrl** key and select the three email messages and click **OK.**
g. Click **Send** (Figure 5-58).

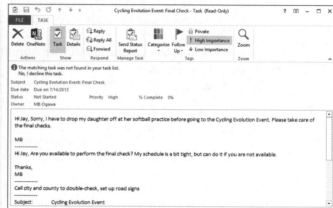

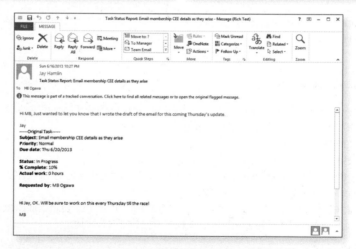

5-58 Completed Guided Project 5-3

Independent Project 5-4

For this project, you prepare for the Placer Hills Real Estate (PHRE) annual strategic planning meeting. You were chosen to lead the meeting and you create a *Tasks List* to keep yourself organized.
[Student Learning Outcomes 5.1, 5.2, 5.3]

Skills Covered in This Project

- Create a new task.
- Modify the task subject, start date, due date, reminder, priority, and message.
- Create a task from a calendar appointment.
- Create a recurring task.
- Email task items as attachments.

---

1. Create a new task with the following information:
   Subject: Reserve Board Room
   Start date: None
   Due date: One week from Monday
   Reminder: Two days from today at 9:00 AM
   Priority: Normal
   Message: Reserve conference room for two weeks from today.

2. Create a new calendar appointment with the following information:
   Subject: Strategic Planning Meeting
   Location: Board Room
   Start time: Two weeks from Monday
   Set the appointment to be an **Event.**
   Body: Planning for the upcoming fiscal year

3. Create a new task from the calendar appointment you created in step 2. Modify the appointment with the following details:
   Subject: Strategic Planning Meeting: Email Reminder to Department Heads
   Message: Send email to all department heads 3 days in advance
   Due Date: Three days before the strategic planning meeting
   Reminder: Three days before the strategic planning meeting at 9:30 AM

4. Create a new task with the following information.
   Subject: Send Agenda to Department Heads
   Start date: None
   Due date: One week from Monday
   Reminder: One week from today at 9:00 AM
   Priority: High
   Message: Develop agenda based on strategies discussed at the last board meeting.

5. Email the three tasks you created to your instructor as Outlook items. Enter the following information in your message:
   To: Instructor's email address
   Cc: Your email address
   Subject: Outlook Independent Project 5-4

Body:
Hi [instructor name],
Attached are my Outlook items for the Independent Project 5-4 exercise.
Sincerely,
[student name]
Attach the three tasks as Outlook Items (Figure 5-59).

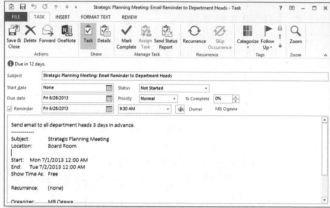

5-59 Completed Independent Project 5-4

Independent Project 5-5

For this project, you use your *Task List* and send out task requests to your peers to prepare for the PHRE strategic planning meeting.
[Student Learning Outcomes 5.1, 5.3, 5.4]

Skills Covered in This Project

- Edit an existing task.
- Assign a task.
- Edit an assigned task message.

- Mark a task as complete.
- Email task items as attachments.

1. Update the task *Reserve Board Room* to reflect the following:
   Subject: Reserve Conference Room A
   Message: Call Cammie for reservation.

2. Mark *Reserve Conference Room A* as complete.

3. Assign the task *Strategic Planning Meeting: Email Reminder to Department Heads* to a partner and include a message asking your partner to send the email reminder to the department heads.

4. Update the task *Send Agenda to Department Heads* to reflect the following:
   Status: In Progress
   % Complete: 50%
   Message: Developed draft agenda.

5. Assign the task *Send Agenda to Department Heads* to a partner with a message that asks them to review the draft available in their shared folder.

6. Email the *Reserve Conference Room A* task and the two messages with assigned tasks to your instructor as Outlook items. Enter the following information in your message:
   To: Instructor's email address
   Cc: Your email address
   Subject: Outlook Independent Project 5-5
   Body:
   Hi [instructor name],

   Attached are my Outlook items for the Independent Project 5-5 exercise.

   Sincerely,

   [your name]
   Attach the three items as Outlook Items (Figure 5-60).

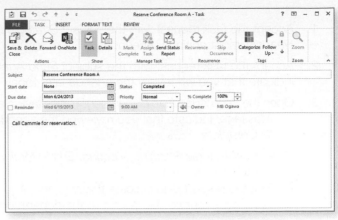

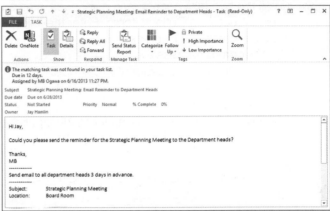

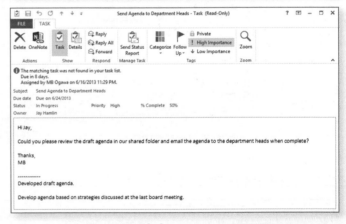

5-60 Completed Independent Project 5-5

Independent Project 5-6

For this project, you receive task requests from your peer to prepare for the PHRE strategic planning meeting. You send an update and complete a task.
[Student Learning Outcomes 5.1, 5.3, 5.4]

Skills Covered in This Project

- Accept a task request.
- Modify a reply to a task request.
- Decline a task request.
- Send a status update to a task request.

1. Accept the task request with the subject *Strategic Planning Meeting: Email Reminder to Department Heads* without editing the response.

2. Accept the task request with the subject *Send Agenda to Department Heads*. Edit the response to indicate that you will review the agenda later today.

3. Open the *Send Agenda to Department Heads* task. Send an update to your partner indicating the following:
   Message: Indicate that you reviewed the agenda and finalized it.
   % Complete: 75%

4. Open the *Strategic Planning Meeting: Email Reminder to Department Heads* request.
   a. Decline the request.
   b. Edit the response to indicate that you reviewed the agenda but think that it would be better received if your partner sent it to the department heads.

5. Email the two task acceptance messages, status update message, and declined task message to your instructor as Outlook items. Enter the following information in your message:
   To: Instructor's email address
   Cc: Your email address
   Subject: Outlook Independent Project 5-6
   Body:
   Hi [instructor name],

   Attached are my Outlook items for the Independent Project 5-6 exercise.

   Sincerely,

   [your name]

   Attach the four items as Outlook Items (Figure 5-61).

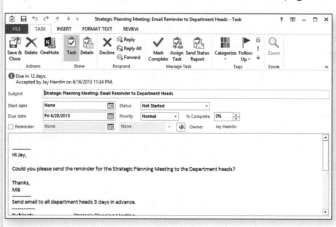

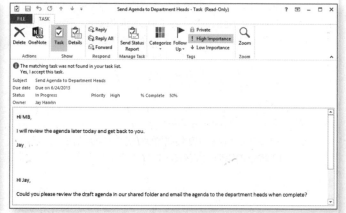

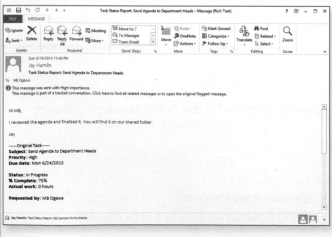

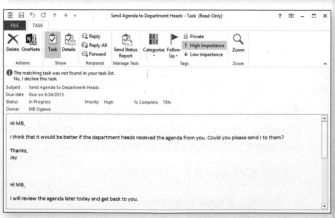

5-61 Completed Independent Project 5-6

Challenge Project 5-7

Create a *Task List* for yourself based on your current school, work, and personal schedules for the current month. Be sure to include items such as homework, projects, activities, and preparation for events such as club activities.
[Student Learning Outcomes 5.1, 5.2, 5.3, 5.5]

- Include all tasks that you will work on in the current month. This should be at least 10 tasks.
- Use categories to keep each of your tasks organized.
- Set appropriate start and end dates.
- Include details for tasks that require them.
- Use recurrence for at least one task.
- Create at least one task from a calendar item or email message. You can use the calendar you created in the previous chapter.
- Mark tasks as complete if you completed them. At least one task should be completed.
- Customize your view to meet your needs.
- Email the tasks to your instructor as email attachments.
- Attach each of the tasks to your email message (attach each task as an *Outlook Item*).
- Change the subject of your message to **Outlook Challenge Project 5-7.**

Challenge Project 5-8

Develop a *Task List* for an organization that you are currently participating in. Be sure to assign tasks to different organization members and include progress for items that are currently being worked on but are not completed. The *Task List* should encompass at least one month of work for the organization.
[Student Learning Outcomes 5.1, 5.2, 5.3, 5.4, 5.5]

- Include all tasks for your organization during the current month. This should be at least 10 tasks. If you do not have at least 10 tasks, you may use tasks from more than one month.
- Use categories to keep each of your tasks organized. This can include preparation tasks for different club activities.
- Set appropriate start and end dates.
- Include details for tasks that require them.
- Include tags, such as priority when appropriate.
- At least one task is partially completed and should include the percentage.
- Assign tasks to different organization members. At least three tasks should be assigned.
- Customize your view to meet your needs.
- Email the tasks to your instructor as email attachments.
- Attach each of the tasks to your email message as an *Outlook* item.
- Change the subject of your message to **Outlook Challenge Project 5-8.**

Challenge Project 5-9

Work with a family member or friend to develop a *Task List* for them. The *Task List* can include items such as chores, homework, projects, and extracurricular activities. Be sure to include categories to keep the *Task List* organized.
[Student Learning Outcomes 5.1, 5.2, 5.3, 5.4, 5.5]

- Include all tasks that your friend or family member will work on in the current month. This should be at least 10 tasks.
- Use categories to keep each of his or her tasks organized.
- Set appropriate start and end dates.
- Include details for tasks that require them.
- Use recurrence for at least one task.
- Mark tasks as complete if they are completed. At least one task should be completed.
- Customize the view to meet his or her needs.
- Email the tasks to your instructor as email attachments.
- Attach each of the tasks to your email message as an *Outlook* item.
- Include a short message describing your friend and how he or she uses *Task Lists* in Outlook and if it is different from how you view or use it.
- Change the subject of your message to **Outlook Challenge Project 5-9.**

Folders, Rules, Quick Steps, and Search Folders

CHAPTER OVERVIEW

After completing the first half of this book, you now have a good understanding of the main components of Outlook—Email, Contacts, Calendar, and Tasks. Building on this essential foundation, we will delve into the numerous ways you can customize Outlook to best meet your needs. Outlook provides you with a range of features to help organize, categorize, and prioritize items within Outlook. Using *folders, Quick Steps, rules,* and *search folders* will help you to become a more efficient and effective Outlook user.

STUDENT LEARNING OUTCOMES (SLOs)

After completing this chapter, you will be able to:

SLO 6.1 Create, arrange, and modify Outlook folders (p. O6-210).

SLO 6.2 Create, apply, and change Outlook rules (p. O6-214).

SLO 6.3 Customize and use *Quick Steps* (p. O6-224).

SLO 6.4 Utilize search folders to find email messages (p. O6-229).

CASE STUDY

For the Pause & Practice projects, you prepare for a group project and class by using folders, rules, Quick Steps, and search folders to help you more effectively and efficiently manage your email.

Pause & Practice 6-1: You create folders to help you keep your email messages organized. You begin by creating folders for your class, instructor, group project partners, and best friend. You delete the folder for your best friend, as she always sends you text messages, as opposed to email messages.

Pause & Practice 6-2: You create two rules. The first rule is to move email from a specific instructor to the folder you created in the first Pause & Practice. The second rule moves all of your email messages from both of your group members into the folder you created in the first Pause & Practice.

Pause & Practice 6-3: You create two *Quick Steps* to help you be more efficient when working with email. For the first *Quick Step,* your instructor indicated that he or she wants you to email with a specific subject line. Rather than ensuring you type the right subject line for each message, you create a *Quick Step* for those messages. For the second *Quick Step,* you create tasks out of email messages for your group project to ensure you can view your work to complete in your tasks instead of searching through many email messages.

Pause & Practice 6-4: You utilize search folders to help you find information quickly. You create a search folder for email messages from your partners with attachments to allow you to easily locate files you are working with. You also want to use a search folder to quickly locate email messages from your instructor with the word *due* to quickly find messages with due dates or changes to due dates.

OUTLOOK

Using Folders

Most of you have some sort of filing system in your home. You might have a filing cabinet with separate folders for bills, insurance, tax papers, investments, and so forth. Can you imagine having just one drawer in your filing cabinet and throwing everything in that drawer? What a mess it would be and how hard it would be to find a specific item.

When using your computer, you create folders to store various files. You might create and use different folders in the *Documents* folder to store tax information files, Grand Canyon road trip files, or recipes, for example. These Windows folders are generic folders in that they can store various types of files: Word, Excel, .pdf, pictures, and others.

In Outlook, folders can be used to help organize and group your emails, contacts, calendar, tasks, notes, and journals. In contrast to the generic type of folders used in Windows, Outlook folders are specific to the type of Outlook items they store. For example, a *Mail* folder is used to store email and a *Task* folder is used to store tasks.

Create a Folder

Creating folders in Outlook is actually very simple. The most important aspect to remember is that each Outlook folder is created to store a specific type of Outlook item. When the **Create New Folder** dialog box is opened, it is important to confirm the type of folder you are creating and the location of the file.

In Outlook the following types of folders can be created:

- *Calendar Items*
- *Contact Items*
- *InfoPath Form Items*
- *Journal Items*
- *Mail and Post Items*
- *Note Items*
- *Task Items*

Follow these steps to create a new *Mail* folder. The steps are the same for creating any type of Outlook folder.

HOW TO: Create a Folder

1. Click the **Mail** button in the *Navigation* pane.
2. Click the **Folder** tab.
3. Click the **New Folder** button in the *New* group (Figure 6-1). The *Create New Folder* dialog box opens (Figure 6-2).
4. Type the name of the new folder to be created.
5. In the *Folder contains* menu, confirm that the folder type is **Mail and Post Items.**

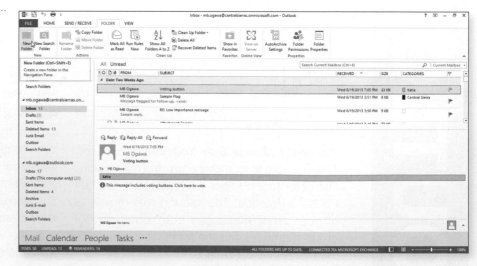

6-1 *New Folder* button

6. In the *Select where to place the folder* section, specify the location in which to save the new folder.

7. Click **OK**.

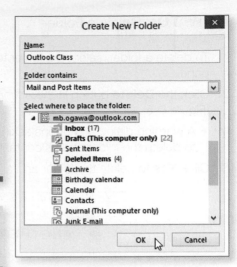

6-2 *Create New Folder* dialog box

> **ANOTHER WAY**
>
> You can create a new folder by right-clicking the folder inside which you would like to create a new folder and then selecting **New Folder.**

> **ANOTHER WAY**
>
> **Ctrl+Shift+E** opens the *Create New Folder* dialog box throughout Outlook.

Move a Folder

There might be times when you add a new folder in the wrong location or you might just want to move a folder from one location to another. The easiest way to move a folder to a new location is to click the folder in the *Navigation* pane and drag and drop it on the new location. The folder and all its contents will be moved to the new location.

Another way to move a folder is to use the ***Move*** feature.

HOW TO: Move a Folder

1. In the *Navigation* pane, select the folder to be moved.

2. Click the **Folder** tab.

3. Click the **Move Folder** button in the *Actions* group (Figure 6-3). The *Move Folder* dialog box opens (Figure 6-4).

4. In the *Move the selected folder to the folder* section, click the desired location to move the folder.

5. Click **OK**. The folder and all its contents will be moved to the new location.

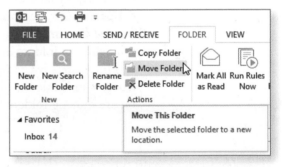

6-3 *Move Folder* button

> **ANOTHER WAY**
>
> You can right-click the folder to be moved and choose **Move Folder,** or you can simply drag and drop the folder to a new location in the *Navigation* pane.

Delete a Folder

Folders are sometimes created to store information temporarily. Folders can be deleted when they are no longer needed. When you delete a folder, all the items in the folder are deleted as well. The deleted folder is stored in the *Deleted Items* folder.

6-4 *Move Folder* dialog box

HOW TO: Delete a Folder

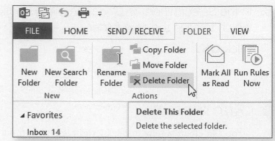

1. To delete a folder, select the folder to be deleted in the *Navigation* pane.
2. Click the **Delete** button in the *Actions* group on the *Folder* tab (Figure 6-5).
   - A warning dialog box opens asking you if you are sure you want to delete the folder and its contents.
3. Click **Yes** to delete the folder and all its contents.

6-5 *Delete Folder* button

> ### ANOTHER WAY
> Right-click the folder to be deleted and choose **Delete Folder**.

> ### ANOTHER WAY
> **Ctrl+D** deletes the selected item. This shortcut will delete a folder or other selected Outlook items.

Use the Folders List

When you are in the Mail, Calendar, Contacts, Tasks, Notes, or Journal areas, only those folders associated with that part of Outlook are displayed in the *Navigation* pane. The **Folders list** (Figure 6-6) is a useful view to display all your Outlook folders in the *Navigation* pane.

The *Folders* list view can be used to view your folder structure in Outlook. This is also a good view to use when you are moving folders from one location to another.

> ### MORE INFO
> In all the areas of Outlook except Mail and the *Folders* list, your folders are not displayed in hierarchical structure. In other words in these other areas, it is hard to know whether or not a folder is located inside of another folder.

The *Folders* list can be displayed in the *Navigation* pane by clicking the *Folders* button at the bottom of the *Navigation* pane.

> ### ANOTHER WAY
> **Ctrl+6** displays the *Folders* list in the *Navigation* pane.

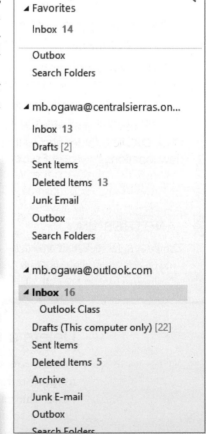

6-6 *Folders* list

For this Pause and Practice project, you create folders to help you keep your email messages organized. You begin by creating folders for your class, instructor, group project partners, and best friend. You delete the folder for your best friend, as she always sends you text messages, as opposed to email messages.

1. Create a folder for your class.
   a. Click the **Mail** button in the *Navigation* pane.
   b. Click the **Folder** tab.
   c. Click the **New Folder** button in the *New* group. The *Create New Folder* dialog box opens.
   d. Type BUS 100 in the *Name* text area.
   e. In the *Folder contains* menu, confirm that the folder type is **Mail and Post Items.**
   f. In the *Select where to place the folder* section, specify your main email account folder.
   g. Click **OK.**

2. Create a folder for your instructor.
   a. Click the **Mail** button in the *Navigation* pane.
   b. Click the **Folder** tab.
   c. Click the **New Folder** button in the *New* group. The *Create New Folder* dialog box opens.
   d. Type your instructor's name in the *Name* text area.
   e. In the *Folder contains* menu, confirm that the folder type is **Mail and Post Items.**
   f. In the *Select where to place the folder* section, specify your main email account folder.
   g. Click **OK.**

3. Create a folder for your group project.
   a. Click the **Mail** button in the *Navigation* pane.
   b. Click the **Folder** tab.
   c. Click the **New Folder** button in the *New* group. The *Create New Folder* dialog box opens.
   d. Type Group Project in the *Name* text area.
   e. In the *Folder contains* menu, confirm that the folder type is **Mail and Post Items.**
   f. In the *Select where to place the folder* section, specify your main email account folder.
   g. Click **OK.**

4. Create a folder for your best friend.
   a. Click the **Mail** button in the *Navigation* pane.
   b. Click the **Folder** tab.
   c. Click the **New Folder** button in the *New* group. The *Create New Folder* dialog box opens.
   d. Type Nicole in the *Name* text area.
   e. In the *Folder contains* menu, confirm that the folder type is **Mail and Post Items.**
   f. In the *Select where to place the folder* section, specify your main email account folder.
   g. Click **OK.**

5. Move the *[instructor name]* and *Group Project* folders into the *[class name]* folder.
   a. In the *Navigation* pane, select *[instructor name]* folder.
   b. Click the **Folder** tab.
   c. Click the **Move Folder** button in the *Actions* group. The *Move Folder* dialog box opens.
   d. In the *Move the selected folder to the folder* section, click the **BUS 100** folder.
   e. Click **OK.**

6. Move the *Group Project* folder into the *BUS 100* folder.
   a. In the *Navigation* pane, select **Group Project folder.**
   b. Click the **Folder** tab.
   c. Click the **Move Folder** button in the *Actions* group. The *Move Folder* dialog box opens.

d. In the *Move the selected folder to the folder* section, click the *[class name]* folder.

e. Click **OK**.

7. Delete the *Nicole* folder.

   a. Select the **Nicole folder** in the *Navigation* pane.

   b. Click the **Delete** button in the *Actions* group on the *Folder* tab.

   c. A warning dialog box opens asking you if you are sure you want to delete the folder and its contents. Click **Yes** to delete the folder and all its contents.

8. Figure 6-7 is a sample of your folder list at the end of Pause & Practice 6-1.

◢ mb.ogawa@outlook.com

◢ Inbox 16

   Outlook Class

   Drafts (This computer only) [22]

   Sent Items

   Deleted Items 5

   Archive

◢ BUS 100

   Group Project

   Professor Ogawa

6-7 Completed Pause & Practice 6-1

Creating and Using Rules

You might receive an enormous amount of emails everyday. You may receive many email messages from each of your instructors for your courses, or from family members keeping in touch with email instead of social networking sites. If all these emails ended up in your Inbox, it would be hard to distinguish which email message was for a specific course you are enrolled in; or you might miss an important message from a family member. You can create folders and set up rules to automatically move email messages from instructors to an appropriate course folder. This will help you to keep your messages organized without the work of moving them.

Rules might be one of the most useful features in Outlook. It can be used to check incoming or outgoing emails and apply some type of action. If you have ever used the *IF* function in Microsoft Excel, rules operate similar to this if/then logical principle. Most rules have two basic parts: a *condition* and an *action*. There is also an *exception* that can be added to the rule.

- *Condition:* The condition is what Outlook is looking for when an email is received or sent. This could be an email that includes a specific word or words in the subject or body, sent from a specific person, received through a specific email account, or marked as high importance.
- *Action:* The action is what is done with the email when the condition is met. This could include moving the email to another folder, marking the email as high importance, categorizing the email with a specific category, deleting the email, or forwarding the email to someone else.
- *Exception:* An exception can be used to nullify an action. For example, a rule can be set up to look for the word "BUS 310" in the subject line and move it to the *BUS 310* folder, except if it comes from the *Dean of the CSIT* area. Exceptions are not commonly used in rules.

Quick Steps are similar to rules, but do not include a condition. So rather than automatically applying an action to an email when it meets a condition, *Quick Steps* can be applied to email on an individual basis. For example, a *Quick Step* can be used to create a meeting request from a received email message.

Create a Quick Rule

A rule can be created quickly based on an email in your Inbox. These quick rules can be used for many of the common rules used in Outlook. These rules have a limited number of options for the condition and action and do not include options for exceptions.

If an email arrives in your Inbox with the subject "Outlook," and you know that there is going to be an email discussion with others based on this topic, a rule can quickly be created to move all emails with the word "Outlook" to an *Outlook* folder to keep all these related messages together.

HOW TO: Create a Rule Based on an Email in Your Inbox

1. In your *Inbox,* open the email for which you would like to create a new rule.
2. Click the **Rules** button in the *Move* group on the *Message* tab.
3. Choose **Create Rule** (Figure 6-8). The *Create Rule* dialog box opens. The three conditions are at the top and the three actions are at the bottom of this dialog box (Figure 6-9).

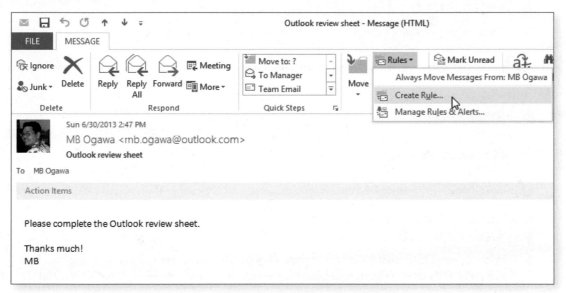

6-8 *Create Rule*

4. In the conditions area (the top half of the dialog box), select the **Subject contains** check box and make sure the word in the subject is correct. If not, correct it.
5. In the actions area (the bottom half of the dialog box), select the **Move the item to folder** check box and click the **Select Folder** button.
6. Select the desired folder from the folder list and press **OK** (Figure 6-10). The *Create Rule* dialog box will still be open. Confirm that the correct folder was selected (Figure 6-10). If not, click the **Select Folder** button and select the correct folder.

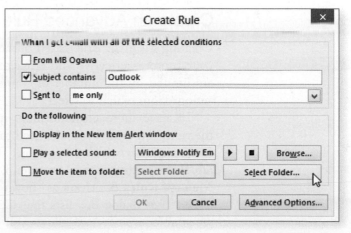

6-9 *Create Rule* dialog box

7. Click **OK.** A *Success* dialog box opens (Figure 6-11).

8. Select the **Run this rule now on messages already in the current folder** check box.

9. Click **OK.**

10. All the emails in your Inbox with a subject that matches the condition will be moved to the specified folder.

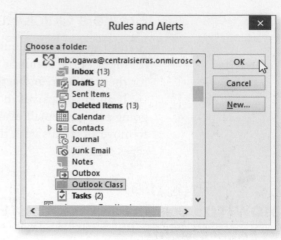

6-10 Select a folder for the rule

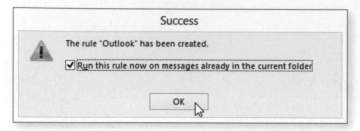

6-11 *Success* dialog box

> **MORE INFO**
>
> If you forget to create a folder before creating a rule, you can create a new folder in the *Rules and Alerts* dialog box by clicking the **New** button.

> **MORE INFO**
>
> When creating a rule that looks for a word in the subject, Outlook looks for *exactly* what you type. Common errors include misspellings and a space after the word. The word you type is not case sensitive.

> **ANOTHER WAY**
>
> When an email is selected in your *Folder* pane, a Quick Rule can be created by clicking the *Rules* button in the *Move* group or by right-clicking the message and choosing **Rules** and then **Create Rule.**

Create an Advanced Rule

Creating a Quick Rule based on an email in your Inbox is effective and efficient, but you are limited by the number of conditions and actions from which to select.

To have more customization options for the rules you create, you will need to open the ***Rules and Alerts*** dialog box (click the **Home** tab, **Rules** button in the *Move* group, and select **Manage Rules & Alerts** as shown in Figure 6-12). This dialog box lists the rules existing on your computer and allows you to create, modify, delete, and order the existing rules.

6-12 *Manage Rules & Alerts*

When you click the *New Rule* button (Figure 6-13), the *Rules Wizard* dialog box opens. The *Rules Wizard* will step you through the creation of your rule. There will be five steps in the *Rules Wizard* dialog box to create your new rule.

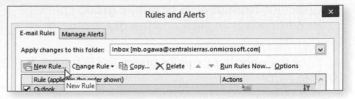

6-13 Create a new rule

- *Step 1:* Choose to use a rule template or create a blank rule. This step will also determine whether this rule is to be applied to incoming or outgoing emails.
- *Step 2:* Select the condition of the rule.
- *Step 3:* Set the action Outlook is to perform if the *condition* is met.
- *Step 4:* Specify any exceptions to the rule.
- *Step 5:* Name and run the rule.

There are rule templates created for the most common types of rules used. When one of these is selected, you will be taken to the next step to specify the condition. You can also choose to start creating a rule from a blank rule.

HOW TO: Create a New Rule

1. Click the **Mail** button in the *Navigation* pane.
2. Create a new folder in your *Inbox.*
3. Click the **Rules** button in the *Move* group on the *Home* tab, and choose **Manage Rules & Alerts.** The *Rules and Alerts* dialog box opens.
4. Click the **New Rule** button. The *Rules Wizard* dialog box opens.
5. Select **Apply rule on messages I receive** in the *Start from a blank rule* section (Figure 6-14).
6. Click **Next.** You will be taken to the next step to select a condition for the rule.

6-14 Create a new blank rule

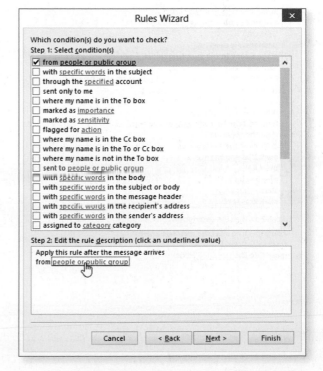

6-15 Click the people or public group link

7. Select the **from people or public group** check box. In the bottom section of this dialog box, the condition is displayed.

8. Click the **people or public group** link in the bottom section (Figure 6-15). The *Rule Address* dialog box opens.

9. Select the name of the individual for the condition of the rule (Figure 6-16).

10. Click **From** and **OK**.
    - The *Rule Address* dialog box will close, and you will be taken back to the *Rules Wizard* dialog box.
    - Notice the person's name appears in the bottom section as the condition for which Outlook is looking.

11. Click **Next.** You will be taken to the *action* step in the *Rules Wizard* dialog box.

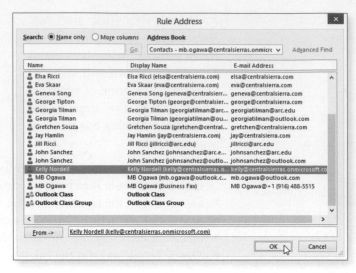

6-16 Select addresses

12. Select the **move it to the specified folder** check box (Figure 6-17).

13. In the bottom section, click the **specified** folder link. The *Rules and Alerts* dialog box opens.

14. Click the desired folder and press **OK** (Figure 6-18). You will be taken back to the *Rules Wizard* dialog box. Always read the rule in the bottom section to make sure the condition and action are correct.

15. Click **Next.** You will be taken to the *exceptions* step.

16. Click **Next.** There will be no exceptions to this rule. The *Finish rule setup* step appears.

17. Customize the name of the rule in the *Step 1* area.

18. Select the **Run this rule now on messages already in "Inbox"** check box (Figure 6-19).

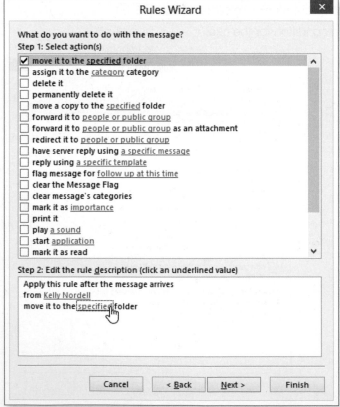

6-17 Select an action

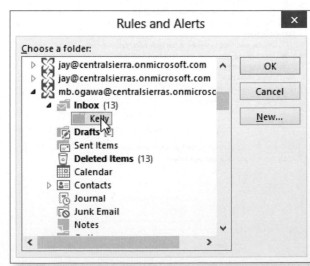

6-18 Select a location

19. Confirm that the **Turn on this rule** box is selected.

20. In the bottom section, read the rule one last time to confirm that the condition and action are correct.

21. Click **Finish.**

- The rule will check the condition on all the emails in your Inbox.
- If the condition is met, Outlook will move all emails matching the condition to the folder you created (see Figure 6-19).

6-19 Setup rule options

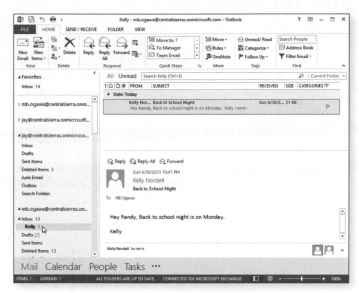

6-20 Email message automatically moved

22. You will be taken back to the *Rules and Alerts* dialog box. Notice the new rule is in the list of rules.

23. Click **Apply** and then **OK.** See how the email from Kelly was automatically moved into the *Kelly* folder (Figure 6-20).

Creating rules might seem like a daunting process, but once you have gone through the steps of creating a rule and understand the logical *condition, action, exception* sequence, you'll realize that creating rules is actually very simple. And not only are rules easy to create and use, but they are also very effective in helping you to organize and customize your Inbox, which will ultimately make you a more proficient and productive Outlook user.

> ### MORE INFO
>
> It is best to keep rules simple: one condition and one action (and an exception if necessary). The more conditions and actions you have in one rule, the greater the chance of either diluting the effectiveness of the rule or causing the rule to not function as intended.

> ### MORE INFO
>
> When using Outlook in a stand-alone environment, your rules are stored on your computer.
> If you are using Outlook in an Exchange environment, your rules are stored on the Exchange server.
> This means that most rules will run wherever you access Outlook, including Outlook Web Access. Some rules are client-only rules, which means they will only run on the computer on which they were created.

Modify a Rule

Once a rule is created, it is very easy to modify the condition, action, or exception. Rules can also be modified to run on different folders within your mailbox.

HOW TO: Modify a Rule

1. Open the *Rules and Alerts* dialog box.
2. Select the rule to be modified, click the **Change Rule** button, and choose **Edit Rule Settings** (Figure 6-21). The *Rules Wizard* dialog box opens. You can also double-click the rule to open the *Rules Wizard* dialog box.
3. You can change the condition, action, exception, name, or folder on which the rule is to run.
4. If you modify a rule, be sure to select the **Run this rule now on messages already in "Inbox"** check box and click **Finish** to apply the changes and run the rule.

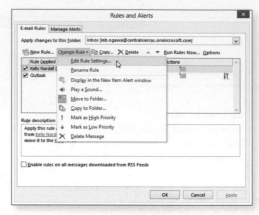

6-21 *Edit Rule Settings*

Delete or Turn On/Off a Rule

There will be times when you will no longer need or want a rule that you created previously. A rule can easily be deleted by selecting the rule in the *Rules and Alerts* dialog box and either pressing the *Delete* button or right-clicking the rule and choosing *Delete*.

Sometimes you might want to turn off a rule but not delete it because you might use it again sometime in the future. Rules can easily be turned off so that no action will be performed.

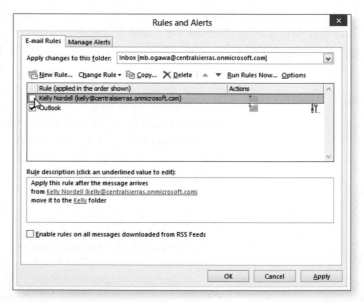

HOW TO: Turn off a Rule

1. Open the *Rules and Alerts* dialog box.
2. Deselect the check box to the left of the rule to turn it off (Figure 6-22).
3. Click **Apply** and then **OK.** The rule is now turned off.

6-22 **Turn a rule off**

A rule can be turned back on by checking the box to the left of the rule in the *Rules and Alerts* dialog box. It is easy to view which rules are on or off by looking at your list of rules in the *Rules and Alerts* dialog box. A check in the check box indicates that a rule is turned on, and no check in the check box indicates that a rule is turned off.

Run a Rule

When a rule that was turned off is turned back on, it is important to run this rule on messages currently in the Inbox. Outlook provides you with a feature to run specific rules without having to step through the *Rules Wizard*.

You will be given the options of selecting the rules to be run, the folder on which to run each rule, and what type of messages on which to apply each rule (*All Messages, Unread Messages,* or *Read Messages*). A ***Rule Description*** is provided in the middle of this dialog box for the selected rule.

HOW TO: Run a Rule

1. Click the **Rules** button [*Home* tab, *Move* group] and select **Manage Rules & Alerts.**
2. Select the *Rule* you want to run and click the **Run Rules Now** button. The *Run Rules Now* dialog box opens (Figure 6-23).
3. Check the rule to run. The *Rule Description* area will display the condition and action (and exception if applicable) of this rule.
4. Specify the folder on which the rule is to run.
5. Specify the types of messages on which to apply the rule.
6. Click **Run Now.**
7. Click **Close** to close the *Run Rules Now* dialog box.

6-23 *Run Rules Now* dialog box

> **ANOTHER WAY**
>
> The *Run Rules Now* dialog box can also be accessed from the *Rules and Alerts* dialog box.

Rearrange Rules

As you begin using rules, you will find more and more uses for them. It will not be long before you have a long list of rules running in Outlook. The rules in Outlook are ***hierarchical***, which means that those at the top of the list are run before those at the bottom. It is important to order rules properly to prioritize the order in which the rules are run and minimize the potential for conflict. For example, if you have a rule to mark an email as important if it comes from a particular person and a rule to move all emails with attachments to an *Attachments* folder, you might have a conflict if you receive an email from that particular person and it has an attachment. If the attachment rule is above the mark as important rule, the email message will be moved to the *Attachments* folder but not marked as important.

You will need to determine which action is the most important and make sure that rule is above the other rules in the *Rules and Alerts* dialog box. There are up and down buttons in the dialog box that can be used to move rules up or down in the rule hierarchy.

HOW TO: Reorder Rules

1. Open the *Rules and Alerts* dialog box.
2. Select the rule to be moved up or down in priority.
3. Click the *Move Up* or *Move Down* button (Figure 6-24).
4. Click **Apply** and **OK**.

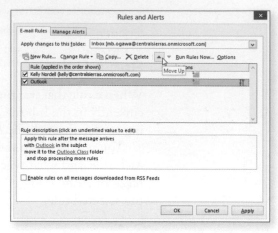

6-24 Move rules up or down

PAUSE & PRACTICE: OUTLOOK 6-2

For this Pause and Practice project, you create two rules. The first rule is to move email from a specific instructor to the folder you created in *Pause & Practice 6-1*. The second rule moves all of your email messages from both of your group members into the folder you created in *Pause & Practice 6-1*.

1. Create a Quick Rule to move email messages from your instructor into the *[instructor name]* folder you created in *Pause & Practice 6-1* (Figure 6-25).
   a. Locate and open a message from your instructor.
   b. Click the **Rules** button in the *Move* group on the *Message* tab.
   c. Choose **Create Rule.** The *Create Rule* dialog box opens.
   d. In the conditions area (the top half of the dialog box), check **From [instructor name]** (the name will vary based on your instructor's name).
   e. In the actions area (the bottom half of the dialog box), check **Move the item to folder** and click the **Select Folder** button.
   f. Select the **[instructor name]** folder from the folder list and press **OK.** The *Create Rule* dialog box will still be open.
   g. Click **OK.**
   h. Select the **Run this rule now on messages already in "Inbox"** check box.
   i. Click **OK.**

2. Create an advanced rule to move emails from your two partners into the *Group Project* folder (Figure 6-25).
   a. Click the **Mail** button in the *Navigation* pane.
   b. Click the **Rules** button in the *Move* group on the *Home* tab and choose **Manage Rules & Alerts.** The *Rules and Alerts* dialog box opens.
   c. Click the **New Rule** button. The *Rules Wizard* dialog box opens.
   d. Select **Apply rule on messages I receive** in the *Start from a blank rule* section.
   e. Click **Next.** You will be taken to the next step to select a condition for the rule.
   f. Check the **from people or public group** box. In the bottom section of this dialog box, the condition is displayed.

g. Click the **people or public group** link in the bottom section. The *Rule Address* dialog box opens.
h. Select the names of your group members if they are in your contacts list or type their email addresses with a semi colon (;) between their email addresses.
i. Click **From** and **OK.**
j. Click **Next.** You will be taken to the *action* step in the *Rules Wizard* dialog box.
k. Check the **move it to the specified folder** box.
l. In the bottom section, click the **specified** folder link. The *Rules and Alerts* dialog box opens.

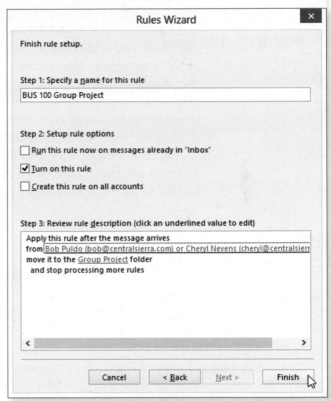

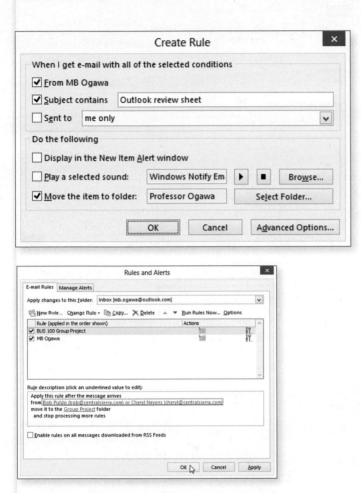

6-25 Completed Pause & Practice 6-2

m. Click the **Group Project** folder and press **OK.** You will be taken back to the *Rules Wizard* dialog box.
n. Click **Next.** You will be taken to the *exceptions* step.
o. Click **Next.** There will be no exceptions to this rule. The *Finish rule setup* step appears.
p. Type Class Name Group Project in the *Step 1* area.
q. Confirm that the **Turn on this rule** box is selected.
r. In the bottom section, read the rule one last time to confirm that the condition and action are correct.
s. Click **Finish.**
t. Click **Apply** and then **OK.**

Using Quick Steps

Quick Steps are powerful tools in Outlook. Similar to a rule, a *Quick Step* performs an action on a selected email. The main difference between a *Quick Step* and a rule is that *Quick Steps* are not based on a condition, but rather they are applied to the emails you select.

Modify an Existing Quick Step

Outlook has some preset *Quick Steps* created for you. When you select an email in your Inbox and click one of the *Quick Steps*, the *Quick Step* will automatically apply the action. For example, the *Reply & Delete Quick Step* (Figure 6-26) will create a reply message to the sender and delete the original message.

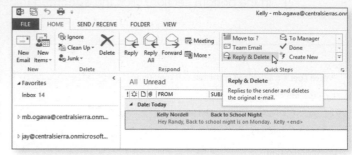

6-26 *Reply & Delete Quick Step*

Some of the *Quick Steps* will need to be customized to specify the action to be performed. For example, the *Team Email Quick Step* needs to have the recipients on your team selected to be able to perform the action.

HOW TO: Modify an Existing Quick Step

1. Select the email in the *Folder* pane or open an email on which to apply the *Quick Step.*

2. In the *Quick Steps* group, click the **Quick Step** to be applied (*Team Email* used in this example). The *Customize Quick Step* (or *First Time Setup*) dialog box opens.

3. Click the **To** button (Figure 6-27) to select the team members to be included in this *Quick Step* and click **OK.** You can also enter the email addresses followed by semicolon.

4. Change the **Name** of the *Quick Step* as desired.

5. Clicking the **Options** button opens the *Edit [Quick Step's name]* dialog box (Figure 6-28). You can add additional actions to this *Quick Step* in this dialog box.

6. Click the **Show Options** link to display more options available for this action. The **Hide Options** link will hide these available options.

7. Click **Save** to close this dialog box and return to the *Customize Quick Step* dialog box.

8. Click **Save** to save this *Quick Step* and apply it to the selected message.

6-27 *First Time Setup* dialog box

6-28 *Edit Quick Step* dialog box

Create a New Quick Step

As you begin using *Quick Steps,* you will find the need to create your own custom *Quick Steps.* These new custom *Quick Steps* will appear in the *Quick Steps* group on the *Home* and *Message* tabs. *Quick Steps* are not limited to one action but can include multiple actions to be performed on a selected email message. For example, you can create a *Quick Step* to mark an email as high importance, mark it as read, and move it to a folder.

HOW TO: Create a New Quick Step

1. Click the **Create New** *Quick Step* button [*Home* tab, *Quick Steps* group] (Figure 6-29). The *Edit Quick Step* dialog box opens (Figure 6-30). You can also click the **New Quick Step** option and select **Custom** from the expand button.
2. Give the *Quick Step* a **Name.**
3. Click the pull-down arrow to display a list of actions that can be performed. *Note: The list of actions includes more than are displayed in the figure below.*
4. Select the action to be performed (see Figure 6-30). If additional criteria are available, the *Show Options* link will appear below the action.
5. Click the **Add Action** button to add another action (Figure 6-31). An action can be deleted by clicking the **X** (delete) button to the right of the action (see Figure 6-31).

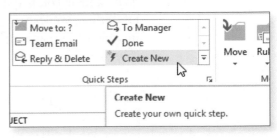

6-29 *Create New Quick Step* button

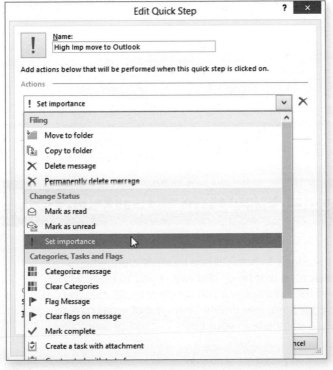

6-30 *Edit Quick Step* dialog box

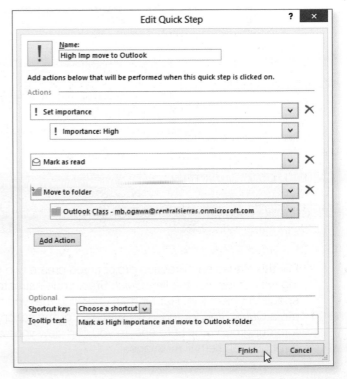

6-31 Completed *Quick Step*

6. In the *Tooltip text* area, type a description for this *Quick Step* (see Figure 6-31). This *Tooltip* will appear when your pointer is placed over the *Quick Step*.

7. When all the actions have been added, click the **Finish** button to create the new *Quick Step* (see Figure 6-31). The new *Quick Step* will be included in the list of *Quick Steps*.

Manage Quick Steps

Like rules, *Quick Steps* can easily be managed. You can open the *Manage Quick Steps* dialog box by clicking the **Manage Quick Steps** option [*Home* tab, *Quick Steps* group, drop-down arrow]. The *Manage Quick Steps* dialog box allows you to create new *Quick Steps* and modify, duplicate, or delete existing ones. You can change the display order of *Quick Steps*, and as you begin to have a lot of them you can create groups in which to organize *Quick Steps* (Figure 6-32).

6-32 *Manage Quick Steps* dialog box

> ## ANOTHER WAY
>
> A shortcut can be added to a *Quick Step* by selecting a shortcut keystroke combination when creating or editing a *Quick Step*.

> ## MORE INFO
>
> The *Restore Defaults* button in the *Manage Quick Steps* dialog box will restore the *Quick Steps* to their original settings.

PAUSE & PRACTICE: OUTLOOK 6-3

For this Pause and Practice project, you create two *Quick Steps* to help you be more efficient when working with email. For the first *Quick Step,* your instructor indicated that he or she wants you to email with a specific subject line. Rather than checking that you typed the right subject line for each message, you create a *Quick Step* for those messages. For the second *Quick Step,* you create tasks out of email messages for your group project to ensure you can view your work to complete in your tasks instead of searching through many email messages.

1. Create a *Quick Step* to email your instructor with the subject *[class name]* (Figure 6-33).
   a. Click the **Create New** *Quick Step* button [*Home* tab, *Quick Steps* group]. The *Edit Quick Step* dialog box opens.
   b. In the *Name* text area type Email [instructor name].
   c. Click the pull-down arrow to display a list of actions that can be performed.
   d. Select **New Message.**
   e. Click the **Show Options** link below the action.
   f. Click the **To** button. Select your instructor's email address and click the **To** button followed by **OK.** If your instructor's email address is not in your Contacts, type it into the *To* field in the *Edit Quick Step* dialog box.
   g. In the *Subject* field, type class name].
   h. In the *Tooltip text* area, type Email to instructor for [class name]**.**
   i. Click the **Finish** button to create the new *Quick Step.*

2. Create a *Quick Step* to create a task with an attachment (Figure 6-33).
   a. Click the **Create New** *Quick Step* button [*Home* tab, *Quick Steps* group]. The *Edit Quick Step* dialog box opens.
   b. In the *Name* text area type Group Project Task.
   c. Click the pull-down arrow to display a list of actions that can be performed.
   d. Select **Create a task with attachment.**
   e. Click the **Add Action** button to add another action.
   f. Click the pull-down arrow to display a list of actions that can be performed.
   g. Select **Delete message.**
   h. In the *Tooltip text* area, type Create task and delete message.
   i. Click the **Finish** button to create the new *Quick Step.*

3. Send an email message to one of your partners to request the draft of the executive summary.
   a. Click the **Mail** button in the *Navigation* pane.'
   b. Click the **New Email** button [*Home* tab, *New* group].
   c. Enter the following information in your message:
      To: partner's email address
      Subject: Executive Summary Request
      Body: Hi [partner name],
      Please email me a draft of the executive summary when you finish it.
      Sincerely,
      [your name]
   d. Click **Send.**

4. Create a task from the message (Figure 6-33).
   a. Locate the email your partner sent. It is in the *Group Project* folder.
   b. Click the **Group Project Task** *Quick Step* [*Home* tab, *Quick Steps* group].
   c. Click the **Save & Close** button.

5. Email the task to your instructor as an Outlook item.
   a. Click the **Mail** button in the Navigation pane.
   b. Click the **New Email** button [*Home* tab, *New* group].
   c. Enter the following information in your message:
      To: [instructor's email address]
      Cc: [your email address]
      Subject: Outlook Pause & Practice 6-3
      Body: Hi [instructor name],
      Attached is the Outlook item for the Pause & Practice 6-3 exercise. Sincerely, [your name]
   d. Click the **Attach Item** button [*Message* tab, *Include* group] and select **Outlook Item.**
   e. Select the **Tasks** option and locate the task you created.

f. Click **OK.**

g. Click **Send.**

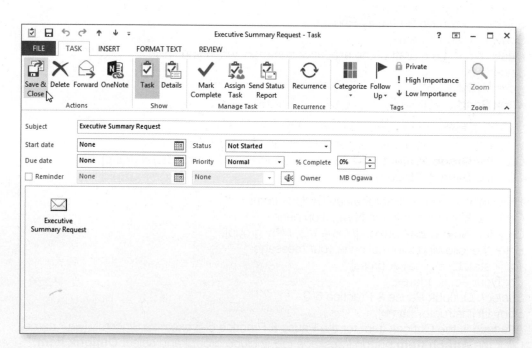

6-33 Completed Pause & Practice 6-3

Using Search Folders

Search folders are somewhat related to rules in that they look for a specific condition or criterion in email messages and, if the condition is met, the message will be displayed in the search folder. Search folders differ from rules in that the message is not physically moved to a different location.

Search folders are virtual folders; they don't actually contain any messages, but rather they display email items that are located in other folders that meet a certain condition. For example, you can create a search folder for *Unread Mail*. Any email message in your mailbox that is unread will be displayed in the *Folder* pane when you click the **Unread Mail** search folder in the *Navigation* pane (Figure 6-34).

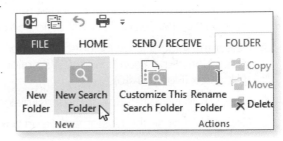

6-34 *Unread Mail* search folder

Create a New Search Folder

Suppose you wanted to create a search folder that looks for all the emails from your professor, but you do not want to create a rule to physically move these messages to a separate folder. A search folder can be created to find and display all the messages from your professor.

> **MORE INFO**
>
> Searching for specific Outlook items will be covered in Chapter 7.

Search folders are very easy to create, customize, and delete.

HOW TO: Create a New Search Folder

1. Click the **Mail** button in the *Navigation* pane.
2. Click the **Folder** tab and then the **New Search Folder** button in the *New* group (Figure 6-35). The *New Search Folder* dialog box opens.
3. Select **Mail from specific people** as the condition (Figure 6-36).
4. Click **Choose** to select a contact. The *Select Names* dialog box opens.
5. Select the name of the contact for the condition of the search folder.
6. Click the **From** button to add the contact or double-click the contact.
7. Click **OK** to close the *Select Names* dialog box.
8. Click **OK** to close the *New Search Folder* dialog box. The new search folder will appear in your list of search folders in the *Navigation* pane (Figure 6-37).

6-35 *New Search Folder* button

6-36 *New Search Folder* dialog box

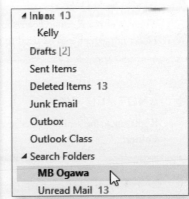

6-37 Search folder

When creating a new search folder, there are many different criteria options available from which to choose. You can also choose the **Create a custom Search Folder** option at the bottom of the *New Search Folder* dialog box for more customization options.

Customize a Search Folder

You can customize search folders by changing the name of the folder, the criteria for the search, and/or the mailbox folders to be included in the search. When you create a new search folder, by default, all the mailbox folders (or personal folders) are included in the search for mail messages meeting the criterion.

HOW TO: Customize a Search Folder

1. Click the **Mail** button in the *Navigation* pane.
2. Select the search folder to be customized.
3. Click the **Folder** tab and then the **Customize This Search Folder** button in the *Actions* group (Figure 6-38). The *Customize* dialog box opens (Figure 6-39).
4. You can change the name of the search folder, select the criteria, or indicate which folders to include in the *Mail from these folders will be included in the Search Folder* selection box.
5. Click the **Browse** button to change the folders to be included in the search. The *Select Folder(s)* dialog box opens.
6. Select the folders to be included in the search for this search folder. Notice the *Search subfolders* option at the bottom of the dialog box (Figure 6-40).
7. Click **OK** to close the *Select Folder(s)* dialog box.
8. Click **OK** to close the *Customize* dialog box.

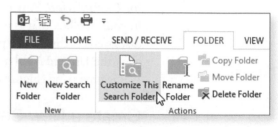

6-38 *Customize This Search Folder* button

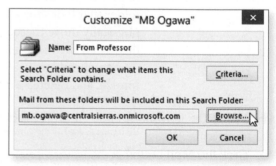

6-39 *Customize Search Folder* dialog box

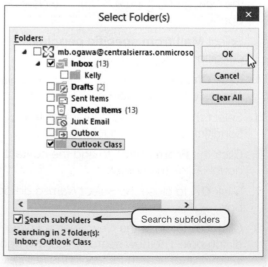

6-40 *Select Folder(s)* dialog box

> **MORE INFO**
>
> There is also a *Rename Folder* button in the *Actions* group on the *Folder* tab, which can be used to rename a search folder.

> **ANOTHER WAY**
>
> Right-click the search folder and choose **Customize This Search Folder.**

Search folders can also be customized to show either the total number of items in the folder or the number of unread items in the folder.

HOW TO: Customize How the Number of Items in the Folder Is Displayed

1. Click one of the search folders.
2. Click the **Folder** tab.
3. Click the **Folder Properties** button in the *Properties* group. The *[Folder's Name] Properties* dialog box opens (Figure 6-41).
4. Click either *Show number of unread items* or *Show total number of items*.
5. Click **Apply** and then **OK.**

> **ANOTHER WAY**
>
> Right-click the search folder and choose **Properties.**

> **MORE INFO**
>
> When a new search folder is created, the default setting is *Show number of unread items.* The number of unread items is displayed in blue parentheses. When *Show total* number of items is selected, the total number of items are displayed in green brackets.

6-41 Search folder properties

Delete a Search Folder

Because search folders are virtual folders, they don't physically contain any email messages. When a search folder is deleted, none of the messages that were displayed in the search folder are deleted.

To delete a search folder, click the search folder in the *Navigation* pane and click the **Delete** button in the *Actions* group on the *Folder* tab or press **Delete** on your keyboard. You can also right-click the search folder and choose **Delete Folder.** When deleting a search folder, a dialog box opens asking if you want to delete the search folder and informing you that the items contained in the search folder will not be deleted (Figure 6-42). Press **Yes** to delete the search folder.

6-42 Delete search folder confirmation

> **ANOTHER WAY**
>
> **Ctrl+D** deletes a selected search folder throughout Outlook.

PAUSE & PRACTICE: OUTLOOK 6-4

For this Pause and Practice project, you utilize search folders to help you find information quickly. You create a search folder for email messages from your partners with attachments to allow you to easily locate files you are working with. You also want to use a search folder to quickly locate email messages from your instructor that contain the word *due* to quickly find messages with due dates or changes to due dates.

1. Create a new search folder to find messages from your partners with attachments.
   a. Click the **Mail** button in the *Navigation* pane.
   b. Click the **Folder** tab and then the **New Search Folder** button in the *New* group. The *New Search Folder* dialog box opens.
   c. Select **Create a custom Search Folder.**
   d. Click **Choose.** The *Custom Search Folder* dialog box opens.
   e. In the *Name* text area, type Group Project Attachments.
   f. Click the **Criteria** button. The *Search Folder Criteria* dialog box opens.
   g. In the *Messages* tab, type your partners' email addresses in the *From* text area or click the **From** button and select their contacts.
   h. Click the **More Choices** tab.
   i. Click the **Only items with** check box and ensure the option is set to **one or more attachments.**
   j. Click **OK** to close the *Search Folder Criteria* dialog box.
   k. Click **OK** to close the *Custom Search Folder* dialog box.
   l. Click **OK** to close the *New Search* Folder dialog box.
   m. The new search folder will appear in your list of search folders in the *Navigation* pane.

2. Customize the *Group Project Attachments* search folder to show the total number of items.
   a. Right-click the *Group Project Attachments* search folder and select **Properties.**
   b. Click the **Show total number of items** radio button.
   c. Click **OK.**

3. Create a new search folder to find messages from your instructor that contain the word *due* in the subject or body of the message.
   a. Click the **Mail** button in the *Navigation* pane.
   b. Click the **Folder** tab and then the **New Search Folder** button in the *New* group. The *New Search Folder* dialog box opens.
   c. Select **Create a custom Search Folder.**
   d. Click **Choose.** The *Custom Search Folder* dialog box opens.
   e. In the *Name* text area, type Class Due Dates.
   f. Click the **Criteria** button. The *Search Folder Criteria* dialog box opens.
   g. In the *Messages* tab, type your instructor's email address in the *From* text area or click the **From** button and select his or her contact.
   h. In the *Search for word(s)* text area type Due.
   i. Click the **In** drop-down arrow and select **subject field and message body.**
   j. Click **OK** to close the *New Search* Folder dialog box.
   k. The new search folder will appear in your list of search folders in the *Navigation* pane.

4. See Figure 6-43 for completed Pause & Practice 6-4.

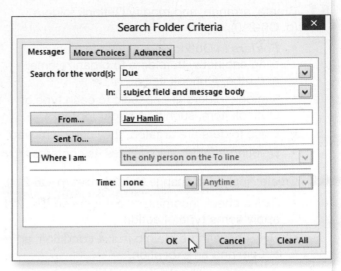

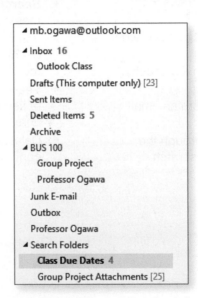

6-43 Completed Pause & Practice 6-4

Chapter Summary

6.1 Create, arrange, and modify Outlook folders (p. O6-210).

- **Folders** in Outlook are similar to a physical filing cabinet with folders to organize email and other Outlook items.
- Outlook folders are specific to each type of Outlook item, such as a folder for tasks.
- Once folders are created, they can be moved.
- Deleting a folder also deletes its contents.

6.2 Create, apply, and change Outlook rules (p. O6-214).

- **Rules** check incoming or outgoing emails and apply some type of action.
- Rules have three main parts: a condition, an action, and an exception.
- **A condition** checks if an email message meets a specific criteria.
- **An action** is what is done with the email when the condition is met.
- **An exception** nullifies an action if a specific criteria is met.
- A Quick Rule can be created from an email message.
- The *Rules Wizard* guides you through the process of creating a rule from scratch.

- Rules can be edited after they are created.
- Rules run **hierarchically;** therefore rules listed at the top run before those listed at the bottom.

6.3 Customize and use *Quick Steps* (p. O6-224).

- **Quick Steps** are similar to rules and can be applied to specific email messages.
- Outlook includes default *Quick Steps,* which you can edit.
- New *Quick Steps* can be created for common tasks.

6.4 Utilize search folders to find email messages (p. O6-229).

- **Search folders** use virtual folders to display messages that meet specific criteria.
- You can create search folders for a variety of criteria including displaying only *Unread* messages.
- Search folders can display either the number of items in the virtual folder or the number of unread items.
- Deleting a search folder does not delete its contents because it is a virtual folder.

Check for Understanding

In the **Online Learning Center** for this text (www.mhhe.com/office2013inpractice), there are a variety of resources that can be used to review the concepts covered in this chapter.

The following Online Learning Resources are available in the Online Learning Center:

- Multiple choice questions
- Short answer questions
- Matching exercises

Guided Project 6-1

For this project, you are a real estate agent for Placer Hills Real Estate (PHRE). You just started working with two new clients, Nina Hu and Jim Cross, who are both looking for new homes. You use folders and rules to keep your messages specific to your client and your company email organized.
[Student Learning Outcomes 6.1, 6.2]

Skills Covered in This Project

- Create folders.
- Move folders.
- Delete a folder.
- Create a Quick Rule.
- Create an advanced rule.
- Run a rule.

1. Create a folder for clients.
    a. Click the **Mail** button in the *Navigation* pane.
    b. Click the **Folder** tab.
    c. Click the **New Folder** button in the *New* group. The *Create New Folder* dialog box opens.
    d. Type Clients in the *Name* text area.
    e. In the *Folder contains* menu, confirm that the folder type is **Mail and Post Items.**
    f. In the *Select where to place the folder* section, specify your main email account folder.
    g. Click **OK.**

2. Create a folder for Nina.
    a. Click the **Mail** button in the *Navigation* pane.
    b. Click the **Folder** tab.
    c. Click the **New Folder** button in the *New* group. The *Create New Folder* dialog box opens.
    d. Type Nina Hu in the *Name* text area.
    e. In the *Folder contains* menu, confirm that the folder type is **Mail and Post Items.**
    f. In the *Select where to place the folder* section, specify your main email account folder.
    g. Click **OK.**

3. Create a folder for PHRE Internal Messages.
    a. Click the **Mail** button in the *Navigation* pane.
    b. Click the **Folder** tab.
    c. Click the **New Folder** button in the *New* group. The *Create New Folder* dialog box opens.
    d. Type PHRE Internal in the *Name* text area.
    e. In the *Folder contains* menu, confirm that the folder type is **Mail and Post Items.**
    f. In the *Select where to place the folder* section, specify your main email account folder.
    g. Click **OK.**

4. Create a folder for Jim Cross.
    a. Click the **Mail** button in the *Navigation* pane.
    b. Click the **Folder** tab.
    c. Click the **New Folder** button in the *New* group. The *Create New Folder* dialog box opens.
    d. Type Jim Cross in the *Name* text area.
    e. In the *Folder contains* menu, confirm that the folder type is **Mail and Post Items.**

    f. In the *Select where to place the folder* section, specify your main email account folder.
    g. Click **OK**.

5. Move the *Nina Hu* folder into the *Clients* folder.
    a. In the *Navigation* pane, select the *Nina Hu* folder.
    b. Click the **Folder** tab.
    c. Click the **Move Folder** button in the *Actions* group. The *Move Folder* dialog box opens.
    d. In the *Move the selected folder to the folder* section, click the *Clients* folder.
    e. Click **OK**.

6. Delete the *Jim Cross* folder since he decided move to another state and will not need your services.
    a. Select the *Jim Cross* folder in the *Navigation* pane.
    b. Click the **Delete** button in the *Actions* group on the *Folder* tab.
    c. A warning dialog box opens asking you if you are sure you want to delete the folder and its contents. Click **Yes** to delete the folder and all its contents.

7. Send an email message to a partner as Nina Hu.
    a. Click the **Mail** button in the *Navigation* pane.
    b. Click the **New Email** button [*Home* tab, *New* group].
    c. Enter the following information in your message:
       To: partner's email address
       Subject: Pre-approval from bank
       Body: Hi [partner's name]
       I just received my pre-approval letter from the bank. I am approved for a purchase up to $375,000 ($75,000 down payment and $300,000 loan).
       Sincerely,
       Nina
    d. Click **Send.**

8. Create a Quick Rule to move email messages from Nina into the *Nina Hu* folder.
    a. Locate and open a message from Nina.
    b. Click the **Rules** button in the *Move* group on the *Message* tab.
    c. Choose **Create Rule.** The *Create Rule* dialog box opens.
    d. In the conditions area (the top half of the dialog box), check **From Nina Hu** (the name may vary based on who sent you the message).
    e. In the actions area (the bottom half of the dialog box), check **Move the item to folder** and click the **Select Folder** button.
    f. Select the **Nina Hu** folder from the folder list and press **OK**. The *Create Rule* dialog box will still be open.
    g. Click **OK.**
    h. Select the **Run this rule now on messages already in "Inbox"** check box.
    i. Click **OK.**

9. Create an advanced rule to move emails from your manager with attachments into the *PHRF Internal* folder.
    a. Click the **Mail** button in the *Navigation* pane.
    b. Click the **Rules** button in the *Move* group on the *Home* tab and choose **Manage Rules & Alerts.** The *Rules and Alerts* dialog box opens.
    c. Click the **New Rule** button. The *Rules Wizard* dialog box opens.
    d. Select **Apply rule on messages I receive** in the *Start from a blank rule* section.
    e. Click **Next.** You will be taken to the next step to select a condition for the rule.
    f. Select the **with specific words in the recipient's address** check box. In the bottom section of this dialog box, the condition is displayed.

g. Click the **specific words** link in the bottom section. The *Search Text* dialog box opens.

h. Type phre.com in the top text area and click **Add.**

i. Click the **OK** button.

j. Click **Next.** You will be taken to the *action* step in the *Rules Wizard* dialog box.

k. Select the **move it to the specified folder** check box.

l. In the bottom section, click the **specified** folder link. The *Rules and Alerts* dialog box opens.

m. Click the **PHRE Internal** folder and press **OK.** You will be taken back to the *Rules Wizard* dialog box.

n. Click **Next.** You will be taken to the *exceptions* step.

o. Click **Next.** There will be no exceptions to this rule. The *Finish rule setup* step appears.

p. Type PHRE Internal in the *Step 1* area.

q. Confirm that the **Turn on this rule** box is selected.

r. In the bottom section, read the rule one last time to confirm that the condition and action are correct.

s. Click **Finish.**

t. Click **Apply** and then **OK** (Figure 6-44).

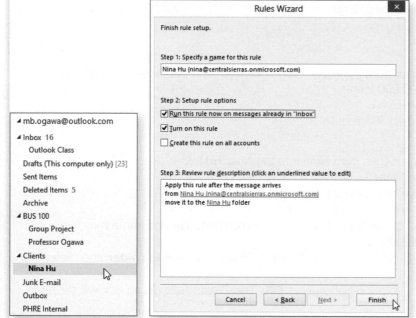
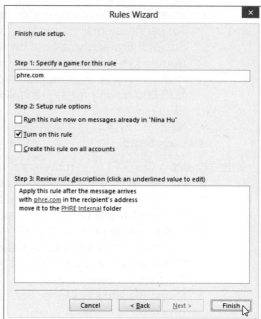

6-44 Completed Guided Project 6-1

Guided Project 6-2

As a real estate agent for PHRE, there are several emails that you send quite often, so you create *Quick Steps* to make your work more efficient. You create a *Quick Step* to forward messages to your manager when you need approval and create an appointment when you meet with your clients.
[Student Learning Outcome 6.3]

Skills Covered in This Project

- Create a *Quick Step.*
- Use the *Forward* feature.
- Use options within actions.
- Add *Tooltips* to *Quick Step.*
- Create an advanced *Quick Step.*
- Create appointments with a *Quick Step.*

---

1. Create a *Quick Step* to email your instructor with the subject *class name.*
   a. Click the **Create New** *Quick Step* button [*Home* tab, *Quick Steps* group]. The *Edit Quick Step* dialog box opens.
   b. In the *Name* text area type Manager Approval.
   c. Click the pull-down arrow to display a list of actions that can be performed.
   d. Select **Forward.**
   e. Click the **Show Options** link below the action.
   f. Click the **To** button. Select your partner's email address and click the **To** button or type it in the *To* text area. If your partner's email address is not in your Contacts, type it into the *To* field in the *Edit Quick Step* dialog box.
   g. In the *Subject* field, type FW: Contract Approval.
   h. In the *Tooltip text* area, type Email to manager for approval.
   i. Click the **Finish** button to create the new *Quick Step.*

2. Create a *Quick Step* to create a task with an attachment.
   a. Click the **Create New** *Quick Step* button [*Home* tab, *Quick Steps* group]. The *Edit Quick Step* dialog box opens.
   b. In the *Name* text area type Client Meeting.
   c. Click the pull-down arrow to display a list of actions that can be performed.
   d. Select **Create an appointment with attachment.**
   e. In the *Tooltip text* area, type Set up client meetings.
   f. Click the **Finish** button to create the new *Quick Step.*

3. Send an email message to your partners to request a meeting about possible locations.
   a. Click the **Mail** button in the *Navigation* pane.
   b. Click the **New Email** button [*Home* tab, *New* group].
   c. Enter the following information in your message:
   To: partner's email address
   Subject: Possible locations?
   Body: Hi [partner name],
   Can we meet next week Monday at 10:00 AM to discuss possible locations for my new home?
   Thanks,
   [your name]
   d. Click **Send.**

4. Create a task from the message.
   a. Locate the email your partner sent. It is in the *Group Project* folder.
   b. Click the **Client Meeting** *Quick Step* [*Home* tab, *Quick Steps* group].
   c. Change the start time to be next week **Monday at 10:00 AM.**
   d. Change the end time to be next week **Monday at 11:00 AM.**
   e. Click the **Save & Close** button.

5. Email the task to your instructor as an Outlook item.
   a. Click the **Mail** button in the *Navigation* pane.
   b. Click the **New Email** button [*Home* tab, *New* group].

c. Enter the following information in your message:
   To: [instructor's email address]
   Cc: [your email address]
   Subject: Outlook Guided Project 6-2
   Body: Hi [instructor name],
   Attached is the Outlook item for the Guided Project 6-2 exercise.
   Sincerely,
   [student name]
d. Click the **Attach Item** button [*Message* tab, *Include* group] and select **Outlook Item.**
e. Select the **Calendar** option and locate the appointment you created.
f. Click **OK.**
g. Click **Send** (Figure 6-45).

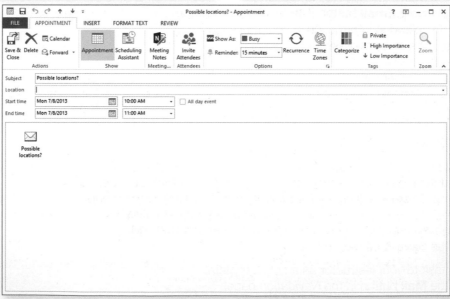

6-45 Completed Guided Project 6-2

Guided Project 6-3

While working with your coworkers and a variety of clients, you identified a handful of email messages that you constantly search for. Therefore, you develop search folders to find messages that deal with executed contracts and messages from your manager with attachments.
[Student Learning Outcome 6.4]

Skills Covered in This Project

- Create a search folder.
- Search for specific words in search folders.
- Search for specific senders in search folders.
- Search for messages with attachments in search folders.
- Use multiple criteria for a search folder.
- Modify the messages shown in search folders.
- Rename search folders.
- Modify a search folder.

---

1. Create a new search folder to find messages regarding executed contracts.
   a. Click the **Mail** button in the *Navigation* pane.
   b. Click the **Folder** tab and then on the **New Search Folder** button in the *New* group. The *New Search Folder* dialog box opens.
   c. Select **Mail with specific words.**
   d. Click **Choose.** The Search Text dialog box opens.
   e. In the first text area, type execute and click **Add.**
   f. In the first text area, type executed and click **Add.**
   g. In the first text area, type contract and click **Add.**
   h. In the first text area, type contracts and click **Add.**
   i. Click **OK** to close the *New Search* Folder dialog box.
   j. The new search folder will appear in your list of search folders in the *Navigation* pane.

2. Modify the search folder to be named *Executed Contracts* and show the total number of items in the search folder.
   a. Right-click the **Group Project Attachments** search folder and select **Properties.**
   b. Replace the text in the first text area with Executed Contracts.
   c. Click the **Show total number of items** radio button.
   d. Click **OK.**

3. Create a new search folder to find messages from your manager with attachments.
   a. Click the **Mail** button in the *Navigation* pane.
   b. Click the **Folder** tab and then on the **New Search Folder** button in the *New* group. The *New Search Folder* dialog box opens.
   c. Select **Create a custom Search Folder.**
   d. Click **Choose.** The *Custom Search Folder* dialog box opens.
   e. In the *Name* text area, type Manager Attachments.
   f. Click the **Criteria** button. The *Search Folder Criteria* dialog box opens.
   g. In the *Messages* tab, type your partners' email addresses into the *From* text area or click the **From** button and select their contacts.
   h. Click the *More Choices* tab.
   i. Click the **Only items with** check box and ensure the option is set to **one or more attachments.**
   j. Click **OK** to close the *Search Folder Criteria* dialog box.
   k. Click **OK** to close the *Custom Search Folder* dialog box.

l. Click **OK** to close the *New Search* Folder dialog box.

m. The new search folder will appear in your list of search folders in the *Navigation* pane (Figure 6-46).

6-46 Completed Guided Project 6-3

Independent Project 6-4

For this project, you are coordinating the Cycling Evolution Event (CEE) for the American River Cycling Club (ARCC). This year, you take registrations via email. Therefore, you create folders and rules to automatically organize registration information for you. You also want to keep email messages you send to the ARCC with updates in a specific folder to ensure you can quickly find the information. [Student Learning Outcomes 6.1, 6.2]

Skills Covered in This Project

- Create folders.
- Move folders.
- Create a Quick Rule.
- Create an advanced rule.
- Run a rule.

---

1. Create a folders to organize ARCC email.
   a. Create a folder named *ARCC*.
   b. Create a folder named *Registrations*.
   c. Create a folder named *Member updates*.
   d. Move the *Registrations* and *Member updates* folders into the *ARCC* folder.

2. Create a rule to organize registration email messages using the following criteria:
   Condition: Messages received with the term *Registration* in the subject.
   Action: Moved into the *Registrations* folder.
   Exception: Unless there is a question mark (?) in the message.

3. Create a rule to organize membership updates messages you send based on the following criteria:
   Condition: Messages sent with the term *Membership update* in the subject.
   Action: Copy to the *Member updates* folder (Figure 6-47).

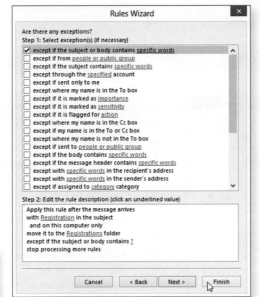
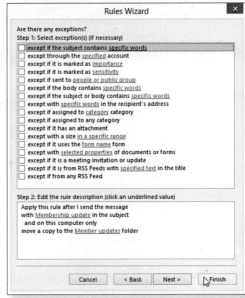

6-47 Completed Independent Project 6-4

Independent Project 6-5

After working on the registration last year, you remember that many of the ARCC members ask similar questions regarding the route. To make your work more efficient, you create a *Quick Step* to reply with the route information. You also create a *Quick Step* to quickly create messages to ARCC members. [Student Learning Outcome 6.3]

Skills Covered in This Project

- Create a *Quick Step*.
- Use the reply feature.
- Use new mail feature.
- Use options within actions.

- Add *Tooltips* to a *Quick Step*.
- Create an advanced *Quick Step*.
- Create appointments with a *Quick Step*.

1. Create a *Quick Step* to reply to ARCC members with the following information:
   Name: Route Reply
   Action: Reply
   Options text: Please see the following URL for the most updated route information: http://www.arcc.org/ceeroute/.
   Tooltip text: Reply with up-to-date route information.

2. Create a *Quick Step* to send email messages to ARCC members with the following information
   Name: Membership update email
   Action: New Message
   To: members@arcc.org
   Subject: Membership update
   Tooltip text: Write membership update messages. (Figure 6-48).

6-48 Independent Project 6-5 completed

Independent Project 6-6

As the CEE coordinator, you recall members asking about receipts for their payments. Since you started giving digital receipts via email, you create a search folder to quickly find receipts to send to participants who accidentally lost the initial message. You also remember participants asking about

their T-shirt size to ensure they receive the correct shirt when they finish the event. Therefore, you create a new search folder to find T-shirt sizes for all participants, which allows you to search within the search folder for a particular member's registration.
[Student Learning Outcome 6.4]

Skills Covered in This Project

- Create a search folder.
- Search for specific words in search folders.
- Search for specific senders.
- Search for messages with attachments in search folders.

- Use multiple criteria for a search folder.
- Modify the messages shown in search folders.
- Rename search folders.
- Modify a search folder.

---

1. Create a new search folder to find messages regarding receipt messages using the following criteria:
   Search folder name: Receipts
   From: [your email address]
   Search for the term *Receipt* in the subject field only.
   Search for items with attachments.
   Show the total number of items for the search folder.

2. Create a new search folder to find T-shirt sizes using the following criteria:
   Search folder name: Shirt size
   To: [your email address]
   Search for the term *size* in the subject field and message body.
   All messages received in the last month.
   Show the total number of items for the search folder (Figure 6-49).

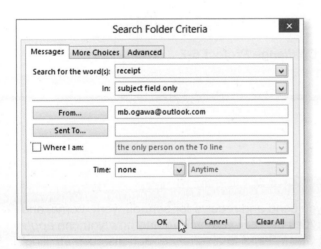
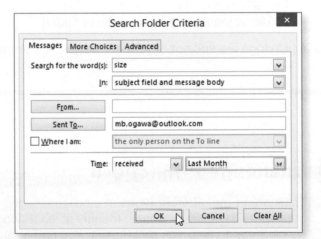

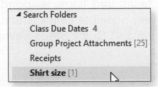

6-49 Completed Independent Project 6-6

O6-245

Challenge Project 6-7

Consider the different types of email you send and receive for school, work, home, and other extra-curricular activities. Identify at least two types of email you receive or send and how you can apply rules to help keep you organized. For example, you can apply rules to emails received from specific people, words in the subject line, or flagged for action. After identifying the types of email you receive, create folders and rules to apply. Email a description of the folders created and rules applied to your instructor.
[Student Learning Outcomes 6.1, 6.2]

- Create at least two rules.
- Create folders for rules when applicable.
- Ensure you have a reason to justify each rule.
- Explain why the rule performs better than a *Quick Step* or search folder.
- Email your instructor using the following message format:
  Rule 1: [reason you are creating a rule for the type of message including why it performs better than *Quick Steps* and search folders]
  Condition: [description of condition]
  Action: [description of action]
  Exception: [description of exceptions]
  Folder 1: [name and description of folder]

  Rule 2: [reason you are creating a rule for the type of message including why it performs better than *Quick Steps* and search folders]
  Condition: [description of condition]
  Action: [description of action]
  Exception: [description of exceptions]
  Folder 2: [name and description of folder]

- Change the subject of your message to **Outlook Challenge Project 6-7.**

Challenge Project 6-8

Think about the different types of email messages you send and receive for school, work, home, and other extracurricular activities. Identify at least two types of email you receive and how you can *apply Quick Steps* to help you be efficient. You can apply *Quick Steps* to a variety of actions such as filing, changing status, creating categories, tasks and flags, responding, creating new appointments, and managing conversations. After identifying possible *Quick Steps,* create folders for those that need it. Email a description of the folders created and *Quick Steps* developed to your instructor.
[Student Learning Outcomes 6.1, 6.3]

- Create at least two *Quick Steps.*
- Create folders for *Quick Steps* when applicable.

- Ensure you have a reason to justify each *Quick Step.*
- Use at least two actions for each *Quick Step.*
- Explain why the *Quick Step* performs better than a rule or search folder.
- Email your instructor using the following message format:

  Quick Step 1: [reason you are created a *Quick Step* for the type of message including why it fits better than rules and search folders]

  Action: [description of action]

  Action: [description of action]

  Folder 1: [name and description of folder]

  Quick Step 2: [reason you are created a *Quick Step* for the type of message including why it performs better than rules and search folders]

  Action: [description of action]

  Action: [description of action]

  Folder 2: [name and description of folder]

- Change the subject of your message to be **Outlook Challenge Project 6-8.**

Challenge Project 6-9

You probably receive many email messages throughout the day for school, work, family, and extracurricular activities. Identify at least two types of emails you send and receive and how you can apply search folders to help you find important messages. After identifying the types of email you send and receive, create search folders for those messages. Email a description of the search folders created to your instructor.
[Student Learning Outcome 6.4]

- Create at least two Search Folders.
- Ensure you have a reason to justify each Search Folder .
- Identify criteria for the Search Folder.
- One of the search folders should contain more than one criteria.
- Email your instructor using the following message format:

  Search Folder 1: [reason you created the search folder including why it fits better than rules and *Quick Steps*]

  Criteria: [description of criteria]

  Search Folder 2: [reason you created the search folder including why it fits better than rules and *Quick Steps*]

  Criteria: [description of criteria]

  Criteria: [description of criteria]

- Change the subject of your message to be **Outlook Challenge Project 6-9.**

CHAPTER 7

Multiple Email Accounts, Advanced Email Options, RSS Feeds, and Search

CHAPTER OVERVIEW

As you begin to use and rely on Outlook to manage your emails and contacts and organize your calendar and tasks, you want to have the ability to customize Outlook to best meet your individual and professional needs. Outlook provides you with the opportunity to have **multiple email accounts** set up and manage these accounts through the use of rules and folders. Also, there are many "under the hood" default settings for email that can be used to tailor how Outlook works for you.

In addition to managing multiple email accounts, Outlook can manage your **RSS feeds.** RSS is an acronym for "really simple syndication." Essentially, RSS feeds are a way of keeping track of the headlines on your favorite web sites, and Outlook can manage your RSS feeds in a similar way to how it manages your email accounts.

STUDENT LEARNING OUTCOMES (SLOs)

After completing this chapter, you will be able to:

SLO 7.1 Connect and use multiple email accounts in Outlook (p. O7-249).
SLO 7.2 Manage multiple email accounts (p. O7-251).
SLO 7.3 Customize advanced email options (p. O7-256).
SLO 7.4 Integrate RSS feeds into Outlook (p. O7-265).
SLO 7.5 Utilize search features to find email and other Outlook items (p. O7-270).

CASE STUDY

For the Pause & Practice projects, you become more proficient with using Outlook with multiple accounts, RSS feeds, and searching for email and other Outlook items that you have difficulty finding. You add accounts to Outlook to ensure you can work with both personal and school- or work-related email messages within the Outlook environment. You also add RSS feeds to enable you to receive news that is important to you and to share it with others. Lastly, you learn to search for information quickly and effectively.

Pause & Practice 7-1: You add an email account to Outlook. If you do not have a secondary email account, you can sign up for a free account at gmail.com or outlook.com. After adding the account, you will change the default account and send a message by selecting the account that is not set as default.

Pause & Practice 7-2: You subscribe to CNN RSS news feeds (available at http://www.cnn.com/services/rss/). You subscribe to an RSS feed, rename the feed folder, and share the feed with your instructor.

Pause & Practice 7-3: You search for the previous Pause & Practice email messages that you sent to your instructor because you did not receive a grade for the *Pause & Practice 7-2* assignment. After you find the message, you forward it to your instructor.

O7-248

Outlook 2013 Chapter 7 Multiple Email Accounts, Advanced Email Options, RSS Feeds, and Search

Setting Up Additional Email Accounts

If you're like most people, you have multiple email accounts: one through your work (an Exchange account) and one through your ISP (Internet service provider) at your home. You might also have a free email account such as Gmail, Outlook.com, or Yahoo Mail.

Outlook gives you the ability to set up multiple email accounts, including multiple Exchange accounts, and to send and receive emails through these accounts. Using Outlook to handle multiple email accounts saves you time because it consolidates your email accounts in one place so that you don't need to go to multiple web sites to check your different email accounts.

> ### MORE INFO
>
> Not all free email accounts can be set up through Outlook. Some types of accounts work seamlessly with Outlook, such as Gmail or Outlook.com. Yahoo Mail accounts will only work with Outlook if you have the Yahoo Plus account, which charges an annual fee.

Auto Account Setup

You don't have to know much about your email account to set it up in Outlook. Outlook 2013 has simplified the process of adding an email account. It determines the type of account (Exchange, Exchange ActiveSync, POP, IMAP, or HTTP) and validates the account settings.

The two pieces of information you will need are your *user name* or *email account* and your *password*. Outlook will automatically detect your email account settings and set up your account in Outlook.

> ### MORE INFO
>
> The different types of email accounts were covered in Chapter 1.

> ### MORE INFO
>
> For some online email accounts, you must enable POP on the online account for your email to be delivered to Outlook. This is typically done by logging into your account on the Internet and editing the settings to enable POP. This will vary from account to account.

HOW TO: Add an Email Account to Outlook

1. Click the **File** tab. The *Backstage* opens.
2. Click **Add Account** (Figure 7-1). The *Add Account* dialog box opens (Figure 7-2).
3. Click the **Email Account** radio button.
4. Fill in the following fields: **Your Name, Email Address, Password,** and **Retype Password.** The password is associated with the email account.

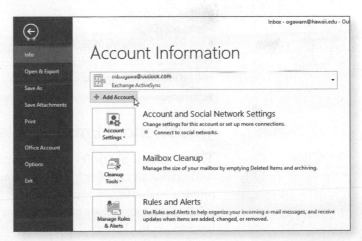

7-1 *Add Account* button

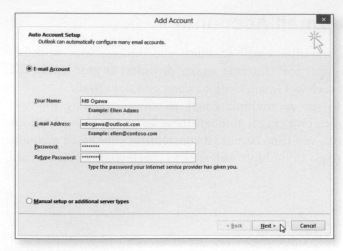

7-2 *Add Account* dialog box

7-3 Auto account setup completion

5. Click **Next.** Outlook will automatically configure and test the account settings. If the account was set up properly, you will see three green check marks and a *"Congratulations!"* message (Figure 7-3).

6. Click **Finish.** The *Account Settings* dialog box appears. Notice your new email account is now included in your list of email accounts.

7. Click **Close.**

> MORE INFO
>
> It is not a good idea to set up all your personal email accounts on your work computer because most employers do not want you to be distracted by personal emails while at work.

If you are using Outlook in an Exchange, Exchange ActiveSync, or IMAP environment you will have folders for each of your accounts. Your email account through Exchange, Exchange ActiveSync, and IMAP will be handled in your username@address.com folders (Figure 7.4), and your personal email accounts will, by default, be handled in your *Personal Folders*.

> MORE INFO
>
> You will also have another set of folders called *Archive Folders*, which will be covered in Chapter 10.

7-4 Account folders

Troubleshoot Email Problems

There might be times when Outlook is not able to automatically detect the account settings for an email account that you are trying to set up. Outlook will try a couple of different options to configure your account.

If this process does not work, you can manually configure your account settings. You might have to go to the email account web site to find specific setup information to configure your account.

HOW TO: Troubleshoot Email Connection Problems

1. If you receive a *Problem Connecting to Server* message, click **Next** to have Outlook try to configure your account using an unencrypted connection (Figure 7-5).

2. If this next step is unsuccessful, check the **Change account settings** box and click **Next.** A new dialog box opens allowing you to choose the type of account.

3. Select the type of email account to be set up, and click **Next.**

4. Confirm that your account information is correct, and click the **Test Account Settings** button (Figure 7-6). A *Test Account Settings* dialog box opens.

5. When this process is complete, click **Close** to close the *Test Account Settings* dialog box.

6. Click **Next** on the open dialog box. A *Congratulations* dialog box opens.

7. Click **Finish** to close the dialog box.

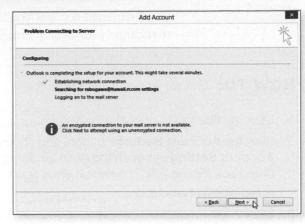

7-5 Unencrypted connection

7-6 Account settings

There might also be times when an existing email account in Outlook will stop sending or receiving for no apparent reason. If this email account was previously working and none of the account settings have been changed, you might try using the **Repair** feature provided in Outlook. This automated feature in the *Account Settings* dialog box will walk you through a couple of steps and try to automatically repair an existing email account.

> ### MORE INFO
>
> A setting change on the email server end might cause an existing email account in Outlook to stop functioning properly. The *Repair* feature might be able to automatically adjust the account settings to restore this account.

SLO 7.2

Managing Multiple Email Accounts

One of the issues with having multiple email accounts in Outlook is keeping them separate in your mail folders. Managing multiple email accounts can become confusing if emails are all being delivered to the same Inbox. Another issue is choosing the account through which you create and send new emails and respond to or forward emails. Having multiple email accounts somewhat complicates this process, but being deliberate about setting your default email account and having emails delivered to different folders can help you to effectively manage multiple email accounts.

Set the Default Account

The default email account is the account that will, by default, be used to send any new email that is created and sent. This should be the account used most often in Outlook. This will be the first email account you set up in Outlook unless you specify a different account. It is easy to change your default email account.

HOW TO: Set an Account as Default

1. Click the **File** tab to open the *Backstage*.
2. Click the **Account Settings** button, and choose **Account Settings** to open the *Account Settings* dialog box (Figure 7-7). The default email account is noted with a check mark.
3. Click the email account you want as your default account.
4. Click the **Set as Default** button. This account will be moved to the top of the list and will be the default email account.

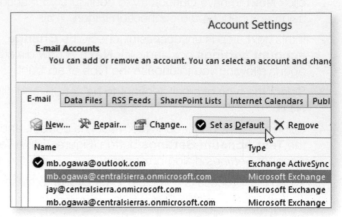

7-7 Set default account

> **MORE INFO**
>
> When you create a new email, the account being used will be displayed to the right of the *From* button. The email will be sent through the default account unless you choose a different account.

> **MORE INFO**
>
> It is probably best to reply to an email using the same account through which the email was received.

Send Email through a Different Account

As mentioned earlier, when you create and send a new email, it will be sent through your default email account. But if you are replying to or forwarding an email, it will be sent through the account through which it was delivered. For example, if you received an email through your Gmail account (assuming this is not your default account), and you reply to or forward this email, it will be sent through your Gmail account unless you choose a different account through which to send this email.

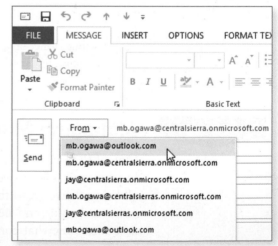

7-8 Set an account to send email

When you have multiple email accounts set up in Outlook, you can decide through which account the email will be sent. This can be done on new emails, replies, or forwards. A *From* button will appear to the right of the *Send* button on all your emails when you have multiple accounts set up in Outlook. You can select the account from which to send an email using the *From* button (Figure 7-8).

HOW TO: Send Email through Another Account

1. Open an existing email.
2. Click the *Reply* or *Forward* button. To the right of the *From* button, the account that will be used to send the email is displayed.
3. Click the **From** button and choose a different account. Notice the account displayed to the right.
4. Click **Send** to send the email through the chosen account.

Change the Email Delivery Folder

On personal email accounts that use POP, you can change the folder to which your email is delivered. You do not have this option with an Exchange account. When managing multiple email accounts, it is probably best to have different accounts delivered to different folders. If your default account is being delivered to your Inbox, you might want to create a *Gmail* folder and have your Gmail always delivered to this folder. You can change the default delivery folder for an email account in the *Account Settings* dialog box.

HOW TO: Change the Email Delivery Folder

1. Click the **File** tab to open the *Backstage* view.
2. Click the **Account Settings** button and choose **Account Settings** to open *Account Settings* dialog box.
3. Click one of your accounts that is not the default account. Notice the *delivery folder* to the right of the *Change Folder* button.
4. Click the **Change Folder** button (Figure 7-9). The *New Email Delivery Location* dialog box opens.
5. Select the new delivery folder (Figure 7-10). A new folder can also be created by clicking the **New Folder** button. Click **OK** to close the *New Email Delivery Location* dialog box.
6. Click **Close** to close the *Account Settings* dialog box. All emails from the chosen account will now be delivered to the folder you chose.

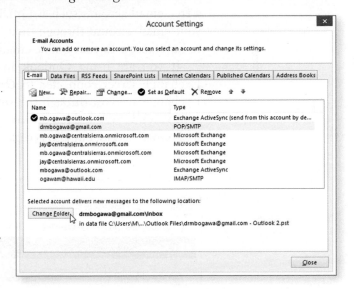

7-9 *Change Folder* button

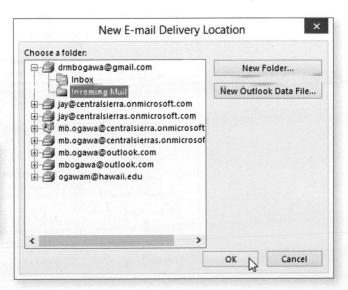

7-10 Select incoming mail folder

> **MORE INFO**
>
> Changing the delivery folder is not available for IMAP email accounts. Rules can be used to deliver email received through these accounts to a different folder.

Create Folders and Use Rules

Rules can also be used to deliver emails from specific accounts to a different folder. The *condition* would be looking for emails received through a specified account (for example, a Gmail or Outlook.com account), and the *action* would be to move it to a specified folder. This rule would do the same thing as changing the default delivery folder, but it could easily be turned off or on.

>
> **MORE INFO**
>
> Rules were covered in Chapter 6.

Outlook Web Access

One of the advantages of using email is the ability to access it from any computer that has Internet access. If you have an email account through your Internet service provider (ISP) or a free email account such as Gmail or Yahoo Mail, you can log on to the Internet and access your email account through their web sites. You need to know your user name and password to have access to your online email account.

If you are using Outlook in an Exchange environment, most companies have their Exchange server connected to *Outlook Web Access* (*OWA*). OWA allows you to access your Exchange account through the Internet. You need to know the URL (web location) of your company's OWA and log on with your username and password. OWA provides you not only with email access, but also access to your calendar, contacts, tasks, and notes (Figure 7-11).

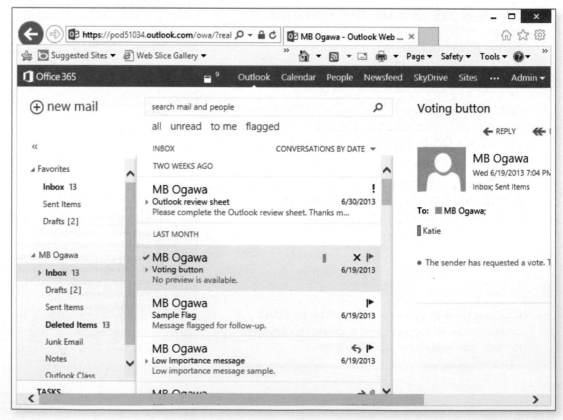

7-11 Outlook Web Access

OWA will be displayed differently depending on the Internet browser you're using (for example, Microsoft Internet Explorer, Google Chrome, or Mozilla Firefox). OWA will look different than Outlook on your computer, but you will still have most of the functionality of your Outlook account.

Outlook for Windows RT

Windows RT, an operating system for Windows tablets will be receiving an update, Windows 8.1, which will include Outlook. Therefore, you will be able to use all of the information you learned in this text while using Microsoft Windows RT based tablet computers.

PAUSE & PRACTICE: OUTLOOK 7-1

For this Pause & Practice project, you add an email account to Outlook. If you do not have a secondary email account, you can sign up for a free account at gmail.com or outlook.com. After adding the account, you will change the default account and send a message by selecting the account that is not set as default.

1. Add a new account to Outlook.
   a. Click the **File** tab. The *Backstage* opens.
   b. Click **Add Account.** The *Add New Account* dialog box opens.
   c. Click the **Email Account** radio button.
   d. Fill in the following fields: **Your Name, Email Address, Password,** and **Retype Password.**
   e. Click **Next.** Outlook will automatically configure and test the account settings. If the account was set up properly, you will see three green check marks and a "*Congratulations!*" message.
   f. Click **Finish.** The *Account Settings* dialog box appears. Notice your new email account is now included in your list of email accounts.
   g. Click **Close.**

2. Change the default email account.
   a. Click the **File** tab to open the *Backstage.*
   b. Click the **Account Settings** button, and choose **Account Settings** to open the *Account Settings* dialog box.
   c. Select the email account you added to Outlook in the first step.
   d. Click the **Set as Default** button.
   e. Click the **Close** button.

3. Send a message by selecting an account (Figure 7-12).
   a. Click the **Mail** button in the *Navigation* pane.
   b. Click the **New Email** button.
   c. Click the **From** button and select the email address that is not the default.
   d. Enter the following information in the new message:
      To: [instructor's email address]
      Cc: [your email address]
      Subject: Outlook Pause & Practice 7-1
      Message: Hi [instructor's name], I added a new address to my Outlook installation. For consistency, I want to be sure you are receiving messages from my school account.
      Thanks,
      [your name]
   e. Click the **Send** button.

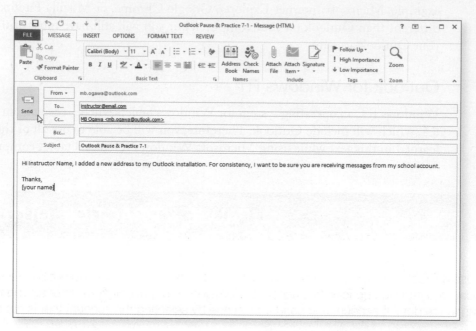

7-12 Completed Pause & Practice 7-1

SLO 7.3

Customizing Email Options

After you have been using Outlook for a while and have become familiar with the main tasks, you might want to change some of the default settings to customize Outlook. Within Outlook there are many customization options available, and you are able to modify many of the default settings throughout Outlook. The **Outlook Options** dialog box within Outlook (Figure 7-13) provides you with one location to change most of the default settings for email, calendar, contacts, tasks, notes, and other global Outlook set-

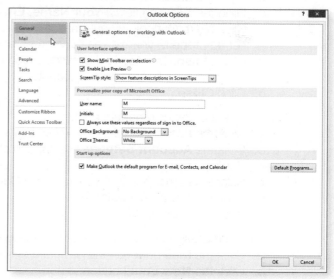

7-13 *Outlook Options* dialog box

tings. The *Outlook Options* dialog box can be accessed by clicking the *File* tab to open the *Backstage* and choosing **Options.**

> **MORE INFO**
>
> The email customization options covered in this section are global or default settings. These differ from message options, which allow you to customize individual email messages. Message options were covered in Chapter 2.

O7-256

Email Options

The **Mail Options** dialog box can be accessed by clicking the *Mail* button in the *Outlook Options* dialog box. In the *Mail Options* dialog box, the different customization options are separated into different sections. Many of these different sections have one or more additional dialog boxes that can be opened for more email options. Clicking the button to the right of the section opens the dialog box for more specific email options.

The following sections are available in *Mail* options:

- *Compose messages*
- *Outlook panes*
- *Message arrival*
- *Conversation Clean Up*
- *Replies and forwards*
- *Save messages*
- *Send messages*
- *MailTips*
- *Tracking*
- *Message format*
- *Other*

Compose Messages

The **Compose messages** section allows you to customize the format of email messages, spell checking, AutoCorrect, signatures, stationery, and themes. The button to the left of each of these areas opens a dialog box with many additional features that you are able to customize.

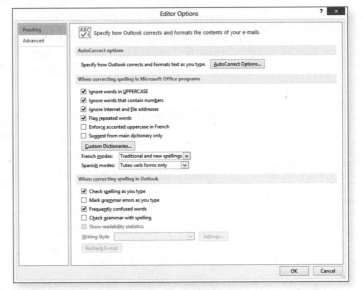

7-14 *Editor Options* dialog box

The *Editor Options* and *Spelling and AutoCorrect* buttons open the *Editor Options* dialog box (Figure 7-14). In this dialog box you are given many options on the *Proofing* and *Advanced* areas.

The *Signatures* and *Stationery and Themes* buttons open the *Signatures and Stationery* dialog box. In this dialog box, you can create and edit signatures, and on the *Personal Stationery* tab you can customize the theme and fonts for emails.

 MORE INFO

Signatures and *Stationery* were covered in Chapter 2.

Outlook Panes

The **Outlook panes** section allows you to control how messages displayed in the *Reading* pane interact with the *Folder* pane. Messages can be set to be marked as read when they are displayed in the *Reading* pane or marked as read when the selection in the *Folder* pane changes (Figure 7-15). Also, the spacebar can be set up and used to move through the text of a message and move to the next message in the *Folder* pane. This is a handy feature to quickly preview and move through messages in the *Reading* pane.

Message Arrival

The *Message arrival* section (Figure 7-16) of *Mail Options* controls what happens in Outlook when a message arrives in your Inbox. By default when a new email message arrives, a sound is played, the pointer briefly changes, an envelope is displayed in the notification area, and a desktop alert is displayed. A *Desktop Alert* is a message that briefly displays the sender's name, subject line, and part of the body of the message in a corner of your screen when a new email message is received in your Inbox (Figure 7-17). The email message can be opened by clicking the alert.

7-15 *Reading Pane* dialog box

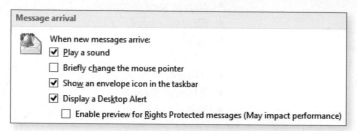

7-16 *Message arrival* options

Conversation Clean Up

The *Conversation Clean Up* section allows you to control what happens when you use the *Clean Up* feature in Outlook to remove redundant emails in a conversation. The conversation arrangement groups related emails together (Figure 7-18).

This section allows you to determine where cleaned-up messages will be moved (the default is in the *Deleted Items* folder) and the type of messages that Outlook will remove when using the *Clean Up* feature.

7-17 Desktop alert

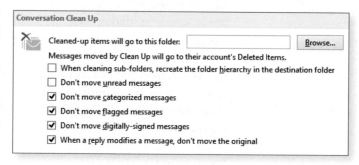

7-18 *Conversation Clean Up* options

> ## MORE INFO
>
> It is good email etiquette to include the original message in the body when replying to or forwarding an email message. By doing this, you provide context for your response.

Replies and Forwards

Outlook allows you to tailor how your email message appears when you receive, or send a reply to, or forward a message (Figure 7-19). By default when you reply to or forward a message, the original message is included below your response in the body of the message.

When **replying** to a message, you have the following options as a default setting (Figure 7-20):

- *Do not include the original message*
- *Attach original message* (this option attaches the original message as an attachment and removes it from the body of the response)
- Include original message text (this is the default setting in Outlook)
- *Include and indent the original message text*
- *Prefix each line of the original message* (the default prefix is >)

When **forwarding** a message, you have the following options as a default setting (Figure 7-21):

- *Attach original message* (this option attaches the original message as an attachment and removes it from the body of the response)
- *Include original message text* (this is the default setting in Outlook)
- *Include and indent the original message text*
- *Prefix each line of the original message* (the default prefix is >)

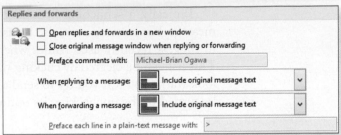

7-19 *Replies and forwards* options

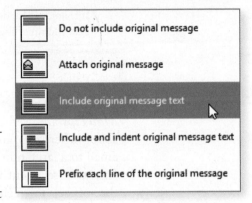

7-20 *Reply* options

Save Messages

Open messages that are either new, a reply, or a forward are by default saved every three minutes in the **Drafts** folder. The time duration and the folder can be customized. Also, by default new messages, replies, and forwards are saved in the *Sent Items* folder (Figure 7-22).

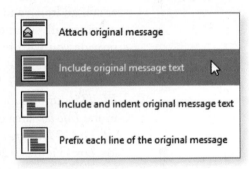

7-21 *Forward* options

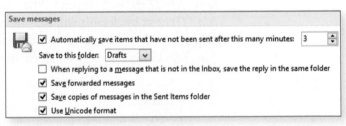

7-22 *Save messages* options

Send Messages

When a new message is created, the default setting for **importance** and **sensitivity** is *Normal*, which means there are no special tags or notifications on the message. In the **Send messages** section (Figure 7-23), you can customize these default settings as well as set a default expiration.

7-23 *Send messages* options

Typically, a semicolon is used to separate recipients' email addresses in the *To* line of a message, but a comma can also be used to separate recipients. The *Auto-Complete List* is used to suggest recently used names when typing names in the *To, Cc,* and *Bcc* lines of an email. This list can be cleared by clicking the **Empty Auto-Complete List** button. By default, Outlook warns you if it you try to send a message that is missing an attachment. This feature can be turned off by unchecking its option.

> **MORE INFO**
>
> It is not a good idea to have all emails marked with *High Importance,* a sensitivity tag, or an expiration date and time. Use these tags only as necessary so they do not lose their effectiveness on recipients.

MailTips

MailTips are used to inform you about when you are sending an email to a large number of recipients, to a recipient who is out of the office, to recipients whose mailbox is full, or to an invalid email address, and about many other email situations. *MailTips* provide you with real-time information about the status of an email message to be sent. The *MailTips* information bar appears in the *Info bar* area of a message.

The *MailTips Options* dialog box (Figure 7-24) allows you to customize the settings for how *MailTips* will appear. The *MailTips* bar by default will only be

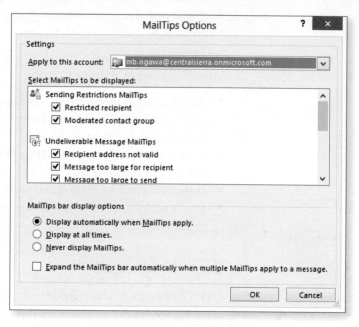

7-24 *MailTips Options* dialog box

displayed when one or more of the *MailTips* apply. You can change the setting so that the *MailTips* bar will appear on all email messages.

> **MORE INFO**
>
> *MailTips* are functional only when using Outlook 2013 in conjunction with an Exchange Server.

> **MORE INFO**
>
> The *MailTips* section does not appear if *MailTips* are not available on your Exchange Server.

Tracking Options

If you are using Outlook in an Exchange environment, Outlook automatically tracks responses when using voting buttons and meeting requests. Outlook will also track receipts received when a read receipt or delivery receipt has been used on an email. The *Tracking options* (Figure 7-25) allows you to determine how Outlook tracks and responds to these items.

You can customize how voting buttons and meeting request responses are processed when they arrive in your Inbox. Also, you can change the default settings for read and delivery receipts for outgoing emails and how Outlook should handle read receipts on emails you receive.

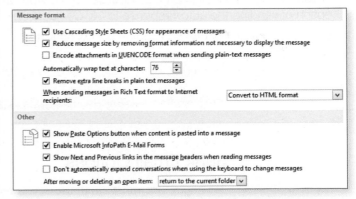

Tracking

Delivery and read receipts help provide confirmation that messages were successfully received. Not all e-mail servers and applications support sending receipts.

For all messages sent, request:
- [ ] Delivery receipt confirming the message was delivered to the recipient's e-mail server
- [ ] Read receipt confirming the recipient viewed the message

For any message received that includes a read receipt request:
- ( ) Always send a read receipt
- ( ) Never send a read receipt
- (•) Ask each time whether to send a read receipt

- [✓] Automatically process meeting requests and responses to meeting requests and polls
- [✓] Automatically update original sent item with receipt information
- [ ] Update tracking information, and then delete responses that don't contain comments
- [ ] After updating tracking information, move receipt to: [Deleted Items ▾] [Browse...]

7-25 *Tracking* options

> **MORE INFO**
>
> Use read and delivery receipts sparingly. It can become very annoying to recipients to receive a read receipt on all emails they receive from you.
>
> Also, if you receive an email that is requesting a read receipt, it is courteous to allow Outlook to send a read receipt.

> **MORE INFO**
>
> Delivery receipts, read receipts, and voting buttons were covered in Chapter 2. Meeting requests were covered in Chapter 4.

Message Format and Other

The last two sections of the *Mail Options* dialog box (Figure 7-26) include some behind-the-scenes options for formatting your email messages. Outlook allows you to customize some of these not so common email formatting options. It is probably best to leave the default settings in these areas unless you have specific reasons to change them.

Message format
- [✓] Use Cascading Style Sheets (CSS) for appearance of messages
- [✓] Reduce message size by removing format information not necessary to display the message
- [ ] Encode attachments in UUENCODE format when sending plain-text messages
- Automatically wrap text at character: [76 ⬍]
- [✓] Remove extra line breaks in plain text messages
- When sending messages in Rich Text format to Internet recipients: [Convert to HTML format ▾]

Other
- [✓] Show Paste Options button when content is pasted into a message
- [✓] Enable Microsoft InfoPath E-Mail Forms
- [✓] Show Next and Previous links in the message headers when reading messages
- [ ] Don't automatically expand conversations when using the keyboard to change messages
- After moving or deleting an open item: [return to the current folder ▾]

7-26 *Message format* and *Other* options

Out of Office Assistant

Most of us have instances when we are away from the office or home when we are not able to respond to emails for an extended time. You might be on vacation or a business trip and don't want to totally ignore those who send you an email. The ***Out of Office Assistant*** is available if you are using an Exchange account and provides you the option of creating an automated response to reply to all emails you receive while you are not able to answer email.

You can set a specific date range for the *Out of Office Assistant*. If you don't specify a date range, the *Out of Office Assistant* will remain on until you turn it off. A message can be created to automatically respond to all those from whom you receive an email. These automated responses can be sent to those within your organization (those connected to your Exchange server), those outside of your organization, or both.

HOW TO: Set up an Out of Office Message

1. Click on the **File** tab to open the *Backstage*.
2. Click on the **Automatic Replies (Out of Office)** button (Figure 7-27). The *Out of Office Assistant* dialog box opens (Figure 7-28).
3. Click on the **Send Out of Office auto-replies.**

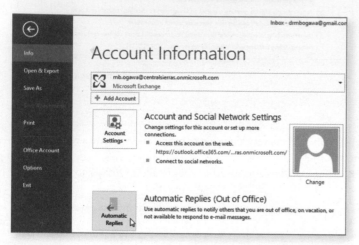

7-27 *Automatic Replies* button

7-28 Set up automatic replies

4. You can set a specific date range if you choose.
5. Compose a brief message in the body.
6. If you want an automated response sent to those outside of your organization, click on the **Outside My Organization** tab and type a brief message. You will have the option of sending the auto-response to *My Contacts only* or *Anyone outside my organization.*
7. Click **OK.** The *Out of Office Assistant* is now activated.

Junk Email Options

If you are like most email users, you receive quite a few junk email messages each day. Antivirus software continues to improve and can identify and move potential junk email messages to a different folder. Online email providers like Gmail, Yahoo Mail, and Outlook.com continue to enhance their efforts to identify spammers (those who send junk mail) and remove junk mail before it is delivered to your Inbox.

But even with these efforts, there are still junk mail messages that make it to your Inbox. Email messages that are identified by Outlook as junk mail are moved to the ***Junk E-mail*** folder in your folder list.

Also, there are times when messages that should make it to your Inbox are identified as junk mail and moved to the *Junk E-mail* folder.

Outlook allows you to customize your junk email settings, add safe senders, add safe recipients, and block senders or domain names.

The ***Junk E-mail Options*** dialog box allows you to control the level of junk email protection in Outlook.

HOW TO: Open Junk E-mail Options

1. Click the **Junk** button in the *Delete* group on the *Home* tab. A menu opens with the junk email options available.
2. Select **Junk E-mail Options.** The *Junk E-mail Options* dialog box opens (Figure 7-29).

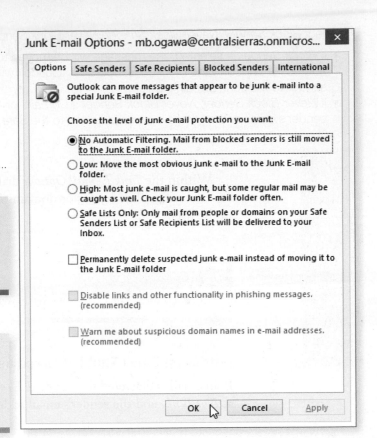

7-29 *Junk E-mail Options* dialog box

Safe and Blocked Senders and Recipients

Within the *Junk E-mail Options* dialog box, you are given the following options to control junk mail messages.

- *Safe Senders:* Senders' email addresses or domains (e.g., @mcgraw-hill.com) can be added to this list to ensure that emails received from these senders or domains are not treated as junk mail.
- *Safe Recipients:* Recipients' email addresses or domains can be added to this list to ensure that emails sent to these recipients or domains are not treated as junk mail.
- *Blocked Senders:* Senders' email addresses or senders' domains can be added to this list to ensure that emails received from these senders or domains will be treated as junk mail and moved to the *Junk E-mail* folder in your folder list.
- *International:* Outlook also allows you to block email messages received in different languages or from different country domains.

Email addresses or domain names can be manually added into these lists (with the exception of international ones) by selecting one of these lists in the *Junk E-mail Options* dialog box by clicking the **Add** button and typing in the email address or domain name.

An email message received in your Inbox can also be added to the *Safe Senders, Safe Recipients,* or *Blocked Senders* list.

HOW TO: Add Senders or Groups to Block or Never Block Lists

1. Open the email to be added to one of these lists.
2. Click the **Junk** button in the *Delete* group.

3. Select *Block Sender, Never Block Sender, Never Block Sender's Domain,* or *Never Block this Group or Mailing List.*
   - If *Block Sender* is selected, the message will be moved to the *Junk E-mail* folder and the sender's email address is added to the *Blocked Senders* list. Outlook will always move email messages received from this sender to the *Junk E-mail* folder.
   - If *Never Block Sender, Never Block Sender's Domain,* or *Never Block this Group or Mailing List* is selected, the sender's email and/or domain name is added to the *Safe Senders* list.

Within the *Junk E-mail Options* dialog box, each of these lists can be edited. You can add or remove email addresses or domains from any of the lists, or you can edit entries included in the lists.

 MORE INFO

Email addresses that you have saved in your *Contacts* folder are, by default, treated as safe senders.

Retrieving Email That Is Marked as Junk

If an email is delivered to your *Junk E-mail* folder and it is not a junk email, it can be marked as ***Not Junk,*** and the sender's email address will be added to the *Safe Senders* list.

HOW TO: Open the Junk E-mail Options Dialog Box

1. Select or open an email in the *Junk E-mail* folder.
2. In the *Delete* group, click the **Junk** button and select **Not Junk.** The *Mark as Not Junk* dialog box opens, and you are given the option to always trust email from this sender.
3. Click **OK.** The email will be moved to the *Inbox* folder, and the sender's email address will be added to the *Safe Senders* list.

ANOTHER WAY

Ctrl+Alt+J marks an email message as *Not Junk.*

ANOTHER WAY

You can also drag an email message from the *Junk E-mail* folder to your *Inbox* or another folder in your folder list.

MORE INFO

It is important to check your *Junk E-mail* folder regularly to ensure that important emails that should be delivered to your Inbox do not get overlooked.

Using RSS Feeds

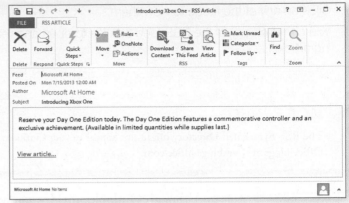

Most of you have watched the news on one of the cable television news shows and have seen the scrolling banner of news headlines at the bottom of the screen. This news feed is similar to an **RSS** (really simple syndication) **feed** from a web site. RSS feeds are headlines of new articles or information on web sites (Figure 7-30). RSS feeds are useful in that when you subscribe to an RSS feed you are automatically sent the new articles from this web site to your RSS feed reader. So, rather than having to visit each of your favorite news, sports, recipe, and entertainment web sites to search for new information, this new information is automatically sent to you as an RSS feed.

Outlook can manage your RSS feeds like it does your email accounts. When a new item is available on a web site, it is delivered to an RSS feed folder. You will receive RSS feeds like an email. These feeds will come with a subject line and a brief summary of the article. There is also usually a link to take you to the web site to read the full article if you're interested.

Subscribe to an RSS Feed

Outlook provides you with an *RSS Feeds* folder to store the RSS feeds to which you subscribe. Outlook also provides you with a menu of RSS feeds from which to easily subscribe. You must first enable the RSS feeds in the *Outlook Options* dialog box. Once enabled, when you click the *RSS Feeds* folder in the *Navigation* pane, the **Outlook Syndicated Content (RSS) Directory** appears in the *Folder* pane. You can click any of these links to subscribe to an RSS feed and automatically add a new folder to your *RSS Feeds* folder.

HOW TO: Subscribe to an RSS Feed

1. Click the **File** button on the *Ribbon* and select **Options.**
2. Click the **Mail** button in the *Navigation* pane.
3. Click the **Advanced** option.
4. Click the **Synchronize RSS Feeds to Common Feed List (CFL) in Windows** check box (Figure 7-31) and click **OK.**
5. Click the **RSS Feeds** folder in the *Mail Folders* list in the *Navigation* pane.
6. Click the **RSS Feeds folder** drop-down arrow to view the available RSS feeds (Figure 7-32).

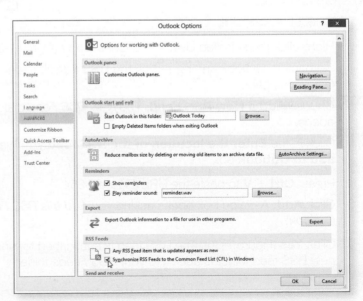

7. Click on any of the feeds to view them.

8. You can click any of the RSS feed articles to open and read any of the interesting articles.

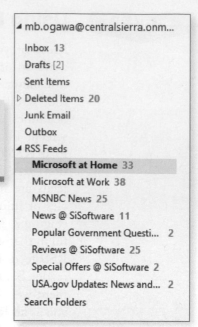

7-32 *RSS Feeds* folder

MORE INFO

The RSS Syndicated Directory might not appear in your Outlook. You can find these Office blogs at www.blogs.office.com.

Although Outlook provides you with many RSS feeds in its RSS Directory, you are not limited to subscribing to only these feeds. Many commercial web sites provide you with RSS links that can be subscribed to in Outlook. Many web sites will also have the RSS feed icon or link to help you to subscribe to the RSS feed link (Figure 7-33).

To subscribe to an RSS feed from a web site, you have to copy the web address (URL) of the RSS feed and paste it into the *New RSS Feed* dialog box.

7-33 **RSS feed for CNN Top Stories**

HOW TO: Subscribe to an RSS Feed from a Web Site

1. Go to the web page of your choice, and locate the RSS feed icon or link. It may take some searching to find the RSS feed icon or link, and not all web sites will have RSS feeds available.

2. Select the RSS URL.

3. Right-click the selected URL and choose **Copy** (Figure 7-34).

4. Go back to Outlook and right-click the **RSS Feeds** folder in the *Navigation* pane.

5. Choose **Add a New RSS Feed.** The *New RSS Feed* dialog box opens.

6. Click in the **Enter the location of the RSS feed you want to add to Outlook** box.

7. Press **Ctrl + V** to paste the URL (Figure 7-35).

8. Click **Add.** A dialog box opens asking you *Add this RSS Feed to Outlook?*

9. Click **Yes** (Figure 7-36). The RSS feed is subscribed to, and a new RSS feed folder is added to your *RSS Feeds* folder.

7-34 **Copy the RSS address**

7-35 *New RSS Feed* dialog box

7-36 *Add this RSS Feed* confirmation

Manage RSS Feeds

Inside the *RSS Feeds* folder you will have a separate subfolder for each subscribed to RSS feed. The subfolders contain the RSS feed emails.

Outlook manages RSS feeds in the *Account Settings* dialog box. By opening the *Account Settings* dialog box and clicking the *RSS Feeds* tab, you can see the RSS feeds to which you are subscribed (Figure 7-37). You can rename a feed, change the delivery location, and change how information in the feed is downloaded.

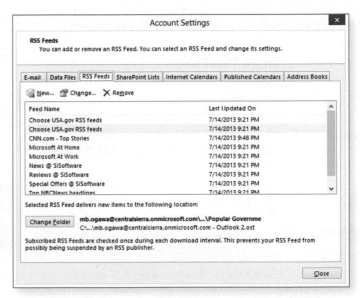

7-37 *RSS Feeds* in account settings

You can also rename the RSS feed folder in the *Navigation* pane.

HOW TO: Rename RSS Feed Folders

1. In the *Navigation* pane, click the RSS feed folder to be renamed.
2. Click the **Folder** tab at the top of the window.

3. Click the **Rename Folder** button in the *Actions* group (Figure 7-38).

4. Type the new name for the RSS feed folder.

5. Press **Enter.** The folder will be renamed.

Share an RSS Feed

RSS feeds can easily be shared with other Outlook users. You might want to send them the URL of the RSS feed and have them add this link as a new RSS feed, but Outlook has provided a much easier way to share an RSS feed.

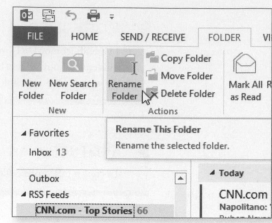

7-38 Rename an RSS feed folder

HOW TO: Share an RSS Feed

1. Click one of the RSS feed folders in the *Navigation* pane. All the RSS feed emails will be displayed in the *Folder* pane.

2. In the *Folder* pane, open one of the RSS feed emails.

3. Click the **Share This Feed** button (Figure 7-39) in the *RSS* group on the *RSS Article* tab. A new email opens (Figure 7-40).

4. Click the **To** button to select recipients and then press **Send.** This RSS feed email will be sent to recipients, and they will be given the option to add this RSS feed to their Outlook.

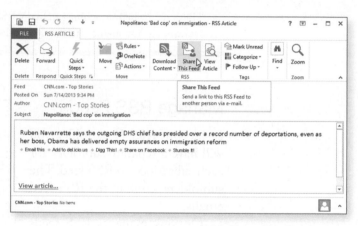

7-39 Share This Feed button

> **ANOTHER WAY**
>
> With an RSS feed email selected in the *Folder* pane, click the **Share This Feed** button in the *RSS* group on the *Home* tab.

When this feed is shared with other Outlook users, they will receive an email in their *Inbox.* They can subscribe to this RSS feed by opening the email and clicking the **Add this RSS Feed** button in the upper left corner of the email (Figure 7-41).

7-40 RSS share email message

Unsubscribe from an RSS Feed

There are a couple of different ways to unsubscribe from an RSS feed. If you want to unsubscribe from an RSS feed and remove the RSS feed folder and all the RSS feed emails, you can right-click the RSS feed folder and choose **Delete Folder.** A dialog box opens asking if you want to delete the folder and all its contents.

> **ANOTHER WAY**
> **Ctrl+D** deletes the selected folder.

You can also unsubscribe from an RSS feed using the *RSS Feeds* tab in the *Account Settings* dialog box.

HOW TO: Unsubscribe from an RSS Feed

1. In the *Account Settings* dialog box, click the **RSS Feeds** tab.
2. Select the RSS feed to be removed and click the **Remove** button.
3. Click **Yes** on the confirmation dialog box (Figure 7-42).
4. Click **Close** to close the *Account Settings* dialog box.

7-41 Add a shared RSS feed

> **MORE INFO**
>
> When unsubscribing from an RSS feed from the *Account Settings* dialog box, the RSS feed subscription is removed but the RSS feed folder and previously received RSS feed emails are not deleted.

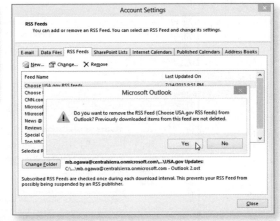

7-42 Remove an RSS feed

PAUSE & PRACTICE: OUTLOOK 7-2

For this Pause & Practice project, you subscribe to CNN RSS news feeds (available at http://www.cnn.com/services/rss/). You subscribe to an RSS feed, rename the feed folder, and share the feed with your instructor.

1. Add the CNN Business feed to your RSS Feeds.
   a. Open a browser and go to the following URL: http://www.cnn.com/services/rss/.
   b. Select the **Technology RSS URL.**
   c. Right-click the selected URL and choose **Copy.**
   d. Go back to Outlook and click the **Mail** button in the *Navigation* pane.
   e. Right-click the **RSS Feeds** folder in the *Folder* pane.
   f. Choose **Add a New RSS Feed.** The *New RSS Feed* dialog box opens.
   g. Click in the **Enter the location of the RSS feed you want to add to Outlook** box.

h. Press **Ctrl + V** to paste the URL.
i. Click **Add.** A dialog box opens asking you *Add this RSS Feed to Outlook?*
j. Click **Yes.**

2. Rename the RSS feed you added in the first step to **CNN Tech.**
   a. Right-click the RSS feed you added in the first step and select **Rename Folder.**
   b. Type CNN Tech and press **Enter.**

3. Share the feed with your instructor (Figure 7-43).
   a. Click the **CNN Tech** feed.
   b. Open the first message.
   c. Click the **Share This Feed** button [*RSS Article* tab, *RSS* group]. A new email opens.
   d. Type your instructor's email address in the *To* field.
   e. Type your email address in the *Cc* field.
   f. Modify to subject to include **Outlook Pause & Practice 7-2** before the RSS feed title.
   g. Add the message: Hi [instructor's name], I thought you would be interested in the CNN Tech feed!
      Thank you,
      [your name]
   h. Click the **Send** button.

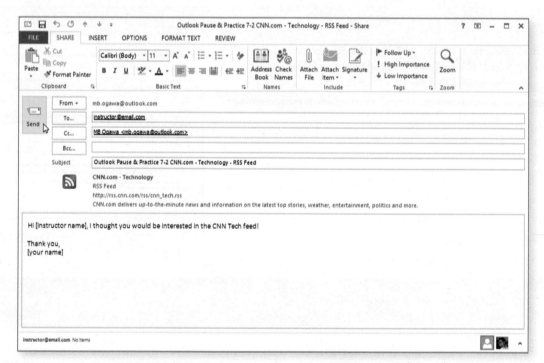

7-43 Completed Pause & Practice 7-2

Searching for Outlook Items

Have you ever tried to find an email item that you sent or received months ago? You might have searched through many different folders looking for a specific email. You might not even remember who sent you the email, the subject of the email, or to whom the email was sent. Even if you don't remember all the specifics about the item for which you are looking, you can use the *Instant Search* feature to find Outlook items.

Instant Search

The ***Instant Search*** feature in Outlook provides you with a tool to quickly search for Outlook items in a specific folder or all folders. It indexes all Outlook items in your folders and searches for items that match the specific criteria for which you are looking. For example, you can search all your mailbox folders for emails from your professor, for all emails with the word "Outlook" in the subject or body, or all contacts who work for McGraw-Hill. Outlook will display in the *Folder* pane all items that match your criteria.

> ### MORE INFO
>
> If you are using Windows Vista, 7, or 8, Outlook *Instant Search* is automatically turned on. If you are using a previous version of Windows, you will have to turn on or enable *Instant Search*.

> ### ANOTHER WAY
>
> **Ctrl+E** activates *Instant Search* on the selected folder. **Ctrl+Alt+A** activates *Instant Search* on *All Mail* Items.

When you click in the *Search* box at the top of the *Folder* pane, the *Search* tab is displayed in Outlook. On the *Search* tab in the *Scope* group, you can select the folders or areas of Outlook to be searched. The *Refine* group will provide you with options to help locate the information for which you are looking. The *Options* group provides you with a list of recent searches and other advanced search tools.

HOW TO: Search for Email Messages

1. Click the **Mail** button in the *Navigation* pane.
2. Click the folder to be searched.
3. Click in the **Search** box at the top of the *Folder* pane (Figure 7-44).
4. Type in the words in the fields to be searched. Outlook will display matching emails in the *Folder* pane.
5. Additional criteria can be selected from the *Refine* group.
6. The *Scope* group will allow you to specify where Outlook performs the search.
7. Click the **Close Search** button (**X**) to the right of the search field to clear the search and close the *Search* area and tab. You can also click one of your mailbox folders to close *Instant Search*.

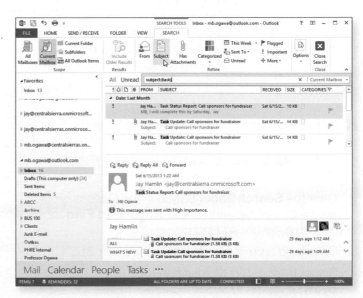

7-44 Search for email messages

When you use *Instant Search*, Outlook will display the matching items in the *Folder* pane, highlight the matching criteria, and list the folder in which the item is located. You can open any of these items from the search results by double-clicking it in the *Folder* pane.

Search Options

You can change the **search options** for *Instant Search* to customize which folders are indexed, how the results are displayed, whether or not the *Deleted Items* folder is included in the search, and the default folders to be searched.

You can open the *Search Options* dialog box by clicking the **Search Tools** button in the *Options* group on the *Search* tab and selecting **Search Options** (Figure 7-45). The *Search Options* are displayed in Figure 7-46.

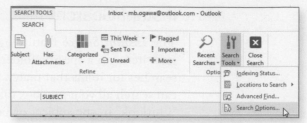

7-45 *Search Options*

> **ANOTHER WAY**
>
> The *Search Options* dialog box can be opened from the Outlook *Backstage*. Click the **File** tab, choose **Options**, and click **Search**.

Advanced Find

When you use *Instant Search* in Mail, Outlook only searches for email items. However, Outlook also provides you with ***Advanced Find*** to search for any type of Outlook item. *Advanced Find* displays Outlook items that match your criteria in the *Advanced Find* dialog box.

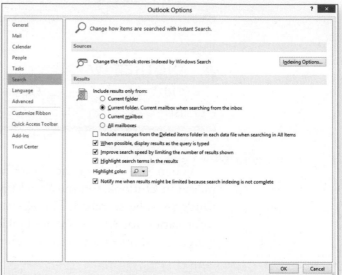

7-46 Search options in *Outlook Options*

HOW TO: Perform an Advanced Search

1. Click in the **Search** box at the top of the *Folder* pane.
2. Click the **Search Tools** button in the *Options* group on the *Search* tab, and select **Advanced Find** to open the *Advanced Find* dialog box.
3. Select the type of item to find in the *Look* area.
4. Select the location to search in the *In* area. Click the **Browse** button to select the folder to search.
5. Type in the search criteria.
   - You can click the *From* or *Sent To* buttons to select contacts.
   - You can also click either the **More Choices** or *Advanced* tabs for more search options.

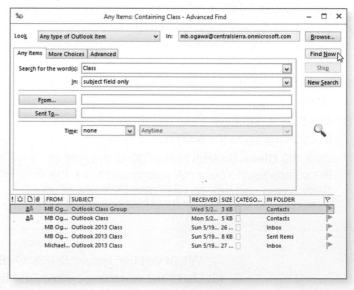

7-47 Search for any Outlook item

6. Click the **Find Now** button to search for items that match your criteria (Figure 7-47). The matching items will be displayed at the bottom of the dialog box.

7. Click **New Search** to clear the current search, or click the **X** in the upper right corner to close the *Advanced Find* dialog box.

> **ANOTHER WAY**
>
> **Ctrl + Shift + F** opens the *Advanced Find* dialog box.

PAUSE & PRACTICE: OUTLOOK 7-3

For this Pause & Practice project, you search for the email messages from *Pause & Practice 7-2* that you sent to your instructor, because you did not receive a grade for the *Pause & Practice 7-2* assignment. After you find the message, you forward it to your instructor.

1. Click the **Mail** button in the *Navigation* pane.

2. Click the **Sent Items** folder.

3. Click in the **Search** box at the top of the *Folder* pane.

4. Click the **Current Mailbox** button [*Search* tab, *Scope* group].

5. Click the **Subject** button [*Search* tab, *Refine* group].

6. Type Pause Practice 7 as the keywords (Figure 7-48).

7. Locate and open the email message for **Outlook Pause & Practice 7-2.**

8. Forward the message to your instructor.
   a. Open the email message for *Outlook Pause & Practice 7-2*.
   b. Click the **Forward** button [*Share* tab, *Respond* group].
   c. Type your instructor's email address in the *To* field.
   d. Type your email address in the *Cc* field.
   e. Modify the subject to include *Outlook Pause & Practice 7-3* before the RSS feed title.
   f. Add the following message: Hi [instructor's name], I am resending my Pause & Practice 7-2 assignment for you to check.
      Thank you,
      [student name]

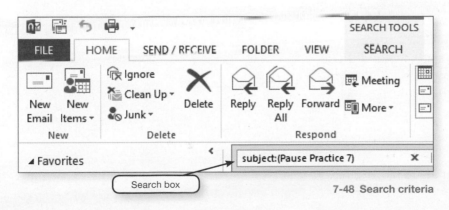

7-48 Search criteria

g. Click the **Send** button (Figure 7-49).

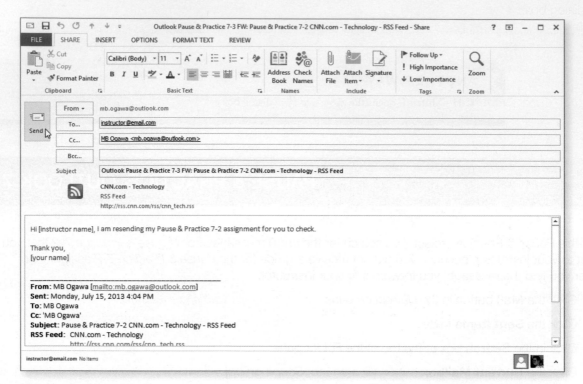

7-49 Completed Pause & Practice 7-3.

Chapter Summary

7.1 Connect and use multiple email accounts in Outlook (p. 249).

- You can manage multiple email accounts in Outlook.
- The **Auto Account Setup** automatically detects and validates account settings using your email account and password.
- You can troubleshoot your account by checking encryption and manually setting up your account if the *Auto Account Setup* is unable to detect the correct settings.
- The **Repair** feature can help to fix accounts that stop working.

7.2 Manage multiple email accounts (p. 251).

- The default email account is used to send any new email.
- You can change the default email account to fit your preference.
- When you create a new message, you can select which account you would like to send the message from, if multiple accounts are set up.
- If you have multiple POP email accounts, you can change the default folder that receives messages.
- Rules can be used to specify delivery folders for email messages.
- When using an Exchange account, you can use **Outlook Web Access (OWA)** to manage your email, tasks, calendar, and contacts from a web browser.
- Windows RT, the Windows based operating system for tablet computers, will have a version of Outlook.

7.3 Customize advanced email options (p. 256).

- Many different options for email can be customized in the *Outlook Options* dialog box.
- The **Compose messages** section allows you to customize the format of email messages, spell checking, autocorrect, signatures, stationery, and themes.
- The **Outlook panes** section allows you to control how messages displayed in the *Reading* pane interact with the *Folder* pane.
- The **Message arrival** section of *Mail Options* controls what happens in Outlook when a message arrives in your Inbox.

- The **Conversation Clean Up** section allows you to select options when you use the *Clean Up* feature in Outlook to remove redundant emails in a conversation.
- The **Replies and forwards** section allows you to tailor how your email message appears when you receive , send a reply to, or forward a message.
- The **Send messages** section allows you to modify how messages are sent.
- The **MailTips** section allows you to modify which *MailTips* are shown. *MailTips* are applicable to Exchange environments.
- The **Tracking Options** section allows you to determine how Outlook tracks and responds to voting buttons, task assignments, and meeting requests..
- The **Message Format** and **Other** sections include behind-the-scenes options for formatting your email messages.
- The **Out of Office Assistant** helps you to create an automated reply message to people within and outside of your company. The *Out of Office Assistant* is applicable to Exchange environments.
- Outlook detects **Junk** email and places it in the **Junk E-mail** folder.
- Junk email options allow you to designate **Safe Senders, Safe Recipients, Blocked Senders,** and **International** messages.

7.4 Integrate RSS feeds into Outlook (p. 265).

- Outlook allows you to receive RSS messages in your mailbox.
- Outlook includes default RSS feeds (Common Feed List).
- You can add RSS feeds that you find on the Internet.
- RSS feeds can be managed from the *Account Settings* dialog box.
- RSS feeds can be shared via email.
- RSS feeds shared via email can be added to your account quickly.
- When unsubscribing from an RSS feed from the *Account Settings* dialog box, all feed messages received are not deleted. They must be deleted manually.

7.5 Utilize search features to find email and other Outlook items (p. 270).

- **Instant Search** allows you to quickly find Outlook items because it indexes them.
- The **Search** box at the top of the screen can be used to quickly enter search criteria.
- The *Scope* of the search defines where you want to search for items, such as a specific folder.

- The *Refine* group in the *Search* tab allows you to set specific fields for your search (e.g., *From, Subject* or *Has Attachments*).
- **Search options** can be customized to determine which folders are indexed, how the results are displayed, whether or not the *Deleted Items* folder is included in the search, and the default folders to be searched.
- **Advanced Find** allows you to search for any type of Outlook item, as opposed to solely email messages.

Check for Understanding

In the **Online Learning Center** for this text (www.mhhe.com/office2013inpractice), there are a variety of resources that can be used to review the concepts covered in this chapter.

The following Online Learning Resources are available in the Online Learning Center:

- Multiple choice questions
- Short answer questions
- Matching exercises

Guided Project 7-1

For this project, you are an academic advisor for Sierra Pacific Community College District (SPCCD). You started using your personal laptop for work because there are many tasks that you need to complete out of the office. Therefore, you have both your personal and work email accounts in Outlook. You decide to change your default email from your personal to work email, as you tend to send messages from your work account.
[Student Learning Outcomes 7.1, 7.2]

Skills Covered in This Project

- Set up an email account.
- Change the default email account.
- Select an account when creating a new message.

---

1. Add a new account to Outlook. (If you completed *Pause & Practice 7-1,* skip this step).
   a. Click the **File** tab. The *Backstage* opens.
   b. Click **Add Account.** The *Add New Account* dialog box opens.
   c. Click the **Email Account** radio button.
   d. Fill in the following fields: **Your Name, Email Address, Password,** and **Retype Password.**

2. Change the default email account to be your work account.
   a. Click the **File** tab to open the *Backstage.*
   b. Click the **Account Settings** button, and choose **Account Settings** to open the *Account Settings* dialog box.
   c. Select your school account (the first one you used to initially set up Outlook in Chapter 1).
   d. Click the **Set as Default** button.
   e. Click the **Close** button.

3. Send a message ensuring the correct **From** address is selected.
   a. Click the **Mail** button in the *Navigation* pane.
   b. Click the **New Email** button.
   c. Click the **From** button and ensure your school account is selected.
   d. Enter the following information in the new message:
      To; [your instructor's email address]
      Cc: [your email address]
      Subject: Outlook Guided Project 7-1
      Message: Hi [instructor's name], I just added my work and personal accounts to my laptop. I wanted to be sure I am sending messages from the correct account. Could you please let me know if this message is coming from my work address?
      Thanks,
      [your name]

e. Click the **Send** button (Figure 7-50).

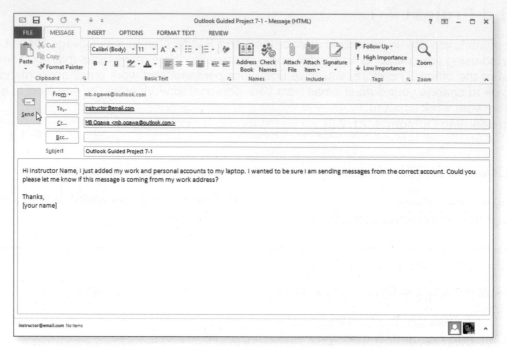

7-50 Completed Guided Project 7-1

Guided Project 7-2

For this project, you want to use Outlook as a central location for information. Therefore, you decide to stay up to date with higher education student services information by subscribing to RSS feeds from the Chronicle of Higher Education (the full RSS feed list is available at http://chronicle.com/sitemap). After reading a few articles, you determine which feed you wanted to keep and which feed you wanted to delete. You decide to share one of the RSS feeds with a colleague.
[Student Learning Outcome 7.4]

Skills Covered in This Project

- Add an RSS feed.
- Rename an RSS feed folder.

- Delete an RSS feed.
- Share an RSS feed.

---

1. Add the ***Chronicle of Higher Education Leadership & Governance*** RSS feed.
   a. Click the **Mail** button in the *Folder* pane.
   b. Right-click the **RSS Feeds** folder in the *Navigation* pane.
   c. Choose **Add a New RSS Feed.** The *New RSS Feed* dialog box opens.
   d. Click in the **Enter the location of the RSS feed you want to add to Outlook** box.
   e. Type http://chronicle.com/section/Leadership-Governance/18/rss.
   f. Click **Add.** A dialog box opens asking you *Add this RSS Feed to Outlook?*
   g. Click **Yes.**

2. Add the ***Chronicle of Higher Education Students*** RSS feed.
   a. Click the **Mail** button in the *Navigation* pane.
   b. Right-click the **RSS Feeds** folder in the *Navigation* pane.
   c. Choose **Add a New RSS Feed.** The *New RSS Feed* dialog box opens.
   d. Click in the **Enter the location of the RSS feed you want to add to Outlook** box.
   e. Type http://chronicle.com/section/Students/19/rss/.
   f. Click **Add.** A dialog box opens asking you *Add this RSS Feed to Outlook?*
   g. Click **Yes.**

3. Rename the ***Chronicle of Higher Education Students*** RSS feed.
   a. Right-click the ***Chronicle of Higher Education Students*** RSS feed and select **Rename Folder.**
   b. Type Chronicle-Students and press **Enter.**

4. Delete the ***Chronicle of Higher Education Leadership & Governance*** RSS feed.
   a. Right-click the ***Chronicle of Higher Education Leadership & Governance*** RSS feed and select **Delete Folder.**
   b. Click **Yes.**

5. Share the ***Chronicle-Students*** feed with your instructor.
   a. Click the ***Chronicle-Students*** feed.
   b. Open the first message.
   c. Click the **Share This Feed** button [*RSS Article* tab, *RSS* group]. A new email opens.
   d. Type your instructor's email address in the *To* field.
   e. Type your email address in the *Cc* field.
   f. Modify the subject to include ***Outlook Guided Project 7-2*** before the RSS feed title.
   g. Add the following message: Hi [instructor's name], Wow, I just found this RSS feed with a lot of great student information. Feel free to add it to your Outlook if you like the information. Let me know if you find any other great feeds, as I enjoy getting this information delivered to me in Outlook.
      Thank you,
      [your name]
   h. Click the **Send** button (Figure 7-51).

7-51 Completed Guided Project 7-2

Guided Project 7-3

You spoke with your colleague about the RSS feed that you shared. He said that he never received it. You were shocked, so for this project, you search for it and resend it when you get to a WiFi hotspot. [Student Learning Outcome 7.5]

Skills Covered in This Project

- Search using *Instant Search.*
- Use *Scope* to narrow search.

- Use *Refine* to narrow search.

---

1. Click the **Mail** button in the *Navigation* pane.

2. Click the **Sent Items** folder.

3. Click in the **Search** box at the top of the *Folder* pane.

4. Click the **Current Folder** button [*Search* tab, *Scope* group].

5. Type RSS Feed as the keywords (Figure 7-52).

6. Click the **Sent To** button [*Search* tab, *Refine* group] and select **Sent to Another Recipient.**

7. Type your instructor's email address as the keywords.

8. Locate and open the email message for ***Outlook Guided Project 7-2.***

9. Forward the message to your instructor.

   a. Open the email message for ***Outlook Guided Project 7-2.***

   b. Click the **Forward** button [*Share* tab, *Respond* group].

   c. Type your instructor's email address in the *To* field.

   d. Type your email address in the *Cc* field.

   e. Modify the subject to include ***Outlook Guided Project 7-3*** before the RSS feed title.

   f. Add the following message: Hi [instructor's name]. Here is the RSS feed we discussed today. Let me know if you receive it. The news really is awesome! Thank you, [your name]

   g. Click the **Send** button (Figure 7-53).

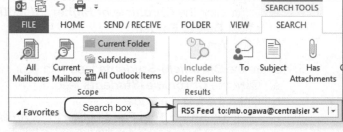

7-52 *Guided Project 7-3 search criteria*

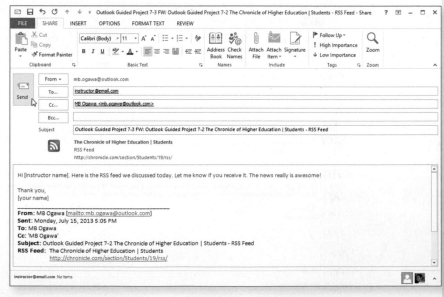

7-53 Completed Guided Project 7-3

Independent Project 7-4

For this project, you are at doctor who works at Courtyard Medical Plaza (CMP). You recently joined the American Medical Association (AMA) using your professional email account. This account is different from your practice account, which you use specifically for email related to your medical practice. Since you use Outlook, you ensure both email accounts are available to make your work more efficient. [Student Learning Outcomes 7.1, 7.2]

Skills Covered in This Project

- Set up an email account.
- Change the default email account.
- Select an account when creating a new message.

---

1. Add a new account to Outlook. (If you completed *Pause & Practice 7-1* or *Guided Project 7-1,* skip this step).

2. Change the default email account to be your work account (school account).

3. Use the information below to send a message to your patient list indicating that you will be out of town at a conference for the next week (Figure 7-54).
   To: [instructor's email address]
   Cc: [your email address]
   Subject: Outlook Independent Project 7-4
   Message: Hi everyone, I just wanted to let you know that I will be out of town at a conference for the next week. For immediate emergencies, contact my assistant, Jane. She can set up appointments with my colleague, Dr. Goron.
   [your name]

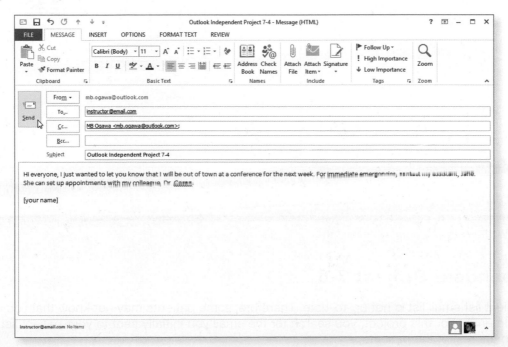

7-54 Completed Independent Project 7-4

Independent Project 7-5

You noticed that more of your patients are discussing stress and nutrition with you. Therefore, for this project, you subscribe to RSS feeds on those subject areas to help you keep abreast of trends.
[Student Learning Outcome 7.4]

Skills Covered in This Project

- Add an RSS feed.
- Rename an RSS feed folder.

- Delete an RSS feed.
- Share an RSS feed.

1. Open a browser and navigate to http://www.mayoclinic.com/health/rss/rss.

2. Locate the RSS feeds for **Stress, Nutrition-wise,** and **All MayoClinic.com Topics.**

3. Add all three RSS feeds to your *RSS Feeds* folder.

4. Rename the **Blog - Stress** RSS feed **Stress Information.**

5. Rename the **Blog – Nutrition-wise** RSS feed **Nutrition Information.**

6. Delete the **All Mayo** Clinic.com **Topics** RSS feed.

7. Share the **Stress Information** and **Nutrition Information** feeds with your instructor. They will be sent as two messages.
   a. Add the text **Outlook Independent Project 7-5** in the subject line before the default subject.
   b. Add your email address to the *Cc* field.
   c. Add a short message to your instructor indicating that you are submitting your completed Independent Project (Figure 7-55).

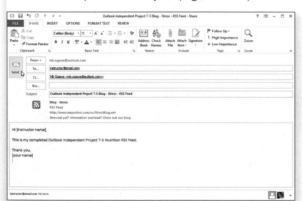 

7-55 Completed Independent Project 7-5

Independent Project 7-6

Your patient list email list is not up-to-date. Therefore, some patients may not know that you are away at a conference. For this project, you search for the email you initially sent to your patient list and forward it to the rest of the patients.
[Student Learning Outcome 7.5]

Skills Covered in This Project

- Search using *Instant Search*.
- Use *Scope* to narrow search.
- Use *Refine* to narrow search.
- Use *Advanced Find*.

---

1. Search for the message you sent in Independent Project 7-4 using *Instant Search* or *Advanced Find*.

2. After locating the message, forward it to your instructor (Figure 7-56).
   a. Be sure to add your address in the *Cc* field.
   b. Add **Outlook Independent Project 7-6** in the subject line.
   c. Add a short message to your instructor with the following information:
      Message: Hi everyone. I am not sure if you received this message, so I am forwarding it to you to ensure you are aware that I will be away. Thanks,
      [your name]
      Below the message to your patients, include the following search information. Only include the features you utilized:
      Keywords: [keywords for search]
      Scope criteria: [criteria and reason for using it]
      Refine criteria: [criteria and reason for using it]
      Advanced Find criteria: [criteria and reason for using it]

Figure 7-56 Completed Independent Project 7-6

Challenge Project 7-7

Most people have more than one email account. Working with multiple accounts and personalizing Outlook to meet your needs is definitely a challenge. For this project, you identify the different email accounts that you have. Determine if you will need additional accounts for different purposes, such as work, school, and personal. Send an email message to your instructor indicating which one would be set as default and why. Also indicate if and when you would use the Web access counterpart, such as Outlook web access. Lastly, you configure Outlook to better meet your needs and email your instructor which customizations you made to your installation and why. You should customize at least three advanced email options.
[Student Learning Outcomes 7.1, 7.2, 7.3]

- Identify the different email accounts that you have.
- Determine if you need additional accounts.
- Determine which account should be the default.
- Determine when the web mail counterpart, such as Outlook Web access would be useful.
- Email your instructor using the following message format:
  Account 1: [purpose for the account]
  Default: [indicate if it is the default account or not and why]
  Web access: [indicate when the Web access counterpart would be useful]
  Account 2: [purpose for the account]
  Default: [indicate if it is the default account or not and why]
  Web access: [indicate when the Web access counterpart would be useful]
  Account 3: [purpose for the account]

Default: [indicate if it is the default account or not and why]
Web access: [indicate when the Web access counterpart would be useful]
Outlook Personalization: [list of features modified]
Feature 1: [indicate modification and reason]
Feature 2: [indicate modification and reason]
Feature 3: [indicate modification and reason]

- Change the subject of your message to Outlook Challenge Project 7-7.

Challenge Project 7-8

Based on your interests, search the web to find at least two RSS feeds that interest you. Add the RSS feeds to your *RSS Feeds* folder and share them with your instructor.
[Student Learning Outcome 7.4]

- Search the web for at least two RSS feeds that interest you.
- Add the feeds to your *RSS Feeds* folder.
- Rename the feeds if you prefer a descriptive title.
- Share the feeds with your instructor (there will be two separate messages).
- Use the following email message format:
    Feed Name: [reason you chose this feed]
    Change the subject of your first message to **Outlook Challenge Project 7-8 Feed 1.**
- Change the subject of your second message to **Outlook Challenge Project 7-8 Feed 2.**

Challenge Project 7-9

Identify one email message and one Outlook item that you created in the past year. Email your message and Outlook item as attachments to your instructor. Include your search criteria to find the message and Outlook item and why you would use the criteria for it.
[Student Learning Outcome 7.5]

- Identify an email message and Outlook item you created in the last year.
- Determine search criteria to find the message and Outlook item.
- You should include keywords in your search.
- For the email message, use one scope and one refine search criteria.
- For the Outlook item, use at least two criteria in addition to keywords.
- Include reasons for your search criteria.
- Email your instructor using the following message format:
    Email message: [Outlook attachment name]
    Keywords: [keywords for search]
    Scope criteria: [criteria and reason for using it]
    Refine criteria: [criteria and reason for using it]
    Outlook item: [Outlook attachment name]
    Keywords: [keywords for search]
    Criteria 1: [criteria and reason for using it]
    Criteria 2: [criteria and reason for using it]
- Change the subject of your message to **Outlook Challenge Project 7-9.**

CHAPTER 8

Advanced Contacts

CHAPTER OVERVIEW

Contacts are an essential part of Outlook and are used when emailing, assigning tasks, and creating meeting requests. The longer you use Outlook, the more you will find that your contacts list will grow and that you are using this stored contact information on a regular basis. You will also realize how your stored contacts integrate with Outlook and other Microsoft Office 2013 programs.

As you become more familiar with the different features available in Outlook, you will want to customize how contacts appear, where they are stored, and how they are categorized. Outlook also provides you with the ability to share contacts with other users or between different programs. Importing and exporting contacts and merging contacts with other programs can save you a huge amount of time.

STUDENT LEARNING OUTCOMES (SLOs)

After completing this chapter, you will be able to:

SLO 8.1   Integrate Outlook contacts with folders and categories (p. O8-286).

SLO 8.2   Create and utilize electronic business cards (p. O8-292).

SLO 8.3   Share contact information by importing to and exporting from Outlook (p. O8-298).

SLO 8.4   Use Outlook Contacts with other Microsoft Office 2013 programs (p. O8-304).

CASE STUDY

For the Pause & Practice projects, you use Outlook contacts to optimize your work by using folders and categories for your contacts. You also export folders to help you quickly build your contact directory.

As a budding professional, you use Outlook to create a business card that will exude a professional persona. For the final Pause & Practice project, you send snail mail thank you letters to your partners and instructor, because they prefer to receive physical letters. You use your Outlook contacts to help you quickly create mail merge address labels so you can easily mail out your letters.

Pause & Practice 8-1: You work with two partners to create a contact folder and use

categories to organize your contacts. After creating and organizing your contacts, you email them to your instructor.

Pause & Practice 8-2: You modify your business card to improve its aesthetics. If possible, you should include an image of yourself.

Pause & Practice 8-3: You export the BUS 100 folder you created in Pause & Practice Outlook 8-1 to a .csv to make it easier to share with others.

Pause & Practice 8-4: You decided to use snail mail to send thank you letters to your partners and instructor. You use Outlook contacts and Word to help you quickly create mailing labels for them.

SLO 8.1

Managing Contacts

As your list of contacts increases and you are using your contacts in Outlook on a more regular basis, you will want to customize your default address book, create folders in which to store contacts, and assign categories to contacts. Using folders and categories will help you to manage an ever-growing list of contacts, and tracking contacts' activities will make you more effective in your use of Outlook.

> **MORE INFO**
>
> Contacts were covered in Chapter 3.
>
> Creating and using categories was covered in Chapter 2.
>
> Creating and using folders was covered in Chapter 6.

Change the Default Address Book

When you create a new email, meeting, or task request and click the **To** button, your default address book opens allowing you to select recipients. If you are using Outlook as a stand-alone program, by default this address book will be your *Contacts folder*.

When you are using Outlook in an Exchange environment, your default address book will be the *Global Address List*. If you work for a medium or large company, this list of contacts could number in the hundreds or thousands. Your most frequently used contacts should be saved in your *Contacts* folder.

You can easily change the default address book so your contacts appear first when selecting recipients. This does not mean that you will not have access to your *Global Address List* or other contact folders. But, the default address book will prevent you from wasting time, by making your select contacts more conveniently located.

HOW TO: Change the Default
Address Book

1. Click the **People** button in the *Navigation* pane.
2. Click the **Address Book** button in the *Find* group on the *Home* tab to open the *Address Book* dialog box.
3. Click the **Tools** menu and choose **Options** (Figure 8-1) to open the *Addressing* dialog box.
4. In the *When opening the address book, show this address list first* field, choose the address book to be set as the default (Figure 8-2).
5. Click **OK**.
6. Close the *Addressing* dialog box.

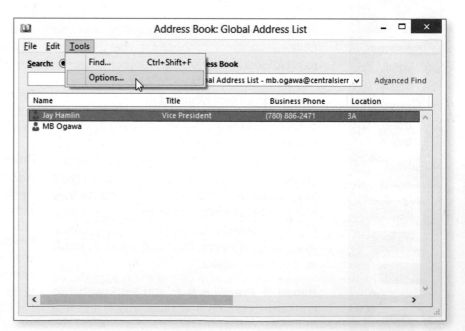

8-1 *Address Book* options

8-2 Select default address book

Create a Contacts Folder

If you use Outlook at both work and home and don't want all your contacts in the *Contacts* folder, you can use folders to organize your contact records (Figure 8-3). Using folders keeps contacts organized so that it is easier to locate contact information.

Creating a folder in Contacts is similar to creating an email folder.

8-3 Contact folders

HOW TO: Create a Contacts Folder

1. Click the **People** button in the *Navigation* pane.
2. Click the **Contacts** folder in the *My Contacts* area of the *Navigation* pane.
3. Click the **Folder** tab.
4. Click the **New Folder** button in the *New* group to open the *Create New Folder* dialog box (Figure 8-4).
5. Type the name of the new folder. Confirm that **Contact Items** is selected in the *Folder contains* area and that the **Contacts** folder is selected in the *Select where to place the folder* area.
6. Click **OK**. The new folder will appear in the list of contact folders (*My Contacts*).

8-4 *Create New Folder* dialog box

> **ANOTHER WAY**
>
> **Ctrl+Shift+E** opens the *Create New Folder* dialog box. Be sure the *Contacts* folder is selected before using this shortcut.

> **ANOTHER WAY**
>
> Right-click the **Contacts** folder and choose **New Folder.**

> **MORE INFO**
>
> Contact folders displayed in the *My Contacts* area are not displayed in hierarchical format; although, by viewing your *Folder List*, you can see the hierarchy of folders.

Once the new folder is created, you can drag and drop contacts from your *Contacts* folder or other contact folders to the new folder. When you click any of the contact folders, the contents of the folder are displayed in the *Folder* pane.

Categorize Contacts

If you are working on a project and have a team of individuals with whom you're working, you might want to group these contacts together, but not necessarily move them to a different contact folder. Grouping these contacts by a category would be an effective use of categories to mark and group contact records. Contacts can be viewed by category in the *List view*.

To assign a contact to a category, you can either use an existing category or create a new category.

> **MORE INFO**
>
> Creating categories was covered in Chapter 2.
> A contact record can be assigned to more than one category. When viewed with *By Category*, the contact will appear in the list in each of the categories for which it is assigned.

HOW TO: Categorize Contacts

1. Click the **People** button in the *Navigation* pane.
2. Click **Contacts** in the *My Contacts* area.
3. Select the contacts to be categorized.

4. Click the **Categorize** button in the *Tags* group on the *Home* tab, and select the desired category (Figure 8-5).

5. Click **List** in the *Current View* section of the *Navigation* pane. Your contacts will be displayed in list format and grouped *By Category* in the *Folder* pane (Figure 8-6).

8-5 Apply a category to a contact

▶ **ANOTHER WAY**

You can assign a category to an open contact by clicking the *Categorize* button in the *Tags* group on the *Contact* tab.

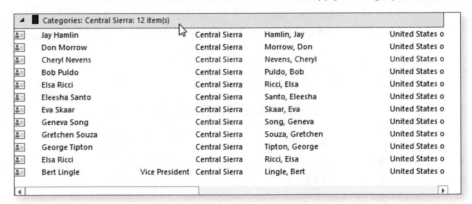

8-6 View contacts by category in List view

When a contact record is open and if it has been assigned to a category, the category will be displayed in the *Info bar* of the contact record. To clear this category or add another category, you can right-click the *Info bar* for the different category option available.

▶ **MORE INFO**

The *Info bar* is available on most Outlook items that have been flagged, categorized, or responded to. Clicking or right-clicking the *Info bar* will provide you with a menu of actions from which to choose.

Update Contacts

When using Outlook in conjunction with an Exchange server, Outlook can automatically **update** your contact records with information from your company's *Global Address List*.

8-7 Update contact from the *Global Address list*

To update a contact, click the **Update** button (Figure 8-7) in the *Update* group on the *Contact* tab. Any changes made to the contact will be displayed in the *Notes* area of the contact record.

Customize Contact Options

In Chapter 7, you learned how to customize many of the different options available for emails. Outlook also allows you to customize some of the options in Contacts.

The Contacts customization options are available by opening the ***Outlook Options*** dialog box [*File* tab, *Options*] and selecting the *People* button on the left (Figure 8-8).

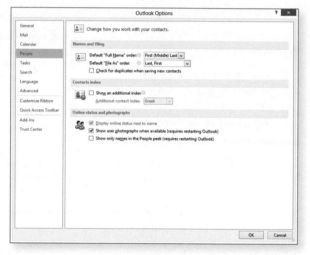

8-8 Outlook options for People

You can customize the order you want Outlook to use for new names and the setting for how Outlook saves new contacts. Outlook can even check for duplicate contacts for you.

The ***Show an additional index*** feature allows you to display an additional language when scrolling through your contact list (Figure 8-9). This feature is especially handy when you are more comfortable with another language.

The ***Online status and photographs*** feature allows you to view your contacts' status and photographs. You can also choose to only display names, as opposed to contact information and photographs, in ***People Peek***. *People Peek* is a contact search tool.

8-9 Additional Greek contact index

For this Pause & Practice project, you work with two partners to create a contact folder and use categories to organize your contacts. After creating and organizing your contacts, you email them to your instructor.

1. Click the **People** button in the *Navigation* pane.

2. Create three new contacts, a new contact for each of your two partners and instructor. Include a first name, last name, email address, and mailing address (you can use the school's address for everyone). You may skip this step if you already have these contacts.

3. Create a folder for your group project.
   a. Click the **Contacts** folder in the *My Contacts* area of the *Navigation* pane.
   b. Click the **Folder** tab.
   c. Click the **New Folder** button in the *New* group to open the *Create New Folder* dialog box.
   d. Type BUS 100 for the name of the folder and press **Enter**.
   e. Click **OK**.

4. Add your two partners and instructor to the *BUS 100* folder.
   a. Click the **People** button in the *Navigation* pane.
   b. Click and drag both of your partners' contacts into the *BUS 100* folder.
   c. Click and drag your professor's contact into the **BUS 100** folder.

5. Create categories for *BUS 100* (blue category), *Student* (green category), and *Professor* (yellow category).

6. Categorize your partners' and instructor's contacts.
   a. Click the **People** button in the *Navigation* pane.
   b. Click **Contacts** in the *My Contacts* area.
   c. Select the students' contacts.
   d. Click the **Categorize** button and select **BUS 100**.
   e. Click the **Categorize** button and select **Student**.
   f. Select the instructor's contact.
   g. Click the **Categorize** button and select **BUS 100**.
   h. Click the **Categorize** button and select **Professor**.

7. Send an email to your instructor with the three contacts as attachments.
   a. Click the **Mail** button in the *Navigation* pane.
   b. Click **New Mail** [*Home* tab, *New* group].
   c. In the *To* field, enter your instructor's email address.
   d. In the *Cc* field, enter your email address.
   e. In the *Subject* field, enter Outlook Pause & Practice 8-1
   f. In the message area, type:

      Dear [instructor's name],
      Attached is my Outlook Pause & Practice 8-1.
      Thank you,
      [student name]

   g. Click the **Business Card** option [*Message* tab, *Include* group, *Attach Item*] and select **Other Business Cards**.
   h. Select the three cards you created and click **OK**.

i. Click the **Send** button (Figure 8-10).

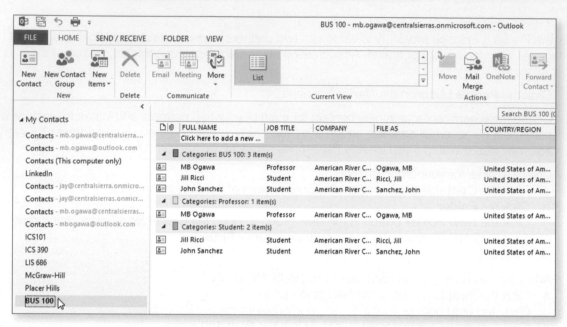

8-10 Completed Pause & Practice 8-1

Using Business Cards

Have you ever been asked to send your contact information to someone via email? This is a very common request, and many times can be done by inserting an existing signature containing this information. But, if you are sending this information to other Outlook users, they will still have to type this information into a new contact record, which is a waste of time.

Outlook allows you to send a contact record (or more than one) as an attachment to an email. You can also add an electronic business card to a signature or customize your business card.

> MORE INFO
>
> In Outlook, the terms **business card** and **electronic business card** are used synonymously. Contact records can be sent as business cards, and, since they are in electronic format, they are in essence electronic business cards.

Send an Electronic Business Card

Sending electronic business cards in an email is similar to attaching a file to an email. The difference is you will be attaching an Outlook item rather than a different type of file, such as a Word document or picture.

HOW TO: Email an Electronic Business Card as an Attachment

1. Open a new email.
2. Select recipients, include a subject, and type a brief message.

3. Click the **Attach Item** button in the *Include* group on the *Message* tab, choose **Business Cards**, and then choose **Other Business Cards** (Figure 8-11). The *Insert Business Card* dialog box opens.

4. Select the **Contacts** folder in the *Look in* area.

5. Select the contacts to be attached (Figure 8-12).

6. Click **OK** to close the *Insert Business Card* dialog box. The selected contacts will be attached to the email, and a graphic of the business card will be inserted in the body of the message.

7. Press the **Send** button to send the email.

8-11 Attach a business card

ANOTHER WAY

You can attach a contact record or other Outlook items by clicking the *Attach Item* button.

MORE INFO

To select multiple contacts, use the **Ctrl** key and your pointer to select nonadjacent items, and use the **Shift** key and your pointer to select a range of items.

8-12 *Insert Business Card* dialog box

You can also send a contact as a business card from the *Contacts* area.

HOW TO: Forward a Business Card

1. Click the **People** button in the *Navigation* pane.

2. Select the **Contacts** folder in *My Contacts*.

3. Select the contacts to whom you want to send a business card.

4. Right-click the contact, choose **Forward Contact,** and select **As a Business Card** (Figure 8-13). A new email opens with the business card attached and a graphic of the business card in the body of the message.

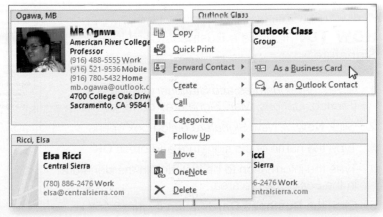

8-13 Forward contact as a business card

5. Select recipients, include a subject, and type a brief message (Figure 8-14).

6. Click **Send**.

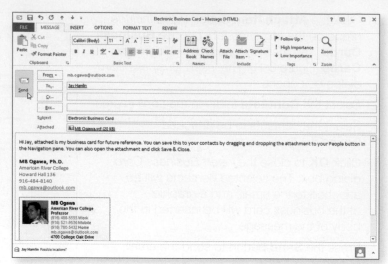

8-14 Contact attached in an email message

Include Your Business Card in a Signature

Another way to include your business card in an email message is to attach it to your signature. You can set up multiple signatures in Outlook, and you might want to create a signature that includes your business card. This will save you from having to manually attach or forward a business card.

When you insert a signature that has a business card attached, the business card will automatically be included as an attachment to the email.

HOW TO: Include a Business Card in a Signature

1. Open the *Signatures and Stationery* dialog box [*File* tab, *Options, Mail, Signatures* button].

2. Click **New**. A *New Signature* dialog box opens.

3. Type the name of the signature and press **OK**.

4. Type the information to be included in the signature in the *Edit signature* area.

5. Click the **Business Card** button (Figure 8-15). The *Insert Business Card* dialog box opens.

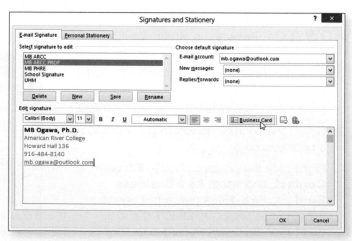

8-15 *Business Card* button

6. Select the contact to be included as a business card (Figure 8-16).

7. Press **OK**. The business card graphic will be included with your signature (see Figure 8-16).

8. Click **Save** to save your signature.

9. Click **OK** to close the *Signatures and Stationery* dialog box.

10. Click **OK** to close the *Outlook Options* dialog box.

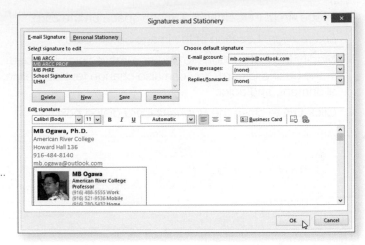

8-16 Business card in a signature

When you insert this signature into an email, the signature and graphic of the business card will be inserted into the body of the email. The graphic of the business card can be deleted without removing the attachment.

> **MORE INFO**
>
> The size of the business card graphic in the signature can be changed. This is done in the *Signatures and Stationery* dialog box.

> **MORE INFO**
>
> It is not necessary to include a signature on every email you send. This is especially true if your business card is attached to the signature.

Customize Your Business Card

When you create a contact record, a business card is automatically generated. Outlook provides a lot of flexibility in customizing the layout, colors, styles, and information of a business card.

HOW TO: Edit a Business Card

1. Open a business card and click the **Business Card** button (Figure 8-17) in the *Options* group on the *Contact* tab. The *Edit Business Card* dialog box opens (Figure 8-18).

2. Modify the **Card Design** options to change the aesthetics.

   Layout: The location of the image

   Background: Background color of the card

   Image: Image to include on the card

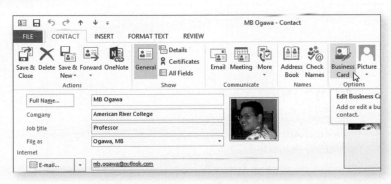

8-17 *Business Card* options button

Image Area: Percentage of image space on the card.

Image Align: Location of the image on the card

3. Modify the **Edit** options to add or remove fields included in the business card. You can also change font size, style, alignment, and color.

4. Click **OK** to close the *Business Card* dialog box.

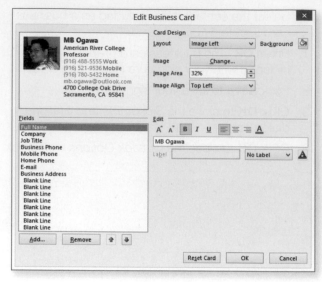

8-18 *Edit Business Card* dialog box

Create a Business Card from an Online Template

There are also many ***online templates*** you can use to customize your business card. A business card template includes layout, graphics, colors, fonts, styles, and fields. You can do an Internet search to find these templates. Microsoft's web site has these templates available.

Once a template has been selected and downloaded, you can customize it in the same manner as customizing a business card described in the previous section.

HOW TO: Find and Edit Business Card Templates

1. Open an Internet browser window and go to www. office.microsoft.com and search the templates for email business cards (Figure 8-19).

2. Select the business card template of your choice and follow the steps to download it. The template will be saved in a temporary location until it is edited and saved in your *Contacts* folder.

3. Enter your contact information (Figure 8-20).

4. You can click the **Business Card** button in the *Options* group to further edit the business card.

5. Click **Save & Close**.

8-19 Search for email business cards

> **MORE INFO**
> Use good judgment when using business card templates, as some creative templates might appear unprofessional in a business environment.

8-20 Modified business card from template

For this Pause & Practice project, you modify your business card to improve its aesthetics. If possible, you should include an image of yourself.

File Needed: *Your image*

---

1. Click the **People** button in the *Navigation* pane.

2. Locate and open your business card.

3. Click the **Business Card** button in the *Options* group on the *Contact* tab. The *Edit Business Card* dialog box opens.

4. Modify the **Card Design** options to change the aesthetics using the following options:
   Layout: **Image Right**
   Background: **Blue**
   Image: Include an image of yourself
   Image Area: **30%**
   Image Align: Top right

   Select all of the text fields that are available on your business card and change the text color to **White**.

5. Click **OK** to close the *Business Card* dialog box.

6. Email the business card to your instructor as an attachment.
   a. Click the **People** button in the *Navigation* pane.
   b. Select the **Contacts** folder in *My Contacts*.
   c. Select your business card.
   d. Right-click the contact, choose **Forward Contact**, and select **As a Business Card**. A new email opens with the business card attached and a graphic of the business card in the body of the message.
   e. Select your instructor as the recipient.
   f. Add your email address in the *Cc* field.
   g. Change the subject to *Outlook Pause & Practice 8-2*.
   h. Type a short message to your instructor indicating that the completed *Pause and Practice Outlook 8-2* project is attached to the message.
   i. Click **Send** (Figure 8-21).

8-21 Completed Pause & Practice 8-2

Importing and Exporting

By now you have created new contacts in Outlook. There are many ways to do this: from scratch, from a received email, from a contact from the same company, and from a contact record sent to you as a business card. What if you had to enter 30, 50, 100, or 1000 new contacts from a database or spreadsheet? This would take a huge amount of time.

Outlook provides *Import* and *Export* features that enable you to both import and export records without spending a long time manually creating them. Outlook can import and export comma-separated values and Personal Folder (PST) files.

The importing and exporting process is one of the more complex tasks in Outlook, but Outlook walks you through it with a step-by-step wizard. After going through the importing and exporting process a couple of times, you'll be amazed at the time saved by using this feature.

> ### MORE INFO
>
> Remember a *field* is one piece of information about a contact such as *First Name, Last Name, Phone,* or *Email.* A *record* (contact record) is a group of related fields. It is important to make this distinction when working with database information.

Import Contacts

The following is an overview of the steps you will take to import contact records. If you are importing from a different type of file, these steps will still work.

1. Create a contact folder in which to import the records.
2. Choose the process: Import.
3. Choose the type of file to import.
4. Choose the file to import.
5. Choose the location to save the imported records.
6. Map fields: This is the process to make sure that the fields from the contacts being imported are mapped (matched) with the fields in the Outlook contact record.
7. Import.

HOW TO: Import Contacts

1. Click the *Contacts* button in the *Navigation* pane.
2. Create a new contact folder in which to save the new contacts (the folder is named *Placer Hills* in this example).
3. Click the **File** tab to open the *Backstage* view.
4. Click **Open and Export** and choose **Import/ Export** (Figure 8-22) to open the **Import and Export Wizard** dialog box.
5. Click **Import from another program or file** and then click **Next** (Figure 8-23) to open the *Import a File* dialog box.
6. Click **Comma Separated Values** as the type of file to import from and click **Next**. The next *Import a File* dialog box opens.

8-22 *Import/Export* files and settings

7. Click the **Browse** button to locate the file on your computer to import, select the file to import, and press **OK** (Figure 8-24).

   - The path to the file appears in the *File to import* text box.
   - *Note: You will be importing the PHRE comma separated value file when you complete the guided project at the end of this chapter.*

8. The *Options* area gives you choices about what action Outlook should perform if duplicate contact records are detected. Click **Next**.

   - Because you are importing into a new folder with no contact records, these options are irrelevant.
   - If you are importing to a folder containing existing contacts, select from one of the options.

9. Choose your newly created folder (*Placer Hills* in this example) as the *destination folder,* the folder into which the new contact records will be imported, and click **Next**.

10. Click the **Map Custom Fields** button. The *Map Custom Fields* dialog box opens.

    - The fields from the CSV file (*Placer Hills Real Estate* in this example) are listed on the left, and the fields available in the Outlook contact record are listed on the right.
    - The fields on the *left* (from CSV) need to be mapped to the fields on the *right* (to Outlook contact record).
    - Outlook makes a guess at fields that are similar; this does not ensure that they are correct.

11. Click the **Clear Map** button. This clears the *Mapped from* fields on the right.

12. Drag each field from the left (CSV) to the corresponding field on the right (Outlook contact) (Figure 8-25). Use the following table to map fields. *Hint: Don't drag a field from the left to a field on the right with a plus by it (e.g., Name). Open (click the plus sign) this field category to see the individual fields.*

From Access	To Outlook Contact
First	First Name
Last	Last Name
Company	Company
Department	Department
Job	Job Title
Street	Business Street
City	Business City
State	Business State
Zip Code	Business Postal
Country	Business Country
Email	Email Address
Phone	Business Phone

8-23 Import from another program or file

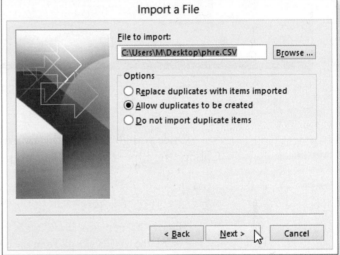

8-24 Select a file to import

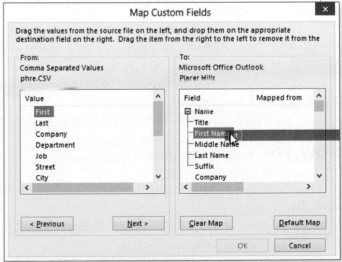

8-25 Match each field from the CSV file to the Outlook contact

13. Once you have mapped all of the fields, click the **Next** button to see the first record displayed on both the left and right. The actual field contents will be displayed next to their corresponding Outlook contact fields.

14. Click **OK** when you have confirmed that all the fields are mapped correctly.

15. Click **Finish** to import the records from the CSV file.

16. Click the new folder (*Placer Hills* in this example) in the *My Contacts* area of the *Navigation* pane. The contents of this folder will be displayed in the *Folder* pane (Figure 8-26).

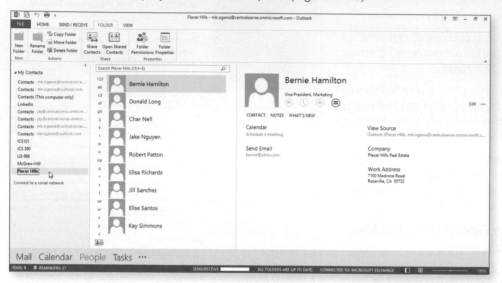

8-26 **Imported Placer Hills Real Estate contacts**

Once you go through this process a couple of times, you'll be able to perform an import in about the time it would take to type one contact record.

> **MORE INFO**
>
> Usually if a mistake is made, it is in mapping fields. If you find a mistake, it is usually quicker to delete the contact records from the contact folder and redo the import.

Export Contacts

Exporting is a similar process to importing, but it is a little easier. Rather than mapping the fields, you just have to drag over the fields from the contact that you want included in the export. Not all of the Outlook contact fields will be exported because many of the fields in a contact record are blank.

HOW TO: Export Contacts

1. Click the folder to be exported (the *Placer Hills* folder in this example) in the *My Contacts* area in the *Navigation* pane.

2. Click the **File** tab and click the **Open & Export** button. The *Import and Export Wizard* dialog box opens (Figure 8-27).

3. Click **Export to a file** and click **Next**.

8-27 *Import and Export Wizard* dialog box

4. Choose **Comma Separated Values** as the type of file to create and click **Next**.

5. Select the contact folder from which to export (the *Placer Hills* folder in this example) and click **Next**.

6. Click **Browse**. The *Browse* dialog box opens. You will name the export file and select a location where to save it (Figure 8-28).

7. In the *File name* box, type the name of the file (*Placer Hills* in this example). Confirm that you are saving as a **Comma Separated Values** file in the *Save as type* box.

8. Click **OK** and then click **Next**.

9. Click the **Map Custom Fields** button. The *Map Custom Fields* dialog box opens.

   • The fields from the Outlook contact are listed on the left, and the fields to be exported to a Comma Separated Values file are listed on the right.
   • You don't want all the fields to be exported because you will have many blank fields in the exported spreadsheet if you do.
   • By default, Outlook does a decent job removing unused fields. You can clear the map and select specific fields to be exported.

10. Click **Clear Map** to clear the fields to be exported.

11. Drag the following fields from the *left* side (Outlook contact) to the *right* side (Excel export): **First Name, Last Name, Company**, **Job Title**, and **Email Address** (Figure 8-29).

12. Click **OK** to close the *Map Custom Fields* dialog box.

13. Click **Finish**. The Excel file is now created with the exported contacts.

14. Open the new *.csv* file to confirm that the records were exported correctly.

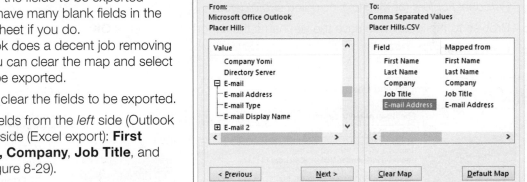

8-28 Select a location and file name

8-29 Select fields to export

After a contact has been exported, the exported file can now be sent to others as an attachment, and they can use this file to import these contact records into Outlook or use it with other programs.

> MORE INFO
> A CSV file can be edited in Microsoft Excel, which makes it easy to add or remove contacts quickly.

Export an Outlook Data File

When you get a new computer, you may dread the amount of time it is going to take to set up all the software and copy all the files. You might wonder how you are going to get all your information from Outlook on your existing computer to the new computer.

If you're working in an Exchange environment, all this information is stored on the Exchange server, so setting up Outlook and retrieving all your information is done when you set up your Exchange account in Outlook on the new computer. But what if you are getting a new home computer and want to transfer all your existing Outlook information to the new computer? Or what if your computer crashes?

Outlook has provided you with a way to transfer and backup your files with ease. Outlook stores all your information in an **Outlook Data File,** which is a *.pst* file. This file resides on your computer and contains all your Outlook information.

If you are changing from one computer to another, Outlook helps you export your *Outlook Data File* and save it as a file. Then this file, which contains all your Outlook information, can be imported into Outlook on the new computer.

HOW TO: Export an Outlook Data File

1. Click the **File** tab and click the **Open & Export** button. The *Import and Export Wizard* opens.
2. Choose **Export to a File** and click **Next** (Figure 8-30).
3. Select **Outlook Data File (.pst)** and click **Next**.
4. Choose the folder to export and click **Next** (Figure 8-31). It is a good idea to export your entire *Personal Folders* (or Mailbox) including *subfolders.*
5. Browse to the location to save the file, name the export file, and click **OK**.
6. Click **Finish**.

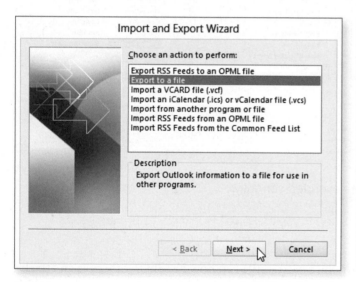

8-30 Export to a file

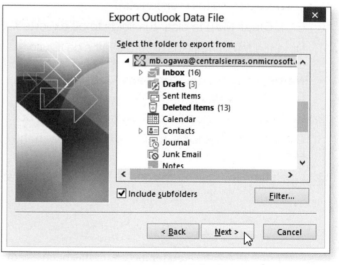

8-31 Select folder to export

> MORE INFO
>
> If you are using Outlook in a stand-alone environment, it is a good idea to occasionally back up (export) your *Outlook Data File* and save this file in a location other than your computer.

Import an Outlook Data File

The process to import an *Outlook Data File* is similar to the importing and exporting process described previously. Importing your *Outlook Data File* is a much more streamlined process than importing contacts from a different file format.

HOW TO: Import an Outlook Data File

1. Click the **File** tab, click the **Open & Export** button, and select **Import/Export**. The *Import and Export Wizard* opens.
2. Choose **Import from another program or file** and click **Next**.
3. Choose **Outlook Data File (.pst)** and click **Next**.
4. Use the **Browse** button to locate and select the *Outlook Data File* to import and then click **Next**.
5. Click **Import items into the same folder in** and choose **Personal Folders**.
6. Click **Finish** (Figure 8-32).

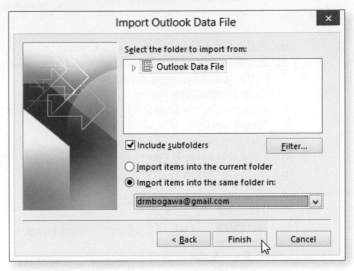

8-32 Import folder location

PAUSE & PRACTICE: OUTLOOK 8-3

For this Pause & Practice project, you export the *BUS 100* folder you created in *Pause & Practice Outlook 8-1*.

1. Click the **People** button on the *Navigation* pane.
2. Click the **BUS 100** folder in the *My Contacts* area in the *Navigation* pane.
3. Click the **File** tab and click the **Open & Export** button. The *Import and Export Wizard* dialog box opens.
4. Click **Export to a file** and click **Next**.
5. Choose **Comma Separated Values** as the type of file to create and click **Next**.
6. Select the **BUS 100** folder as the contact folder from which to export and click **Next**.
7. Click **Browse**. The *Browse* dialog box opens.
8. Select the location on your computer where to save the export file.
9. In the *File name* box, type BUS 100 [your initials] as the name of the file. Confirm that you are saving as a **Comma Separated Values** file in the *Save as type* box.
10. Click **OK** and then click **Next**.
11. Click the **Map Custom Fields** button. The *Map Custom Fields* dialog box opens.
12. Click **Clear Map** to clear the fields to be exported.
10. Drag the following fields from the *left* side (Outlook contact) to the *right* side (Excel export): **First Name, Last Name, Email Address, Business Street, Business City, Business State,** and **Business Postal**.
14. Click **OK** to close the *Map Custom Fields* dialog box.
15. Click **Finish**.
16. Send an email to your instructor with the *.csv* file you exported as an attachment.
    a. Click the **Mail** button in the *Navigation* pane.
    b. Click **New Mail** [*Home* tab, *New* group].
    c. In the *To* field, enter your instructor's email address.

d. In the *Cc* field, enter your email address.
e. In the *Subject* field, enter Outlook Pause & Practice 8-3.
f. In the message area, type:
Dear [instructor's name],
Attached is my Outlook Pause & Practice 8-3.
Thank you,
[student name]
g. Click the **Attach File** button [*Message* tab, *Include* group] and select the exported file.
h. Click the **Send** button (Figure 8-33).

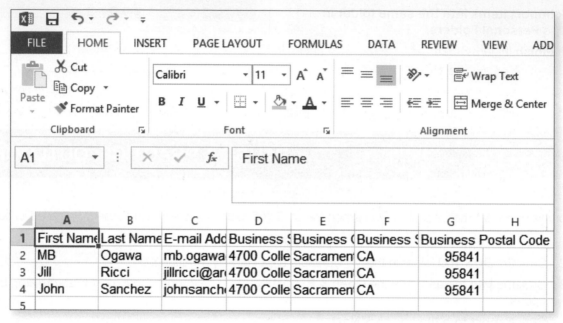

8-33 Completed Pause & Practice 8-3

Using Contacts with Other Office 2013 Programs

An advantage of using Microsoft Office products is the ability to share information between programs. You can easily use your Outlook Contacts to create mailing labels, envelopes, and business letters. Contacts can also be used in conjunction with Excel and Access, as comma separated value files are easy to import and manage.

Use Contacts to Create Mailing Labels in Word

Outlook 2013 has streamlined the process of using information in your contact records in a ***Mail Merge.*** Outlook works in conjunction with Microsoft Word to create labels, envelopes, or form letters. You can use all the contacts in a folder, or you can choose the contacts to be included in the merge. You don't have to be an expert in Word to create mailing labels; you can use the Mail Merge feature, which will walk you through this process.

The following example will walk you through the process of creating mailing labels from all the contacts you imported into the Placer Hills contacts folder.

HOW TO: Use Mail Merge with Outlook Contacts

1. In the *Navigation* pane, select the *Contacts* folder to be used in the merge.
2. Click the **Mail Merge** button in the *Actions* group on the *Home* tab. The *Mail Merge Contacts* dialog box opens (Figure 8-34).
3. In the *Mail Merge Contacts* dialog box, select **All contacts in current view** and select the *Document file* to be a **New document**.
4. In the *Merge options* section, select **Mailing Labels** and merge to **New Document**.
5. Click **OK**. Microsoft Word opens, and a dialog box opens informing you to set up your mailing labels.
6. Click **OK**. The *Mail Merge Helper* dialog box opens.
7. Click **Setup** (Figure 8-35). The *Label Options* dialog box opens.
8. Select your label brand and type (Avery 5160 is a standard label type) and click **OK** (Figure 8-36).
9. Close the **Mail Merge Helper** dialog box.
10. In the open Word document, click the **Mailings** tab.
11. Click the **Start Mail Merge** button and choose **Step by Step Mail Merge Wizard**. The *Mail Merge wizard* opens to the right of the document.
12. You will be on *Step 3 of 6;* click **Next: Arrange your labels**.
13. *Step 4 of 6:* Click the **Address Block** link. The *Insert Address Block* dialog box opens.
14. Select how you want your address block to appear and click **OK** (Figure 8-37).

8-34 Mail Merge Contacts dialog box

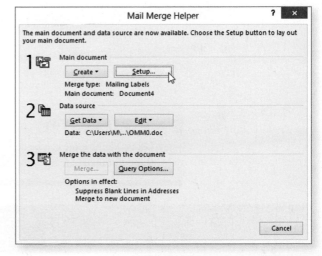

8-35 Mail Merge Helper dialog box

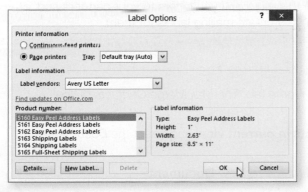

8-36 Select your label brand and type

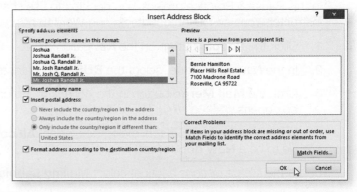

8-37 Select your address block appearance

15. Click the **Update all labels** button and click **Next** (Figure 8-38).

16. *Step 5 of 6:* Your labels will appear in the document. Click **Next: Complete the Merge**.

17. Select the entire document (**Ctrl+A**), change the paragraph spacing to **0 pt. before** and **after**, and change the line spacing to **Single**.

18. *Step 6 of 6:* You can either select **Print** or **Edit individual labels**. Figure 8-39 includes the completed mail merge.

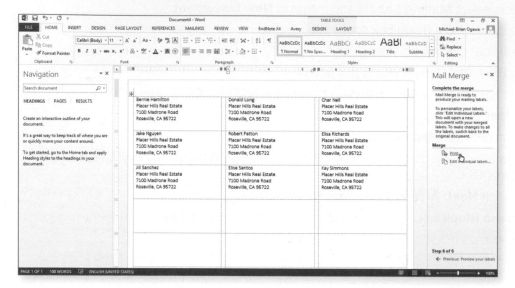

8-39 Completed mail merge

8-38 Update all labels

> **ANOTHER WAY**
>
> Using Mail Merge can be done directly from Word. The *Mail Merge Wizard* in Word will walk you through the mail merge process. Outlook contacts can be selected as a data source.

PAUSE & PRACTICE: OUTLOOK 8-4

In this Pause & Practice project, you decided to use snail mail to send thank you letters to your partners and instructor. You use Outlook contacts and Word to help you quickly create mailing labels for them.

1. Click the **People** button on the *Navigation* pane.

2. In the *Navigation* pane, select the **BUS 100** contacts folder.

3. Click the **Mail Merge** button in the *Actions* group on the *Home* tab. The *Mail Merge Contacts* dialog box opens.

4. In the *Mail Merge Contacts* dialog box, select **All contacts in current view** and select the *Document file* to be a **New document**.

5. In the *Merge options* section, select **Mailing Labels** and merge to **New Document**.

6. Click **OK**.

7. Click **OK** to close the dialog box and open the **Mail Merge Helper** dialog box.

8. Click **Setup**. The *Label Options* dialog box opens.

9. Select **Avery 5160** and click **OK**.

10. Close the **Mail Merge Helper** dialog box.

11. In the open Word document, click the **Mailings** tab.

12. Click the **Start Mail Merge** button and choose **Step by Step Mail Merge Wizard**. The *Mail Merge wizard* opens to the right of the document.

13. You will be on *Step 3 of 6;* click **Next: Arrange your labels**.

14. *Step 4 of 6:* Click the **Address Block** link. The *Insert Address Block* dialog box opens.

15. Click **OK**.

16. Click the **Update all labels** button and click **Next**.

17. *Step 5 of 6:* Your labels will appear in the document. Click **Next**.

18. Select the entire document (**Ctrl+A**), change the paragraph spacing to **0 pt. before** and **after**, and change the line spacing to **Single**.

19. *Step 6 of 6:* Select **Edit individual labels**. The **Merge to New Document** dialog box opens.

20. Select **All** and click **OK**.

21. In Word, click the **File** button and select **Save As**. Save the file as *outlookpp8-4* (Figure 8-40).

22. Send an email to your instructor with the completed mail merge as an attachment.
    a. Click the **Mail** button in the Navigation pane.
    b. Click **New Mail** [*Home* tab, *New* group].
    c. In the *To:* field, enter your instructor's email address.
    d. In the *Cc:* field, enter your email address.
    e. In the *Subject* field, enter: Outlook Pause & Practice 8-4
    f. In the message area, type:
       Dear [instructor name],
       Attached is my Outlook Pause & Practice 8-4.
       Thank you,
       [student name]
    g. Click the **Attach File** button [*Message* tab, *Include* group] and select the completed mail merge file.
    h. Click the **Send** button.

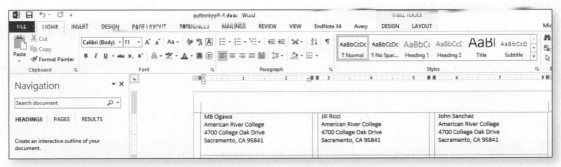

8-40 Completed Pause & Practice 8-4

Chapter Summary

8.1 Integrate Outlook contacts with folders, categories, and activities (p. O8-286).

- Folders and categories help you to organize and manage your list of contacts.
- You can change your default address book to help you quickly select contacts in Outlook.
- Using folders can help you keep contacts grouped together similar to the way folders work in Windows.
- You can drag and drop contacts into Folders.
- Categories allow you to label contacts without moving them into folders.
- You can update contacts using the *Global Address List* if your company uses an Exchange Server.
- The People button in the *Outlook Options* window allows you to customize how you view and work with contacts.

8.2 Create and utilize electronic business cards. (p. O8-292).

- Sending your business card allows other Outlook users to quickly add you as a contact.
- Business cards are attached to email messages as Outlook items.
- Business cards can be included in signatures.
- Outlook allows you to customize the appearance of your business card.
- You can download business card templates from the Internet and use them as a starting point for a business card.

8.3 Share contact information by importing to and exporting from Outlook (p. O8-298).

- Outlook allows you to import and export content to make your work more efficient.
- You can import and export contacts and folders in .pst and .csv file types.
- When importing contacts, it is a good idea to manually match the fields, as Outlook may not guess the fields it is trying to match correctly.
- It is important to export contacts based on how you want to import them.
- Exporting and importing Outlook data can help you to quickly move your Outlook information to a new computer.
- If you are using an Exchange environment, your Outlook data is saved on the server, so importing and exporting is less useful.

8.4 Use Outlook Contacts with other Microsoft Office programs (p. O8-304).

- Outlook contacts can be used with other Microsoft Office products such as Word, Excel, and Access.
- You can quickly create mail merges including mailing labels, envelopes, and business letters in Word.
- Contact data exported in .csv format can easily be imported into Excel or Access.

Check For Understanding

In the **Online Learning Center** for this text (www.mhhe.com/office2013inpractice), there are a variety of resources that can be used to review the concepts covered in this chapter.

The following Online Learning Resources are available in the Online Learning Center:

- Multiple choice questions
- Short answer questions
- Matching exercises

Guided Project 8-1

In this project, you are a real estate agent for Placer Hills Real Estate (PHRE). You decided to set up your home computer to include your contacts from work. Therefore, you exported your contacts in your office computer to a .csv file. In this project, you are looking to import your contacts from work and organize them using folders and categories.

[Student Learning Outcomes 8.1, 8.2, 8.3]

Skills Covered in This Project

- Create a contacts folder.
- Import contacts from a .csv file.
- Map fields.

- Select an account when creating a new message.
- Assign categories to contacts.
- Email business cards as attachments.

---

1. Click the *Contacts* button in the *Navigation* pane.

2. Create a new **Contacts** folder in which to save the new contacts, and name this folder **Placer Hills**.
   a. Click the **Contacts** folder in the *My Contacts* area of the *Navigation* pane.
   b. Click the **Folder** tab.
   c. Click the **New Folder** button in the *New* group to open the *Create New Folder* dialog box.
   d. Type Placer Hills for the name of the folder and press **Enter**.
   e. Click **OK**.

3. Click the **File** tab to open the *BackStage* view.

4. Click **Open and Export** and choose **Import/Export** to open the *Import and Export Wizard* dialog box.

5. Click **Import from another program or file** and click **Next** to open the *Import a File* dialog box.

6. Click **Comma Separated Values** as the type of file to import from and click **Next**. The next *Import a File* dialog box opens.

7. Click the **Browse** button to locate and select the **phre.csv** file on your computer and press **OK**.

8. In the *Options* area, select **replace duplicates with items imported** and click **Next**.

9. Choose **Placer Hills** as the *destination folder,* the folder into which the new contact records will be imported, and click **Next**.

10. Click the **Map Custom Fields** button. The *Map Custom Fields* dialog box opens.

11. Click the **Clear Map** button.

12. Drag each field from the left (CSV) to the corresponding field on the right (Outlook contact). Use the following table to map fields.

From Access	To Outlook Contact
First	First Name
Last	Last Name
Company	Company
Department	Department
Job	Job Title
Street	Business Street
City	Business City
State	Business State
Zip Code	Business Postal
Country	Business Country
Email	Email Address
Phone	Business Phone

13. Once you have mapped each of the fields, click the **Next** button to see the first record displayed at both the left and right. The actual field contents will be displayed next to their corresponding Outlook contact fields.

14. Click **OK** when you have confirmed that all the fields are mapped correctly.

15. Click **Finish** to import the records from the CSV file.

16. Click the **Placer Hills** folder in the *My Contacts* area of the *Navigation* pane. The contents of this folder will be displayed in the *Folder* pane (see Figure 8-26).

17. Create a category named **PHRE Agent** with the color **blue**.

18. Select the contacts for **Char Nell, Robert Patton,** and **Elisa Richards**. Click the **Categorize** button [*Home* tab, *Tags* group] and select **PHRE Agent** (Figure 8-41).

19. Email **Char Nell, Robert Patton,** and **Elisa Richards'** business cards to your instructor as an attachment.
    a. In the *To:* field, enter your instructor's email ddress.
    b. In the *Cc:* field, enter your email address.
    c. In the *Subject* field, enter: Outlook Guided Project 8-1
    d. In the message area, type:
       Dear [instructor's name],
       Attached is my Outlook Guided Project 8-1.
       Thank you,
       [your name]
    e. Click the **Business Card** option [*Message* tab, *Include* group, *Attach Item*] and select **Other Business Cards**.
    f. Select the three cards you categorized as **PHRE Agent** and click **OK**.
    g. Click the **Send** button.

8-41 Completed Guided Project 8-1

Guided Project 8-2

In this project, you are Robert Patton, an agent for PHRE. You recently realized that the appearance of your Outlook business card is very important because it is viewed both internally by members of the PHRE team and externally by clients. Therefore, you decide to download a template from Microsoft's web site and modify it to improve its aesthetics.
[Student Learning Outcome 8.2]

Skills Covered in This Project

- Download a contact template from office.microsoft.com.
- Edit the contents of a contact template.
- Modify the appearance of a contact template.

---

1. Click the **People** button in the *Navigation* pane.

2. Select **Robert Patton's** entry and press **Delete**.

3. Open an Internet browser window and go to www.office.microsoft.com, and search the templates for **email business card**.

4. Select a design of your choice, and follow the steps to download it. The template will be saved in a temporary location until it is edited and saved in your *Contacts* folder. The **E-mail business card (Grid design)** is used in this example.

5. Enter Robert Patton's contact information.
   Name: Robert Patton
   Company: Placer Hills Real Estate
   Job title: Agent
   E-mail: robert@phre.com
   Business Phone: (780) 886-2475
   Business Address: 7100 Madrone Road
   Roseville, CA 95722

6. Modify the **Card Design** options to change the aesthetics using the following options.
   a. Click the **Background Color** button and select a **dark blue**.
   b. Select each of the text fields that are available on your business card and change the text color to **White**.

   c. Select the **Mobile Phone** option in the *Fields* area and click **Remove**.

7. Click **OK** to close the *Business Card* dialog box.

8. Click the **Categorize** button and select **PHRE Agent**.

9. Click the **Save & Close** button. Figure 8-42 displays the completed business card for Robert Patton.

10. Click and drag Robert Patton's business card to the **Placer Hills** folder.

11. Email the Business card to your instructor as an attachment.
    a. Click the **People** button in the *Navigation* pane.
    b. Select the **Placer Hills** folder in *My Contacts*.
    c. Select your Business card.

d. Right-click the contact, choose **Forward Contact,** and select **As a Business Card**. A new email opens with the business card attached and a graphic of the business card in the body of the message.

e. Select your instructor as the recipient.

f. Add your email address in the *Cc:* field.

g. Change the subject to *Outlook Guided Project 8-2*.

h. In the message field, type:
   Dear [instructor's name],
   Attached is my Outlook Guided Project 8-2.
   Thank you,
   [your name]

i. Click **Send**.

8-42 Completed Guided Project 8-2

Guided Project 8-3

In this project, you are Jake Nguyen, President of PHRE. You decided to have a surprise Christmas party for your staff. Since it is a surprise, you decide to send the invitation to each individual employee via snail mail. You decide to use mail merge to help you create shipping labels for each of your employees.
[Student Learning Outcome 8.4]

- Create a mail merge from Outlook contacts.
- Create mail merge mailing labels.

---

1. Click the **People** button on the *Navigation* pane.

2. In the *Navigation* pane, select the **Placer Hills** contacts folder.

3. Click the **Mail Merge** button in the *Actions* group on the *Home* tab. The *Mail Merge Contacts* dialog box opens.

4. In the *Mail Merge Contacts* dialog box, select **All contacts in current view** and select the *Document file* to be a **New document**.

5. In the *Merge options* section, select **Mailing Labels** and merge to **New Document**.

6. Click **OK**.

7. Click **OK**. The *Mail Merge Helper* dialog box opens.

8. Click **Setup**. The *Label Options* dialog box opens.

9. Select **Avery 5160** and press **OK**.

10. Close the **Mail Merge Helper** dialog box.

11. In the open Word document, click the **Mailings** tab.

12. Click the **Start Mail Merge** button and choose **Step by Step Mail Merge Wizard**. The *Mail Merge wizard* opens to the right of the document.

13. You will be on *Step 3 of 6;* click **Next: Arrange your labels**.

14. *Step 4 of 6:* Click the **Address Block** link. The *Insert Address Block* dialog box opens.

15. Click **OK**.

16. Click the **Update all labels** button and click **Next**.

17. *Step 5 of 6:* Your labels will appear in the document. Click **Next**.

18. Select the entire document (**Ctrl+A**), change the paragraph spacing to **0 pt**. **before** and **after,** and change the line spacing to **Single**.

19. In Word, click the **File** button and select **Save As**. Save the file as *outlookgp8-3* (Figure 8-43).

20. Send an email to your instructor with the completed mail merge as an attachment.
    a. Click the **Mail** button in the Navigation pane.
    b. Click **New Mail** [*Home* tab, *New* group].
    c. In the *To:* field, enter your instructor's email address.
    d. In the *Cc:* field, enter your email address.
    e. In the *Subject* field, enter: Outlook Guided Project 8-3
    f. In the message area, type:
       Dear [instructor's name],
       Attached is my Outlook Guided Project 8-3.
       Thank you,
       [your name]

g. Click the **Attach File** button [*Message* tab, *Include* group] and select the completed mail merge file.

h. Click the **Send** button.

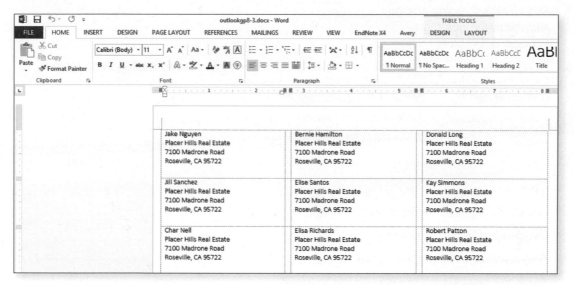

8-43 Completed Guided Project 8-3

Independent Project 8-4

In this project, you are an academic advisor for Sierra Pacific Community College District (SPCCD). After looking through your contact list, you noticed that you had contacts that were administrative or academic advisors from a variety of campuses. Based on your job history, you decided to organize your contacts using categories to allow you to find people by position or institution.
[Student Learning Outcomes 8.1, 8.3]

File Needed: *spccd.csv*

Skills Covered in This Project

- Create a contacts folder.
- Import contacts from a CSV file.
- Map fields.

- Select an account when creating a new message.
- Assign categories to contacts.

---

1. Create a contact folder named **SPCCD**.

2. Import the file **spccd.csv** to the **SPCCD** contact folder.

3. Ensure the fields are mapped correctly.

4. Create the following categories:
   SPCCD North, color: green
   SPCCD South, color: red
   SPCCD East, color: yellow
   SPCCD West, color: orange
   Administrator, color: gray
   Advisor, color: blue

5. Apply Categories to the contacts in the SPCCD contact folder using the following table:

First	Last	Category 1	Category 2
Jim	Cooke	SPCCD North	Advisor
Jake	Duane	SPCCD North	Advisor
Denise	Fong	SPCCD West	Advisor
Debbie	Huan	SPCCD East	Advisor
Nellie	Nelson	SPCCD West	Administrator
Virginia	Pulson	SPCCD South	Advisor
Marcie	Ritt	SPCCD South	Administrator
Melisa	Somora	SPCCD East	Administrator
Joey	Tomlin	SPCCD North	Administrator

6. Figure 8-44 displays Contact list for SPCCD.

7. Export the SPCCD folder as a .pst file named *spccd-contacts*.

8. Email the .pst file to your instructor as an attachment based on the information below.
   a. In the *To:* field, enter your instructor's email address.
   b. In the *Cc:* field, enter your email address.
   c. In the *Subject* field, enter: Outlook Independent Project 8-4.
   d. In the message area, type:
      Dear [instructor's name],
      Attached is my Outlook Independent Project 8-4.
      Thank you,
      [your name]

8-44 Completed Independent Project 8-4

Independent Project 8-5

In this project, you are Jim Cooke, an academic advisor for Sierra Pacific Community College District (SPCCD). Since the SPCCD has become more collaborative over the past year, you felt it was time to spruce up your Outlook business card.
[Student Learning Outcome 8.2]

File Needed: *jim.jpg*

Skills Covered in This Project

- Edit the contents of a contact template.
- Modify the appearance of a contact template.

1. Add Jim's picture to his business card.

2. Modify the **Card Design** options to ensure the following:
    a. Jim's picture is located on the left side of the card.
    b. The image area is **50%**.
    c. Jim's image is aligned to the **Center Left** of the card.

3. Modify the text fields in the following ways:
    a. Italicize the *Company*.
    b. Change the *E-mail* to have a **Green** font color.

4. Figure 8-45 displays Jim's Outlook business card.

5. Email the Business card to your instructor as an attachment.
    a. Change the subject to **Outlook Independent Project 8-5**.
    b. Type a short message to your instructor indicating that the completed Independent Project 8-5 is attached to the message.

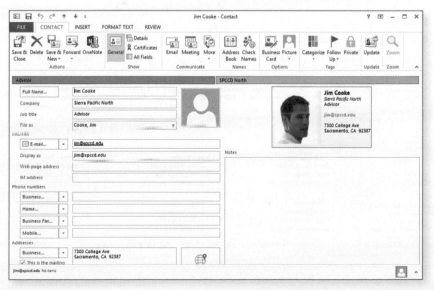

8-45 Completed Independent Project 8-5

Independent Project 8-6

In this project, you are Melissa Somora, Provost for SPCCD. It is that time of the year to send reminders to students about registration. Since SPCCD uses postal mail to send official reminder letters to each advisor to remind them about registration, you decide to use the mail merge feature to create mailing labels.
[Student Learning Outcomes 8.1, 8.4]

Skills Covered in This Project

- Create a mail merge from Outlook contacts.
- Create mail merge mailing labels.

---

1. Create a new contact folder and copy all of the advisors to it.

2. Create a mail merge for all academic advisors.

3. Create Mailing labels using **Avery 5160** as the template.

4. Make formatting changes to ensure text is viewable on all labels.

5. Save the completed Word file as *outlookip8-6* (Figure 8-46).

6. Send an email to your instructor with the completed mail merge as an attachment.
   a. Click the **Mail** button in the Navigation pane.
   b. Click **New Mail** [*Home* tab, *New* group].
   c. In the *To:* field, enter your instructor's email address.
   d. In the *Cc:* field, enter your email address.
   e. In the *Subject* field, enter: Outlook Independent Project 8-6.
   f. In the message area, type:
      Dear [instructor name],
      Attached is my Outlook Independent Project 8-6.
      Thank you,
      [student name]

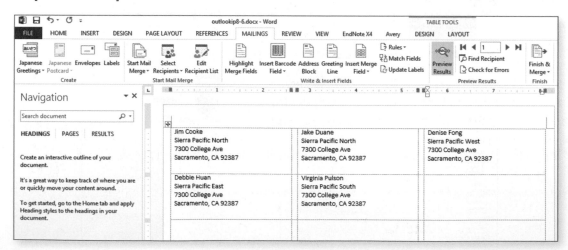

8-46 Completed Independent Project 8-6

Challenge Project 8-7

Most people have a slightly different way of organizing information. In this challenge project, you will take your contacts and organize them using folders and categories. Even though this sounds like a simple task, you will need to explain how it is organized to your instructor. To submit the assignment, you will export the contacts from Outlook and share them with your instructor as an email attachment.
[Student Learning Outcomes 8.1, 8.3]

- Include at least 10 contacts.
- Identify how you will organize your contacts.
- Both folders and categories should be implemented.
- Email your instructor using the following message format:
  Folder list: [include the name of each folder and why it was created]
  Category list: [include the name of each category and indicate why it was created]
- Change the subject of your message to be **Outlook Challenge Project 8-7**.
- Export your contacts and include them as an attachment to your instructor.

Challenge Project 8-8

Business cards include a lot more information about you than your contact information. The way a business card appears can also be seen as an extension of how you represent yourself. Therefore, it is important to have a business card that expresses who you are and defines your professionalism. In this Challenge Project, you will create a business card for yourself and send it to your instructor. You may use a template as a starting point, but be sure to further customize it, as it is likely that more than one person uses each template.
[Student Learning Outcome 8.2]

- Create a personalized business card.
- You may optionally start with a template.
- Be sure to identify a purpose for your business card.
- Email your completed business card to your instructor as an attachment.
- In the body of the message to your instructor, explain your purpose and how you customized your business card to meet it.
- Change the subject of your message to be **Outlook Challenge Project 8-8**.

Challenge Project 8-9

The mail merge in Word, used in conjunction with Outlook contacts, can be a powerful tool that makes your work more effective and efficient. Identify a purpose for a mail merge, such as thank you or invitation cards, and use Outlook contacts with Word to create a mail merge to meet your need.
[Student Learning Outcomes 8.1, 8.3, 8.4]

- Identify a purpose for a mail merge.
- Create a contact group for the merge.
- Create a mail merge using the contact group.
- Export your contact group as a .csv file.
- Email your completed mail merge and contact group to your instructor as attachments.
- Change the subject of your message to be **Outlook Challenge Project 8-9**.

Advanced Calendars and Sharing

OUTLOOK

CHAPTER OVERVIEW

Now that you are comfortable using an electronic calendar to help organize your daily life, you are ready to incorporate some of the additional Outlook calendar features. In this chapter, you will learn how to create and use multiple calendars, incorporate advanced calendar features, customize the default calendar options, and print and share calendars.

A distinct advantage of Outlook in an Exchange environment is its ability to share your information with others. Many of you collaborate with others on work projects. The **Delegates** feature in Outlook allows you to give access to certain areas of Outlook to others with whom you work.

> ### MORE INFO
>
> If you need to review the basics of the Outlook calendar, they are covered in Chapter 4.

STUDENT LEARNING OUTCOMES (SLOs)

After completing this chapter, you will be able to:

SLO 9.1 Create and use multiple Outlook calendars (p. O9-322).

SLO 9.2 Customize your Outlook calendar using calendar options (p. O9-324).

SLO 9.3 Incorporate printing and sharing with your Outlook calendar (p. O9-326).

SLO 9.4 Utilize advanced calendar features (p. O9-334).

SLO 9.5 Assign and collaborate with Outlook delegates (p. O9-340).

CASE STUDY

For the Pause & Practice projects, you create a new calendar for your BUS 100 class. Since you are working with a new calendar, you will need to create appointments and categorize them to improve the overall organization. You attach your homework to the recitation session for class to ensure it is easy for you to find. Lastly, you realize that you will be out of town and have minimal access to the Internet. Therefore, you asked a partner to serve as a delegate for your Calendar so you can stay abreast of your group work.

Pause & Practice 9-1: You create a new calendar for your class, BUS 100. You create three appointments and share your calendar with your instructor. You also forward your group meeting appointment to your instructor so that he knows when you are meeting for your project.

Pause & Practice 9-2: You improve the organization of your BUS 100 Calendar by using categories. You also attach your homework file to the BUS 100 Recitation appointment to make it easy for you to find. Since your lecture occurs weekly, you set the Calendar item to recur weekly till the end of the semester (10 weeks).

Pause & Practice 9-3: You will be out of town with minimal Internet access. Therefore, you choose one of your partners to be a delegate while you are away. Since you are concerned about the Calendar, you give your partner *Author* permissions so that he can add group meeting dates while you are away. You selected *Author* permission to prevent your partner from accidentally deleting any of your current calendar items.

<table><tr><td>SLO 9.1</td></tr></table>

Using Multiple Calendars

Up to this point, you probably have been keeping all your calendar items on the default Outlook calendar. But what if you wanted to keep all your personal calendar items on one calendar and all your business-related calendar items on a separate calendar? Or you might be involved in a professional organization, club, or charity organization and would like to have a separate calendar for the activities associated with each of these groups.

Outlook provides you with the option of having multiple calendars, which can help keep you organized by having separate calendars for different personal and business areas of your life.

Create a New Calendar

Creating a new calendar is similar to creating a new *Inbox* or *Contacts* folder. When you create a new calendar, it will appear in the *My Calendars* list in the *Navigation* pane.

HOW TO: Create a New Calendar

1. Click the **Calendar** button in the *Navigation* pane.
2. Click the **Folder** tab and then on the **New Calendar** button in the *New* group (Figure 9-1). The *Create New Folder* dialog box opens.
3. Type the **Name** of the new calendar (Figure 9-2). Confirm that the folder contains *Calendar Items* and that the new calendar will be placed in the *Calendar* folder.
4. Click **OK**. The new calendar will be created and will appear in your *My Calendars* area in the *Navigation* pane.

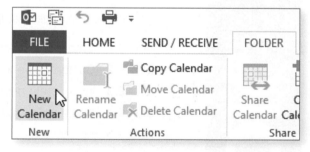

9-1 *New Calendar* button

> **ANOTHER WAY**
>
> Right-click **Calendar** in the *My Calendar* list and choose **New Calendar.**

You can delete a calendar by selecting the calendar and clicking the **Delete Calendar** button in the *Actions* group on the *Folder* tab. The default Outlook calendar cannot be deleted.

9-2 *Create New Folder* dialog box

View Multiple Calendars

By default, your main calendar (Calendar) will be displayed in the *Folder* pane. The check box to the left of the calendars listed in the *My Calendars* area indicates which calendars will be displayed in the *Folder* pane (Figure 9-3).

An additional or different calendar can be displayed in the *Folder* pane by checking the box to the left of the calendar name in the *My Calendars* area in the *Navigation* pane.

9-3 Select multiple calendars

> **MORE INFO**
> At least one calendar must be selected at all times; Outlook will not allow you to deselect all the calendars in the calendars list.

When multiple calendars are displayed in the *Folder* pane, they can be viewed in **side-by-side mode** or in **overlay mode.** When calendars are viewed in side-by-side mode (Figure 9-4), the items on each of the calendars are smaller and more difficult to read. The overlay mode allows you to easily switch between calendars in the *Folder* pane. Each calendar will appear in a different color.

The tab at the top of each calendar displays the name of the calendar. When you are in overlay mode (Figure 9-5), click a tab to display the selected calendar on top of the other calendar.

There are small arrows to the left of each of the calendar names (see Figure 9-5). By clicking one of these arrows you can switch the display mode.

When you view your calendars in overlay mode, the items on the nondisplayed calendar will appear on the displayed calendar. Calendar items on the nondisplayed calendar will appear on the displayed calendar in a different color.

In side-by-side mode, calendar items can be copied from one calendar to another by clicking a calendar item and dragging and dropping it on the other calendar.

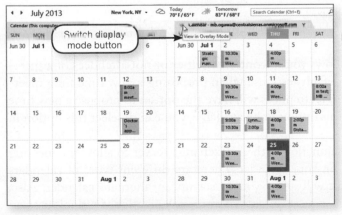

9-4 Multiple calendars in side-by-side mode

9-5 Multiple calendars in overlay mode

Customizing Calendar Options

In the *Outlook Options* dialog box, Outlook provides you with many features to customize the default settings of your calendar, including changing the work week options, changing the calendar color, adding holidays, changing the default reminder setting, adding time zones, and customizing the *Scheduling Assistant*. You can access calendar options by clicking the **File** tab to open the *Backstage,* selecting **Options,** and choosing **Calendar** in the *Outlook Options* dialog box (Figure 9-6).

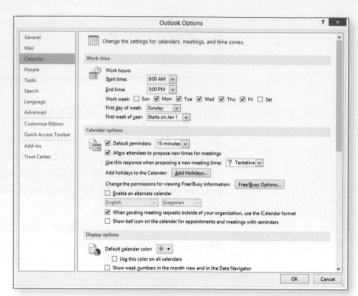

9-6 *Calendar Options*

Work Time Options

By default, Outlook is set up like a regular calendar with Sunday as the first day of the week. What if you don't work a standard Monday–Friday work week? You can customize your Outlook calendar to begin on whichever day you choose by changing the settings in the *Work time* area of the *Calendar Options* dialog box.

When a calendar is displayed in *Week* view, you have the options of *Show work week* or *Show full week.* If you work a Wednesday–Sunday work week, you can change the settings to reflect your work week on your Outlook calendar.

Calendar Options

The default setting for a reminder on an appointment is 15 minutes, which means an electronic reminder opens on your computer 15 minutes before a scheduled appointment. The default reminder can be changed, or reminders can be changed when you create or edit an appointment.

> **MORE INFO**
>
> The default reminder for an event is 18 hours.

The *Calendar Options* area also allows you to control whether or not attendees of a meeting can propose new times and the default response when proposing a new time for a meeting. When you set up a meeting request, attendees will have the option to propose a new time for the meeting. If you do not want this option to be available, you can deselect this option in the *Calendar Options* dialog box.

Free/Busy Options are used in conjunction with an Exchange server to allow the meeting organizer to see free and busy time on your calendar. There are different types of calendars used throughout the world. Outlook will allow you to set up an alternate calendar. Also, by default when you send a meeting request outside of your organization, Outlook uses an *iCalendar* format, which enables other email users to view the meeting information.

Outlook can automatically add **holidays** to your Outlook calendar, and you can choose the country or countries from which to add holidays.

HOW TO: Add Holidays to Your Calendar

1. Click the **File** tab and choose **Options.** The *Outlook Options* dialog box opens.
2. Click the **Calendar** button. The *Calendar Options* dialog box opens.
3. Click the **Add Holidays** button. The *Add Holidays to Calendar* dialog box opens (Figure 9-7).
4. Select the country or countries of your choice.
5. Click **OK.** The holidays will be added to your calendar.
6. Click **OK** to close the *Calendar Options* dialog box.
7. Click **OK** to close the *Outlook Options* dialog box.

9-7 Add holidays to your calendar

> ### MORE INFO
>
> Most countries have a lot of holidays. Be careful not to add too many countries' holidays, so as not to clutter up your calendar.

Display Options

The color of the default Outlook calendar can be changed (Figure 9-8). When you view multiple calendars in the *Folder* pane, Outlook will automatically select a different color for each calendar displayed in the *Folder*

9-8 Display options

pane. You have the option of making all the displayed calendars the same color by checking the **Use this color on all calendars** box. It is probably best to have each calendar be a different color to help you distinguish between calendar items.

Week numbers (1–52) can be added so they will be displayed in *Month* view and in the *Date Navigator.* By default, Outlook does not display week numbers.

Schedule view displays a single calendar or multiple calendars in the timeline view to assist you in scheduling appointments and meetings. The last two check boxes allow you to control how calendars and free appointments are viewed when using *Schedule* view. By default, free appointments are not displayed in *Schedule* view.

Time Zones

What if you regularly do business with a company or individual from a different time zone? Outlook will allow you to change the time zone on your calendar or

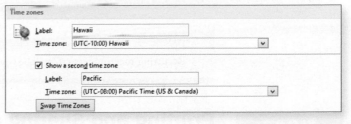

9-9 Select multiple time zones

add an additional time zone to your calendar (Figure 9-9). If you add an additional time zone to your calendar, both time zones will be displayed when you view your calendar in *Day* or *Week* view. You can also add labels to each of the time zones, which will be displayed on the calendar in *Day* and *Week* views.

Scheduling Assistant

The **Scheduling** Assistant (Figure 9-10) can be used when creating meetings, appointments, or events on your calendar. It displays your calendar in timeline view in the body of a new calendar item to assist you in selecting a day and time for the calendar item. By default calendar details are displayed in both ScreenTips and the scheduling grid.

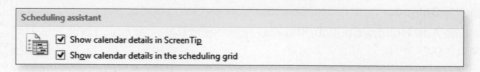

9-10 *Scheduling assistant* options

Automatic Accept or Decline

Outlook also gives you the option of automatically accepting meeting requests, declining meeting requests, and removing cancelled meetings (Figure 9-11). You can also change the default settings to control how Outlook handles meeting requests that conflict with other calendar items and how Outlook handles recurring meeting requests.

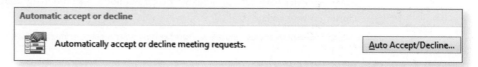

9-11 *Automatic accept or decline* options

Weather

You can view the weather in the Outlook calendar. The Outlook *Weather* options (Figure 9-12) allow you to view the temperature based on Celsius or Fahrenheit based on your preference. You can also remove it if you prefer not to see the weather when viewing the calendar.

If you want to add a weather location, you can click on the drop-down arrow next to the City/State and type a location. Outlook will search and allow you to select a location to fit your needs.

9-12 *Weather* options

> **MORE INFO**
> Recurring meeting requests will be covered later in this chapter.

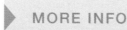

Printing and Sharing an Outlook Calendar

It's great being able to keep all your appointments and events on your calendar, but there might be times when you need a hard copy of your calendar or you want to share your calendar with others. Outlook provides you with a variety of ways to both print and share your Outlook calendar.

Print an Outlook Calendar

There are times when you might be away from your computer but you would like to have your calendar available. Outlook allows you to print your calendar in various formats. You can print your calendar in the following styles: *Daily Style, Weekly Style, Monthly Style, Tri-fold Style,* and *Calendar Details Style.*

HOW TO: Print a Calendar

1. Click the **File** tab to open the *Backstage* view.
2. Click the **Print** button to display the print options on the *Backstage* view (Figure 9-13).
3. Select the style of calendar to print in the *Settings* area.
4. Click the **Print Options** button to open the *Print* dialog box.
5. Click **Print** to print the calendar.

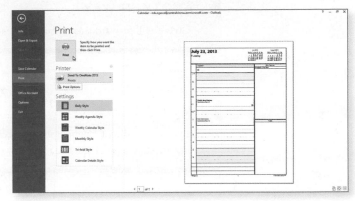

9-13 *Print* menu

Forward an Appointment

When you create and send a meeting request, the meeting is automatically placed on the recipient's Outlook calendar. There might be times when a meeting request is not needed or not appropriate but you still want to send a calendar item to another Outlook user. You can easily forward a calendar item as an attachment to an email to other Outlook users.

HOW TO: Forward an Appointment

1. Open an item on your calendar.
2. Click the **Forward** button in the *Actions* group on the *Appointment* (or *Event*) tab (Figure 9-14). A new email opens with the calendar item as an attachment (Figure 9-15).
3. Select the recipients and include any necessary information in the body.
4. Click **Send.**

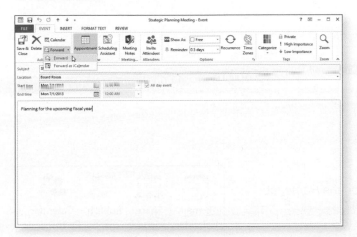

9-14 Forward an appointment

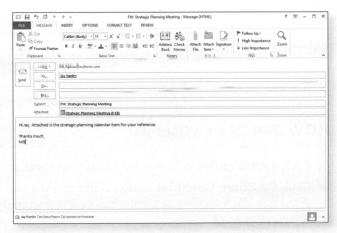

9-15 Forwarded appointment email

> **ANOTHER WAY**
>
> You can also right-click a calendar item and choose **Forward.** A new email opens with the calendar item attached.

> **ANOTHER WAY**
>
> **Ctrl+F** will forward a calendar item when the item is selected on your calendar.

> **MORE INFO**
>
> If you are sending a calendar item to recipients who are not using Outlook, it is probably best to forward it as an iCalendar so they can view the details of the calendar item.

When a calendar item is received as an attachment to an email, it can be added to the recipient's calendar by dragging and dropping the attachment on the **Calendar** button in the *Navigation* pane or by opening the attached calendar item and clicking **Save & Close.** The calendar item will automatically be placed on the correct date on the calendar.

Share a Calendar in an Exchange Environment

If you are using Outlook in an Exchange environment, you can share your calendar with others on the same Exchange server. This will enable them to view your calendar and use it to facilitate scheduling of events, appointments, and/or meetings. Later in this chapter you will see how sharing an Outlook calendar works in conjunction with planning a meeting and AutoPick a meeting time.

When you share your calendar with other Outlook users on the same Exchange server, an email will be sent to those users informing them that you have shared your calendar with them. You can request that they share their calendar with you also. Those with whom you share your calendar will only have *Reviewer* (read-only) permission when viewing your calendar.

> **MORE INFO**
>
> Permission levels and delegates will be covered later in the chapter.

HOW TO: Share a Calendar

1. Click the **Calendar** button in the *Navigation* pane.
2. Click the **Share Calendar** button in the *Share* group on the *Home* tab (Figure 9-16). A sharing request email opens (Figure 9-17).
3. Select recipients.
4. Select the **Request permission to view recipient's Calendar** check box to gain access to your recipients' calendars.

9-16 Share Calendar button

5. Make sure **Allow recipient to view your Calendar** is checked. Select one of the following options:
   - *Availability only:* Times are listed as *Free, Busy, Tentative, Working Elsewhere,* or *Out of Office.*
   - *Limited details:* Includes availability and subjects of calendar items.
   - *Full details:* Includes the availability and full details of calendar items.

6. Add any necessary information in the body.

7. Click **Send.** A dialog box opens asking you to confirm that you want to share your calendar (Figure 9-18).

8. Click **Yes** to send the sharing request email.

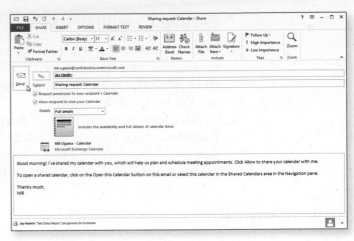

9-17 Share calendar request email

> **MORE INFO**
>
> By default, Outlook will share your main calendar. You can share other calendars you have created by right-clicking the calendar, choosing **Sharing,** and selecting **Share Calendar.**

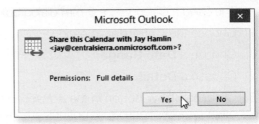

9-18 Share calendar confirmation

When your calendar has been shared with others, they will receive an email message informing them they now have access to your calendar. The **Allow** button will share the recipient's calendar with the sender (as requested). The **Open this Calendar** button opens the sender's calendar (Figure 9-19). Shared calendars will appear in the *Shared Calendars* area in the *Navigation* pane.

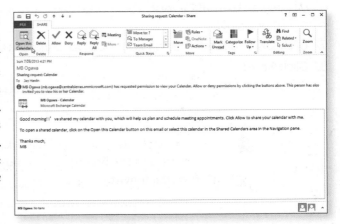

9-19 Open a shared calendar

> **MORE INFO**
>
> The **Calendar Permissions** button in the *Share* group on the *Home* tab will provide you with a summary of those with whom you have shared your calendar (Figure 9-20).

> **MORE INFO**
>
> If you try to share your Outlook calendar with a recipient who is not on your Exchange system, a dialog box opens informing you of this and giving you the option of sending the calendar through email.

9-20 Calendar permissions

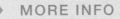

Send a Calendar via Email

What if you want to send your calendar to someone outside your Exchange environment or to someone who does not even use Outlook? Outlook will allow you to send a calendar via email. You can specify the calendar to send, the date range to send, the details to be included, and the layout of the email.

This feature creates a type of *Internet calendar* to be attached to the email and a *Calendar Snapshot*, which displays the calendar information in the body of the email. Recipients can view your calendar in the body of the email they receive. If they are Outlook users, they will be able to open your calendar from the attached Internet calendar.

HOW TO: Email a Calendar

1. Click the **E-mail Calendar** button [*Home* tab, *Share* group]. The *Send a Calendar via E-mail* dialog box opens (Figure 9-21).

2. Choose the **Calendar** to send.

3. Choose a **Date Range.**

4. Choose a **Detail.**

5. Click the **Show** button in the *Advanced* area to display other detail options. Your options are *Include details of items marked private* or *Include attachments with calendar item.*

6. Choose an **E-mail Layout.** Your options are *Daily schedule* or *List of events.*

7. Click **OK** to close the *Send a Calendar via E-mail* dialog box.

8. Click **Send.**

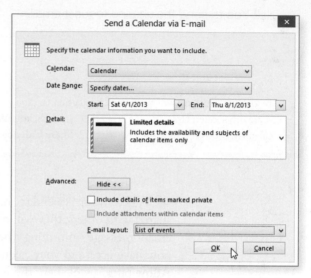

9-21 *Send a Calendar via E-mail* dialog box

Recipients will receive an email with your Internet calendar attached and the *Calendar Snapshot* in the body of the message (Figure 9-22). The Internet calendar can be opened from the attachment.

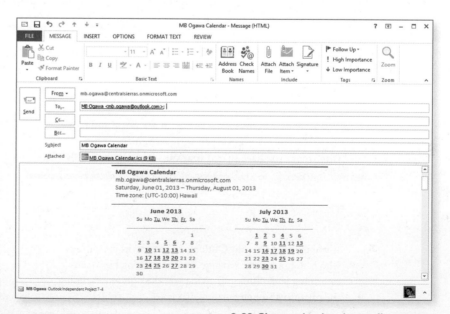

9-22 Share calendar via email message

Publish and Share a Calendar

Suppose you belong to a cycling club and keep a separate Outlook calendar for all the club rides, events, and activities. If you are using a Microsoft account and update regularly, you don't want to have to send out a new Internet calendar through email each time there is an update. A much more effective method would be to publish your calendar online.

An Outlook calendar using a *Microsoft account* is automatically synced with the *Microsoft Calendar.* This service allows you to publish your calendar and then invite others to subscribe to and view your calendar. Alternatively, you can create a link to your calendar and distribute it to others. A published calendar will be synchronized on a regular basis so that those viewing the calendar will be seeing current calendar information. To share your Outlook calendar, you must have a Microsoft account.

HOW TO: Share a Calendar

1. Open a browser and go to www.outlook.com.
2. Enter your user name and password and click **Sign in.**
3. Click the **Outlook** drop-down arrow and select **Calendar** (Figure 9-23).
4. Click the **Share** button and select your calendar (Figure 9-24).
5. You can add each of the users' Microsoft accounts with whom you want to share the calendar with and give them permissions (Figure 9-25). The following permission levels are available:

   - *Co-owner:* Can create, view, edit, and delete items
   - View, edit, and delete items
   - View details
   - View free/busy times, titles, and locations
   - View free/busy times

6. Click the **Share** button.
7. You can also create a link to a calendar so others can view it online. To do so, click the **Get a link** hyperlink (see Figure 9-25).

   - Select *either Links to free/busy times* or *Links to event details.*
   - Select one of the links [HTML (web browser), ICS (import to other calendar programs), or XML (Feed reader)].
   - Send the link to your desired users.

9-23 Calendar option on Outlook.com

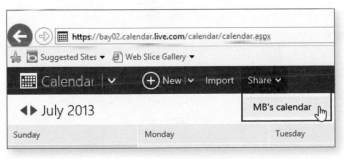

9-24 Share your calendar online

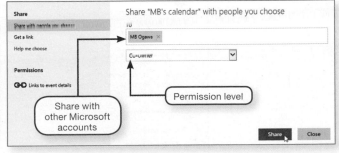

9-25 Microsoft account sharing options

Recipients will receive an email message informing them of the availability of this online calendar. They will be given the option to *Accept* or *Decline* the shared calendar.

If a recipient chooses **Accept,** the calendar will be available in the *Calendars* list in the *Navigation* pane. Outlook will periodically check online for updates to this calendar and synchronize it with the published calendar.

When sharing a link, users will be able to view the calendar using a browser (HTML), in a calendar program (ICS), or using a feed reader (XML).

In addition to being listed in the *Other Calendars* area in the *Navigation* pane, all the Internet calendars to which you are subscribed will be listed in the *Account Setting* dialog box under the *Internet Calendars* tab. You can add or delete a subscription to an Internet Calendar (ICS) in this dialog box.

> **ANOTHER WAY**
>
> Select the calendar to be deleted and click the **Delete Calendar** button in the *Actions* group on the *Folder* tab.

View a Shared Calendar

When others have shared their Outlook calendars with you, these calendars will appear in the *Shared Calendars* area in the *Navigation* pane. When you have subscribed to Internet calendars, these calendars will appear in the *Other Calendars* area of the *Navigation* pane.

To view a shared calendar or one you have subscribed to, check the box to the left of the calendar name. The calendar will be displayed in the *Folder* pane (Figure 9-26). When you deselect the calendar check box, the calendar will no longer be displayed in the *Folder* pane.

To remove any of the calendars from the *Shared Calendars* list, right-click the calendar and choose **Delete Calendar.** This will remove the calendar from the *Shared Calendars* list, but it will not remove your permission to view this calendar. Only the owner of the calendar can change the permission settings.

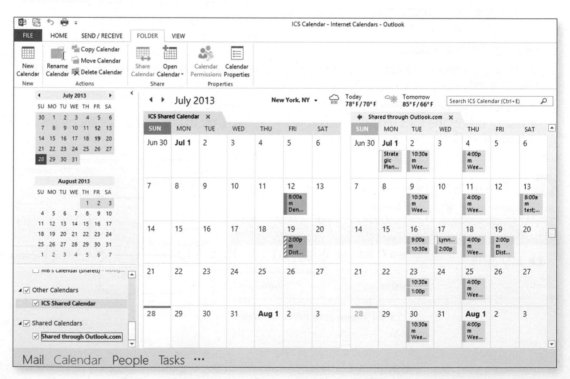

9-26 Shared calendars

For this Pause & Practice project, you create a new calendar for your class, BUS 100. You create three appointments and share your calendar with your instructor. You also forward your group meeting appointment to your instructor so that he knows when you are meeting for your project.

1. Click the **Calendar** button in the *Navigation* pane.

2. Create a new calendar for your BUS 100 class.
   a. Click the **Folder** tab and then the **New Calendar** button in the *New* group. The *Create New Folder* dialog box opens.
   b. Type BUS100 as the **Name** of the new calendar. Confirm that the folder contains **Calendar Items** and that the new calendar will be placed in the **Calendar** folder.
   c. Click **OK.**

3. Create an appointment with the following information:
   Subject: BUS 100 Lecture
   Location: HH132
   Start time: Next week Tuesday at 9:00 AM
   End time: Next week Tuesday at 10:30 AM

4. Create another appointment with the following information:
   Subject: BUS 100 Recitation
   Location: Online
   Start time: Next week Friday at 4:30 PM
   End time: Next week Friday at 6:00 PM

5. Create a third appointment with the following information:
   Subject: BUS 100 Group Meeting
   Location: Cafe
   Start time: Next week Wednesday at 10:30 AM
   End time: Next week Wednesday at 11:30 AM

6. Forward the **BUS 100 Group Meeting** appointment to your instructor.
   a. Double-click the **BUS 100 Group Meeting** appointment (Figure 9-27).
   b. Click the **Forward** button [*Appointment* (or *Event*) tab, *Actions* group]. A new email opens with the calendar item as an attachment.
   c. Select your instructor as the recipient.
   d. Add your email address to the *Cc* field.
   e. Modify the subject to Outlook Pause & Practice 9-1a.
   f. In the message area, type:
   Dear [instructor's name],
   Attached is my Outlook Pause & Practice 9-1a.
   Thank you,
   [your name]
   g. Click **Send.**

7. Share your calendar with your instructor.
   a. Click the **Share Calendar** button in the *Share* group on the *Home* tab. A sharing request email opens.
   b. Select your instructor as the recipient.
   c. Modify the subject to Outlook Pause & Practice 9-1b.
   d. In the message area, type:
   Dear [instructor's name],
   This is my Outlook Pause & Practice 9-1b.
   Thank you,
   [your name]

e. Click **Send.**

f. Click **Yes** to send the sharing request email.

9-27 Completed Pause & Practice 9-1

Using Advanced Calendar Features

Outlook provides you with many advanced calendar features to help you organize your calendar items and schedule meetings. Calendar items can be assigned to a category. Files and other Outlook items, such as an email or contact, can be attached to a calendar item. Calendar items can be marked as private so others with whom your calendar is shared cannot see the details of an event or appointment. Outlook can also work in conjunction with shared calendars to assist you in scheduling meetings.

Categorize Calendar Items

Just as with emails, contacts, and tasks, *categories* can be used to group calendar items. A category can be assigned to a calendar item by selecting the calendar item, clicking the **Categorize** button in the *Tags* group, and selecting the category. Also, with a calendar item open, you can assign it to a category by clicking the **Categorize** button in the *Tags* group on the *Event* or *Appointment* tab.

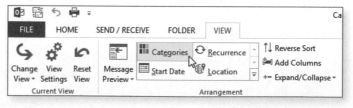

9-28 *Categories* view

The default view for your calendar is *Calendar* view. There are many other preset views available in Outlook by which to view your calendar. Some of these other views display your calendar in list view in the *Folder* pane.

To view calendar items by category, you will need to be in a list view. Click the **View** tab, click the **Change View** button, and select **List**. Next, click the **Categories** button in the *Arrangement* group on the *View* tab (Figure 9-28). Choose **Calendar** view in the *Change View* menu to return to the default calendar view.

MORE INFO

Creating, editing, and assigning categories was covered in Chapter 2.

MORE INFO

Using one of the calendar list views is an easy way to find, edit, and/or delete calendar items.

Add Attachments to a Calendar

Suppose you have created a vacation event on your calendar. You might want to attach the email confirmation you received from the hotel or airline to the calendar item. You might also want to attach a Word document that contains your itinerary and/or a contact record of a friend you are planning on visiting during your vacation. You can do this in Outlook.

HOW TO: Attach Items to a Calendar Item

1. Open the calendar item.
2. Click the **Outlook Item** button [*Insert* tab, *Include* group] (Figure 9-29). The *Insert Item* dialog box opens (Figure 9-30) and allows you to select the type of Outlook item to attach.
3. Select the Outlook items to attach to the calendar item and click **OK**.
4. Click the **Attach File** button in the *Include* group to attach a file such as a Word or Excel document. The *Insert File* dialog box opens.
5. Browse to find the file(s) on your computer, select the file(s), and click **Insert**.
6. Click **Business Card** and choose **Other Business Cards**. The *Insert Business Card* dialog box opens.
7. Select the business cards to attach and click **OK**.
8. Click **Save & Close** [*Appointment* or *Event* tab]. Figure 9-31 is a calendar item with attachments.

9-29 Attach *Outlook Item* button

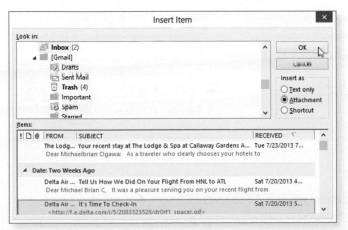
9-30 *Insert Item* dialog box

9-31 Calendar item with attachments

Private Calendar Items

When you have a shared calendar, it might be a good idea to mark some calendar items as *private*. When a calendar item is selected or open, the *Private* button is available in the *Tags* group (Figure 9-32). When a calendar item is marked as private, those with whom you share your calendar will be able to see the calendar item but not the details of the calendar item.

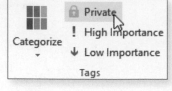

9-32 Mark a calendar item as private

When printing a calendar, you have the option of hiding the details of a private calendar item.

HOW TO: Print a Calendar without Private Appointments

1. Click the **File** tab to open the *Backstage* view.
2. Click the **Print** button.
3. Click the **Print Options** button. The *Print* dialog box opens.
4. Select the **Hide details of private appointments** check box in the *Print range* area (Figure 9-33).

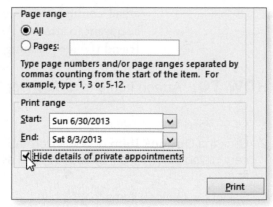

9-33 Hide private appointments when printing

Recurring Appointments

If you have a weekly brainstorming meeting, you can create a meeting request that recurs on a scheduled interval. Creating a recurring meeting request is similar to creating a recurring appointment or event. This recurring meeting will appear on your calendar for each date and time when it is to recur.

HOW TO: Create a Recurring Appointment

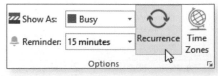

9-34 *Recurrence* button

1. Create a new appointment.
2. Enter **Subject, Location, Start time,** and **End time.**
3. Click **Invite Attendees** in the *Attendees* group.
4. Click the **To** button, select attendees, and click **OK.**
5. Click the **Recurrence** button in the *Options* group (Figure 9-34). The *Appointment Recurrence* dialog box opens (Figure 9-35). Confirm the appointment start and end times and duration.
6. Set a **Recurrence pattern.** This determines the frequency of the recurring meeting.
7. Set the **Range of recurrence.** This determines the date range of the recurring meeting.

8. Click **OK** to close the *Appointment Recurrence* dialog box.

9. Click **Send.**

When a recipient accepts a meeting request, the recurring meeting request will be saved on his or her calendar.

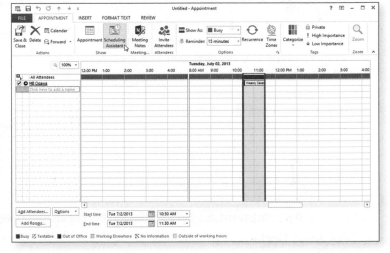

9-35 *Appointment Recurrence* dialog box

> **ANOTHER WAY**
>
> **Ctrl+G** opens the *Appointment Recurrence* dialog box.

Scheduling Assistant

When creating an appointment or meeting request, you will sometimes have to check your calendar for other calendar items on that date. Rather than having to switch between Outlook windows, you can use the *Scheduling Assistant* to show you appointments, events, or meetings currently on your calendar.

To use the *Scheduling Assistant*, click the **Scheduling Assistant** button in the *Show* group (**Schedule**

9-36 *Scheduling Assistant*

button in the *Show* group for non-Exchange environments). The *Scheduling Assistant* will display your calendar items in timeline format in the body section of the new appointment (Figure 9-36). You can adjust the date and/or time of the appointment based on your other calendar items.

The *Scheduling Assistant* can be particularly helpful when you are creating a meeting request. Attendees will appear in the list at the left of the body. If the attendees have shared their calendars with you, their appointments and events will be displayed in timeline format below your calendar items, which will facilitate selecting a meeting date and time.

> **MORE INFO**
>
> The *Scheduling Assistant* is available when using Outlook in both an Exchange and stand-alone environment, but displaying others' calendars is only available when using Outlook on an Exchange server.

AutoPick a Meeting Time

There are times when a scheduled meeting needs to be changed. If you have already sent out a meeting request and others have responded to it, you can make changes to the meeting request and send an update to attendees.

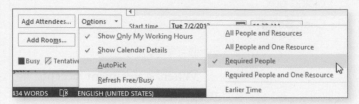

9-37 *AutoPick* options

Outlook has an *AutoPick* feature that can automatically pick a new time for the meeting based on the shared calendars of others. To use this feature, you must be working on an Exchange server and the attendees must also be on the same Exchange server. Clicking the **AutoPick** option in the *Scheduling Assistant* (Figure 9-37) will pick the next time available for those to whom the meeting request was sent.

HOW TO: AutoPick a Meeting Time

1. From your calendar, open the meeting to be rescheduled.
2. Click the **Scheduling Assistant** button in the *Show* group.
   - The list of attendees will appear on the left.
   - If attendees shared their calendars with you, they will appear in timeline view in the body of the meeting request.
3. Click the **Options** button and select one of the following *AutoPick* options (Figure 9-38):
   - *All People and Resources*
   - *All People and One Resource*
   - *Required People*
   - *Required People and One Resource*
   - *Earlier Time*
4. Click the **Appointment** button to return to the meeting request.
5. Click **Send Update.** An update will be sent to all the recipients of the original meeting request.

9-38 *AutoPick* based on *Required People's* schedules

PAUSE & PRACTICE: OUTLOOK 9-2

For this Pause & Practice project, you improve the organization of your BUS 100 calendar by using categories. You also attach your homework file to the *BUS 100 Recitation* appointment to make it easy for you to find. Since your lecture occurs weekly, you set the calendar item to recur weekly through the end of the semester (10 weeks).

File Needed: ***sales.xlsx***

1. Click the **Calendar** button in the *Navigation* pane.
2. Select the **BUS 100** calendar.

3. Create the following categories:
   a. *Name:* Class Session; *Color:* Red
   b. *Name:* Group Session; *Color:* Blue

4. Apply categories to the three appointments you created in *Pause & Practice Outlook 9-1.*
   a. Select the **BUS 100 Lecture** appointment.
   b. Click the **Categorize** button [*Appointment* tab, *Tags* group].
   c. Click **Class Session.**
   d. Select the **BUS 100 Recitation** appointment.
   e. Click the **Categorize** button [*Appointment* tab, *Tags* group].
   f. Click **Class Session.**
   g. Select the **BUS 100 Group Meeting** appointment.
   h. Click the **Categorize** button [*Appointment* tab, *Tags* group].
   i. Click **Group Session.**

5. Attach the file *sales.xlsx* to the **BUS 100 Recitation** appointment.
   a. Open the **BUS 100 Recitation** appointment.
   b. Click the **Attach File** button [*Insert* tab, *Include* group]. The *Insert File* dialog box opens.
   c. Browse to find the file *sales.xlsx* on your computer, select the file(s), and click **Insert.**
   d. Click **Save & Close** [*Appointment* or *Event* tab, *Actions* group].

6. Mark the **BUS 100 Recitation** appointment as private.
   a. Open the **BUS 100 Recitation** appointment.
   b. Click the **Private** button [*Appointment* or *Event* tab, *Tags* group].
   c. Click **Save & Close** [*Appointment* or *Event* tab, *Actions* group].

7. Forward the **BUS 100 Recitation** appointment to your instructor.
   a. Double-click the **BUS 100 Group Meeting** appointment.
   b. Click the **Forward** button [*Appointment* (or *Event*) tab, *Actions* group]. A new email opens with the calendar item as an attachment.
   c. Select your instructor as the recipient.
   d. Add your email address in the *Cc* field.
   e. Modify the subject to Outlook Pause & Practice 9-2a.
   f. In the message area, type:
      Dear [instructor's name],
      Attached is my Outlook Pause & Practice 9-2a.
      Thank you,
      [your name]
   g. Click **Send.**

8. Set the **BUS 100 Lecture** appointment to recur weekly for the next 10 weeks.
   a. Open the **BUS 100 Lecture** appointment.
   b. Click the **Recurrence** button [*Appointment* or *Event* tab, *Options* group]. The *Appointment Recurrence* dialog box opens.

9-39 Completed Pause & Practice 9-2

   c. In the *Recurrence pattern* section, select **Weekly, Recur every 1 week,** on **Tuesday.**
   d. In the *Range of recurrence* section, select **End after 10 occurrences.**
   e. Click **OK** to close the *Appointment Recurrence* dialog box.
   f. Click **Save & Close** (Figure 9-39).

Sharing Your Outlook with Others

Earlier in this text we discussed sharing your Outlook calendar with others. Outlook also allows you to share other areas of Outlook with coworkers who are on the same Exchange server. The *Delegate* feature gives you control over who has access to your Outlook information and how much access they have. This feature will only work with those who are on the same Exchange server.

Delegates and Permissions

A *delegate* is someone to whom you have given access to certain of your Outlook folders. This feature is commonly used with administrative assistants and members of a work team so they have access to the emails, calendars, contacts, tasks, notes, and/or journals of others.

The *Delegate* feature gives you more flexibility than simply sharing a calendar. Not only can you specify what areas of Outlook to share, but also the *permissions,* or the level of access granted to a delegate. For example, when sharing a calendar with another Outlook user, the default permission he or she has is a *Reviewer,* which means they can see your calendar but cannot create, delete, or edit an appointment.

The permission settings for a delegate can be customized for each area of Outlook. There are four different permissions that can be granted to a delegate.

- *None:* Delegate does not have access to this area of Outlook.
- *Reviewer:* Can read items but does not have access to create, delete, or edit items.
- *Author:* Can read and create items but does not have access to delete or edit items.
- *Editor:* Can read, create, delete, or edit items.

Assign a Delegate

The advantage of using the *Delegate* feature rather than the *Sharing* feature is that the role for each area of Outlook can be set and customized from one area. It's easy to view or change permissions from this one dialog box.

HOW TO: Assign a Delegate

1. Click the **File** tab, click the **Account Settings** button, and choose **Delegate Access.** The *Delegates* dialog box opens (Figure 9-40).
2. Click the **Add** button. The *Add Users* dialog box opens.
3. Select the name of the delegate to be added and click **Add.** You can select multiple delegates and customize the permission level for each delegate.
4. Click **OK** to close the *Add Users* dialog box. The *Delegate Permissions* dialog box opens (Figure 9-41).
   - You can set the permission level for this delegate for each area of Outlook.
   - Different roles can be set for different areas of Outlook.
5. Select the **Automatically send a message to delegate summarizing these permissions** check box. This will automatically generate and send an email message to the delegate informing him or her of the permissions granted.

9-40 Add delegate

6. If you want the delegate to see your private items, select the **Delegate can see my private items** check box.
7. Click **OK** to close the *Delegate Permissions* dialog box.
8. Click **OK** to close the *Delegates* dialog box.
9. Click the **File** tab to return to Outlook.

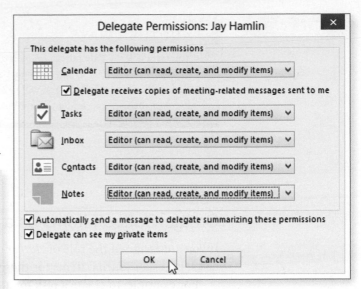

9-41 *Delegate Permissions*

> ### MORE INFO
>
> Just like sharing a calendar, you can share other areas of Outlook by clicking the *Permissions* button in the *Properties* group on the *Folder* tab. When you share areas of Outlook with others, the default permission level is *Reviewer*. The *Delegate* feature gives you more options for customizing the permissions of delegates.

> ### MORE INFO
>
> Be careful about granting permission to others, especially if you are granting *Editor* permission. Delegates with this permission have full control of the area of Outlook for which you assign them the role of *Editor*.

Open Another Outlook User's Folders

When an Outlook user on your Exchange server assigns you as a delegate, you will most likely receive an email summarizing your permission levels for the different areas of Outlook.

Once you have been granted permission, you can open that user's folders in your Outlook. For example, you can open the user's calendar and view it in your Outlook.

HOW TO: Open Outlook Folders as a Delegate

1. Click the **Calendar** button in the *Navigation* pane.
2. Click the **Open Calendar** button [*Home* tab, *Manage Calendars* group] and choose **Open a Shared Calendar.** The *Open a Shared Calendar* dialog box opens (Figure 9-42).
3. Click the **Name** button to open the *Select Name* dialog box.
4. Select the name of the contact and click **OK.** The calendar will appear in the *Shared Calendars* list in the *Navigation* pane.

9-42 *Open a Shared Calendar*

> ### MORE INFO
>
> You can follow the preceding steps to open another user's calendar to open other areas of Outlook to which you were granted permission.

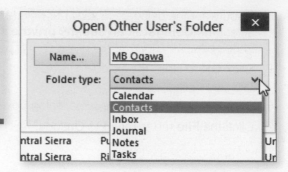
9-43 Select a shared folder from the
Open Other User's Folder dialog box

Create Outlook Items as a Delegate

If you are assigned the role of *Author* or *Editor,* you can create emails, calendar items, contacts, tasks, notes, or journal items for those to whom you are a delegate.

For example, to create a task for another user, you must first open his or her *Tasks* folder so you can view it in your Outlook.

When his or her *Tasks* folder is selected from the *Shared Tasks* area in the *Navigation* pane, it is displayed in the *Folder* pane. You can create a task in his or her *Tasks* folder in the same way you would create a task in your folder. The task that you create as a delegate will appear in his or her Outlook task list.

Remove a Delegate

In the *Delegates* dialog box, you can change the permission settings for a delegate by clicking the *Permissions* button (Figure 9-44) and making the desired changes.

To delete a delegate, select the delegate to be removed and press the **Remove** button (see Figure 9-44). The delegate will be removed from the delegate list and will no longer have access to your Outlook.

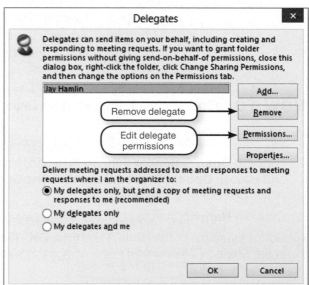

9-44 Edit or remove delegates from the *Delegates*
dialog box

For this Pause & Practice project, you will be out of town with minimal Internet access. Therefore, you designate one of your partners to be a *Delegate* while you are away. Since you are concerned about the calendar, you give your partner *Author* permissions so that he can add group meeting dates while you are away. You selected *Author* permission to prevent your partner from accidentally deleting any of your current calendar items.

1. Add a partner as a delegate.
   a. Click the **File** tab, click the **Account Settings** button, and choose **Delegate Access.** The *Delegates* dialog box opens.
   b. Click the **Add** button. The *Add Users* dialog box opens.
   c. Select your partner's name and click **Add.**
   d. Click **OK** to close the *Add Users* dialog box. The *Delegate Permissions* dialog box opens.
   e. Click the **drop-down** arrow next to **Calendar** and select **Author.**
   f. Click the **drop-down** menu next to **Tasks, Inbox, Contacts,** and **Notes** and change the permissions to **None.**
   g. Select the **Automatically send a message to delegate summarizing these permissions** check box.
   h. Deselect the **Delegate can see my private items** check box.
   i. Click **OK** to close the *Delegate Permissions* dialog box.
   j. Click **OK** to close the *Delegates* dialog box.
   k. Click the **File** tab to return to Outlook.

2. Open your partner's calendar.
   a. Click the **Calendar** button in the *Navigation* pane.
   b. Click the **Open Calendar** button [*Home* tab, *Manage Calendars* group] and choose **Open a Shared Calendar.** The *Open a Shared Calendar* dialog box opens.
   c. Click the **Name** button to open the *Select Name* dialog box.
   d. Select your partner's name and click **OK.** The calendar will appear in the *Shared Calendars* list in the *Navigation* pane.

3. Create a new appointment for a group meeting using the following information:
   Subject: BUS 100 Group Meeting
   Location: Cafe
   Start time: One week after your first meeting on Wednesday at 10:30 AM
   End time: One week after your first meeting on Wednesday at 11:30 AM
   Categorize the appointment as a **Group Session** (Figure 9-45).

4. Remove your partner as a delegate.
   a. Click the **File** tab, click the **Account Settings** button, and choose **Delegate Access.** The *Delegates* dialog box opens.
   b. Select your partner and click **Remove.**
   c. Click **OK** to close the *Delegates* dialog box.

5. Forward the *Delegate* designation message to your instructor.
   a. Click the **Mail** button in the *Navigation* pane.
   b. Select the *Delegate* message. It should have the subject **You have been designated as a delegate for [name].**
   c. Click the **Forward** button.
   d. Select your instructor as the recipient.
   e. Add your email address in the *Cc* field.
   f. Modify the subject to **Outlook Pause & Practice 9-3.**

g. In the message area, type:
Dear [instructor's name],
Attached is my Outlook Pause & Practice 9-3.
Thank you,
[your name]
h. Click **Send.**

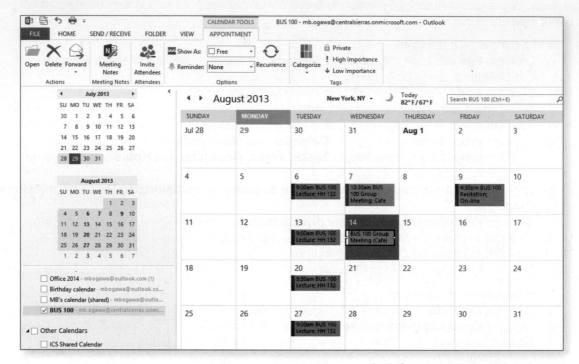

9-45 Completed Pause & Practice 9-3

Chapter Summary

9.1 Create and use multiple Outlook calendars (p. O9-322).

- You can create multiple calendars in Outlook.
- You can view multiple calendars simultaneously.
- Calendars can be viewed in *side-by-side* or *overlay* mode.

9.2 Customize your Outlook calendar using calendar options (p. O9-324).

- The *Outlook Options* dialog box includes calendar specific items.
- You can specify your work week if it is not Monday–Friday.
- On Exchange servers, you can control whether or not recipients of meeting requests can propose new times.
- Outlook can automatically add *holidays* based on region to your calendar.
- Display options can be modified to change calendar color, include week numbers, and view by *Schedule* view.
- You can select multiple time zones for your calendar which is useful when you work with others from different regions.
- The *Scheduling Assistant* options allow you to view details in ScreenTips and a scheduling grid.
- *Automatic accept or decline* options can be used in conjunction with an Exchange server to automatically respond to meeting requests.
- *Weather* options allow you to view weather for a location within your calendar.

9.3 Incorporate printing and sharing with your Outlook calendar (p. O9-326).

- Calendars can be printed in *Daily, Weekly, Monthly, Trifold,* or *Calendar Details* style.
- You can forward an appointment if you want to let the recipient know about a meeting without it automatically being added to his or her calendar.
- When using an Exchange server, you can share your calendar with other Exchange users. You can allow them to view *Availability only, Limited details,* or *Full details.*

- You can share your calendar with others via email as an Outlook attachment.
- If you are using a *Microsoft account,* you can share your calendar via Outlook.com.
- Outlook.com allows you to share a calendar with others and give others variable permissions.
- Outlook.com allows you to share a calendar link over HTML (web), ICS (import to other calendar programs), or XML (feed reader).

9.4 Utilize advanced calendar features (p. O9-334).

- Calendar items can be categorized.
- Calendar items can include file attachments and Outlook items.
- Marking calendar items as private sets permissions to not allow others who share your calendar to see those items.
- You have the option to print calendars without private items.
- Recurrence can be used when calendar items come up on a regular basis.
- The *Scheduling Assistant* allows you to see others' schedules and helps you to select a meeting time.

9.5 Collaborate with Outlook delegates (p. O9-340).

- The *Delegate* feature allows others to have control and access over specific parts of your Outlook information when using an Exchange server.
- The *Delegate* feature includes the following permission levels:
  - *None:* Delegate does not have access to this area of Outlook
  - *Reviewer:* Can read items, but does not have access to create, delete, or edit items.
  - *Author:* Can read and create items, but does not have access to delete or edit items.
  - *Editor:* Can read, create, delete, or edit items.
- You can change permissions for delegates based on each aspect of Outlook.
- You can add, remove, or modify permissions for delegates at any time.

O9-345

Check for Understanding

In the **Online Learning Center** for this text (www.mhhe.com/office2013inpractice), there are a variety of resources that can be used to review the concepts covered in this chapter.

The following Online Learning Resources are available in the Online Learning Center:

- Multiple choice questions
- Short answer questions
- Matching exercises

Guided Project 9-1

For this project, you are an insurance agent for Central Sierra Insurance (CSI). Your Outlook calendar is too cluttered with your home and work commitments since you initially used your default Outlook calendar to host both your home and work calendars. You create a new calendar specifically for your work. You add a few appointments and share your new calendar with a colleague.
[Student Learning Outcomes 9.1, 9.3, 9.4]

Skills Covered in This Project

- Create a new calendar.
- Mark a calendar item as private.

- Forward a calendar item.
- Share a calendar.

---

1. Click the **Calendar** button in the *Navigation* pane.
   a. Click the **Folder** tab and then the **New Calendar** button in the *New* group. The *Create New Folder* dialog box opens.
   b. Type Central Sierra as the **Name** of the new calendar. Confirm that the folder contains **Calendar Items** and that the new calendar will be placed in the *Calendar* folder.
   c. Click **OK.**

2. Create an appointment with the following information:
   Subject: Staff Breakfast
   Location: Conference Room A
   Start time: Next week Monday at 8:00 AM
   End time: Next week Monday at 9:30 AM

3. Create another appointment with the following information:
   Subject: New Client: Jim Santiago
   Location: My office
   Start time: Next week Wednesday at 2:30 PM
   End time: Next week Wednesday at 3:30 PM

4. Mark the **New Client: Jim Santiago** appointment as private.
   a. Open the **New Client: Jim Santiago** appointment.
   b. Click the **Private** button [*Appointment* or *Event* tab, *Tags* group].
   c. Click **Save & Close** [*Appointment* or *Event* tab, *Actions* group].

5. Create a third appointment with the following information:
   Subject: **Agents Meeting**
   Location: **Beach Cafe**
   Start time: Next week Thursday at 12:00 PM
   End time: Next week Thursday at 1:30 PM (Figure 9-46)

6. Forward the **New Client: Jim Santiago** appointment to your instructor.

9-46 Completed Guided Project 9-1

 a. Double-click the **New Client: Jim Santiago** appointment.

 b. Click the **Forward** button [*Appointment* (or *Event*) tab, *Actions* group]. A new email opens with the calendar item as an attachment.

 c. Select your instructor as the recipient.

 d. Add your email address in the *Cc* field.

 e. Modify the subject to Outlook Guided Project 9-1a.

 f. In the message area, type:
Dear [instructor's name],
Attached is my Outlook Guided Project 9-1a.
Thank you,
[your name]

 g. Click **Send.**

7. Share your calendar with your instructor.

 a. Click the **Share Calendar** button in the *Share* group on the *Home* tab. A sharing request email opens.

 b. Select your instructor as the recipient.

 c. Modify the subject to Outlook Guided Project 9-1b.

 d. In the message area, type:
Dear [instructor's name],
This is my Outlook Guided Project 9-1b.
Thank you,
[your name]

 e. Click **Send.**

 f. Click **Yes** to send the sharing request email.

Guided Project 9-2

For this project, you are an insurance agent for CSI. Your new calendar is a little disorganized since you created appointments without categorizing them. Therefore, you categorize them to make each item more easily noticeable when you glance at your schedule. You also attach a preparation file for your new client meeting with Jim. You include a business card to remind you to give Jim a physical card when you see him. Also, your supervisor told you that the agents' meeting would occur every other week, so you make it a recurrence in your calendar.
[Student Learning Outcomes 9.3, 9.4]

File Needed: ***insurance.xlsx***

Skills Covered in This Project

- Create categories.
- Apply categories to calendar items.
- Attach a file to a calendar item.

- Attach an Outlook item to a calendar item.
- Forward a calendar item.
- Set recurrence for a calendar item.

---

1. Click the **Calendar** button in the *Navigation* pane.

2. Select the **Central Sierra** calendar.

3. Create the following categories:
   Name: Staff; *Color:* **Green**
   Name: Clients; *Color:* **Yellow**

4. Apply categories to the three appointments you created in *Guided Project 9-1.*
   a. Select the **Staff Breakfast** appointment.
   b. Click the **Categorize** button [*Appointment* tab, *Tags* group].
   c. Click **Staff.**
   d. Select the **New Client: Jim Santiago** appointment.
   e. Click the **Categorize** button [*Appointment* tab, *Tags* group].
   f. Click **Clients.**
   g. Select the **Agents Meeting** appointment.
   h. Click the **Categorize** button [*Appointment* tab, *Tags* group].
   i. Click **Staff.**

5. Attach the file ***insurance.xlsx*** and your business card to the **New Client: Jim Santiago** appointment.
   a. Open the **New Client: Jim Santiago** appointment.
   b. Click the **Attach File** button [*Insert* tab, *Include* group]. The *Insert File* dialog box opens.
   c. Browse to find the file ***insurance.xlsx*** on your computer, select the file(s), and click **Insert.**
   d. Click **Business Card** [*Insert* tab, *Include* group], and choose **Other Business Cards.** The *Insert Business Card* dialog box opens.
   e. Select your business card and click **OK** (it is okay if your business card is the one you created in a previous project).
   f. Click **Save & Close** [*Appointment* or *Event* tab, *Actions* group] (Figure 9-47).

9-47 Completed Guided Project 9-2

6. Forward the **New Client: Jim Santiago** appointment to your instructor.
   a. Double-click the **New Client: Jim Santiago** appointment.
   b. Click the **Forward** button [*Appointment* (or *Event*) tab, *Actions* group]. A new email opens with the calendar item as an attachment.
   c. Select your instructor as the recipient.
   d. Add your email address in the *Cc* field.
   e. Modify the subject to Outlook Guided Project 9-2.
   f. In the message area, type:
   Dear [instructor's name],
   Attached is my Outlook Guided Project 9-2.
   Thank you,
   [your name]
   g. Click **Send.**

7. Set the **Agents Meeting** appointment to recur every other week without an end date.
   a. Open the **Agents Meeting** appointment.
   b. Click the **Recurrence** button [*Appointment* or *Event* tab, *Options* group]. The *Appointment Recurrence* dialog box opens.
   c. In the **Recurrence pattern** section, select **Weekly, Recur every 2 weeks,** on **Thursday.**
   d. In the **Range of recurrence** section, select **No end date.**
   e. Click **OK** to close the *Appointment Recurrence* dialog box.
   f. Click **Save & Close.**

Guided Project 9-3

For this project, you are an insurance agent for CSI. You will be going on vacation in two weeks. Even though you are on vacation, work does not stop. You assign your assistant as a *Delegate*. Your assistant only needs access to your calendar and tasks with *Author* permission. While you are away, your assistant sets up a follow-up meeting with Jim.
[Student Learning Outcome 9.5]

Skills Covered in This Project

- Add a delegate.
- Set permissions for a delegate.
- Open a calendar as a delegate.
- Create a calendar item as a delegate.
- Remove a delegate.

---

1. Add a partner as a delegate.
   a. Click the **File** tab, click the **Account Settings** button, and choose **Delegate Access.** The *Delegates* dialog box opens.
   b. Click the **Add** button. The *Add Users* dialog box opens.
   c. Select the name of the delegate (your partner) to be added and click **Add.**
   d. Click **OK** to close the *Add Users* dialog box. The *Delegate Permissions* dialog box opens.
   e. Click the **drop-down** arrow next to **Calendar** and **Tasks** and select **Author.**
   f. Click the **drop-down** menu next to **Inbox, Contacts,** and **Notes** and change the permissions to **None.**
   g. Select the **Automatically send a message to delegate summarizing these permissions** check box.
   h. Deselect the **Delegate can see my private items** check box.
   i. Click **OK** to close the *Delegate Permissions* dialog box.
   j. Click **OK** to close the *Delegates* dialog box.
   k. Click the **File** tab to return to Outlook.

2. Open your partner's calendar.
   a. Click the **Calendar** button in the *Navigation* pane.
   b. Click the **Open Calendar** button [*Home* tab, *Manage Calendars* group] and choose **Open a Shared Calendar.** The *Open a Shared Calendar* dialog box opens.
   c. Click the **Name** button to open the *Select Name* dialog box.
   d. Select your partner's name and click **OK.** The calendar will appear in the *Shared Calendars* list in the *Navigation* pane.

3. Create a new appointment for a group meeting using the following information.
   Subject: Jim: Follow up on life Insurance policy
   Location: Conference Room A
   Start time: Three weeks from today on Wednesday at 10:30 AM
   End time: Three weeks from today on Wednesday at 11:30 AM
   Categorize the appointment as a **Clients** (Figure 9-48).

4. Remove your partner as a delegate.
   a. Click the **File** tab, click the **Account Settings** button, and choose **Delegate Access.** The *Delegates* dialog box opens.
   b. Select your partner and click **Remove.**
   c. Click **OK** to close the *Delegates* dialog box.

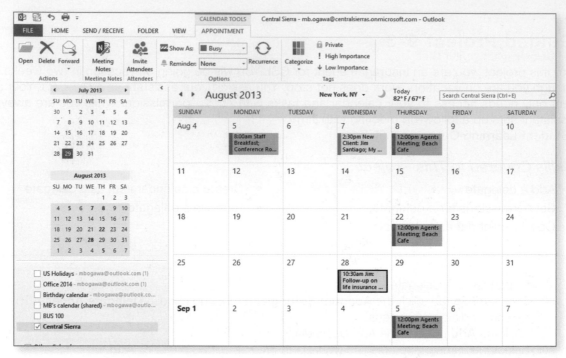

9-48 Completed Guided Project 9-3

5. Forward the *Delegate* designation message to your instructor.
   a. Click the **Mail** button in the *Navigation* pane.
   b. Select the *Delegate* message. It should have the subject You have been designated as a delegate for [name].
   c. Click the **Forward** button.
   d. Select your instructor as the recipient.
   e. Add your email address in the *Cc* field.
   f. Modify the subject to Outlook Guided Project 9-3.
   g. In the message area, type:
      Dear [instructor's name],
      Attached is my Outlook Guided Project 9-3.
      Thank you,
      [your name]
   h. Click **Send.**

Independent Project 9-4

For this project, you are a coordinator for the American River Cycling Club (ARCC). Since you are new to the position, you use Outlook to help you organize the events for ARCC. You create a new calendar in Outlook and start creating calendar items for the event. You also share the calendar with a co-coordinator, so you can both view the calendar as needed.
[Student Learning Outcomes 9.1, 9.3, 9.4]

Skills Covered in This Project

- Create a new calendar.
- Mark a calendar item as private.
- Forward a calendar item.
- Share a calendar.

---

1. Create a new calendar named **ARCC**.

2. Create an appointment with the following information:
   Subject: ARCC Membership Meeting
   Location: American River Coffee House
   Start time: Next week Wednesday at 7:00 AM
   End time: Next week Wednesday at 8:00 AM

3. Create another appointment with the following information:
   Subject: Test CEE Route
   Location: ARC Stadium
   Start time: Next week Thursday at 5:00 PM
   End time: Next week Thursday at 7:00 PM
   Message: Executive members only
   Mark the meeting as *Private* (Figure 9-49).

4. Forward the **Test CEE Route** appointment to your instructor.
   a. Select your instructor as the recipient.
   b. Add your email address in the *Cc* field.
   c. Modify the subject to Outlook Independent Project 9-4a.
   d. In the message area, type:
   Dear [instructor's name],
   Attached is my Outlook Independent Project 9-4a.
   Thank you,
   [your name]
   f. Click **Send**.

5. Share the **ARCC** calendar with your instructor.
   a. Select your instructor as the recipient.
   b. Modify the subject to Outlook Independent Project 9-4b.
   c. In the message area, type:
   Dear [instructor's name],
   This is my Outlook Independent
   Project 9-4b.
   Thank you,
   [your name]
   d. Click **Send**.
   e. Click **Yes** to send the sharing request email.

9-49 Completed Independent Project 9-4

Independent Project 9-5

For this project, you are a coordinator for ARCC. Since you created the calendar, you noticed that you could barely tell the difference between the different items, since some included information that should not be released yet, while others were perfectly okay for public dissemination. You use categories to help you quickly see the difference between each item. You also attach a file to a calendar item, forward an item, and set an item to recur.

[Student Learning Outcomes 9.3, 9.4]

File Needed: ***ceeroute.pdf***

Skills Covered in This Project

- Create categories.
- Apply categories to calendar items.
- Attach a file to a calendar item.

- Forward a calendar item.
- Set recurrence for a calendar item.

---

1. Click the **Calendar** button in the *Navigation* pane.

2. Select the **Central Sierra** calendar.

3. Create the following categories:
   Name: Confidential; *Color:* **Red**
   Name: Public; *Color:* **Green**

4. Apply categories to the two appointments you created in *Independent Project 9-4.*
   a. Categorize **ARCC Membership Meeting** as **Public.**
   b. Categorize **Test CEE Route** as **Confidential** (Figure 9-50).

9-50 Completed Independent Project 9-5

5. Attach the file ***ceeroute.pdf*** to the **Test CEE Route** appointment.

6. Forward the *Test CEE Route* appointment to your instructor.
   a. Select your instructor as the recipient.
   b. Add your email address in the *Cc* field.
   c. Modify the subject to Outlook Independent Project 9-5.
   d. In the message area, type:
      Dear [instructor's name],
      Attached is my Outlook Independent Project 9-5.
      Thank you,
      [your name]
   e. Click **Send.**

7. Set the *ARCC Membership Meeting* appointment to recur monthly on the first Wednesday of each month without an end date.

Independent Project 9-6

For this project, you are a coordinator for ARCC. Your work started to pick up, so you enlisted the help of one of your co-coordinators to serve as a delegate for you until your work slows down. You give your co-coordinator *Author* privilege for your tasks, calendar, and notes.
[Student Learning Outcome 9.5]

Skills Covered in This Project

- Add a delegate.
- Set permissions for a delegate.
- Open a calendar as a delegate.
- Create a calendar item as a delegate.
- Remove a delegate.

---

1. Add a partner as a delegate with the following permissions:
   a. **Author:** Tasks, Calendar, and Notes
   b. **None:** Inbox and Contacts
   c. Select the **Automatically send a message to delegate summarizing these permissions** check box.
   d. Deselect the **Delegate can see my private items** check box.

2. Open your partner's calendar and create a new appointment for a coordinators' meeting using the following information:
   Subject: CEE Coordinators' Meeting
   Location: American River Coffee Bar
   Start time: Two weeks from today on Tuesday at 7:00 AM
   End time: Two weeks from today on Tuesday at 8:00 AM
   Categorize the appointment as **Public** (Figure 9-51).

3. Remove your partner as a delegate.

4. Forward the *Delegate* designation message to your instructor.
   a. Select your instructor as the recipient.
   b. Add your email address in the Cc field.
   c. Modify the subject to Outlook Independent Project 9-6.
   d. In the message area, type:
   Dear [instructor's name],
   Attached is my Outlook Independent Project 9-6.
   Thank you,
   [your name]
   e. Click **Send**.

9-51 Completed Independent Project 9-6

Challenge Project 9-7

Create a new calendar in Outlook for a club or association that you are involved with. Be sure to include activities for the organization and categorize them to better organize each appointment or event. To submit the assignment, you will print the calendar and share it with your instructor via Outlook.com or your Exchange account.
[Student Learning Outcomes 9.1, 9.2, 9.3, 9.4]

- Create a new calendar.
- Include at least 10 appointments or events for an organization you are involved in.
- Attach items to each appointment or event when necessary.
- Create at least three categories and apply them appropriately to each calendar item.
- The calendar should account for at least two months of activities.
- Share your calendar with your instructor via Outlook.com or an Exchange server.
- Print a hard copy of the calendar in *Weekly Style* and submit it.

Challenge Project 9-8

Create a new calendar specifically for your school work. Include categories for each class that you are taking. Work with two partners on a group project for a specific class and give them permission to view your calendar with details. Mark all of your school work for your other classes as private so that they can only see items specific to the class you are taking together. Submit this project to your instructor by sharing your calendar.
[Student Learning Outcomes 9.1, 9.2, 9.3, 9.4]

- Create a new calendar.
- Include your class meeting times and assignment due dates for two months of the semester.
- Attach items to each appointment or event when necessary.
- Create categories for each of your classes.
- Mark appointments for other classes as private.
- Share the calendar with two of your classmates giving them *Limited details* permission.
- Share your calendar with your instructor giving him or her *Full details* permission.
- Print a copy of your calendar in *Weekly* format including calendar items marked as private and submit it to your instructor.

Challenge Project 9-9

Consider a job that you are interested in having in the future. Think about how you could use delegates in the workplace and the types of permissions you would give to different users, such as a personal assistant. Email at least two uses of delegates for the position you are considering to your instructor. [Student Learning Outcome 9.5]

- Identify a job that you are interested in.
- Determine how you could use delegates in the position.
- Include at least two delegates for your position. If you do not have two delegates, you can use two different possible jobs.
- Email your instructor using the following message format:
  Job title: [responsibilities]
  Delegate 1: [position in relation to your future job]
  Calendar: [permission level: reason for permission]
  Tasks: [permission level: reason for permission]
  Inbox: [permission level: reason for permission]
  Contacts: [permission level: reason for permission]
  Delegate 2: [position in relation to your future job]
  Calendar: [permission level: reason for permission]
  Tasks: [permission level: reason for permission]
  Inbox: [permission level: reason for permission]
  Contacts: [permission level: reason for permission]
- Change the subject of your message to **Outlook Challenge Project 9-9.**

CHAPTER 10

Notes, Journal, Shortcuts, Archiving, and Security

CHAPTER OVERVIEW

There are still more Outlook tasks and features available to help keep you organized. Outlook **Notes** store information that might not fit neatly into a task or calendar item. Outlook **Journal** can be used to track the time spent on Outlook items and other Microsoft Office documents.

Shortcuts can be incorporated into Outlook to quickly locate areas regularly used in Outlook. The **Archive** feature creates a different set of folders to store older information.

Security has become an increasingly important topic when dealing with digital information. Outlook provides many security features to protect your information from viruses and other potential threats.

STUDENT LEARNING OUTCOMES (SLOs)

After completing this chapter, you will be able to:

SLO 10.1 Create and use Notes in Outlook (p. O10-359).

SLO 10.2 Integrate the Outlook Journal with Outlook items and Microsoft Office documents (p. O10-361).

SLO 10.3 Incorporate shortcuts in Outlook (p. O10-363).

SLO 10.4 Use archiving to store Outlook items (p. O10-367).

SLO 10.5 Incorporate security features in Outlook (p. O10-371).

CASE STUDY

For the Pause & Practice projects in this chapter, you continue to work with your BUS 100 group. You use Outlook's Notes feature to remind yourself of discussions your group had. You also use the Journal to keep track of work completed and create a shortcut to it to make it easier to find. You also want to use a digital signature with your email messages, so you import one and add it to your messages.

Pause & Practice 10-1: You continue working with your BUS 100 group. Your group decided to keep track of each member's contribution, so you write a note to remind yourself of the decision. Since your group decided to use the *Journal* feature in Outlook frequently, you create a shortcut to it. Lastly, you create a journal entry to keep track of time spent on your part of the group project.

Pause & Practice 10-2: You set up a digital ID to ensure your recipients can verify that your messages are not tampered with. If your institution provides you with a digital ID, you can import it. Otherwise, you can use a free digital ID service, such as Comodo.

OUTLOOK

Using Notes

Do you have sticky notes stuck to your computer monitor, bathroom mirror, or refrigerator? If you're like most people, you use these sticky notes to write down reminders or random pieces of information. Outlook provides you with a feature similar to paper sticky notes. *Notes* (Figure 10-1) can be used to store information that does not necessarily fit as a task or calendar item. These items can be used to store a book wish list, a user name to a web site, a grocery list, a mileage rate for travel reimbursement, or other miscellaneous pieces of information.

10-1 Outlook *Notes*

> ### ANOTHER WAY
>
> **Ctrl+5** opens Notes in Outlook.

> ### MORE INFO
>
> Be careful about storing sensitive information in Notes if you are using Outlook in a stand-alone environment where others have access to your Outlook account.

> ### MORE INFO
>
> If you prefer to have the *Notes* button visible in the *Navigation* pane, you can customize it to show more than four buttons. See Chapter 5 for details on customizing the *Navigation* pane to meet your work style.

Create a Note

The *Notes* button is located on the . . . (more button) in the *Navigation* pane. By clicking the *Notes* button (see Figure 10-1), the *Notes* folders are displayed in the *My Notes* list in the *Navigation* pane, and your notes are displayed in the *Folder* pane.

(Note: Throughout the chapter, when the Notes *button is referred to, it is the* Notes *button on the* Navigation *pane; the . . . (more button) will not be included in each step.)*

HOW TO: Create a Note

1. Click the **Notes** button in the *Navigation* pane.
2. Click the **New Note** button (Figure 10-2). A new note will display.

3. Type in the information to be included in the note.
4. Click the **X** in the upper right corner to save and close the note. The first line of the note will be the name of the note that will be displayed in the *Folder* pane.

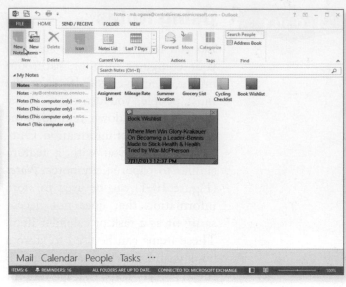

10-2 *New Note* button

ANOTHER WAY

In Notes, **Ctrl+N** opens a new note. **Ctrl+Shift+N** opens a new note anywhere in Outlook.

Edit a Note

Notes are very basic; you do not have as many formatting options available for notes as you have when customizing an email, task, signature, or calendar item. To edit a note, simply double-click the note to be edited in the *Folder* pane. The note opens, appearing similar to a sticky note on your computer screen, and you will be able to change the contents of the note. To save and close the note, click the **X** in the upper right corner.

Categorize Notes

As with other Outlook items, notes can be assigned to a category. When a note is assigned to a category, the color of the note changes to the color of the category to which it was assigned.

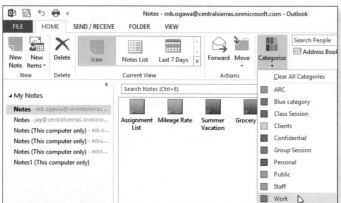

10-3 **Categorize notes to organize them**

HOW TO: Categorize Notes

1. Select the notes to be categorized.
2. Click the **Categorize** button [*Home* tab, *Tags* group] (Figure 10-3).
3. Click the selected category. The notes will change to the color of the assigned category.

ANOTHER WAY

Right-click the selected notes, click **Categorize,** and select the category.

Note Views

Notes can be displayed in a variety of ways. The different views are available in the *Current View* area in the *Navigation* pane. The default

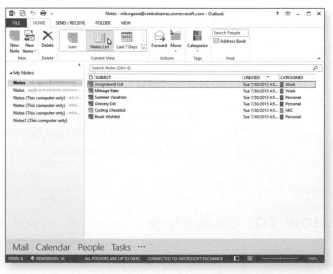

10-4 *Notes List* view

view is *Icon* (see Figure 10-3). Other note views include *Notes List* (Figure 10-4) and *Last 7 Days*. Both *Notes List* and *Last 7 Days* look similar, but *Last 7 Days* only shows notes created or edited within the last week.

Notes can also be displayed on your computer desktop (just like putting a sticky note on your computer screen). To display a note on your desktop, drag the note from the *Folder* pane and drop it on the desktop. A copy of the note is placed on the desktop.

Within *Icon* view, the notes can be displayed as large icons, small icons, or as a list. Click the **View** tab to display the different options in the *Arrangement* group (Figure 10-5).

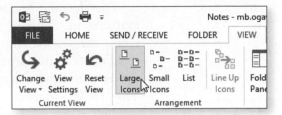

10-5 Arrangement options for *Notes* views

Forward a Note

Notes can be forwarded as an attachment via email to other Outlook users. When a recipient receives a forwarded note, he or she can drag the attached note to the *Notes* button and the note will be saved in his or her *Notes* folder.

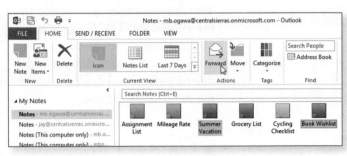

10-6 Forward a note

HOW TO: Forward a Note

1. Select the note to be forwarded.
2. Click the **Forward** button [*Home* tab, *Actions* group] (Figure 10-6). A new email opens with the note attached.
3. Select recipients, type a subject, and include necessary information in the body (Figure 10-7).
4. Click **Send** to send the note.

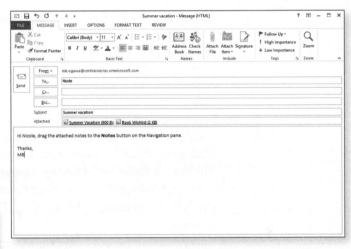

10-7 Forwarded note email message

> **ANOTHER WAY**
> **Ctrl+F** can be used to forward selected notes. A new email message opens with the selected notes.

> **ANOTHER WAY**
> Right-click the selected notes and choose **Forward.**

SLO 10.2

Using the Journal

Outlook *Journal* (Figure 10-8) is a feature used to track the amount of time you have spent working on a particular document or task. You can also use a journal to track activities related to a particular contact. An Outlook journal can be particularly useful if you or your company charges customers based on the time spent working on activities for them. A journal entry can be manually created and tracked, or you can have Outlook automatically create and track certain types of documents or specific contacts.

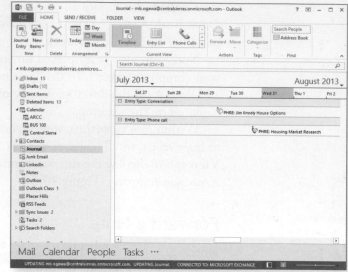

The *Journal* button is not available in Outlook 2013. To access the *Journal* feature, click the **Folder** button in the *Navigation* pane and select **Folder**. The *Folder* button is located on the ... (more button) in the *Navigation* pane (Figure 10-9). The *Journal* folder is available in the *Folders* list. The *Folder* button in the *Navigation* pane is similar to the *Notes* button; they are hidden by default and can be made visible through the *Navigation Options*.

10-8 Outlook *Journal* feature

> ## ANOTHER WAY
>
> **Ctrl+8** opens the *Journal*.

Record a Journal Entry

A journal entry can be created to track the amount of time spent on numerous activities. The different activities that can be tracked with a journal entry are: *Conversation, Document, Email message, Fax, Letter, Meeting, Meeting cancellation, Meeting request, Meeting response, Microsoft Access, Microsoft Excel, Microsoft*

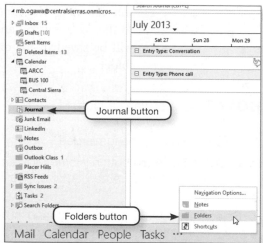

10-9 *Folder* button

PowerPoint, Microsoft Word, Note, Phone call, Remote session, Task, Task request, and *Task response.*

When you manually create a journal entry, you can record the **Subject, Entry type, Company, Start time,** and **Duration.** You can use the **Start Timer** button to automatically record the amount of time you spent on a journal entry, or you can manually enter the time into the journal.

HOW TO: Record a Journal Entry

1. Click the **Folder** button in the *Navigation* pane.
2. Click the **Journal Entry** button (Figure 10-10). A new journal entry opens (Figure 10-11).
3. Fill in the **Subject.**
4. Select the **Entry type.**
5. Select the *Start time* or click **the Start Timer** button. If you are not using the timer, select the *Duration* for the journal entry.

10-10 *Journal Entry* button

6. Add any details to the body.

7. Click **Save & Close.**

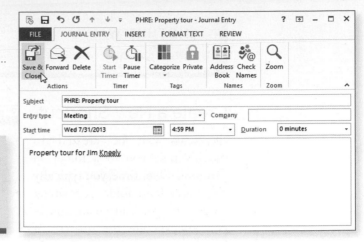

10-11 Sample journal entry

ANOTHER WAY

When you are in *Journal,* **Ctrl+N** opens a new journal entry. **Ctrl+Shift+J** opens a new journal entry anywhere in Outlook.

Journal Views

Outlook has numerous preset views by which you can see your journal entries in the *Folder* pane. Some of the views display your journal entries in timeline format, while others display them in list format. The preset journal views are:

- *Timeline* (timeline view)
- *Entry List* (list view)
- *Phone Calls* (list view)
- *Last 7 Days* (list view)

Journal entries in the timeline view can be displayed in a day, week, or month arrangement.

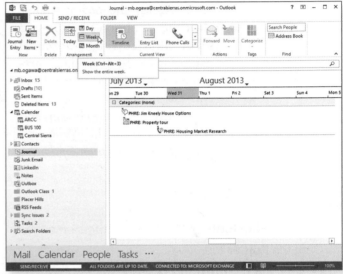

10-12 View journal by week

These different arrangement options are provided in the *Arrangement* group on the *Home* tab (Figure 10-12).

ANOTHER WAY

You can also change the scale of the timeline (day, week, month) by right-clicking the timeline in the *Folder* pane and selecting either *Day, Week,* or *Month.*

SLO 10.3

Using Shortcuts

In addition to *Mail, Calendar, Contacts, Tasks, Notes, Folder List,* and *Folder,* Outlook provides you with another *Navigation* pane view. The **Shortcuts** view in the *Navigation* pane gives you the ability to create shortcut links to Outlook folders, other folders, programs, and documents on your computer, and web sites. **Groups** of related shortcuts can also be created. If the link in the *Shortcuts* area is to an Outlook folder, the Outlook folder will be displayed in the *Folder* pane when the link is clicked. If the link in the *Shortcuts* area is to a program or file, the program or file opens in a new window when you click the shortcut.

> **ANOTHER WAY**
>
> **Ctrl+7** opens the *Shortcuts* view in Outlook.

Create a New Shortcut

Shortcuts can be created to quickly take you to a folder in Outlook. Over time, you typically build up a large folder repository. Therefore, you can create short-cuts to expedite the process of locating your most commonly used folders.

To access the *Shortcuts* area, click the . . . (more) button and select **Shortcuts** in *Navigation* pane (Figure 10-13). The *Short-cuts* button is similar to the *Notes* and *Folder* buttons; it is located within the . . . (more) button and can be placed in the *Navigation* pane in the *Navigation Options*.

10-13 Outlook *Shortcuts*

HOW TO: Create a Shortcut

1. Click the **Shortcuts** button on the *Navigation* pane.
2. Click the **Folder** tab.
3. Click the **New Shortcut** button in the *New* group (Figure 10-14). The *Add to Folder Pane* dialog box opens and will display all your Outlook folders (Figure 10-15).
4. Select an Outlook folder to be added as a shortcut.
5. Click **OK** to add the shortcut to the *Folder* pane.
6. The shortcut will appear in the *Folder* pane. When the shortcut is clicked, the folder will appear in the main document area.

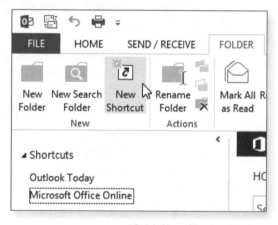

10-14 *New Shortcut* button

> **ANOTHER WAY**
>
> Right-click a shortcut group and choose **New Shortcut**.

Create a New Group

Shortcut Groups can be created within the *Shortcuts* area (of related items). To cre-ate a new group, right-click in the **Short-cuts** area in the *Navigation* pane and select

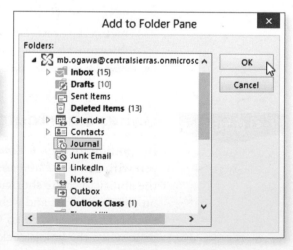

10-15 *Add to Folder Pane* dialog box

New Shortcut Group (Figure 10-16). A new group will be created in the *Navigation* pane, and you will need to type the name of the new group.

Edit a Shortcut or Group

Shortcuts and shortcut groups can be rearranged by dragging the shortcut up or down in the list of shortcuts or right-clicking the shortcut and choosing *Move Up* or *Move Down* (Figure 10-17). Shortcuts can also be renamed by right-clicking the shortcut, choosing **Rename Shortcut,** and typing the new shortcut name. Groups can be rearranged or renamed similarly to how a shortcut link is rearranged or renamed.

You can delete shortcuts and groups by right-clicking the shortcut or group and choosing *Delete Shortcut* or *Delete Group.* If you remove a group, all the shortcuts within that group will be deleted.

10-16 Create a New Shortcut Group right-click options

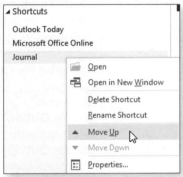

> **MORE INFO**
>
> When you delete a shortcut, the actual item is not deleted; just the shortcut to the item is deleted.

10-17 Edit a shortcut or group using the right-click options

PAUSE & PRACTICE: OUTLOOK 10-1

For this Pause & Practice project, you continue working with your BUS 100 group. Your group decided to keep track of each member's contribution, so you write a note to remind yourself of the decision. Since your group decided to use the *Journal* feature in Outlook frequently, you create a shortcut to it. Lastly, you create a journal entry to keep track of time spent on your part of the group project.

1. Create a note indicating that your group will keep track of work using the *Journal* feature.
   a. Click the **Notes** button in the *Navigation* pane.
   b. Click the **New Note** button. A new note will be displayed.
   c. Type the following text into the note: BUS 100 group decided to track individual time spent using the Journal.
   d. Click the **X** in the upper right corner to save and close the note.

2. Create a shortcut to the *Journal* folder.
   a. Click the **Shortcuts** button in the *Navigation* pane.
   b. Click the **Folder** tab.
   c. Click the **New Shortcut** button in the *New* group. The *Add to Folder Pane* dialog box opens and will display all your Outlook folders.
   d. Select the **Journal** folder.
   e. Click **OK** to add the shortcut to the *Folder* pane.

3. Create a journal entry indicating that you spent two hours on research.
   a. Click the **Shortcuts** button in the *Navigation* pane.
   b. Click the **Journal** shortcut.
   c. Click the **Journal Entry** button. A new journal entry opens.
   d. In the *Subject* field, type BUS 100 Library Research.
   e. In the *Entry type* field, select **Task.**
   f. In the *Start time* fields, select **yesterday's date** at **2:30 PM.**
   g. In the *Duration* field, select **2 hours.**
   h. Click **Save & Close** (Figure 10-18).

4. Send an email to your instructor with the note and journal entry as attachments.
   a. Click the **Mail** button in the *Navigation* pane.
   b. Click **New Mail** [*Home* tab, *New* group].
   c. In the *To* field, enter your instructor's email address.
   d. In the *Cc* field, enter your email address.
   e. In the *Subject* field, enter Outlook Pause & Practice 10-1.
   f. In the message area, type:
      Dear [instructor's name],
      Attached is my Outlook Pause & Practice 10-1.
      Thank you,
      [your name]
   g. Click the **Outlook Item** button [*Insert* tab, *Include* group].
   h. Select your note and click **OK.**
   i. Click the **Outlook Item** button [*Insert* tab, *Include* group].
   j. Select your journal entry and click **OK.**
   k. Click the **Send** button.

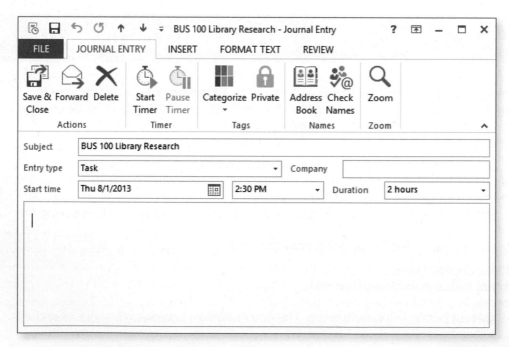

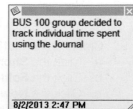

BUS 100 group decided to track individual time spent using the Journal

8/2/2013 2:47 PM

10-18 Completed Pause & Practice 10-1

Archiving Outlook Folders

After you have been using Outlook for some time, you will have numerous old email and calendar items taking up storage space. If you are using Outlook in a stand-alone environment, space is typically not a problem, but if you are on an Exchange server, you only have a limited amount of space on the server to store all your Outlook data. If you keep all your old email and calendar items, you might receive an email message warning you that you are close to or over your allotted space on the server.

Outlook provides you with a solution to this space limitation. *Archiving* is moving older Outlook items from their location (personal folders or mailbox folders) to a set of *archive folders* (Figure 10-19). When *AutoArchive* runs, a set of archive folders is created and stored locally on your computer rather than on the Exchange server. This set of folders mirrors the folders in your mailbox or personal folders and contains the older archived Outlook items. This helps control the amount of space you are using on the Exchange server while still allowing you to save and have access to these older Outlook items.

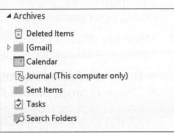

10-19 Archive folders

AutoArchive can be set to run periodically and will automatically move older Outlook items to your archive folders. You can customize the *AutoArchive* settings to move older mail, calendar, tasks, notes, and journals to the archive folders. You can also customize the archive settings for individual Outlook folders.

> **MORE INFO**
>
> Contacts are not archived because they are not time sensitive like emails, calendar items, tasks, notes, and journals.

> **MORE INFO**
>
> If you archive items on your local computer, you will not be able to retrieve them from OWA (Outlook Web Access) as the items have been removed from the Exchange server and are only available locally.

AutoArchive Settings

AutoArchive is by default turned on in Outlook. The *AutoArchive* dialog box has many settings that you can customize. *AutoArchive* can be set to run automatically at a regular interval (e.g., every 14 days), and you can be prompted before *AutoArchive* runs. If you choose *Prompt before AutoArchive runs,* a dialog box opens asking you if you want to run *AutoArchive.* If this option is not selected, *AutoArchive* will run automatically on the set schedule. In the *AutoArchive* dialog box, you have the option to either delete older Outlook items or move (archive) them to another set of folders. The default setting is to move older items to the archive folders, which are stored locally on your computer rather than on the Exchange server. In the *Clean out items older than* area, you can specify when you want your older items archived. This setting can be set from one day to 60 months. *AutoArchive* can also be set to delete expired email items. You can specify the location on your computer where you want archive folders saved. This set of folders is saved as an Outlook Data File (*.pst*).

The settings made in the *AutoArchive* dialog box are global and can be applied to all Outlook folders by clicking the *Apply these settings to all folders now* button.

HOW TO: Modify AutoArchive Settings

1. Click the **File** button on the *Ribbon* to open the *Backstage* view.
2. Click **Options.** The *Outlook Options* dialog box opens.
3. Select **Advanced** and click the **AutoArchive Settings** button (Figure 10-20). The *AutoArchive* dialog box opens (Figure 10-21).
4. Make the desired changes to the *AutoArchive* settings. A few general guidelines to follow are:

   - **Run AutoArchive every:** 14 days (2 weeks)
   - Check **Prompt before AuroArchive runs,** as your computer may slow down a little depending on the speed during the archiving process.
   - Check **Delete expired items (e-mail folders only)** if you do not intend to revisit expired items.
   - Check **Archive or delete old items.**
   - Check **Show archive folder in folder list.**
   - Clean out items older than **6 months** if you normally do not revisit items older than half a year.
   - Select **Move old items to** and select an archive location on your computer that you will remember. This will allow you to revisit items archived if you need to and will help to keep your Outlook *.pst* file smaller to improve overall performance.

5. Click **OK** to close the *AutoArchive* dialog box.
6. Click **OK** to close the *Outlook Options* dialog box.

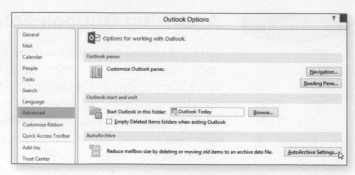

10-20 *AutoArchive Settings* button

10-21 *AutoArchive* dialog box

> ### MORE INFO
>
> Expired email was covered in Chapter 2.
>
> Outlook Data Files (*.pst*) were discussed in Chapter 8.

> ### MORE INFO
>
> It is a good idea to archive rather than delete older items so that you have access to them if you need them in the future. If you delete older Outlook items, they will not be stored in the archive folders.

Custom AutoArchive Settings

There might be some folders in Outlook that you do not want to archive or you want to archive at different *AutoArchive* settings than the default ones. For example, you might not want to archive your Inbox and tasks, but you might want to archive your calendar more or less frequently than your current default (global) *AutoArchive* settings. Outlook allows you to customize the archive settings on individual folders.

When customizing *AutoArchive* settings for individual folders, you are given the following three options (Figure 10-22):

- **Do not archive items in the folder:** This option turns off *AutoArchive* on the selected folder.
- **Archive items in this folder using the default settings:** This option uses the default *AutoArchive* settings for the selected folder.
- **Archive this folder using these settings:** This option allows you to customize the *AutoArchive* settings for the selected folder.

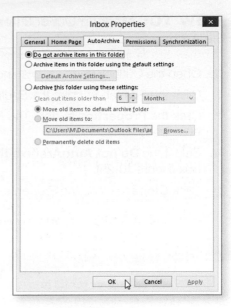

10-22 AutoArchive Inbox folder settings

HOW TO: Customize AutoArchive Settings

1. Select the folder on which to customize *AutoArchive* settings.
2. Click the **Folder** tab and then the **AutoArchive Settings** (or **Folder Properties**) button in the *Properties* group. The *[Folder name] Properties* dialog box opens.
3. Select one of the three custom *AutoArchive* options and make any desired changes to the *AutoArchive* settings.
4. Click **Apply.**
5. Click **OK** to close the dialog box (Figure 10-23).

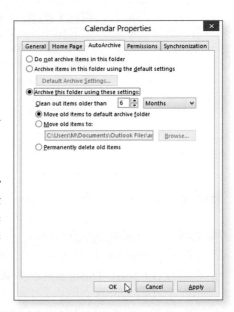

These custom settings will now be the *AutoArchive* settings for this folder and will override the default *AutoArchive* settings in Outlook. You can customize the *AutoArchive* settings on any of your folders that will be archived in Outlook.

10-23 *AutoArchive Calendar* folder settings

> **ANOTHER WAY**
>
> You can right-click any Outlook folder and choose **Properties** to open the *Properties* dialog box (Figure 10-24). You will then need to click the **AutoArchive** tab.

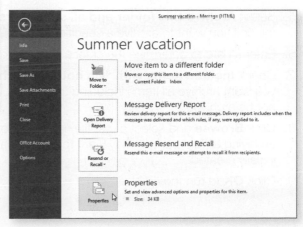

Outlook allows further customization regarding the archiving of specific items in Outlook. Individual Outlook items can be set so they are not archived even if they are in a folder that will be archived.

10-24 Properties for Outlook items

HOW TO: Mark an Outlook Item to Not be Archived

1. Open the Outlook item you wish not to be archived.
2. Click the **File** tab to open the *Backstage.*
3. Click the **Properties** button. The *Properties* dialog box opens.
4. Select the **Do not AutoArchive this item** check box (Figure 10-25).
5. Click **Close** to close the *Properties* dialog box.

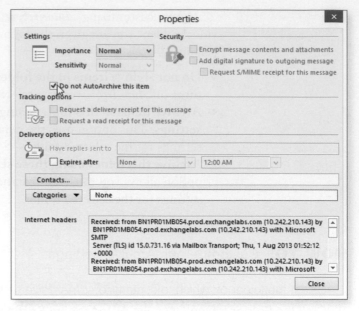

10-25 Ensure an Outlook item is NOT archived

Run AutoArchive

After you initially set up *AutoArchive*, it should run on its own for the first time based on the criteria you defined. *AutoArchive* should also continue to run based on the schedule you set. However, there are times that you want to archive your folders manually, such as seeing your quota almost being filled.

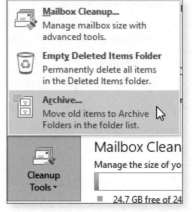

10-26 *Archive* button to manually archive folders

HOW TO: Manually Archive Folders

1. Select the folder you want to archive.
2. Click the **File** tab to open the *Backstage.*
3. Select **Cleanup Tools** and click **Archive** (Figure 10-26). The *Archive* dialog box opens (Figure 10-27).
4. Select **Archive all folders according to their AutoArchive settings** if you want to archive all folders.
5. Select **Archive this folder and all subfolders** and click on a folder if you want to archive a specific folder.
6. Enter a date to determine the criteria in which to archive items.
7. Check **Include items with "Do not AutoArchive" checked** if you want archive all items including the ones you indicated would not be archived.
8. Click **Browse** and select a *.pst* file name and location. If you are archiving all folders, you may want to use the same *.pst* file you initially created.
9. Click **OK** to run the archive.

10-27 *Archive* dialog box

Customizing Security Settings

As increasingly more communication is being done through email, security has become an important issue to protect your computer and information from viruses and malicious attacks. Outlook provides options for controlling which emails are treated as junk mail. Microsoft has also provided Office users with a **_Trust Center_** to give you control over many security aspects of online information from one central area.

Outlook Trust Center

The Outlook Trust Center (Figure 10-28) allows you to tailor your Outlook security in the following areas: _Trusted Publishers, Privacy Options, Email Security, Attachment Handling, Automatic Download, Macro Settings,_ and _Programmatic Access._

The Outlook _Trust Center_ can be opened by clicking the **File** tab, selecting **Options,** and choosing **Trust Center.**

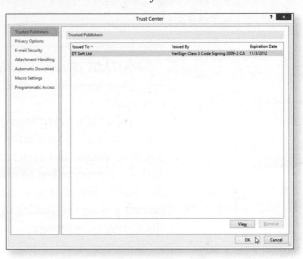

10-28 _Trusted Publishers_ in the _Trust Center_

Trusted Publishers

Trusted publishers (see Figure 10-28) are those organizations that are reputable and have a digital signature assigned to the macro or program that you allow to run on your computer. The Outlook _Trust Center_ stores this information to validate this publisher or developer. If a macro or other code is run on your computer from a source that is not a trusted source, you will receive a warning message prompting you to allow or deny the action.

Privacy Options

The **_Privacy Options_** (Figure 10-29) area of the _Trust Center_ allows you to control what information is sent to and received from Microsoft. These options can provide additional functionality and resources in Outlook, as well as monitoring your Outlook usage to help with product improvement.

In this area, you can also control available translation and research options.

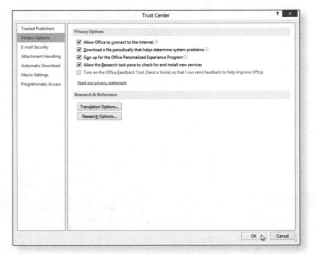

10-29 _Privacy Options_

Email Security

The **_Email Security_** area (Figure 10-30) allows you to control the use of encrypted emails and digital IDs.

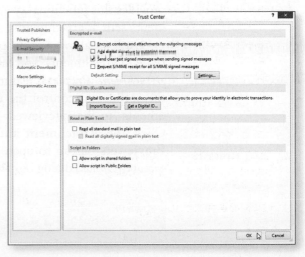

10-30 _E-mail Security_

Encrypting is a way to add another level of security to the messages and attachments you send. You can also choose to automatically include a *digital signature* to each message you send.

> **MORE INFO**
>
> Digital signatures will be covered later in this section.

S/MIME (Secure/Multipurpose Internet Mail Extensions) can be used to confirm that an email was sent and received unaltered and provides details about when the email was opened and read.

Digital IDs (certificates) can be used to verify your identity and electronically sign documents of high importance. Digital IDs are used in conjunction with encryption to secure email messages and attachments. To encrypt a document, the sender must have a digital ID and use a *private key* to encrypt the data. The receiver of the encrypted message must have the *public key* that matches the private key of the sender to view the encrypted message.

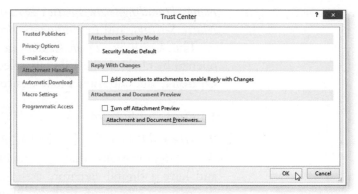

Attachment Handling

The *Trust Center* allows you to control how documents attached to an email are handled in Outlook (Figure 10-31). By default Outlook blocks some attachments it views as potentially dangerous.

10-31 *Attachment Handling*

> **MORE INFO**
>
> Microsoft Access documents are not allowed as attachments in an Outlook email message. To be able to send an Access file, you must compress or zip the file and attach the compressed or zipped folder.

You can use the *Add properties to attachments to enable Reply with Changes* feature. Most Microsoft Office documents allow you to include comments and changes, but this feature provides this functionality on other documents sent as attachments.

Outlook allows you to preview many types of attachments. You can turn off the *Attachment Preview* feature or change the settings to control the types of documents to be previewed in Outlook. Click the **Attachment and Document Previewers** button to open the *File Previewing Options* dialog box (Figure 10-32).

10-32 *File Previewing Options*

> **MORE INFO**
>
> Previewing attachments was covered in Chapter 1.

Automatic Download

Most of you have received an email message with embedded HTML content—pictures and text that look similar to a web page. By default Outlook does not download pictures and graphics embedded in these messages (Figure 10-33).

When you receive an email with HTML content, Outlook automatically blocks the content. The *InfoBar* will give you the option of downloading the content of the email. When HTML content is downloaded from a server, the sender of the message knows that your email account is active and you might start receiving more unsolicited emails—junk mail. In the **Automatic Download** area (Figure 10-34), you can customize how Outlook handles this type of email.

Macro Settings

Macros are simply a set of programming instructions. They are very common in electronic documents, and most perform some necessary actions in a document. But many viruses are spread by the use of macros, so Outlook tries to protect you from these malicious macros by proactively warning you about macros that are detected in email messages or attachments (Figure 10-35).

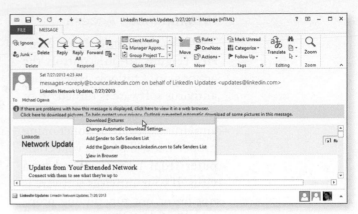

10-33 Pictures are not automatically downloaded in email messages

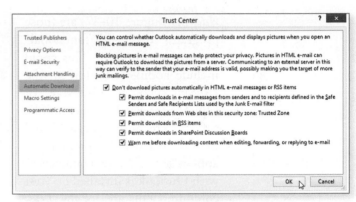

10-34 *Automatic Download* options

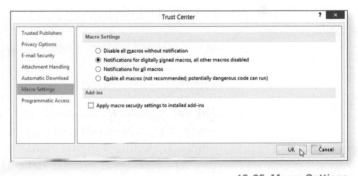

10-35 *Macro Settings*

> ### MORE INFO
>
> As with most of the default settings in the *Trust Center*, it is probably best to leave the default macro setting at *Notifications for digitally signed macros; all other macros are disabled*.
>
> The Melissa and ILOVEYOU viruses were spread by accessing Outlook and sending a message containing a virus to contacts stored in Outlook.

Programmatic Access

The **Programmatic Access Security** (Figure 10-36) controls the actions in Outlook when your antivirus software is turned off or not functioning properly. If your antivirus software is functioning properly, it will protect your computer from being accessed by a virus. If your antivirus software is not on or not functioning properly, Outlook will warn you when suspicious activity is detected.

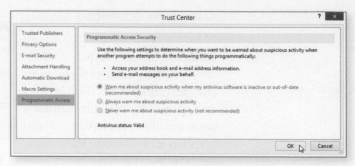

10-36 *Programmatic Access* options

Add-Ins

Add-ins (Figure 10-37) are those programs that add functionality to your Outlook. This could include adding a button on the *Ribbon* such as OneNote or Outlook Social Connector. The add-ins are automatically listed in this area when a program or application used in conjunction with Outlook is installed on your computer. This area of the *Trust Center* lists *Active, Inactive,* and *Disabled Application Add-ins*. The area below the *Add-Ins* list gives you the publisher, location (on your computer), and description of the selected add-in.

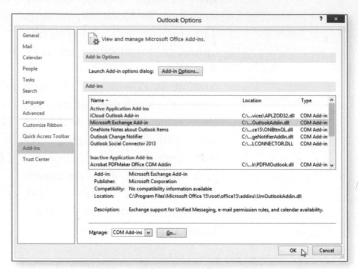

10-37 Outlook *Add-Ins*

Digital Signatures

Digital signatures are used to verify the authenticity of the sender. Including a digital signature in a message is not the same as including a signature in a message. A digital signature uses a certificate to verify who you are and a public key that can be used by the receiver of the message to access encrypted information. Digital IDs can be obtained through your Exchange administrator; most digital IDs are issued by third-party sources.

10-38 Add a digital signature to outgoing messages

If you have a digital ID, you can include a digital signature on all outgoing email by changing the settings in the *Email Security* area of the *Trust Center* to *Add digital signature to outgoing messages* (Figure 10-38).

You can also add a digital signature individually to an email.

HOW TO: Add a Digital Signature To a Message

1. Open a new email or an email to which you are going to reply.

2. Click the **expand** button on the bottom right of the *Tags* group on the *Message* tab. The *Properties* dialog box opens.

3. Click the **Security Settings** button. The *Security Properties* dialog box opens (Figure 10-39).

4. Check **Add digital signature to this message.** In this dialog box, you can encrypt a message or add a digital signature to the message.

5. Click **OK** to close the *Security Properties* dialog box.

6. Click **OK** to close the *Properties* dialog box.

10-39 Add a digital signature to an email message

> **MORE INFO**
>
> Use digital signatures only when it is necessary to either certify your identity or secure information.
>
> Digital signatures were covered in Chapter 2.

PAUSE & PRACTICE: OUTLOOK 10-2

For this Pause & Practice project, you set up a digital ID to ensure your recipients can verify that your messages are not tampered with. If your institution provides you with a digital ID, you can import it. Otherwise, you can use a free digital ID service, such as Comodo. If you have a digital ID or received one from your institution, start at step 1. If you need to download one, start at step 2.

1. Import your digital ID.
   a. Click the **File** button and select **Options.**
   b. Select **Trust Center** and click the **Trust Center Settings** button.
   c. Select **E-mail Security** and click the **Import/Export** button.
   d. Click the **Browse** button and locate your digital ID.
   e. Enter your password and click **OK.**

2. Acquire a digital ID.
   a. Click the **File** button and select **Options.**
   b. Select **Trust Center** and click the **Trust Center Settings** button.
   c. Select **E-mail Security** and click the **Get a Digital ID** button. Your browser will open.
   d. Select one of the services, such as Comodo, and follow the on-screen instructions to install the ID.

3. Send an email to your instructor with the note and journal entry as attachments.
   a. Click the **Mail** button in the *Navigation* pane.
   b. Click **New Mail** [*Home* tab, *New* group].
   c. Click the **expand** button on the bottom right of the *Tags* group on the *Message* tab.

d. Click the **Security Settings** button.
e. Check **Add digital signature to this message.**
f. Click **OK** to close the *Security Properties* dialog box.
g. Click **OK** to close the *Properties* dialog box.
h. In the *To* field, enter your instructor's email address.
i. In the *Cc* field, enter your email address.
j. In the *Subject* field, enter Outlook Pause & Practice 10-2.
k. In the message area, type:
   Dear [instructor's name],
   This is an email message with my digital ID.
   Thank you,
   [student name]
l. Click **Send** (Figure 10-40).

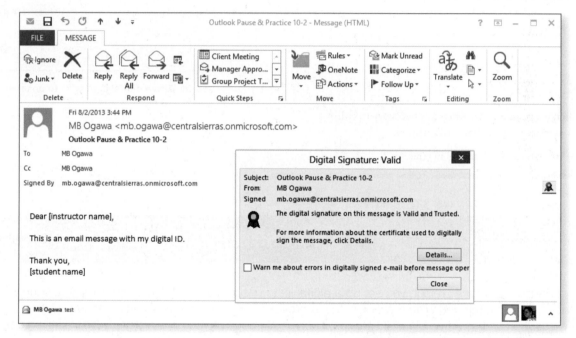

10-40 Completed Pause & Practice 10-2

Chapter Summary

10.1 Create and use Notes in Outlook (p. O10-359).

- Outlook **Notes** are digital versions of sticky notes.
- Information that cannot easily be classified into a task or calendar item could be created as a note.
- Like other Outlook items, Notes can be categorized.
- Notes can be viewed as icons or lists depending on your preference.
- You can forward notes to others using email.

10.2 Integrate the Outlook Journal with Outlook items and Microsoft Office documents (p. O10-361).

- The **Journal** feature helps you track the amount of time you spent on a particular activity.
- The Journal is located in the *Folder* list.
- You can manually input the duration of a journal entry or use the **Start Timer** and **Stop Timer** feature to keep track of time.
- Like other Outlook items, journals can be categorized.
- The Journal can be viewed in a timeline or list view.

10.3 Incorporate shortcuts in Outlook (p. O10-363).

- The **Shortcuts** view allows you to create links to Outlook folders, items on your computer, and online.
- Shortcuts can be organized within the **Shortcut Group.**
- Shortcut groups and shortcuts can be reordered, renamed, or deleted using the right-click menu.

10.4 Use archiving to store Outlook items (p. O10-367).

- **Archiving** moves older Outlook items such as email, calendar, tasks, notes, and journal items, from their current location to a set of **archive folders**.

- **AutoArchive** can automatically run an archive for you based on criteria you set.
- *AutoArchive* settings can be set globally or by folder.
- You can choose to omit specific Outlook folders and items from being archived.
- You can manually archive folders.

10.5 Incorporate security features in Outlook (p. O10-371).

- The **Trust Center** allows you to customize your Outlook security.
- **Trusted publishers** are organizations that are reputable and have a digital signature assigned to their macro or program.
- **Privacy Options** allow you to control information sent to and received from Microsoft.
- **Email Security** allows you to control the use of encrypted emails and digital IDs.
- **Encryption** is a way of adding security by scrambling a message.
- **S/MIME** can be used to confirm that an email was sent and received unaltered.
- **Digital IDs** are used to verify your identity as the sender.
- **Attachment Handling** allows you to control how attachments are handled, such as potentially dangerous file types.
- **Automatic Download** controls how emails are viewed, such as emails in HTML format with embedded pictures.
- **Macros** are a set of programming instructions that Outlook tries to protect you from because some of the code may be malicious.
- **Programmatic Access Security** checks to ensure your antivirus is functioning properly or not, and warns you when suspicious activity is detected.
- **Add-ins** are programs that add functionality to Outlook. You can control which add-ins are enabled or disabled.

Check for Understanding

In the **Online Learning Center** for this text (www.mhhe.com/office2013inpractice), there are a variety of resources that can be used to review the concepts covered in this chapter.

The following Online Learning Resources are available in the Online Learning Center:

- Multiple choice questions
- Short answer questions
- Matching exercises

Guided Project 10-1

For this project, you are a receptionist at Courtyard Medical Plaza (CMP). You recently noticed that your desk and computer monitor are getting cluttered with sticky notes, so you start using Outlook Notes for messages. While sorting your messages in Outlook, you noticed that it was hard to find your frequently used folders, so you create shortcuts and a shortcut group for your work with CMP. [Student Learning Outcomes 10.1, 10.3]

Skills Covered in This Project

- Create a note.
- Categorize a note.
- Create a shortcut group.
- Create a shortcut.
- Forward notes.

---

1. Create a new mail folder named CMP Articles.

2. Create a category named **Business** with a green color.

3. Create a category named **Personal** with an orange color.

4. Create a note for Dr. Saito.
   a. Click the **Notes** button in the *Navigation* pane.
   b. Click the **New Note** button. A new note will be displayed.
   c. Type the following text into the note: Dr. Saito: Dr. Callaway called at 2:00 regarding the article you are writing.
   d. Click the **X** in the upper right corner to save and close the note.

4. Categorize the note as **Business.**
   a. Select the note.
   b. Click the **Categorize** button and select **Business.**

5. Create a note for Dr. Sharuma.
   a. Click the **Notes** button on the *Navigation* pane.
   b. Click the **New Note** button. A new note will be displayed.
   c. Type the following text into the note: Dr. Sharuma: Your wife called and wants you to pick up the dry cleaning on the way home.
   d. Click the **X** in the upper right corner to save and close the note.

6. Categorize the note as **Personal.**
   a. Select the note.
   b. Click the **Categorize** button and select **Personal.**

7. Create a shortcut group named **CMP.**
   a. Click the **Shortcuts** button in the *Navigation* pane.
   b. Click the **Folder** tab.
   c. Right-click in the **Shortcuts** area in the *Navigation* pane and select **New Shortcut Group.**
   d. Type CMP and press **Enter.**

8. Create a shortcut to the *CMP Articles* folder.
   a. Click the **Shortcuts** button in the *Navigation* pane.
   b. Click the **Folder** tab.

c. Click the **New Shortcut** button in the *New* group. The *Add to Folder Pane* dialog box opens and will display all your Outlook folders.

d. Select the **CMP Articles** folder.

e. Click **OK** to add the shortcut to the *Folder* pane (Figure 10-41).

9. Send an email to your instructor with the notes as attachments.

a. Select the two notes you created (hold the **Ctrl** key and click on each of the notes).

b. Click the **Forward** button [*Home* tab, *Actions* group].

c. In the *To* field, enter your instructor's email address.

d. In the *Cc* field, enter your email address.

e. In the *Subject* field, enter Outlook Guided Project 10-1.

f. In the message area, type:
Dear [instructor's name],
Attached is my Outlook Guided Project 10-1.
Thank you,
[your name]

g. Click the **Send** button.

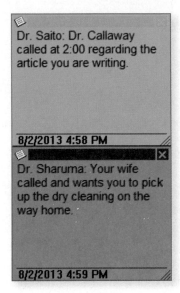

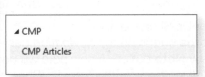

10-41 Completed Guided Project 10-1

Guided Project 10-2

For this project, you are a receptionist for CMP who recently learned that the office will be undergoing a reorganization. You were asked to keep journal logs of your day to help with the reorganization process.

[Student Learning Outcome 10.2]

Skills Covered in This Project

- Create a journal entry.
- Modify entry type.
- Modify duration.

---

1. Create a journal entry indicating that you spent one hour organizing files.
   a. Click the **Folders** button in the *Navigation* pane.
   b. Click **Journal.**
   c. Click the **Journal Entry** button. A new journal entry opens.
   d. In the *Subject* field, type: Organizing files.
   e. In the *Entry type* field, select **Task.**
   f. In the *Start time* fields, select **today's date** at **1:00 PM.**
   g. In the *Duration* field, select **1 hour.**
   h. Click **Save & Close.**

2. Create a journal entry indicating that you spent 15 minutes on the phone with a pharmaceutical salesman.
   a. Click the **Folders** button in the *Navigation* pane.
   b. Click **Journal.**
   c. Click the **Journal Entry** button. A new journal entry opens.
   d. In the *Subject* field, type Conversation with pharmaceutical salesman.
   e. In the *Entry type* field, select **Phone call.**
   f. In the *Start time* fields, select **today's date** at **4:00 PM.**
   g. In the *Duration* field, select **15 minutes.**
   h. Click **Save & Close** (Figure 10-42).

3. Send an email to your instructor with the journal entries as attachments.
   a. Click the **Mail** button in the *Navigation* pane.
   b. Click **New Mail** [*Home* tab, *New* group].
   c. In the *To* field, enter your instructor's email address.
   d. In the *Cc* field, enter your email address.
   e. In the *Subject* field, enter Outlook **Guided Project 10-2.**
   f. In the message area, type:
      Dear [instructor's name],
      Attached is my Outlook Guided Project 10-2.
      Thank you,
      [your name]
   g. Click the **Outlook Item** button [*Insert* tab, *Include* group].
   h. Hold the **Ctrl** key and select your journal entries and click **OK.**
   i. Click the **Send** button.

 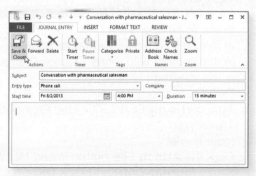

10-42 Completed Guided Project 10-2

Guided Project 10-3

For this project, you have been asked to email your journal entries as an archive to the CMP management for review. You begin by marking a journal item to not be *AutoArchived.* Next, you archive your journal entries and send them with a digital signature to ensure it is not modified in transit.
[Student Learning Outcomes 10.4, 10.5]

Skills Covered in This Project

- Mark an Outlook item to not be archived.
- Run a manual archive.

- Email using a digital signature.

---

1. Mark your **BUS 100 Library Research** journal entry to not be archived.
   a. Click the **Folders** button in the *Navigation* pane.
   b. Click **Journal.**
   c. Double-click the **BUS 100 Library Research** item.
   d. Click **File** and select the **Properties** button.
   e. Check **Do not AutoArchive** this item.
   f. Click **Close.**
   g. Click the **Save & Close** button.

2. Run a manual archive.
   a. Click **File** to open the *Backstage* view.
   b. Click the **Cleanup Tools** button and select **Archive.**
   c. Select **Archive this folder and all subfolders.**
   d. Select your **Journal.**
   e. Change the date for **Archive items older than** to **tomorrow's date** to ensure you include the journal items you created today.
   f. Click the **Browse** button and select a location on your computer. Save the file as journal-CMP.
   g. Click **OK.**

3. Send an email to your instructor with the journal entry as attachments.
   a. Click the **Mail** button in the *Navigation* pane.
   b. Click **New Mail** [*Home* tab, *New* group].
   c. Click the **expand** button at the bottom right of the *Tags* group on the *Message* tab.
   d. Click the **Security Settings** button.
   e. Check **Add digital signature to this message.**
   f. Click **OK** to close the *Security Properties* dialog box.
   g. Click **OK** to close the *Properties* dialog box.
   h. In the *To* field, enter your instructor's email address.
   i. In the *Cc* field, enter your email address.
   j. In the *Subject* field, enter Outlook Guided Project 10-3.
   k. In the message area, type:
      Dear [instructor's name],
      Attached is my Outlook Guided Project 10-3.
      Thank you,
      [your name]
   l. Click the **Attach File** button [*Insert* tab, *Include* group].
   m. Select *journal-CMP* and click **OK.**

n. Click the **Send** button. Outlook may warn you about sending a potentially unsafe file. This is why you wanted to digitally sign the email to ensure it was not modified in transit. Outlook will also warn the recipient about the attachment (Figure 10-43).

> **MORE INFO**
>
> You will rarely, if ever, send a *.pst* file over email. This Guided Project should be used to help you understand how to archive folders. You should also be aware that sending and receiving *.pst* files can be dangerous, as viruses can be embedded within those files.

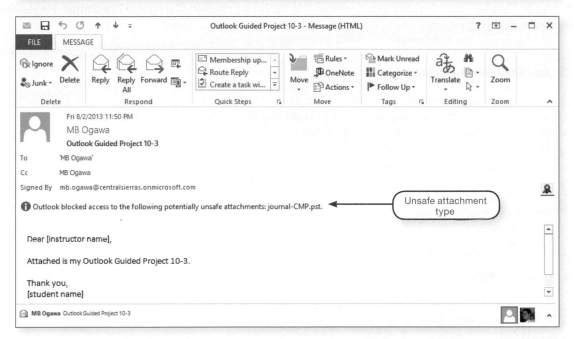

10-43 Completed Guided Project 10-3

Independent Project 10-4

For this project, you are an academic advisor for the Sierra Pacific Community College District (SPCCD). You recently found yourself having trouble keeping your notes straight from your meetings because they are a mix of notes on sticky notes, note pads, and loose sheets of paper. You take your laptop computer to meetings to help you take notes and keep them organized.
[Student Learning Outcome 10.1]

Skills Covered in This Project

- Create notes.
- Categorize notes.

- Forward notes.

1. Create the following categories:
   a. *Category:* Undergraduate Advising; *Color:* **Blue**
   b. *Category:* Freshmen Retention; *Color:* **Red**
   c. *Category:* Administrative Duties; *Color:* **Purple**

2. Create and categorize the following notes:
   a. *Note:* New undergraduate core requirements available at campus web site; *Category:* **Undergraduate Advising**
   b. *Note:* Brainstorm campus engagement opportunities for freshman; *Category:* **Freshmen Retention**
   c. *Note:* Create 5 survey questions for incoming freshmen packet; *Category:* **Freshmen Retention**
   d. *Note:* Advising requirement updated to be one session per academic year; *Category:* **Undergraduate Advising**
   e. *Note:* New form 27 for students applying for graduation, update records; *Category:* **Administrative Duties** (Figure 10-44)

3. Send an email to your instructor with the notes as attachments.
   a. Select the five notes you created (hold the **Ctrl** key and click on each of the notes).
   b. Click the **Forward** button [*Home* tab, *Actions* group].
   c. In the *To* field, enter your instructor's email address.
   d. In the *Cc* field, enter your email address.
   e. In the *Subject* field, enter Outlook Independent Project 10-4.
   f. In the message area, type:
      Dear [instructor's name],
      Attached is my Outlook Independent Project 10-4.
      Thank you,
      [your name]
   g. Click the **Send** button.

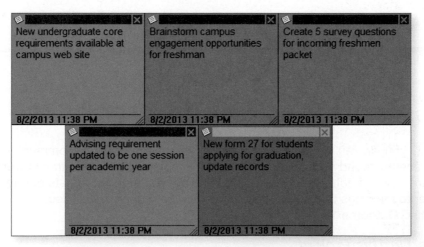

10-44 Completed Independent Project 10-4

Independent Project 10-5

For this project, you are an academic advisor for the SPCCD. Recently, the dean asked all academic advisors to keep track of time spent advising undergraduate students to help the administration understand student needs. To help you keep track of advising sessions, you begin using the *Journal* feature to track duration.
[Student Learning Outcome 10.2]

Skills Covered in This Project

- Create a journal entry.
- Modify entry type.
- Modify duration.

---

1. Create a journal entry for a face-to-face advising session using the following information:
   Subject: Randon Catallina (Freshman)
   Entry type: **Meeting**
   Start time: **tomorrow's date** at **9:00 AM**
   Duration: **1 hour**
   Message: Major exploration

2. Create a *Journal* entry for a face-to-face advising session using the following information:
   Subject: Janelle Shin (Incoming Freshman)
   Entry type: **Phone Call**
   Start time: **tomorrow's date** at **10:30 AM**
   Duration: **30 minutes**
   Message: Registration inquiry

3. Create a journal entry for a face-to-face advising session using the following information:
   Subject: Shirley Santiago (Junior)
   Entry type: **Meeting**
   Start time: **tomorrow's date** at **2:00 PM**
   Duration: **1 hour**
   Message: Study skills assistance (Figure 10-45)

4. Send an email to your instructor with the journal entries as attachments.
   a. In the *To* field, enter your instructor's email address.
   b. In the *Cc* field, enter your email address.
   c. In the *Subject* field, enter Outlook Independent Project 10-5.
   d. In the message area, type:
      Dear [instructor's name],
      Attached is my Outlook Independent Project 10-5.
      Thank you,
      [your name]
   e. Click the **Send** button.

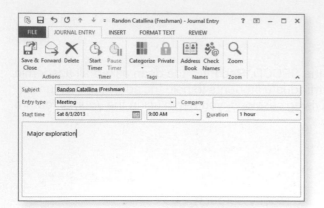

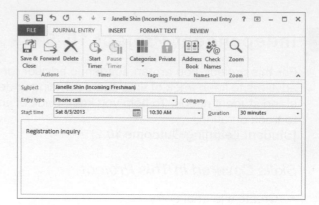

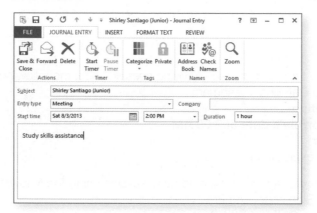

10-45 Completed Independent Project 10-5

Independent Project 10-6

For this project, you are an advisor for SPCCD. You received an inquiry from another advisor, Megan Sharp, who also wants to use the *Journal* feature. She is having difficulty finding the *Journal* feature, so you email her instructions on how to create a shortcut.

You also became more concerned about your emails being modified when sent to receivers, since your IT department emailed all faculty and staff regarding recent information security issues. You use a digital signature to ensure the receivers of your message do not get a message that has been modified. [Student Learning Outcomes 10.3, 10.5]

Skills Covered in This Project

- Create a shortcut.
- Use a digital signature.

---

1. Send an email to your instructor as Megan Sharp describing how to create a shortcut to the *Journal* folder.
   a. In the *To* field, enter your instructor's email address.
   b. In the *Cc* field, enter your email address.

c. In the *Subject* field, enter Outlook Independent Project 10-6.

d. In the message area, describe to Megan how you can create a shortcut to the *Journal* folder.

2. Add your digital signature (Figure 10-46).

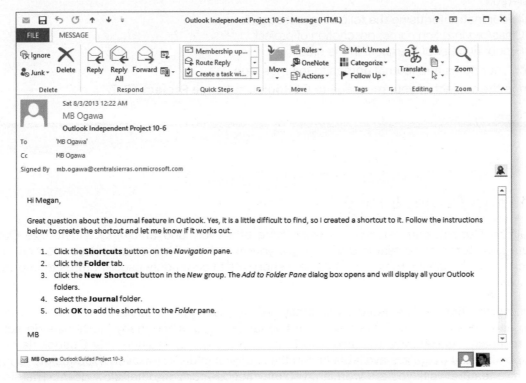

10-46 Completed Independent Project 10-6

Challenge Project 10-7

Working in teams, whether in school, clubs, organizations, or business, can be challenging. Notes can help you to keep track of many things that arise, such as collaboration details on group decisions. In these instances, Notes can be more efficient than tasks or calendar items. It can also be difficult to keep track of who was responsible for each task and how much time the task took to complete, to ensure work completed can be reported accurately. For this project, consider a team project that you participated in, whether it be for a class, club, work, or other organization. Use Notes to write notes for documentation during the group project. Also, use the *Journal* tool to create a timeline of the tasks completed.
[Student Learning Outcomes 10.1, 10.3]

- Identify a team project that you worked on.
- Create at least two notes for the group project.
- Each note should be categorized.
- Create at least two journal entries detailing work completed and duration.

- Each journal entry should be categorized.
- Create a secondary category for journal entry with each team member's name.
- Apply each team member's name to each journal entry to make it easier to track work completed per person.
- Email your instructor using the following message format:
  Class/organization name: description of project
  Group: number of members in the group
- Attach your notes and journal entries to the message.
- Change the subject of your message to **Outlook Challenge Project 10-7.**

Challenge Project 10-8

Personalizing Outlook can help you to work more effectively and efficiently. Customize Outlook's *Shortcuts* and *AutoArchive* features to improve your workflow. Shortcuts help you to find information quickly, rather than searching for it. Create shortcuts to commonly used features to improve your productivity.

Customizing the *AutoArchive* feature can really help to make your installation of Outlook run faster. It is also convenient to have Outlook perform this task for you, since many individuals do not like to archive manually. *AutoArchive* will also help to keep you organized, since only Outlook items newer than a specific date range are available (not in the *Archives* folder). However, if Outlook is running the *AutoArchive* feature while you are working, you may notice your computer slow down. Therefore, it is important to set up *AutoArchive* to run at a time when you will not likely be using the computer. You will also want to know when you need to search the *Archive* folder to find an Outlook item.

For this Project, you create shortcuts and set up *AutoArchive* to fit your needs and explain why and how you set it up.
[Student Learning Outcome 10.4]

- Create at least three shortcuts to commonly used features.
- Explain why you created each shortcut.
- Identify the *AutoArchive* settings that fit your work style.
- Describe why each setting fits you.
- Identify folders or Outlook items that you would not archive.
- Describe why you would not archive each folder or item.
- Email your instructor using the following message format:
  Shortcuts
  Shortcut name 1: [what it links to and why you created it]
  Shortcut name 2: [what it links to and why you created it]
  Shortcut name 3: [what it links to and why you created it]
  AutoArchive
  Run AutoArchive every: __ days: [reason for setting]
  Check/Do not check Prompt before AutoArchive runs: [reason for setting]

Check/Do not check Delete expired items (e-mail folders only): [reason for setting]
Check/Do not check Archive or delete old items: [reason for setting]
Check/Do not check Show archive folder in folders list: [reason for setting]
Check/Do not check Clean out items older than __ Months/Weeks/Days: [reason for setting]
Select Move old items to: or Permanently delete old items: [reason for setting]
Folder to not archive: [reason for not archiving]
Outlook item to not archive: [reason for not archiving]

- Change the subject of your message to **Outlook Challenge Project 10-8.**

Challenge Project 10-9

Although the default security options in Outlook work well for many people, there are times when you want to make additional changes based on your preferences. Open the *Trust Center* and identify changes you would make and indicate why. Examples of changes include the addition of a digital signature to outgoing messages or turning off attachment previews. This project should help you to customize Outlook's security options to meet your needs.
[Student Learning Outcome 10.5]

- Identify Outlook security options that you would like to modify.
- Describe why you would like to change the security option.
- Email your instructor using the following message format:
    Security Option Name 1: reason for modification
    Security Option Name 2: reason for modification
    Security Option Name 3: reason for modification
- Change the subject of your message to **Outlook Challenge Project 10-9.**

O10-389

appendices

Setting Up Outlook for an On-site or Online Classroom Environment

The text was developed to promote collaboration and digital organization among Outlook users. In an on-site course, students will be able to experience all the benefits of using Outlook in an Exchange environment and practice using the features of Outlook with classmates in a computer lab environment. But many Outlook courses are taught in an online environment. In this appendix, you'll be provided with some tips to help you set up your Outlook course whether it is an on-site or online course.

On-site Course

If you're teaching this course on-site, you should create a set of student accounts on an Exchange server. These accounts can be generic accounts that get recycled from semester to semester. It is probably best to have a separate domain for the classroom Exchange server so it does not conflict with your campus or district Exchange server. Using a separate server also helps prevent students from having access to the entire *Global Address List* of your school, district, or company.

Creating User Accounts

These accounts can easily be managed through ***Exchange admin center.*** The student accounts are given a generic name (e.g., *D01, D02, D03*, etc.), and a generic password is used (e.g., student). Here is the process that can be used to create the generic student accounts.

HOW TO: Create User Accounts

1. Open *Exchange admin center* in a browser. The URL is typically https://<Servername>/ecp if you are working within the organization's firewall.
2. Ensure the **mailboxes** link is selected. You can access it through the *recipients* link on the left navigation.
3. Create a *New User* by clicking the **+ (plus)** sign and selecting **User mailbox** (Figure A-1). A new browser window will open with the new user's information.

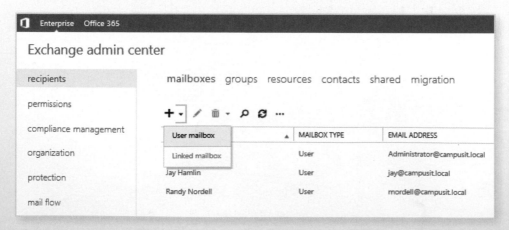

A-1 Create new users in *Exchange admin center*

4. Type in the user information (Figure A-2)

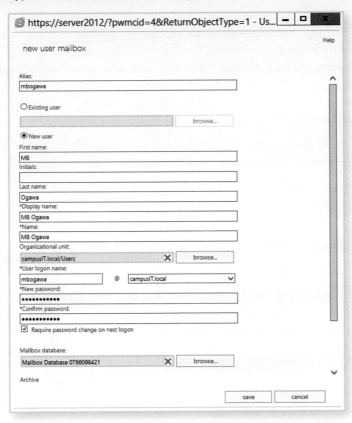

A-2 Enter user information

5. Click **Save** to add the user. The user will be added to the user list in the *mailboxes* link.

6. You can create additional accounts by using the same process.

7. You can edit multiple users at once by selecting them (hold the **Ctrl** key and click on each user or hold the **Shift** key and select the first and last user in a range). Edit the details, such as *Contact Information, Organization,* etc. using the options on the right side of the page (Figure A-3).

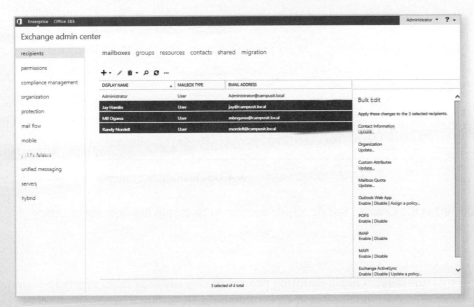

A-3 Edit multiple users

Recycling User Accounts

At the end of each semester, these Exchange email accounts can be recycled so they can be used again for subsequent semesters. The recycling process consists of deleting and re-creating the accounts.

HOW TO: Recycle User Accounts

1. Open *Exchange admin center* and navigate to the *mailboxes* link.
2. Select the accounts to be deleted, and delete them by clicking the **Delete** button and selecting **Delete** (Figure A-4).

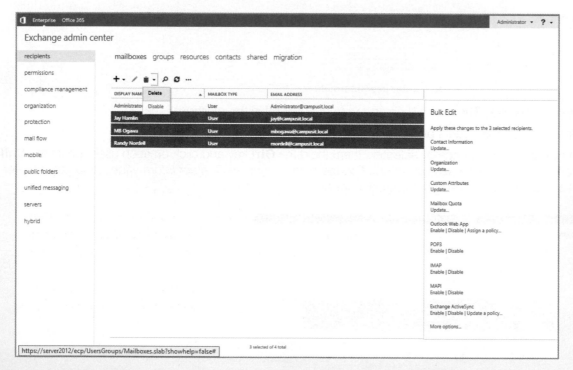

A-4 Delete multiple accounts

3. Follow the steps previously outlined in the *Create User Accounts* section to re-create the new set of user accounts.

Although this might seem like a daunting process, it actually only takes about 15 minutes. Most likely this process will be done by the person who manages the Exchange server at your institution. This person can easily set up a separate domain for the class Exchange server.

Online Course

When teaching an Outlook course in an online environment, there will be some decisions that need to be made by the instructor. The following are some issues to think about before setting up your course, and some suggestions to help make your online course as effective as possible.

Email

One of the major issues of teaching Outlook online is email accounts. Do students use their personal email accounts, school accounts, or new email accounts? Contacts are another issue. How do students obtain the contact information for other students in the course?

There are a couple of reasons why it is probably not a good idea to have students use their personal email accounts for a course such as this. Students will be interacting via email with others in the course. They do not necessarily want all students in the class to have their personal email accounts. Also, there will be a large volume of emails being sent and received in this class. It will be much better if class emails are not intermingled with personal emails.

Below are a couple of suggestions:

- **Generic Email Accounts:** You can set up generic email accounts for your class using one of the free email services such as Gmail or Microsoft Outlook Mail. You could use a generic format such as ARC-Student1@outlook.com or ARC-Student2@outlook.com. At the end of the semester, you could recycle these accounts by deleting all emails and changing passwords.

    At the beginning of the semester, each student would be given an email account and a list of the email addresses for other students and the professor in the class. Students would type in the email addresses of other students and the professor. Contacts are covered in Chapter 3.

- **Student-Created Email Accounts:** Students could create a new email account to be used specifically for this course. These email addresses could then be sent to the professor. A list of email addresses could then be created and distributed to all students in the class.

- **School-Created Email Accounts:** Many schools provide email accounts for students. Depending on the type of account, it is possible that these accounts can be set up and used in Outlook. If these school-created accounts are either POP3 or IMAP accounts, they can be set up in Outlook.

    It would still be a good idea to have the email administrator set up a unique set of student accounts that can be used specifically for this course. These accounts could then be recycled each semester.

In Chapter 7, students will be adding an additional account. At this point, they will create a new account and share their email addresses with other classmates. They will have enough knowledge of email and contacts to easily get this new information to others in the class, without the professor having to handle this administrative task.

Using SimNet

One of the difficulties of teaching an Outlook course in an online environment is that students are not on a common Exchange server. Also, students will not be able to experience all the benefits of using Outlook in conjunction with an Exchange server.

For an online course, using this text in conjunction with *SimNet,* which will allow you to create lessons and tests that can be used with the students, is recommended. The features that are unique to using Outlook in an Exchange environment can be covered in SimNet. Appendix D lists many of the features that are unique to Outlook in an Exchange environment.

Screen Shots

Many of the topics covered in this text, such as Calendar, Notes, Journal, and user interface, will not require students to send emails. The instructor might require students to take screen shots (**Ctrl+Print Screen**) or use the Snipping Tool in Windows 8. These screen shots could then be pasted into a Word document, saved, and submitted as an attachment to an email. If students are using Microsoft Office 2010 or later, they can insert a screen shot from the *Insert* tab.

Outlook Keyboard Shortcuts

Global Outlook Commands

Activity	Shortcut
Go to Mail	Ctrl+1
Go to Calendar	Ctrl+2
Go to Contacts	Ctrl+3
Go to Tasks	Ctrl+4
Go to Notes	Ctrl+5
Go to Folder List	Ctrl+6
Go to Shortcuts	Ctrl+7
Go to Journal	Ctrl+8
New item	Ctrl+N
New email message	Ctrl+Shift+M
New calendar appointment	Ctrl+Shift+A
New meeting request	Ctrl+Shift+Q
New contact	Ctrl+Shift+C
New contact group	Ctrl+Shift+L
New task	Ctrl+Shift+K
New task request	Ctrl+Alt+Shift+U
New note	Ctrl+Shift+N
New folder	Ctrl+Shift+E
Save	Ctrl+S
Save as	F12
Move item	Ctrl+Shift+V
Print	Ctrl+P
Open	Ctrl+O
Close an open Outlook item or dialog box	Esc or Alt+F4
Copy	Ctrl+C
Cut	Ctrl+X
Paste	Ctrl+V
Undo	Ctrl+Z
Bold	Ctrl+B
Italicize	Ctrl+I
Underline	Ctrl+U
Select all	Ctrl+A

Activity	Shortcut
Select range of items	Shift+click on first and last item in range
Select nonadjacent items	Ctrl+click
Help	F1
Search	F3 or Ctrl+E
Advanced find	Ctrl+Shift+F
Open Address Book	Ctrl+Shift+B
Switch between panes	F6
Activate *Ribbon*/menu	F10
Send/receive all folders	F9
Move forward one field	Tab
Move back one field	Shift+Tab
Repeat command or typing	Ctrl+Y
Forward selected item	Ctrl+F
Delete selected item	Ctrl+D

Mail

Activity	Shortcut
Go to Mail	Ctrl+1
New email message	Ctrl+N
New email message (anywhere in Outlook)	Ctrl+Shift+M
Open selected email	Ctrl+O
Close an open email	Esc or Alt+F4
Reply	Ctrl+R
Reply all	Ctrl+Shift+R
Reply with meeting	Ctrl+Alt+R
Forward	Ctrl+F
Forward email as an attachment	Ctrl+Alt+F
Send	Alt+S
Mark as read	Ctrl+Q
Mark as unread	Ctrl+U
New mail folder	Ctrl+Shift+E
Delete selected email or folder	Ctrl+D
Ignore conversation	Ctrl+Delete
Clean up conversation	Alt+Delete
Display Address Book	Ctrl+Shift+B

Calendar

Activity	Shortcut
Go to Calendar	Ctrl+2
New appointment	Ctrl+N
New appointment (anywhere in Outlook)	Ctrl+Shift+A
New meeting request	Ctrl+Shift+Q
Open selected calendar item	Ctrl+O
Close an open calendar item	Esc or Alt+F4
Forward calendar item	Ctrl+F
Open *Recurrence* dialog box	Ctrl+G
Create new calendar	Ctrl+Shift+E
Delete selected calendar item or calendar	Ctrl+D
Display calendar in *Day* view	Ctrl+Alt+1
Display calendar in *Work Week* view	Ctrl+Alt+2
Display calendar in *Week* view	Ctrl+Alt+3
Display calendar in *Month* view	Ctrl+Alt+4
Display calendar in *Schedule* view	Ctrl+Alt+5

Contacts

Activity	Shortcut
Go to Contacts	Ctrl+3
New contact	Ctrl+N
New contact (anywhere in Outlook)	Ctrl+Shift+C
New contact group	Ctrl+Shift+L
Open selected contact	Ctrl+O
Close an open contact	Esc or Alt+F4
Open Address Book	Ctrl+Shift+B
New contact folder	Ctrl+Shift+E
Forward contact as a business card	Ctrl+F
Delete selected contact or folder	Ctrl+D

Tasks

Activity	Shortcut
Go to Tasks	Ctrl+4
New task	Ctrl+N
New task (anywhere in Outlook)	Ctrl+Shift+K
New task request	Ctrl+Alt+Shift+U
Open selected task	Ctrl+O
Close an open task	Esc or Alt+F4
Open *Recurrence* dialog box	Ctrl+G
New task folder	Ctrl+Shift+E
Delete selected contact or folder	Ctrl+D

Notes

Activity	Shortcut
Go to Notes	Ctrl+5
New note	Ctrl+N
New note (anywhere in Outlook)	Ctrl+Shift+N
Open selected note	Ctrl+O
Close an open note	Esc or Alt+F4
Forward note	Ctrl+F
New note folder	Ctrl+Shift+E
Delete selected note or folder	Ctrl+D

Journal

Activity	Shortcut
Go to Journal	Ctrl+8
New journal entry	Ctrl+N
Open selected journal	Ctrl+O
Close an open journal	Esc or Alt+F4
Forward journal	Ctrl+F
Open Address Book	Ctrl+Shift+B
New journal folder	Ctrl+Shift+E
Delete selected journal or folder	Ctrl+D

Formatting

Activity	Shortcut
Copy	Ctrl+C
Cut	Ctrl+X
Paste	Ctrl+V
Undo	Ctrl+Z
Select all	Ctrl+A
Bold	Ctrl+B
Italicize	Ctrl+I
Underline	Ctrl+U
Align left	Ctrl+L
Align center	Ctrl+E
Align right	Ctrl+R
Align justified	Ctrl+J
Add bullet	Ctrl+Shift+L
Insert hyperlink	Ctrl+K
Increase indent	Ctrl+M
Decrease indent	Ctrl+Shift+M
Increase font size	Ctrl+> (Ctrl+Shift+.)
Decrease font size	Ctrl+< (Ctrl+Shift+,)
Clear all formatting	Ctrl+spacebar

Outlook Quick Reference Guide

Global Outlook Features

Task	Action	Alternative Method	Keyboard Shortcut
Advanced Find	Click in the *Search* box above the *Folder* pane • Search *Ribbon* • *Options* group • *Search Tools* button • *Advanced Find*		**Ctrl+Shift+F**
Archive, folder settings	Select folder • *Folder Ribbon* • *Properties* group • *AutoArchive Settings*	Right-click on folder • *Properties* • *AutoArchive* tab	
Archive, global settings	*File* tab • *Options* • *Advanced* • *AutoArchive Settings*		
Categories, assign	With Outlook item open • *Tags* group • *Categorize* button • select category	In list view, right-click on the *Category* column • select category	
Categories, create new	*Home* tab • *Tags* group • *Categorize* button • *All Categories*	Open Outlook item • *Tags* group • *Categorize* button • *All Categories*	
Categories, set *Quick Click*	*Home* tab • *Tags* group • *Categorize* button • Set *Quick Click*	*File* tab • *Options* • *Advanced* • *Other* section • *Quick Click*	
Delegate, assign	*File* tab • *Account Settings* • *Delegate Access* • *Add*		
Delegate, edit permissions	*File* tab • *Account Settings* • *Delegate Settings* • select delegate • *Permissions*		
Delegate, remove	*File* tab • *Account Access* • Delegate access • *Remove*		
Email account, create new	*File* tab • *Add Account*	*File* tab • *Account Settings* • *Account Settings* • *New*	
Email account, edit	*File* tab • *Account Settings* • *Account Settings* • *Change*		
Empty Deleted Items, manually	Click on *Deleted Items* folder in the *Navigation* pane • *Folder Ribbon* • *Clean Up* group • Empty *Folder* button	Right-click on *Deleted Items* folder • *Empty Folder*	
Empty Deleted Items upon exiting, default setting	*File* tab • *Options* • *Advanced* • Empty *Deleted Items* folder when exiting Outlook		
Export Outlook data file	*File* tab • *Options* • *Advanced* • *Export* • Export to a file • Outlook Data File (*.pst*)		
Folder, create new	*Folder Ribbon* • *New* group • *New Folder* button	In the *Navigation* pane, right-click on folder in which the new folder will be created • *New Folder*	**Ctrl+Shift+E**

Task	Action	Alternative Method	Keyboard Shortcut
Folder, delete	*Folder Ribbon* • *Actions* group • *Delete Folder* button	In the *Navigation* pane, right-click on folder to be deleted • *Delete Folder*	**Ctrl+D**
Folder, move	*Folder Ribbon* • *Actions* group • *Move Folder* button	In the *Navigation* pane, drag the folder to the desired location in the list of folders	
Folder, rename	*Folder Ribbon* • *Actions* group • *Rename Folder* button	In the *Navigation* pane, right-click on folder to be renamed • *Rename Folder*	
Import Outlook data file	*File* tab • *Open* • *Import* • Import from another program or file • Outlook Data File (*.pst*)		
Instant Search	Click in the *Search* box above the *Folder* pane		**Ctrl+E**
Modifying views	*View Ribbon* • *Current View* group • *Change View* button • *Manage Views*		
Navigation buttons	*More* (. . .) button • *Navigation Pane Options*		
Navigation pane options	*Configure Buttons* • *Navigation Pane Options*	*File* tab • *Options* • *Advanced* • *Outlook Panes* section • *Navigation* pane	
Outlook Today, customize	Click on *Mailbox* folder • *Customize Outlook Today*		
Outlook Today, default start window	*File* tab • *Options* • *Advanced* • Start Outlook in this folder	Click on *Mailbox* folder • *Customize Outlook Today* • check *When starting, go directly to Outlook Today*	
Quick Access toolbar, customize	Click on *Customize Quick Access Toolbar* button • *More Commands*	*File* tab • *Options* • *Quick Access Toolbar*	
Reading pane	*View Ribbon* • *Layout* group • *Reading Pane* button		
Ribbon, customize	*File* tab • *Options* • Customize Ribbon	Right-click on a *Ribbon* or tab • *Customize the Ribbon*	
Security settings	*File* tab • *Options* • *Trust Center* • *Trust Center Settings*		
Shortcut, create new	Click on *Shortcuts* button in *Navigation* pane • *Folder Ribbon* • *New* group • *New Shortcut*	Click on *Shortcuts* button in *Navigation* pane • Right-click on *Shortcuts* • *New Shortcut*	
Shortcut, delete	Right-click on shortcut • Delete shortcut		
Shortcut group, create new	Right-click on *Shortcuts* • *New Shortcut Group*		
Shortcut group, delete	Right-click on *Shortcuts* • *Delete Group*		

Task	Action	Alternative Method	Keyboard Shortcut
View, add columns (in list views only)	*View Ribbon • Arrangement* group • *Add Columns* button	Right-click on column heading in the *Folder* pane • *Field Chooser*	
View, custom view	*View Ribbon • Current View* group • *Change View* button • *Manage Views • New*		
View, modify	*View Ribbon • Current View* group • *View Settings* button	*View Ribbon • Current View* group • *Change View* button • *Manage Views • Modify*	
View, show in groups	*View Ribbon • Arrangement* group • *More* button • *Show in Groups*	*View Ribbon • View* group • *View Settings* button • *Group By*	
View, sorting	Click on column header to sort by column • click to toggle between ascending and descending sort	*View Ribbon • Current View* group • *View Settings* button • *Sort*	

Mail

The context of most of these commands is with a new email open, or replying to or forwarding an email.

Task	Action	Alternative Method	Keyboard Shortcut
Attach, file	*Message Ribbon • Include* group • *Attach File* button	*Insert Ribbon • Include* group • *Attach File* button	
Attachment, preview	Click on attachment • Attachment will be displayed in body of message		
Attachment, print	Click on attachment • *Attachment Ribbon • Actions* group • *Quick Print*	Right-click on attachment • *Quick Print*	
Attachment, save	Click on attachment • *Attachment Ribbon • Actions* group • *Save As*	Right-click on attachment • *Save As*	
Attach, Outlook item	*Message Ribbon • Include* group • *Attach Item* button • *Other Outlook* item	*Insert Ribbon • Include* group • *Outlook Item* button	
Bcc	*Options* tab • *Show Fields* group • *Bcc*	*To* button • *Bcc*	
Category	Select email in *Folder* pane • *Home Ribbon • Tags* group • *Categorize*	Right-click on email in *Folder* pane • *Categorize*	
Change email format, default setting	*File* tab • *Options • Mail •* Compose message in this format		
Change email format, individual email	*Format Ribbon • Format Text* group • select format		
Delay Delivery	*Options Ribbon • More Options* group • *Delay Delivery* button		
Delete email	*Home* or *Message Ribbon • Delete* group • *Delete* button	Right-click on email in *Folder* pane • *Delete*	**Ctrl+D**

Task	Action	Alternative Method	Keyboard Shortcut
Delivery Receipt	*Options Ribbon* • *Tracking* group • Request a delivery receipt	*Message Ribbon* • *Tags* group • *Expand* button • Request a delivery receipt for this message	
Desktop Alert settings	*File* tab • *Options* • *Mail* • *Message arrival* area • *Desktop Alert* settings		
Direct Replies To	*Options Ribbon* • *More Options* group • *Direct Replies To*	*Message Ribbon* • *Tags* group • *Expand* button • *Have replies sent to*	
Email account, set default	*File* tab • *Account Settings* button • *Account Settings* • select account • *Set as Default*		
Email, change default delivery folder	*File* tab • *Account Settings* button • *Account Settings* • select account • *Change Folder*		
Email, options	*File* tab • *Options* • *Mail*		
Email, send through different account	Create new email or choose *Reply, Reply All,* or *Forward* on existing email • *From* button • Select account		
Expiration date/ time on email	*Message Ribbon* • *Tags* group • *Expand* button • *Expires after*	*Options Ribbon* • *More Options* group • *Expand* button • *Expires after*	
Favorites, add folder	Select folder to add to *Favorites* • *Folder Ribbon* • *Favorites* group • *Show in Favorites*	Right-click folder to add to *Favorites* • *Show in Favorites*	
Favorites, remove folder	Select folder to remove from *Favorites* • *Folder Ribbon* • *Favorites* group • *Show in Favorites*	Right-click folder to remove from *Favorites* • *Show in Favorites*	
Flag for Recipients	*Message Ribbon* • *Tags* group • *Follow Up* button • *Custom* • *Flag for Recipients*		
Follow Up flag	*Message Ribbon* • *Tags* group • *Follow Up*		
Font, default	*File* tab • *Options* • *Mail* • *Stationery and Fonts* • *Personal Stationery* tab		
Format text	*Message Ribbon* • *Basic Text* group	*Format Text Ribbon*	
Forward email as attachment	*Home* or *Message Ribbon* • *Respond* group • *More* button • *Forward as Attachment*		**Ctrl+Alt+F**
Importance	*Message Ribbon* • *Tags* group • *High Importance*	Click on *Expand* button in *Tags* group • *Importance*	
Junk email, block sender	Select email to be blocked • *Home Ribbon* • *Delete* group • *Junk* button • *Block Sender*	Open email to be blocked • *Message Ribbon* • *Delete* group • *Junk* button • *Block Sender*	
Junk email, manage lists	*Home Ribbon* • *Delete* group • *Junk* button • *Junk Email Options* • choose list to manage	Open email • *Message Ribbon* • *Delete* group • *Junk* button • *Junk Email Options* • choose list to manage	

Task	Action	Alternative Method	Keyboard Shortcut
Junk email, never block sender or sender's domain	Select email • *Home Ribbon* • *Delete* group • *Junk* button • *Never Block Sender* or *Never Block Sender's Domain*	Open email • *Message Ribbon* • *Delete* group • *Junk* button • *Never Block Sender* or *Never Block Sender's Domain*	
Junk email, options	*Home Ribbon* • *Delete* group • *Junk* button • *Junk Email Options*		
Mark email as unread/read	Click on email in *Folder* pane • *Home Ribbon* • *Tags* group • *Unread/read* button	Right-click on email in *Folder* pane • *Mark as Unread/read*	**Ctrl+U (mark as unread)** **Ctrl+Q (mark as read)**
Out of Office Assistant	*File* tab • *Automatic replies (Out of Office)*		
Print email	*File* tab • *Print*	*Quick Print* button on *Quick Access* toolbar	**Ctrl+P**
Quick Steps, create new	*Home Ribbon* • *Quick Steps* group • *Create New*	*Home Ribbon* • *Quick Steps* group • *More* button • *New Quick Step*	
Quick Steps, manage	*Home Ribbon* • *Quick Steps* group • *More* button • *Manage Quick Step*		
Quick Steps, use existing	*Home Ribbon* • *Quick Steps* group • select *Quick Step* to use		
Read reccipt	*Options Ribbon* • *Tracking* group • *Request a Read Receipt*	*Message Ribbon* • *Tags* group • *Expand* button • Request a read receipt for this message	
Recall sent message	*Sent Items* folder • Open email to be recalled • *Message Ribbon* • *Move* group • *Actions* button • *Recall This Message*	*Sent Items* folder • Open email to be recalled • *File* tab • *Recall* or *Resend* button • *Recall This Message*	
Reminder	*Message Ribbon* • *Tags* group • *Follow Up* • *Add Reminder*	Right-click on email in *Folder* pane • *Follow Up* • *Add Reminder*	
Resend sent message	*Sent Items* folder • Open email to be recalled • *Message Ribbon* • *Move* group • *Actions* button • *Resend This Message*	*Sent Items* folder • Open email to be recalled • *File* tab • *Recall* or *Resend* button • *Resend This Message*	
RSS feed, delete	*File* tab • *Account Settings* button • *Account Settings* • *RSS Feed* tab • select RSS feed • *Remove*	Right-click on RSS feed folder to delete • *Delete Folder*	**Select RSS feed folder to delete • Ctrl+D**
RSS feed, share	Open an existing RSS feed email • *RSS Article Ribbon* • *RSS* group • *Share This Feed*	Right-click on an RSS feed email • Share this feed	
RSS feed, subscribe	*File* tab • *Account Settings* button • *Account Settings* • *RSS Feeds* tab • *New*	In the *Navigation* pane, right-click on the RSS Feeds folder • Add a New RSS Feed	
Rules, create	*Home Ribbon* • *Move* group • *Rules* button • *Manage Rules & Alerts* • *New Rule*	Right-click on email message • *Rules* • *Create Rule*	

Task	Action	Alternative Method	Keyboard Shortcut
Rules, delete	*Home Ribbon* • *Move* group • *Rules* button • *Manage Rules & Alerts* • select rule • *Delete*		
Rules, edit	*Home Ribbon* • *Move* group • *Rules* button • *Manage Rules & Alerts* • select rule • *Change Rule* • *Edit Rule Settings*	*Home Ribbon* • *Move* group • *Rules* button • *Manage Rules & Alerts* • double-click on rule	
Rules, order	*Home Ribbon* • *Move* group • *Rules* button • *Manage Rules & Alerts* • select rule • *Move Up* or *Move Down* button		
Rules, run now	*Folder Ribbon* • *Clean Up* group • *Run Rules Now* button • select rules to run • *Run Now*	*Home Ribbon* • *Actions* group • *Rules* button • *Manage Rules & Alerts* •*Run Rules Now* button • select rules to run • *Run Now*	
Rules, turn on/off	*Home Ribbon* • *Move* group • *Rules* button • *Manage Rules & Alerts* • select rule • select or deselect check box		
Save email, draft	*Save* button on *Quick Access* toolbar	*File* tab • *Save*	**Ctrl+S**
Save email, outside of Outlook	*File* tab • *Save As*		**F12**
Save Sent Item To	*Options Ribbon* • *More Options* group • *Save Sent Items To* button • *Other Folder*		
Search folder, create new	*Folder Ribbon* • *New* group • *New Search Folder*	Right-click on *Search Folders* • *New Search Folder*	**Ctrl+Shift+P**
Search folder, customize	Select search folder • *Folder Ribbon* • *Actions* group • *Customize This Search Folder*		
Search folder, delete	Select search folder • *Folder Ribbon* • *Actions* group • *Delete Folder*	Right-click on search folder • *Delete Folder*	**Ctrl+D**
Security	*Message Ribbon* • *Tags* group • *Expand* button • *Security Settings*		
Sensitivity	*Message Ribbon* • *Tags* group • *Expand* button • *Sensitivity*	*Options Ribbon* • *More Options* group • *Expand* button • *Sensitivity*	
Signature, create	*File* tab • *Options* • *Mail* • *Signatures* • *New*	*Message Ribbon* • *Include* group • *Signature* button • *Signatures*	
Signature, default	*File* tab • *Options* • *Mail* • *Signatures* • set default signature account and type	Open email • *Message Ribbon* • *Include* group • *Signatures* button • *Signatures* • set default signature account and type	
Signature, insert	*Message Ribbon* • *Include* group • *Signatures* button • select signature	*Insert Ribbon* • *Include* group • *Signatures* button • select signature	

Task	Action	Alternative Method	Keyboard Shortcut
Theme, individual email	*Options Ribbon* • *Themes* group • *Themes* button		
Theme, set default	*File* tab • *Options* • *Mail* • *Stationery and Fonts* • *Theme*		
Voting buttons, custom	*Options Ribbon* • *Tracking* group • *Use Voting Buttons* button • *Custom*	*Message Ribbon* • *Tags* group • *Expand* button • *Use voting buttons* checkbox • type voting buttons separated by a semicolon	
Voting buttons, preset	*Options Ribbon* • *Tracking* group • *Use Voting Buttons* button • select preset voting buttons	*Message Ribbon* • *Tags* group • *Expand* button • *Use voting buttons* checkbox	
Voting buttons, track responses	Open email with voting response • click on *InfoBar* • View voting responses	Open original email with voting buttons from *Sent Items* folder • *Message Ribbon* • *Show* button • *Tracking*	
Voting buttons, vote	Open email with voting button • *Respond* group • *Vote* button • select response		

Calendar

Task	Action	Alternative Method	Keyboard Shortcut
Add holidays	*File* tab • *Options* • *Calendar* • *Calendar options* area • *Add Holidays*		
Appointment	*Home Ribbon* • *New* group • *New Appointment* button	Type appointment on calendar in *Day* or *Week* view	**Ctrl+N (when in Calendar)** **Ctrl+Shift+A (anywhere in Outlook)**
Attach business card to calendar item	Open new or existing calendar item • *Insert Ribbon* • *Include* group • *Business Card* • *Other Business Cards*		
Attach file to calendar item	Open new or existing calendar item • *Insert Ribbon* • *Include* group • *Attach File*		
Attach Outlook item to calendar item	**Open new or existing calendar item** • *Insert Ribbon* • *Include* group • *Outlook Item*		
AutoPick meeting times	Open new or existing meeting request • *Meeting Ribbon* • *Show* group • *Scheduling Assistant* button • *Options* button • *AutoPick Next*		
Calendar, create new calendar folder	*Folder Ribbon* • *New* group • *New Calendar* button	Right-click on the *Calendar* folder in the *Navigation* pane • *New Calendar*	**Ctrl+Shift+E**

Task	Action	Alternative Method	Keyboard Shortcut
Calendar item, copy	Select calendar item • hold down **Ctrl** key • drag to new location		**Ctrl+C (copy)** **Ctrl+V (paste)**
Calendar item, delete	Select calendar item • *Actions* group • *Delete* button	Open existing calendar item • *Appointment, Event,* or *Meeting Ribbon* • *Actions* group • *Delete* button	**Ctrl+D**
Calendar item, move	Open calendar item • change start and end times • *Save & Close*	Drag the calendar item to new location on the calendar	**Ctrl+X (cut)** **Ctrl+V (paste)**
Calendar view, *Day*	*Home Ribbon* • *Arrangement* group • *Day View* button	*View Ribbon* • *Arrangement* group • *Day View* button	**Ctrl+Alt+1**
Calendar view, *Month*	*Home Ribbon* • *Arrangement* group • *Month View* button	*View Ribbon* • *Arrangement* group • *Month View* button	**Ctrl+Alt+4**
Calendar view, other views	*View Ribbon* • *Current View* group • *Change View* button • select view		
Calendar view, *Schedule*	*Home Ribbon* • *Arrange* group • *Schedule View* button	*View Ribbon* • *Arrangement* group • *Schedule View* button	
Calendar view, *Week*	*Home Ribbon* • *Arrange* group • *Week View* button	*View Ribbon* • *Arrangement* group • *Week View* button	**Ctrl+Alt+3**
Calendar view, *Work Week*	*Home Ribbon* • *Arrange* group • *Work Week View* button	*View Ribbon* • *Arrangement* group • *Work Week View* button	**Ctrl+Alt+2**
Convert email to calendar item	Select email • *Home Ribbon* • *Quick Steps* • *Create Appointment*	Drag email to *Calendar* button	
Event	*Home Ribbon* • *New* group • *New Appointment* button • *All day event*	Type event on calendar in *Event* area of *Day, Week,* or *Month* view	
Forward calendar item	Select calendar item • *Appointment Ribbon* • *Actions* group • *Forward* button	Open calendar item • *Appointment, Event,* or *Meeting Ribbon* • *Actions* group • *Forward* button	**Ctrl+F**
Forward calendar item, as iCalendar	Select calendar item • *Appointment Ribbon* • *Actions* group • small arrow below the *Forward* button • *Forward as iCalendar*	Open calendar item • *Appointment, Event,* or *Meeting Ribbon* • *Actions* group • small arrow to the right of the *Forward* button • *Forward as iCalendar*	
Meeting, create	*Home Ribbon* • *New* group • *New Meeting* button	Open existing appointment or create new appointment • *Appointment Ribbon* • *Attendees* group • *Invite Attendees* button	**Ctrl+Shift +Q**

Task	Action	Alternative Method	Keyboard Shortcut
Meeting, respond	Open meeting request email • *Meeting Ribbon* • *Respond* group • select response		
Meeting, track	From your Calendar, open the meeting request you created • *Meeting Ribbon* • *Show* group • *Tracking* button	From your Calendar, open the meeting request you created • tracking summary in the *InfoBar*	
Meeting, update	From your Calendar, open the meeting request you created • *Meeting Ribbon* • make desired changes • *Send Update*		
Print calendar	*File* tab • *Print* • select *Settings* • *Print*	*Print* button on *Quick Access* toolbar	**Ctrl+P**
Private calendar item	Open new or existing calendar item • *Appointment, Event,* or *Meeting Ribbon* • *Tags* group • *Private* button	Right-click on calendar item • *Private*	
Recurring calendar item	Open new or existing calendar item • *Appointment, Event,* or *Meeting Ribbon* • *Options* group • *Recurrence* button	Select calendar item • *Appointment Ribbon* • *Recurrence* button	**Ctrl+G**
Reminder, default settings	*File* tab • *Options* • *Calendar* • *Calendar options* area • *Default reminders*		
Reminder, set	Open calendar item • *Appointment, Event,* or *Meeting Ribbon* • *Options* group • *Reminder*		
Scheduling Assistant, default settings	*File* tab • *Options* • *Calendar* • *Scheduling assistant* area		
Scheduling Assistant, use	Open existing or new calendar item • *Appointment, Event,* or *Meeting Ribbon* • *Show* group • *Scheduling Assistant* button		
Send calendar via email	*Home Ribbon* • *Share* group • *Email Calendar*	Right-click on calendar • *Share* • *Email Calendar*	
Share calendar	*Home Ribbon* • *Share* group • *Share Calendar*	Right-click on calendar • *Share* • *Share Calendar*	
Time zones	*File* tab • *Options* • *Calendar* • *Time zones* area		
Weather bar location	*Location* • *Add Location*		
Work time options	*File* tab • *Options* • *Calendar* • *Work time* area		

Contents

Task	Action	Alternative Method	Keyboard Shortcut
Add multiple email addresses	Open new or existing contact record • click on arrow next to *Email* button • select *Email 2* or *Email 3*		
Change default Address Book	*Home Ribbon* • *Find* group • *Address Book* • *Tools* menu • *Options*		
Change field name	Open new or existing contact record • click on arrow next to field name • select new field name		
Contact, add from Global Address List	Open *Global Address List* • right-click on contact to be added • *Add to Contacts*	Open *Global Address List* • select contact to be added • *File* menu • *Add to Contacts*	
Contact, create new	*Home Ribbon* • *New* group • *New Contact* button		**Ctrl+N (when in Contacts)** **Ctrl+Shift+C (anywhere in Outlook)**
Contact, from received email	With email open or in *Reading* pane, right-click on name or email address • *Add to Outlook Contacts*	With email open or in *Reading* pane, move pointer on name or email address • click on + (plus) button • *Add to Outlook Contacts*	
Contact, new from same company	With existing contact open • *Contact Ribbon* • *Actions* group • small arrow next to the *Save & New* button • *Contact from the Same Company*		
Contact folder, new	*Folder Ribbon* • *New* group • *New Folder* button	Right-click on *Contacts* • *New folder*	**Ctrl+Shift+E**
Contact group, add members	Open new or existing contact group • *Contact Group Ribbon* • *Members* group • *Add Members* button		
Contact group, create new	*Home Ribbon* • *New* group • *New Contact Group*		**Ctrl+Shift+L**
Contact group, delete	Select contact group • *Home Ribbon* • *Delete* group • *Delete* button	Right-click on contact group • *Delete*	**Ctrl+D**
Contact group, remove members	Open new or existing contact group • select members to be removed • *Contact Group Ribbon* • *Members* group • *Remove Member* button	Open new or existing contact group • select members to be removed • *Delete*	
Contact options	*File* tab • *Options* • *Contacts*		
Create mailing labels using Contacts	*Home Ribbon* • *Actions* group • *Mail Merge* button		
Customize business card	Open existing contact • *Contact Ribbon* • *Options* group • *Business Card* button		

Task	Action	Alternative Method	Keyboard Shortcut
Delete contact	Select contact • *Home Ribbon* • *Delete* group • *Delete* button	Right-click on contact • *Delete*	**Ctrl+D**
Export contacts	*File* tab • *Options* • *Advanced* • *Export* • *Export to a file*		
Forward business card	Select contact • *Home Ribbon* • *Share* group • *Forward Contact* • *As a Business Card*	Right-click on contact • *Forward Contact* • *As a Business Card*	**Ctrl+F**
Import contacts	*File* tab • *Open* • *Import* • *Import from another program or file*		
Include business card in signature	*File* tab • *Options* • *Mail* • *Signatures* • *Business Card*		
Map contact address	Open existing contact with address • *Map It* button	Open existing contact with address • *Contact Ribbon* • *Communicate* group • *More* button • *Map It*	
Picture, add	Open new or existing contact • click *Add Contact Picture* button	Open new or existing contact • *Contacts Ribbon* • *Options* group • *Picture* button • *Add Picture*	
Picture, remove	Open new or existing contact • *Contacts Ribbon* • *Options* group • *Picture* button • *Remove Picture*		
Send email to contact	Select contact • *Contact Ribbon* • *Communicate* group • *Email*	Right-click on contact • *Create* • *Email*	

Tasks

Task	Action	Alternative Method	Keyboard Shortcut
Attach file to task	Open new or existing task • *Insert Ribbon* • *Include* group • *Attach File* button		
Attach Outlook item to task	Open new or existing task • *Insert Ribbon* • *Include* group • *Outlook Item* button		
Mark task as complete	Select task • *Home Ribbon* • *Manage Task* group • *Mark Complete*	Right-click on task • *Mark Complete*	
Private	Select task • *Home Ribbon* • *Tags* group • *Private* button	Open new or existing task • *Task Ribbon* • *Tags* group • *Private* button	
Recurring task	Open new or existing task • *Task Ribbon* • *Recurrence* group • *Recurrence* button		**Ctrl+G**
Reminder	Open new or existing task • check *Reminder* • set reminder date and time	Select task • *Home Ribbon* • *Follow Up* group • *Custom* button • *Reminder*	

Task	Action	Alternative Method	Keyboard Shortcut
Task, create new	*Home Ribbon* • *New* group • *New Task* button		**Ctrl+N (when in Tasks)** **Ctrl+Shift+K (anywhere in Outlook)**
Task, delete	Select task • *Home Ribbon* • *Delete* group • *Delete* button	Right-click on task • *Delete*	**Ctrl+D**
Task, new from email	Drag email to *Tasks* button	Select email • *Home Ribbon* • *Move* group • *Move* button • *Copy to Folder* • *Tasks*	
Task options	*File* tab • *Options* • *Tasks*		
Task request, accept	Open task request email • *Task Ribbon* • *Respond* group • *Accept*		
Task request, assign	Open new or existing task • *Task Ribbon* • *Manage Task* group • *Assign Task* button	Right-click on task • *Assign Task*	
Task request, create new	*Home Ribbon* • *New* group • *New Items* button • *Task Request*	Open new task • *Task Ribbon* • *Manage Task* group • *Assign Task* button	**Ctrl+Alt+ Shift+U**
Task request, mark complete	Select an accepted task • *Home Ribbon* • *Manage Task* group • *Mark Complete*	Right-click on accepted task • *Mark Complete*	
Task request, send status report	Open an accepted task • *Task Ribbon* • *Manage Task* group • *Send Status Report*		
To-Do bar, view	*View Ribbon* • *Layout* group • *To-Do bar* button • select options	Click the X next to each option to remove it from the *To-Do bar*	

Notes and Journal

Task	Action	Alternative Method	Keyboard Shortcut
Journal, manually record	*Home Ribbon* • *New* group • *Journal Entry*		**Ctrl+N (when in Journal)** **Ctrl+Shift+J (anywhere in Outlook)**
Note, create new	*Home Ribbon* • *New* group • *New Note*		**Ctrl+N (when in Notes)** **Ctrl+Shift+N (anywhere in Outlook)**
Note, delete	Select note to be deleted • *Home Ribbon* • *Delete* group • *Delete* button	Right-click on note to be deleted • *Delete*	**Ctrl+D**
Note, edit	Double-click on note • make editing changes		**Ctrl+O**
Note, forward	Select note • *Home Ribbon* • *Actions* group • *Forward* button	Right-click on note • *Forward*	**Ctrl+F**

Exchange Server versus Stand-Alone Usage

Outlook Features Available When on an Exchange Server

Some features of Outlook are available only when it is operating within an Exchange environment. Microsoft Exchange, on a business network, handles all the incoming and outgoing mail. Each individual user of Exchange is actually a client of this Exchange network, and the network administrator sets up an account for each individual user. In addition to handling email, Exchange also stores all the data associated with calendars, contacts, tasks, notes, and journals. All this information is stored on the Exchange server.

Outlook in an Exchange environment has the same user interface as in a stand-alone environment, but Outlook with an Exchange server does allow you more functionality.

Global Address List

The Global Address List (Figure D-1) is the list of Outlook contact records of all the employees in an organization. If an organization is using an Exchange server, each individual in the organization has a unique email address. This email address, as well as other contact information such as title, department, and phone, is stored in the *Global Address List*. It usually includes contact groups as well. The *Global Address List* is maintained by the person who is responsible for maintaining the Exchange server.

Contact records that you use frequently can be added from the *Global Address List* to your *Contacts* folder.

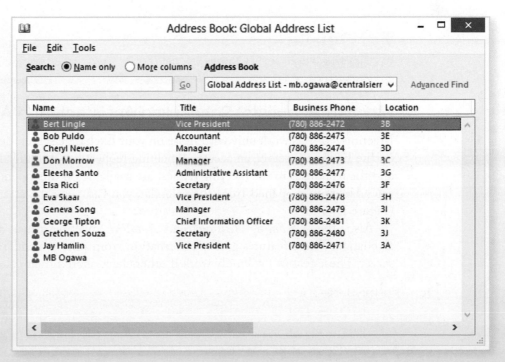

D-1 *Global Address List*

> **MORE INFO**
>
> *The Global Address List* is covered in Chapters 3 and 8.

Tracking

Outlook can track the responses to meeting requests, task requests, and emails with voting buttons (Figure D-2). When you recall an email message, Outlook will also track whether or not the recall succeeded or failed. When you use one of these tasks in Outlook, you will be provided with a summary of responses to voting buttons, meeting requests, task requests, or success and failures of email recalls. Tracking is a very powerful tool and is unique to using Outlook on an Exchange server.

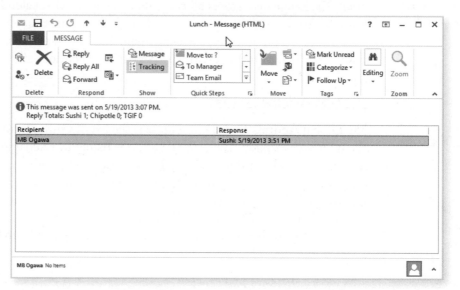

D-2 Track responses

> **MORE INFO**
>
> Tracking is discussed in Chapters 2, 4, and 7.

Meeting Requests, Scheduling Assistant, and AutoPick

Meeting requests work only with those on your Exchange server. Because calendars are stored on the Exchange server, an accepted meeting request is automatically saved on your calendar, and the responses to the meeting request are available on this calendar item. When a meeting calendar item is opened from the calendar, you can view the attendees and their responses (Figure D-3).

Also, the *Scheduling Assistant* and *AutoPick* meeting times are available when using Exchange. These features gather information from other calendars stored on the Exchange server. These features will only work if others have shared their calendar with you.

> **MORE INFO**
>
> *Meeting Requests* are covered in Chapter 4, and sharing calendars, the *Scheduling Assistant,* and *AutoPick* are discussed in Chapter 9.

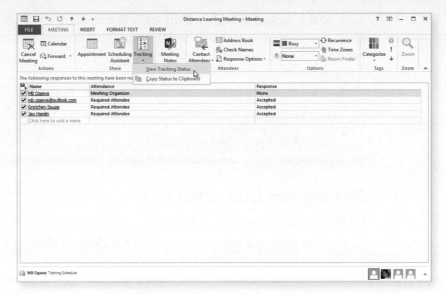

D-3 Track meeting responses

Task Requests

When a task request is sent to another user on your Exchange system and that task is accepted, it is recorded in your Tasks. You will see a different task icon displayed in the *Task List* to indicate that a task has been assigned and accepted. When an assigned task has been completed, the originator of the task will receive a message and the task will automatically be marked as complete (Figure D-4).

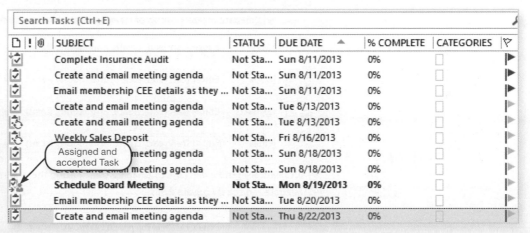

D-4 Track tasks

> **MORE INFO**
>
> Task requests are covered in Chapter 5.

Voting Buttons

Using voting buttons on an email is a great way to get information from others. If you wanted to find out the restaurant preference for the members of your team, you could set up voting buttons with three choices of restaurants from which they could choose. The benefit of using voting buttons as opposed to having recipients just type their selections in the body of the messages is that Outlook will consolidate the voting results for you (see Figure D-2). For voting buttons to work properly, the recipients must be using Outlook on an Exchange server.

▶ MORE INFO

Voting buttons are covered in Chapter 2.

Sharing and Delegates

One of the advantages of using Outlook in conjunction with an Exchange server is the ability to share different parts of your Outlook (Mail, Calendar, Contacts, Tasks, etc.) with others on your Exchange system (Figure D-5). Since your Outlook information is stored on an Exchange server, you can allow others to access your Outlook information and control the amount of access they have by setting the permission level. This feature is particularly helpful for scheduling meetings and appointments. When you have access to view others' calendars, you can open a shared calendar in your Outlook to view available times and dates. Sharing and delegate permissions work in all areas of Outlook.

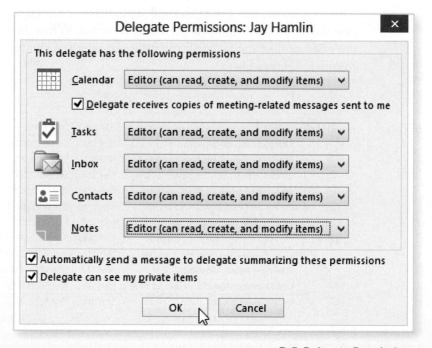

D-5 *Delegate Permissions*

▶ MORE INFO

Sharing calendars and delegates are covered in Chapter 9.

Outlook Web Access

If you have an email account at work, most likely it is set up on an Exchange server. If so, then you most likely have access to your email and other Outlook information through the Internet on Outlook Web Access (OWA).

If you are on a business trip, working from home, or away from your office computer, you can still access your Exchange mailbox by using OWA (Figure D-6). You can connect to OWA through the Internet and a web browser. You can log into your OWA account with your user name and password. The information stored on the Exchange server is available to you in OWA.

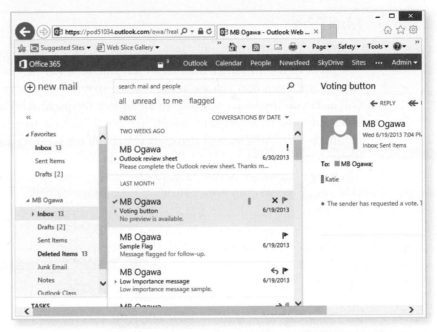

D-6 Outlook Web Access

> **MORE INFO**
>
> Outlook Web Access is discussed in Chapter 7.

Out of Office Assistant

The *Out of Office Assistant* is available when using Outlook in a stand-alone environment. But you are given additional *Out of Office options* when using Outlook in an Exchange environment. You can set up your *Out of Office* replies to those inside of your organization (on the same Exchange server) and those outside of your organization (Figure D-7). You can set up a different message and different criteria for these two groups.

D-7 Automatic Replies

▶ MORE INFO

The *Out of Office Assistant* is covered in Chapter 7.

MailTips

MailTips alert the Outlook user to potential issues with an email to be sent. For example, if you press *Reply All* rather than *Reply* and the recipient list is large, *MailTips* will provide an alert to warn you that you are about to send an email to a large number of recipients. *MailTips* will alert you if you are sending an email to a recipient who is out of the office, to an invalid email address, to a recipient whose mailbox is full, or to a recipient who is outside of your organization. *MailTips* will also alert you if you are sending an attachment that is too large or if the attachment is too large for the recipient. *MailTips* will only work in conjunction with Microsoft Exchange Server (Figure D-8).

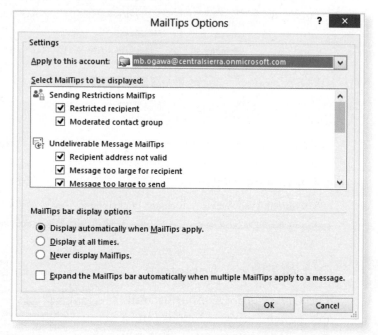

D-8 *MailTips Options*

▶ MORE INFO

MailTips are covered in Chapter 7.

Quick Tips and Troubleshooting

Email Accounts: Outlook provides you with an email account *Setup Wizard* to help you easily set up email accounts. The following are some troubleshooting tips if your email account is not working properly. (Email accounts are discussed in Chapters 1, 2, and 7.)

- **User name and password:** Make sure your user name and password are correct. Typically user names are not case sensitive while passwords are case sensitive.

- **Repair feature:** If your account is not working properly, you might try using the *Repair* feature. In the *Accounts Settings* dialog box, there is a *Repair* button, and Outlook will automatically make account setting changes in an attempt to repair an existing email account.

- **Default account:** If you have multiple email accounts, the first account you create will be your default account. The default account is the account by which new email will be sent. On each email message, you can change the account through which the email is sent. You can also change your default email account in the *Account Settings* dialog box.

Address Books: A common error is confusing or not distinguishing between the *Global Address List* and *Contacts*. (*Contacts*, the *Global Address List*, and address books are covered in Chapters 3 and 8)

- *Global Address List:* The *Global Address List* is only available when you are using Outlook in an Exchange environment. You cannot add to or make changes to the *Global Address List* because this list is maintained by your Exchange server administrator.

- **Contacts folder:** Whether you are using Outlook as a stand-alone program or in an Exchange environment, you will have a *Contacts* folder. The *Contacts* folder is by default the folder in which new contacts are saved. You can add, edit, or delete contacts from this folder.

- **Default address book:** When using Outlook in an Exchange environment, the *Global Address List* is the default address book. You can change the settings to make your *Contacts* folder the default address book (see Chapter 8).

- **Address Book:** When the *Address Book* dialog box is open, you can select the address book to use from the *Address Book* pull-down list.

- **Save contact to a different folder:** By default new contacts will be saved to your *Contacts* folder. To save to a different folder, click the **File** tab to open the *Backstage*, click the **Move to Folder** button, and select the desired folder.

- **Contacts folder not displayed in *Address Book*:** If you have multiple *Contacts* folders, these folders can be made available in your address book by changing the properties of the folders. Right-click on the contacts folder to add to the address book, choose **Properties,** click on the **Outlook Address Book** tab, check **Show the folder as an email Address Book,** and press **OK** to close the dialog box.

Rules—Troubleshooting: See the following for some common errors pertaining to rules and some troubleshooting tips. (Rules are covered in Chapter 6.)

- **Incorrect folder:** Be sure to specify the folder on which the rule is to run. Normally this should be the Inbox, but a common error is having the rule running on a different folder. This will cause the rule to not function as intended.

- **Misspellings and extra spaces:** If the rule is looking for a word or group of words, a misspelled word or an extra space after the last word will cause the rule to not function properly.

- **Deleted folder:** If a *Mail* folder that is referenced in a rule is deleted, Outlook will recognize the error in the rule and the rule will not function properly. An error message will appear when you open the *Rules and Alerts* dialog box, and the rule will be marked as having an error.

- **Run rules after modifying:** After modifying a rule, you must select **Run Rules Now** in order for the rule to run on those items in your Inbox or the folder on which the rule is to run.

Rules—Effectiveness: It is important to create rules that are effective and efficient. See the following tips to increase the effectiveness of your rules. (Rules are covered in Chapter 6.)

- **Keep rules simple.** Rules are most effective when they are simple. The effectiveness of a rule can be diluted if there are too many conditions, actions, and exceptions.

- **Break up a complex rule.** If a rule has multiple conditions, actions, and/or exceptions, try breaking the rule into two or more rules.

- **Ordering rules.** Rules run in the order in which they are listed in the *Rules and Alerts* dialog box. When creating, editing, and managing rules, you must think about the order in which they appear and the conflicts that might occur.

Quick Steps: *Quick Steps* can be used and customized to perform one-click actions on email messages. (*Quick Steps* are covered in Chapter 6.)

- **Using default *Quick Steps:*** Outlook provides a number of preset *Quick Steps.* On some of these *Quick Steps,* you will need to set the criteria of the action. Once the criteria are defined, Outlook will remember and perform the action.

- **Modifying *Quick Steps:*** To modify *Quick Steps,* click on the **More** button in the *Quick Steps* group and choose **Manage Quick Steps.** You can customize an existing *Quick Step* or reset a *Quick Step* to its original default setting. A *Quick Step* can also be modified to perform multiple actions.

- **Creating *Quick Steps:*** A new *Quick Step* can be created, or an existing *Quick Step* can be duplicated and modified.

Voting Buttons: Voting buttons are an excellent way to gather and track responses to a question via email in Outlook. Voting buttons are unique to working with Outlook in an Exchange environment. (Voting buttons are covered in Chapter 2.)

- **Custom voting buttons:** When creating custom voting buttons, be sure to separate each choice with a semicolon.

- **Tracking responses:** You can track voting responses in two ways. After responses have been received, you can open the original email (from the *Sent Items* folder) and click on the **Tracking** button to view the responses. You can also open a voting response received in your Inbox and click on the **InfoBar** to view responses.

- **Voting buttons not working:** Voting buttons will only work consistently within your Exchange server system. If you are sending an email to recipients outside of your Exchange system, the voting buttons will not track properly.

Signatures: Information can be saved as a signature and inserted into an email. Signatures are not limited to name and company information but can include other commonly used information such as a paragraph or multiple paragraphs of text. Signatures can be inserted individually in an email message or default signatures can be set. (Signatures are covered in Chapter 2.)

- **Default signature:** A signature can be set to automatically appear on all new email messages and/or replies and forwards. Default signatures are set in the *Signatures and Stationery* dialog box. Signatures can also be inserted individually in an email message.

- **Different default signatures for different email accounts:** If you are using multiple email accounts in Outlook, you can set up different default signatures for different email accounts. This can be done in the *Signatures and Stationery* dialog box by selecting the email account and then choosing the default signature.

- **Multiple signatures in an email message:** Only one signature can be used in an email message. If you insert a second signature, it will replace the previous signature.

- **Signature appears different:** When a signature is inserted into an email to which you are replying, it might appear different than you created. If the message is a Plain Text message, the signature will appear as plain text without any styles or colors. Also, if the original message to which you are replying has a theme applied, your signature might appear different.

Search Folders: These folders are virtual folders that display email items that meet the criteria of the folder. These folders don't actually contain email messages but rather just display them from other folders. Outlook comes with some preset search folders. (Search folders are covered in Chapter 6.)

- **Customizing a search folder:** You can customize search folders by specifying which folders are to be searched to locate items matching the criteria.

- **Too many items displayed:** A common error is having the search folder look in all your *Mailbox* folders rather than specifying just the Inbox and subordinate folders. It is probably not a good idea to have your search folders look in the *Deleted Items* and *Sent Items* folders.

- **Deleting search folders:** When you delete a search folder, none of the emails displayed in that folder will be deleted because these items being displayed are actually located in a different folder.

- **Deleting email in a search folder:** When you delete an email from within a search folder, the email will be deleted.

HTML Content in Email Messages: Email messages with embedded HTML (Hypertext Markup Language) are becoming more common. Outlook, by default, will block the images in these messages. (HTML content is covered in Chapter 10.)

- **Displaying HTML content:** When an email message with HTML content is received, the images are blocked by Outlook. To display these images, click on the **InfoBar** and choose **Download Pictures.**

- **Add to Safe Sender List:** If a sender is added to your *Safe Sender List* (junk email options), the HTML content will automatically be displayed when you receive an email from this sender.

***Tasks* and *To-Do Lists*:** The *Tasks List* and the *To-Do List* can be confusing at first glance. Each of these lists has a unique purpose in Outlook. (The *Tasks List, To-Do List,* and *To-Do bar* are covered in Chapter 5.)

- ***To-Do List:*** The *To-Do List* is more inclusive than the *Tasks List.* Any Outlook item marked with a flag is included in the *To-Do List.* This list can include email messages, tasks, and contacts.

- ***Tasks List:*** The *Tasks List* only includes tasks. When a task is created, it is automatically marked with a *Follow Up* flag and is included in both the *Tasks* and *To-Do* lists.

- ***To-Do bar:*** The *To-Do bar* provides you with a list of the items in the *To-Do List.* The *To-Do bar* also includes a date navigator and upcoming calendar items.

glossary

A

action What Outlook does when a condition to a rule is met.

Add-Ins Third party software programs that add functionality to Outlook.

address book The collection of names and email addresses from a *Contacts* folder or Global Address List. An address book can be used to populate an email message, meeting request, or task request.

appointment A calendar item that is less than 24 hours in duration.

arrangement The way Outlook items are grouped or sorted for display in the *Folder* pane.

attachment A file or other Outlook item attached to an email message, contact, calendar item, task, or journal.

Auto Account Setup An Outlook feature to automatically detect email account settings and use these settings to create an account in Outlook.

AutoArchive The automatic process of removing older Outlook items and storing them in a separate set of folders in Outlook.

AutoPick An Outlook calendar feature that will pick available meeting times.

B

Backstage The window displayed when the **File** tab is clicked. It allows you to manage how your Outlook works, along with your account information.

Bcc Acronym for blind carbon copy and can be used to hide a recipient's name and email address from other recipients of an email message.

business card (or electronic business card) An Outlook item created from a contact record that can be sent to other Outlook users.

C

Calendar Snapshot Displays calendar details in the body of an email message.

Category A grouping tool that can be used on all Outlook items. Categories can be customized by name and color.

Cc Acronym for carbon copy and is used when someone is not the main recipient of the email message.

Clean Up A feature that will delete redundant items related to an email conversation.

condition The specific information Outlook rules look for before performing an action.

contact group A selected set of contacts that are saved together in a group.

contact A group of related pieces of information (fields) about an individual or company.

Context Sensitive Groups and buttons will change based on the context of the selection. For example, the *Home Ribbon* will display different groups and buttons depending on whether *Mail* or *Calendar* is selected.

conversation An Outlook arrangement that groups together messages with the same subject.

D

Daily Task List A list of current tasks that appears at the bottom of the calendar in the *Folder* pane when viewing the calendar in *Day, Week,* or *Work Week* views.

Database A file consisting of related groups of information (records), and each record consists of individual pieces of information (fields).

Date Navigator A calendar thumbnail that appears in the *To-Do bar.* Clicking on a date on the date navigator will display that day in the *Folder* pane.

default settings Those settings that come preset in Outlook. Many default settings can be changed in the *Options* dialog box.

Delay Delivery A feature used to delay the sending of an email message.

delegate An Outlook user who has access to Outlook folders of another Outlook user on an Exchange server.

Delivery Receipt An Outlook feature that can be used to send a receipt to the sender of a message when the recipient(s) receive the email message.

desktop alert A notification that appears when you receive an email message.

dialog box A separate window that opens and provides additional selection options.

digital signature A method of authenticating an email message.

draft An email message that has been created and saved but not yet sent. A draft message is stored in the Drafts folder.

E

email The commonly used term for an electronic message.

Encrypt An email message option that scrambles the message and/or attachment to add security to a message.

event A calendar item that is a full day or more in duration.

exception An optional part of the rule that would cause an action to not be performed when a condition is met.

Exchange ActiveSync A method that allows users to set up a Microsoft account in Outlook.

expand button At the bottom right corner of some groups is an expand button that will open a dialog box with additional selections.

export The process of sending Outlook data to another file format.

F

Favorites The area of Outlook in the *Navigation* pane that contains links to commonly used mail folders.

field An individual piece of information.

Field Chooser The dialog box that allows users to choose fields to be displayed in the *Folder* pane.

File button The button or tab to the left of the *Home* tab that opens the Outlook *Backstage*.

Flag for Recipient A flag and *Info bar* message added to an email that recipients receive.

Folder List The selection that displays all of the Outlook folders in the *Navigation* pane.

Folder pane The section of Outlook to the right of the *Navigation* pane. The contents of the folder selected in the *Navigation* pane are displayed in the *Folder* pane.

Follow Up flag A flag that can be added to an Outlook item that serves as a reminder for the user. When an Outlook item is marked with a follow up flag, that item will also be included in the *To-Do List*.

G

Global Address List The collection of contact records available when using Outlook in conjunction with an Exchange server.

groups Each *Ribbon* has buttons and options categorized by groups. Some groups can be expanded to open a dialog box with additional options. Groups can also refer to how items are grouped and displayed in the *Folder* pane.

H

HTML (Hypertext Markup Language) A message format that is the standard format for email messages. This format supports the use of different fonts, styles, colors, and HTML content.

HTTP (Hypertext Transfer Protocol) A type of email account that uses hypertext transfer protocol for sending and receiving email.

I

iCalendar A calendar format that can be sent via email and is compatible with many other software programs.

Ignore An Outlook feature that will move current and future email messages related to a particular conversation to the *Deleted Items* folder.

IMAP (Internet Message Access Protocol) A standard Internet protocol for sending and receiving email.

importance A tag that can be added to Outlook items. Importance can be set at high, normal, or low.

import The process of bringing data from another file into Outlook.

Info bar An informational bar that appears above the *From* line in an email message and provides additional information for the recipient(s).

Instant Search An Outlook feature to quickly search for Outlook items in a specific folder or all folders.

Internet Service Provider (ISP) A company that offers access to the Internet and provides email accounts for users.

J

journal An Outlook item used to record the amount of time spent working on a document or other task.

junk email An email message that is identified by Outlook as potentially dangerous or from a disreputable source.

M

macro A set of programming instructions.

MailTip Alert that warns the user of potential email issues.

meeting (or meeting request) A calendar item that can be used to invite other Outlook users to an appointment or event.

member A contact who is part of a contact group.

Microsoft Exchange Server A file server used to manage Outlook accounts and data within a company.

N

Navigation pane The section of Outlook at the bottom left-hand side of the window used to navigate between the different Outlook features and provide access to the folders in each of these areas.

O

Out of Office Assistant An Outlook feature that allows the user to create an automated reply to emails received.

Outlook Data File Outlook stores user data in a *.pst* file.

Outlook Rich Text Format (RTF) A message format that is unique to Outlook and supports the use of different fonts, styles, colors, and HTML content.

Outlook Today The opening window that is displayed in the *Folder* pane when Outlook is started.

Outlook Social Connector Allows Outlook users to keep track of friends and colleagues. Related Outlook items are displayed in the People pane.

Outlook Web Access (OWA) The online environment to access your Outlook exchange account.

P

panes Separate areas within the Outlook window, which include the *Navigation* pane, *Folder* pane, and *Reading* pane.

People Card A new way of viewing contacts in Outlook 2013. The *People Card* includes contact information in a single place and allows you to schedule meetings, send email, or call from a single location.

People pane Displays Outlook items associated with an individual. The *People* pane appears below the *Reading* pane in the main Outlook interface and at the bottom of received email messages, contacts, meetings, and task requests.

permission The amount of access a delegate has to an area of Outlook.

Plain Text A message format that only supports basic text.

POP3 (Post Office Protocol) A standard Internet protocol for sending and receiving email.

Private A tag that can be used on calendar items, contacts, tasks, and journal entries that hides details of these items from delegates or other users with whom areas of Outlook are shared.

Private Key A tool used by the message sender to encrypt an email message.

Public Key An authentication tool used by the receiver of a message to unencrypt and view an encrypted message.

Q

Quick Access toolbar The toolbar at the top left of the Outlook window that contains buttons for commonly used features. The *Quick Access* toolbar is available on all Microsoft Office products.

Quick Steps Provide one-click access to email actions.

R

Read Receipt An Outlook feature that can be used to send a receipt to the sender of a message when the recipient(s) open the email message.

Reading pane The *Reading* pane can appear below or to the right of the *Folder* pane. The *Reading* pane displays the Outlook item selected in the *Folder* pane. The *Reading* pane can also be turned off.

Recall An Outlook feature used to recall a previously sent message.

record A group of related fields about an individual or company.

recurrence A calendar item or task can be set to recur at a specified interval.

reminder A reminder can be set on Outlook items and a reminder dialog box will open to alert the user.

Resend An Outlook feature used to resend a previously sent message.

Ribbon Each Outlook *Ribbon* provides users with groups and buttons for easy access to Outlook features and commands. Each *Ribbon* is accessed by clicking on its tab.

RSS Feed Acronym for Really Simple Syndication and can be retrieved by Outlook to allow easy access to headlines of new articles or information from a web site.

rule An Outlook feature that controls the handling of email messages. Rules operate on a logical condition(s), action(s), and exception(s) sequence.

S

Schedule view A calendar view that displays calendar(s) in timeline format.

Scheduling Assistant An Outlook calendar feature that displays multiple calendars in timeline format to help facilitate meeting, appointment, and event scheduling.

ScreenTip A small label that appears when the pointer is placed on a button or area of a *Ribbon*.

Search folder A virtual folder that will display email items from other folders that match specified criteria.

sensitivity A tag on an email message that provides a managing conduct to the recipient.

signature A stored group of text that can be automatically or manually inserted into an email, meeting request, or task request.

Stand-Alone Refers to Outlook being used without being connected to a Microsoft Exchange server.

T

tab Each *Ribbon* in Outlook has a tab which displays the name of that *Ribbon*.

Task A piece of work to be completed.

Task List A list of all of the tasks in Outlook.

Task Request A task that is assigned to another Outlook user.

theme A set of fonts, colors, background, and fill effects in the body of an email message.

To-Do bar The area at the right of the Outlook window that displays a date navigator, upcoming calendar items, and the *To-Do* items.

To-Do items All Outlook items marked with a follow up flag.

To-Do List A list of Outlook items that have been marked with a follow up flag. This list is available in Tasks.

Tracking A Microsoft Exchange feature that provides the sender with a summary of responses to meeting requests, voting buttons, and read and delivery receipts.

Trust Center The area of Outlook that allows users to customize the security settings.

trusted publisher Reputable organizations that have a digital signature assigned to a macro or program to be run on a user's computer.

V

view How items are displayed in the *Folder* pane.

voting buttons These preset or custom buttons can be used on an email message to gather responses from recipients.

W

weather bar Displays the weather in the calendar.

index

A

Accept button, O4-158, O5-185, O5-201
Accept option, O4-144, O4-146, O9-332
Accept or Decline option, O9-331
Accept task button, O5-181
Accepting Task dialog box, O5-181
Access file, sending compressed or zipped, O10-372
account. *See also* Microsoft account
    adding to Outlook, O7-277
    inputting information, O1-16
    manually configuring settings, O7-250
    setting to send email, O7-252
Account Settings button, O7-252, O7-253, O7-277
    Delegate Access, O9-351
Account Settings dialog box, O7-250, O7-252, O7-255, O7-277
    changing default delivery folder, O7-253
    under the Internet Calendars tab, O9-332
    Repair, O7-251
    RSS feeds in, O7-267
    RSS Feeds tab, O7-269
Account Settings option, O7-277
action, O7-254
    in a rule, O6-214
Actions button, O1-25, O1-26
Active (List view), O4-138
activities, tracking amount of time, O10-362
Add a New RSS Feed, O7-266, O7-269, O7-278, O7-279
Add Account, O7-277
Add Account dialog box, O1-15, O1-16, O7-250
Add Account option, O7-249
Add Action button, O6-226, O6-227
Add button, O7-263, O9-351
Add Columns button, O5-190
Add Contact Picture dialog box, O3-103, O3-104
Add digital signature to outgoing messages option, O10-374
Add digital signature to this message check box, O10-375, O10-376, O10-382
Add Holidays button, O9-325
Add Holidays to Calendar dialog box, O9-325
Add Members button, in the Members group, O3-113, O3-115, O3-117
Add New Account dialog box, O1-15, O7-249, O7-255, O7-277
Add New Category dialog box, O2-62
Add New Member dialog box, O3-117
Add Picture option, O3-110, O3-123

Add properties to attachments to enable Reply with Changes feature, O10-372
Add this RSS Feed button, O7-268
Add this RSS Feed to Outlook dialog box, O7-266, O7-270, O7-279
Add to Contacts, O3-99, O4-100
Add to Contacts check box, O3-117
Add to Folder Pane dialog box, O10-364, O10-365, O10-380
Add to Outlook Contacts, O3-97
Add Users dialog box, O9-340, O9-343, O9-351
Adding dialog box, O8-287
add-ins, described, O10-374
Add-ins settings, in Trust Center, O10-374
address block, selecting appearance of, O8-305
Address Block link, O8-307, O8-314
Address Book button, O3-99, O8-286
Address Book drop-down menu, O3-110–O3-111
address field, O3-102
addresses, adding to contact records, O3-102–O3-103
Addressing dialog box, O8-286
advanced calendar features, O9-334–O9-338
Advanced Find, O7-272
advanced rule, creating, O6-216, O6-222
Advanced View Settings button, O2-63
Advanced View Settings dialog box, O5-192, O5-193
Advanced View Settings List dialog box, O3-109
All Categories, O2-61, O2-62
All contacts in current view, O8-305, O8-306, O8-314
All day event check box, O4-133, O4-139, O4-143, O4-145
Allow recipient to view your Calendar check box, O9-329
Always use my fonts option, O2-77
antivirus software, O10-374
Apply rule on messages I receive, O6-217, O6-222, O6-237
Apply these settings to all folders now button, O10-367
appointment(s), O4-132
    appearing on calendar, O4-134
    canceling, O4-158
    categorizing, O9-351
    converting to events, O4-133, O4-139
    copying, O4-140
    creating, O4-138–O4-139, O4-141, O4-142, O4-155, O4-157, O9-333, O9-347, O9-351
    creating for a group meeting, O9-343
    default reminder time for, O4-139

    displayed in Month view, O4-136
    forwarding, O9-327–O9-328, O9-333, O9-339, O9-347–O9-348, O9-350
    marking as private, O9-339, O9-347
    moving, O4-140
    recurring, O4-141
    setting to recur every other week, O9-350
    setting to recur weekly, O9-339
    typing a new, O4-136
Appointment button, in the Show group, O4-148
appointment date, updating, O4-158
Appointment Recurrence dialog box, O4-141, O9-336, O9-337, O9-339, O9-350
Appointment tab, O2-61
Appointments, in the To-Do bar, O5-179
Approve;Reject button, O2-69
Archive all folders according to their AutoArchive settings, O10-370
Archive button, to manually archive folders, O10-370
archive folders, O10-367
Archive items in this folder using the default settings, O10-369
Archive items older than tomorrow's date, O10-382
Archive or delete old items, selecting, O10-368
archive settings, customizing on individual folders, O10-368
Archive this folder and all subfolders, O10-370, O10-382
Archive this folder using these settings, O10-369
archiving, defined, O10-367
Arrange By option, O5-191
arrangement, of email messages, O1-32–O1-33
Arrangement group, O5-191
    on the Home tab, O10-363
    on the View tab, O1-33, O3-108, O5-189
arranging, in Outlook, O5-190
As a Business Card option, O3-101, O3-110, O3-112, O8-293
As an Outlook Contact option, O3-124
ascending sort, O3-108, O5-189
Assign Task button, O5-180, O5-185, O5-199
Attach File button, O1-28, O1-44, O8-304, O8-307, O8-315, O9-335, O9-339, O9-349, O10-382
Attach File option, O5-171
Attach Item button, O1-32, O5-200, O6-227, O6-240, O8-293
    Outlook Item, O4-143, O4-156, O4-157, O4-158, O5-171, O5-177, O5-186, O5-198, O5-202

security settings
   customizing, O10-371–O10-375
   in the Properties dialog box, O2-54
Security Settings button, O2-54, O10-375, O10-376, O10-382
Select Attendees and Resources dialog box, O4-144
Select Folder button, O6-215, O6-222, O6-237
Select Folder(s) dialog box, O6-230
Select Members dialog box, O3-113, O3-116
Select Names dialog box, O1-18, O1-21, O3-110, O3-111, O3-114, O3-115, O6-229, O9-341, O9-343, O9-351
semicolon (;), separating email addresses, O1-17, O7-260
Send a Calendar via Email dialog box, O9-330
Send Anyway button, O1-28
Send button, O1-21, O1-27, O1-38, O1-41, O1-42, O1-43, O1-44, O2-60, O2-68, O2-79, O2-80, O2-84, O2-86, O2-87
   in a meeting request, O4-133
   on a task request, O5-180
   sending an email message, O3-122
   sending email to a contact group, O3-114
Send Cancellation button, O4-150, O4-158
Send Items folder, O1-27
Send messages section, of Mail options, O7-259–O7-260
Send Out of Office auto-replies, O7-262
Send Response Now radio button, O2-73
Send Status Report, in the Manage Task group, O5-183
Send Status Report button, O5-185, O5-201
Send the Response Now option, O2-70, O2-71, O4-146, O4-158, O5-181
Send To, Compressed (zipped) Folder, O1-29
Send Update, O4-149
Send Update button, O4-150, O4-158
Send update to all attendees option, O4-150
Send updates to only added or deleted attendees option, O4-150
sensitivity
   default setting for, O7-259–O7-260
   of email, O2-53–O2-54
Sent Items folder, O1-21, O1-24, O2-55, O2-56, O7-259, O7-273, O7-280
Sent Items option, O4-157, O4-158
Sent to Another recipient, O7-280
Sent To button, O7-280
Set as Default button, O7-252, O7-255, O7-277
Set Quick Click dialog box, O2-64, O2-66
Setup rule options, O6-219
Share button, O9-331
Share Calendar button, O9-328, O9-333–O9-334, O9-348
Share calendar request email, O9-329
Share This Feed button, O7-268, O7-270, O7-279
shared calendar, viewing, O9-332

Shared Calendars area, in the Navigation pane, O9-329, O9-332
Shared Calendars list
   in the Navigation pane, O9-343, O9-351
   removing calendars from, O9-332
shared folder, selecting from Open Other User's Folder dialog box, O9-342
shared RSS feed, adding, O7-269
SharePoint
   OSC connecting with, O2-79
   Social Connector and People pane integrating with, O1-10
sharing, a calendar, O9-328–O9-329
Sharing feature, compared to Delegate feature, O9-340
Shift key
   selecting adjacent contacts, O3-111
   selecting attachment items, O1-32
   selecting contact records, O3-107
   selecting items, O8-293
   selecting multiple files, O1-28
   selecting recipients, O1-18
Shift+Tab, moving back one field at a time, O5-168
shortcut groups
   creating, O10-379
   editing, O10-365
Shortcut Key drop-down arrow, O2-62
shortcuts
   creating new, O10-364
   creating to the Journal folder, O10-365
   deleting, O10-365
   editing, O10-365
   renaming, O10-365
   using, O10-363–O10-365
Shortcuts area
   accessing, O10-364
   in the Navigation pane, O10-364, O10-379
Shortcuts button, O10-364, O10-365, O10-366, O10-379
Shortcuts view, O10-363
Show an additional index feature, O8-290
Show archive folder in folder list, O10-368
Show Columns dialog box, O5-190
Show Favorites button, O5-188
Show full week option, O9-324
Show High Detail option, O4-135
Show in Favorites option, O5-188
Show in Groups option, O5-191
Show Low Detail option, O4-135
Show Medium Detail option, O4-135
Show Message button, O1-29
Show number of unread items, O6-231
Show Options link, O6-224, O6-225, O6-227, O6-239
Show Tabs and Commands, selecting, O1-10
Show total number of items radio button, O6-232, O6-241
Show work week option, O9-324
side-by-side mode, displaying multiple calendars, O9-323
signature(s)
   creating, O2-73–O2-75, O2-79, O2-83
   defined, O2-73

   editing, O2-83
   including business cards in, O8-294–O8-295
   including in the body of a task, O5-172
   manually inserting, O2-75–O2-76
   setting a default, O2-75
   setting up multiple, O8-294
Signature button, O2-75, O2-76, O2-79, O2-80, O2-83, O2-86, O2-87
Signatures and Stationery dialog box, O2-74, O2-83, O7-257, O8-294, O8-295
   New button, O2-79
   opening, O2-75
   Personal Stationery tab, O2-77
small bell icon, O1-35
S/MIME (Secure/Multipurpose Internet Mail Extensions), O10-372
Snooze drop-down menu, O4-140
snoozing, a task, O5-170
social networks, connecting to, O3-106–O3-107
Solve Names dialog box, O3-103
Sort, view options, O5-192
sorting
   contacts, O3-108
   in Outlook, O5-190
space limitation, in Exchange server, O10-367
spammers, identifying, O7-262
specific words link, O6-238
specified folder link, O6-238
stand-alone environment, rules stored on your computer, O6-219
stand-alone program, Outlook as, O1-13
start date, for a task, O5-169
Start Mail Merge button, O8-305, O8-307, O8-314
Start time, for an appointment, O4-139, O4-143
Start Timer button, recording time spent on a journal entry, O10-362
Startup check box, O5-187
Stationery and Fonts button, O2-77
Stationery and Themes button, O7-257
Status of a task, O5-170
status report, sending about a task, O5-182–O5-183, O5-201
status update message, emailing, O5-201–O5-202
Step by Step Mail Merge Wizard, O8-305, O8-307, O8-314
sticky notes, O1-5
style of calendar, selecting to print, O9-327
Styles area, choosing the style of Outlook Today, O5-187
Subject, O4-143
   of an appointment, O4-139
Subject button, O7-273
Subject contains check box, O6-215
Subject field, O1-41, O1-43, O2-83, O2-85, O2-87, O3-122, O3-124
Subject line, O1-20
Success dialog box, O6-216
Synchronize RSS Feeds to Common Feed List (CFL) in Windows check box, O7-265